Ancient States and Infrastructural Power

EMPIRE AND AFTER

Clifford Ando, Series Editor

A complete list of books in the series
is available from the publisher.

Ancient States and Infrastructural Power

Europe, Asia, and America

Edited by

Clifford Ando and Seth Richardson

PENN

UNIVERSITY OF PENNSYLVANIA PRESS

PHILADELPHIA

Copyright © 2017 University of Pennsylvania Press

All rights reserved. Except for brief quotations used for purposes of review or scholarly citation, none of this book may be reproduced in any form by any means without written permission from the publisher.

Published by
University of Pennsylvania Press
Philadelphia, Pennsylvania 19104-4112
www.upenn.edu/pennpress

Printed in the United States of America on acid-free paper
10 9 8 7 6 5 4 3 2 1

A catalogue record for this book is available from the Library of Congress.

ISBN 978-0-8122-4931-6

CONTENTS

Introduction: States and State Power in Antiquity   1
CLIFFORD ANDO

Chapter 1. Before Things Worked: A "Low-Power" Model of Early Mesopotamia   17
SETH RICHARDSON

Chapter 2. Property Claims and State Formation in the Archaic Greek World   63
EMILY MACKIL

Chapter 3. Western Zhou Despotism   91
WANG HAICHENG

Chapter 4. The Ambitions of Government: Territoriality and Infrastructural Power in Ancient Rome   115
CLIFFORD ANDO

Chapter 5. Populist Despotism and Infrastructural Power in the Later Roman Empire   149
JOHN WEISWEILER

Chapter 6. Territorializing Iran in Late Antiquity: Autocracy, Aristocracy, and the Infrastructure of Empire   179
RICHARD PAYNE

Chapter 7. Kinship and the Performance of Inca Despotic and Infrastructural Power   218
R. ALAN COVEY

Chapter 8. Statehood, Taxation, and State Infrastructural
Power in Visigothic Iberia   243
    DAMIÁN FERNÁNDEZ

Chapter 9. Did the Byzantine Empire Have "Ecumenical" or
"Universal" Aspirations?   272
    ANTHONY KALDELLIS

List of Contributors   301

Index of Subjects   303

Index of Citations   307

Introduction: States and State Power in Antiquity

CLIFFORD ANDO

This volume seeks to assess the power—the reach, if you will—of ancient states. Its method is historical and comparative rather than ideal-typical. That is to say, the project does not commence from an idealist understanding of states and state power, according to which states occupy bounded territories whose space and population they both know and control and within which they exercise a monopoly on fiscal matters and the authorization of the use of violence, as well as law-making and law-applying institutions.[1] The choice of method does not arise from an objection to ideal-typical or more broadly sociological analyses of the state as such.[2] It is rather that contemporary ideals of the state and state power are—as has long been recognized—historically contingent. This applies very precisely to notions of territoriality, the control and knowledge of persons, and the generation of norms.[3] The study of ancient states in the light of modern idealist literatures therefore always risks a double fault, of becoming at once little more than a portrait of deficiency, on the one hand, while premodern states and their aspirations to power become mere way stations on the way to ourselves, on the other.

The volume is historical insofar as the chapters take a strictly empiricist approach to the questions posed by its project, which include: What powers did ancient states claim for themselves? What capacity did they have or develop to actualize such claims? What spaces and social fields existed outside the state, and what was their relation to state authority? What possibilities for cooptation or resistance existed between non-statal resources and systems of social dependency and state elites? It is historical also in respecting the evidentiary regimes and traditions of interpretation that exist within the separate fields and disciplines on which it draws: the authors work in departments of anthropology, art history, classics, history, and Near Eastern studies.

The volume is comparative in the double sense that, despite their different points of disciplinary origin and the varied empirical objects of their investigations, the authors shared not only a set of motivating questions but also a reading list of theoretical and historical studies. These included Seth Richardson's "Early Mesopotamia: The Presumptive State," a study of the relationship between claims to powers and the actuality and efficacy of those powers on the part of states of the ancient Near East; William Novak's "The Myth of the Weak American State," which employs Michael Mann's notion of infrastructural power in order to surmount an ideological distinction in American politics between federal, state, and local governments; Mann's own essay "The Autonomous Power of the State"; and James C. Scott's *Seeing Like a State*, which was intended to provoke thoughts not simply about the relationship between knowledge, power, and state institutions but also about the relationship between forms of power and forms of resistance. What is more, both Richardson's essay and Scott's volume reflect explicitly on the limits of state power—which is to say, on the weakness of the state—and how we might theorize that weakness in itself, as well as the gap between claims to power and the ability of states to actualize those claims.[4] (I will have more to say about the contribution that these readings made to the project below.)

Beyond the sharing of questions and readings, the papers were delivered and drafts circulated among the authors prior to preparation of the final publication. In this way, one might say, the authors were also invited to think *beyond* the evidentiary regimes or traditions of interpretation of their respective fields, which are, after all, shaped *also* by ideological considerations, alongside other historical forces. This is a principal mechanism by which comparative conversation enriches the imagination: one's models of historical reality—of both causation and social action—become more complex, as gaps and elisions in our information and understanding are conjecturally mapped by analogical and comparative reasoning. It should therefore be clear that our object was not to situate the societies under study in relation to each other along one or another index of *Staatlichkeit*, but rather to further inquiry by specialists into their own contexts through engagement with the creative responses of others to the evidentiary regimes within which we each work.

In what follows, I first survey select trends in the study of ancient states as these bear on this project, particularly in light of late twentieth-century studies of the (legitimate) powers of modern (national) states—modern nation-states being the context of contemporary theory, whatever its content and however much it claims disinterest for itself. I then attempt to draw out some themes of the current project, in order to indicate some ways of reading the present volume.

Ancient States in Modern Perspective

Contemporary literature on ancient states has tended to focus on empires.[5] This is particularly true of comparativist projects with roots in the ancient Mediterranean. To a point this is both intelligible and easily justified, and, indeed, this volume might be said to follow in this trend. However, it does so with a skeptical eye, and to appreciate why and how this is so, it might be useful to reflect on some of the normative and theoretical commitments that have inflected analysis of this kind in the past. I do so in two parts, focusing first on the bracketing of the city-states of the classical Mediterranean from inquiry in this field and next on recent literature on ancient empires.

The focus on empires amounts to an affirmation of several interrelated and often unarticulated claims about power relations in the varied political forms of ancient life. At an empirical level, the overwhelming majority of translocal and transregional powers in the premodern world were empires, just as a startling number of purely local powers nurtured imperial ambitions.[6] This empirical pattern may lie behind a common, often unstated normative assumption to the effect that premodern forms of political or statal domination are those exercised by one people over another. In part, this focus on empires also issues from the success enjoyed by ancient city-state elites in naturalizing the power relations inherent in their notionally democratic and republican orders. To the extent that scholars in the modern West have understood their own political systems to operate in succession to Greece and Rome, they have had an interest in collaborating in this project. As a result, literature on the Greek polis, for example, has tended to privilege concepts such as social cooperation and coordination within the population that elite Greek males defined as fully human and therefore worthy of citizenship; correlatively, it has tended to neglect slavery, domination, and predation as key to understanding their developed political economies, even as literature on the emergence of the polis has indexed its history to the development of monumentalized public spaces.⁷ The result, and perhaps the point, of these choices has been to index "our" histories of Greek politics to "their" definitions of who counts as political, what counts as political action, and where legitimate politics takes place. This identification of empires as states but cities and villages as communal, egalitarian, and democratic has had at least one further consequence of relevance to this project: it has required that one efface from study the relations of domination exercised by city-based elites over populations in their hinterland specifically and the rural economy more generally.⁸

For their part, ancient empires have not lacked for attention or, indeed, admiration—a consequence of the fetishization of despotic over infrastructural power, as well as the identification of despotic power with monarchy, and states with empire. Their extraordinary self-confidence (witness the valediction of Sargon II in select correspondence, which might be paraphrased, "Obey or die! Yours, Sargon"); the seeming stability of the rule of law that they claimed to impose (a confusion of enactment with efficacy, and a modern privileging of positive law over all other forms of norms, have led some to argue that ancient law sought the selfsame goods as law ever has: protecting private property, reducing risk, and promoting predictability and efficiency in exchange); the vastness of their suzerainty; and the firmness of the peace they imposed, being proportionate to the strife we perceive as otherwise endemic to worlds of sub-political ethnicities and religious groups: these aspects of ancient imperial power contributed to an early modern fetishization of empires as loci of sovereignty and practitioners of *étatisme* avant la lettre. As a circular matter, the sense that ancient states had wielded such power amplified and legitimated early modern longings for robust realizations of state control. Indeed, despite the collapse of such views of ancient government along many fronts, nostalgia for empire continues to animate political theory and public argument across many spheres.

But collapse those views did. The diminution in late twentieth-century esteem for ancient imperial states took place under pressure from theoretical and empirical advances in numerous domains, of which several have special relevance to this project. First, continental social theorists in the third quarter of the twentieth century attended with remarkable empiricism and critical insight to the break that (supposedly) differentiated modernity from what came before. Much of this work focused on the aspirations of early modern government to know and hence to interpellate individual subjects of rule and to police social and economic conduct; much stress was also laid on the communicative technology regimes and revolutions in knowledge that subtended these developments. An important if often unstated implication of this work was the relegation of premodern government to the status of primitive.[9]

Second, historians working on ancient contexts themselves came to question the actuality of governmental power on the ground. In Roman history, Fergus Millar's splendid essay "The World of the Golden Ass" may stand as emblematic of this work (Millar 1981). Reading the novel of Apuleius, written at the height of Roman power, Millar posed the question of why representatives of imperial government were so absent from the provincial landscape traversed by the characters. The answer, he suggested, was an actual absence of direct representatives of Rome from the provincial imaginary, which he took to be a proxy for the light footprint of Roman power in the lived realities of the ancient Mediterranean. As brilliant and helpful as his observations were, Roman historians generally failed to respond with any theorization or comparative assessment of Roman state power: how might one assess or qualify Millar's observations? Do they have implications for a history of governmentality or the intensity or penetration of state power? Is the implication that the Roman state was weak in general, or infrastructurally weak? If so, was it weak in the same way, or along the same axes of analysis, that second millennium B.C.E. Near Eastern states were weak?

A third area of research that contributed to contemporary negative assessments of state power in antiquity concerns the character or, if you will, the ambitions of ancient government. In the case of the ancient Mediterranean, a significant percentage of the evidence for actions of ancient government derives from correspondence between the governed (whether individuals or communities) and the central power; and a significant portion of that material was inscribed locally, rather than in the metropole. Formal qualities of this material have been interpreted to suggest that the character of ancient government was fundamentally reactionary.[10] Far from having any interest in proactive policy or imposing norms, ancient rulers and officials adjudged only what others brought before them. Governmental knowledge was thus highly contingent, and norms spread in large measure through citation and interpretation by interested lay parties. Likewise, a vast number of the preserved wood and bamboo legal documents of Qin and Han period China are in fact formularies: they therefore attest a metropolitan desire to render local legal and social relations—and, indeed, the operations of their own functionaries—legible, in

Scott's terms, but whether they can attest to more than the aspirations of the central power is a historical question that the formal qualities of the formularies cannot by their very nature answer (Korolkov 2011; 2016).

In a fourth move, scholars influenced by postcolonial epistemologies and analysis—and, indeed, modern theories of political communication—have directed attention to the political and interpretive agency exercised by subjects of imperial power, who might formerly have been taken merely as its addressees. In one tradition, vastly greater agency is now accorded to the collaborative work of ruler and ruled in the sustaining of order. This is true of the articulation and vindication of validity claims as regards legitimacy of rule, as well as the constitution of local social orders and matters of civil law and procedure.[11] At the same time, modern students of governmental power have been forewarned against processualist readings of public speech in authorized fora: forms of power produce their own forms of knowing resistance, particularly but not exclusively at the vanguard of politicization.[12]

As a related matter, over the past two generations a great deal of truly excellent historical scholarship has focused on local or regional experience. At times, this has occurred because of methodological or epistemic commitments of the discipline, as when the particularities of epigraphic and archaeological evidence are first interpreted in light of their immediate context. Nor can there be any doubt that the dynamics of daily life often exhibit little of the tidiness of metropolitan knowledge or, for that matter, modern analytic frameworks.

Finally, considerable theoretical energy has been expended in recent years on empire as a political form, distinguishing ancient and modern; monarchic and aristocratic; sea-, land- and steppe-based empires; commercial and colonial; and primary and shadow empires, to name only some of the most relevant distinctions.[13] What is more, an important foil in all such work has been modern theories of the state.[14] Hence, where modern states develop and propagate institutions to extend state power and cultivate a national culture uniformly throughout their territory, and likewise insist that they alone can authorize the use of violence and generate laws within that territory, macro- and trans-regional governments in the ancient world governed through the cultivation and management of difference: they devolved considerable authority to local institutions, which betimes operated according to norms avowedly generated locally, in large measure in (rational) response to material constraints on the power of the notional hegemon.[15]

Unsurprisingly, in consequence of pressure from very similar trends in postmodern critique, recent decades have witnessed massive shifts in perspective in the study of the post-Westphalian state. Sovereigntism is dead; constitutional history as a history of legislators and black-robed judges has yielded to new and exciting forms of legal history; legal history itself has given way to greatly enriched perspectives on the sources and contestation of normative orders; and understandings of the space and scope of political deliberation have become vastly more capacious. Power is more pervasive, but neither power nor politics are limited to spaces, instruments, and authorities commanded by state ideologies. In consequence, statal orders are no longer granted the ontological security that they claim for themselves, but are understood as requiring continuous renewal and reconstitution. A philologist might well say that the origins of "state" in Latin *statio* are at last revealed. *Statio*, meaning "position" or "condition," itself derived from a perfective passive participle: a *statio* is not a fact about a thing or the world, but something established through agential action. Statal orders are not historical givens, but forever captured *in statu nascendi*.

Infrastructural Power in Ancient States

These new critical approaches to sovereigntism are now spurring important reflection among historians of antiquity, as well as anthropologists and social theorists inquiring into the history of the state. Some have argued that, far from resting on an uncontested lodging of power in monarchic points of singularity, the legitimacy and stability of ancient states were secured discursively.[16] To the extent that this is so, a window is opened onto other areas, not least the historical problematics of subjectivity and governmentality, that remain insufficiently explored.[17] In other words, we need to investigate not simply Sargon's valediction, but the anticipation of his power by those subordinates who offered to die if they should fail the king. More seriously, we need proper histories of the processes charted in this volume and elsewhere by Seth Richardson, in which the presumptive claiming by states of certain powers leads historically not simply to later states also claiming those powers, but also to the surrender to those claims by civil society, in Mann's terms, which concedes something like monopoly authority in those domains to the state.

Among ancient historians, these trends have issued in several projects with broad empirical range and considerable theoretical heterogeneity. Thus, Peter Bang and Walter Scheidel's *Oxford Handbook of the State in the Ancient Near*

East and Mediterranean (2013) observes a loosely developmental framework, from the "origins" to "the end" of the ancient state, but the individual chapters declare affiliation to a great variety of conceptions of both the state and social power. Scheidel's pathbreaking projects on Rome and China, by contrast, sharpen the apparent cogency of the comparative enterprise by adopting highly formalist or narrowly quantitative lenses upon their material (2009, 2015). The "Imperium et Officium" project of the Austrian Wissenschaftsfonds is something of a hybrid. On the one hand, its stated ambition is to assess each of the societies under study in light of Weberian theories of bureaucratic rationality (notwithstanding the fact that its primary form of evidence, archived correspondence from within administrative apparatus, will tend to exhibit formal qualities easily interpreted as rationalist). On the other, many of the participants in the project are editors of documentary sources, with all the respect for particularist historicism that this entails. In addition, a number of projects have sought to devise or adopt quantitative indices by which to assess the actual reach and penetration of state power and bypass the hermeneutic problems that inhere in evaluating the efficacy of any given discursive claim to power.[18]

The present volume makes a distinctive contribution to this literature and responds to the larger trends outlined above. Its distinctiveness rests in part on its effort to address a number of theoretical issues. First, we seek to bridge the divide between metropolitan discourse and the historical materiality of practice. Sophisticated studies of imperial ideology abound, of course, as do treatments of government or law on the ground. The existence of these separate fields derives in large measure from their attestation in very different bodies of evidence, even if participants in one or the other tradition advance political or even moral claims for their perspective. Contributors were invited to consider one recent effort to surmount this split, through reflection on Seth Richardson's recent study of what he terms "the presumptive state" (2012). Richardson documents both the grandiose claims to authority, power, and efficacy made by second-millennium Near Eastern polities, as well as the reasons regularly advanced to withhold credence in respect of them. Viewing his objects of study against the backdrop of developmental histories of state power, Richardson not only poses the question of whether modern scholars have been seduced by the self-representations of ancient states into attributing to them capacities they did not have; he also wonders whether claiming those capacities was not a principal mechanism of bringing them into being. Richardson then suggests that, over time, states' awareness of themselves as historical entities in dialogue with earlier powers helped to validate their claims to legitimacy qua states and monopoly on specific powers, even as it also contributed to solidifying the ontology of the state qua form of social power.

Second, we have adopted a capacious notion of state power. Following the historical sociology of Michael Mann (1986–2013), we understand state infrastructural power to embrace both personnel and materiel, studied within the spatial and institutional configurations that announced and amplified their authority. Furthermore, we follow the lead of William Novak in his recent invocation of Mann, in his now famous essay "The Myth of the Weak American State" (Novak 2008). Novak sought to account for (and largely bracket) the refusal by the American state of expansive despotic power and directed attention instead to the burgeoning histories of "the conscious and continuing construction of new forms of state power throughout American history" (76). To achieve this end, he drew on Mann's notion of infrastructural power, not least because it allowed him to play down the interpretive and practical significance of distinctions between federal, state, and local government. In similar fashion, where relevant, we have tentatively sought to establish metropolitan, imperial, and local structures of social and institutional authority in a continuum rather than in oppositional relationship to each other. No one doubts but that ancient empires sought the cooperation of local elites, or that (some) local elites collaborated, so as to cement and extend their local hegemony. A history of government and governmentality needs a way to understand the resulting networks of power, despite the ideological claims to juridical or ethnic difference that were advanced notionally to disjoin their constituent parts. For such analysis, the notion of civil society as exploited by Mann is not merely anachronistic; it is largely inapposite to ancient empires.[19] At the level of ideology critique, it might suffice to show that formally treating indigenous and local institutions of government as external to themselves allowed empires to create those local institutions as a kind of constitutive outside.[20] For the purposes of the present volume, we have sought to understand the matrices of imperial and local governmental power as part of a single whole.

The returns on this way of proceeding are perhaps especially visible when one turns to the study of built infrastructure. In recent years, for all its necessary commitment to particularism, archaeology has become a major locus of research on statal and social power.[21] In part this has come about through more strictly critical approaches to aesthetics: we are more wary now of ancient and modern tendencies to monumentalize power and find it beautiful, and to assimilate historical and political categories to aesthetic ones. In part this has come about through recognizing that traditional areas of attention in archaeological inquiry (cities, temples, palaces, etc.) have in fact operated as proxies for notions of the state, subtended to concepts like culture and civilization. One result is that where we might once have taken claims to power by sovereigns residing in monumentalized urban cores at face value, the assertion of power over territory is now understood historically as a claim that required vindication, even as the construction of monumentalized public spaces should itself be regarded as part of a claim to sovereignty and not the natural outcome of its success.[22]

So, for example, the implanting of Roman colonies, with their distinctive architecture and distributions and monumentalization of public and religious power, was once regarded as a principle mechanism by which a particular vision of legitimate public power and its lodging in depersonalized institutions were conveyed.[23] And it remains true that the control and development of urban cores and the elaboration of road systems were in many places a significant instrument for the extension of metropolitan, imperial power.[24] That said, the material sites of social power can also be co-opted to resist empire (not least by its own agents); and no study of the creation and subscription of social power in such sites can proceed without considering how the symbolism and practicalities of the varied rituals, ceremonies, and procedures conducted in such spaces channeled, conveyed, and constrained both assent and dissent to ruling ideologies.[25]

Often in ancient states, the elaboration and—nota bene—the maintenance of state infrastructure required the mobilization of networks of social dependency notionally outside the state apparatus. In some cases, this issued in what we might term an accidental homeomorphy of institutional structures between the imperial and local, with the effective result being the material extension of state power into local landscapes, achieved via local labor.[26] In other cases, the infrastructure in question lay at the borders of the state, and the mobilization of labor and resources in the sustaining of state infrastructural projects also operated to circulate regional potentates away from the networks that they controlled and on which they depended: the drawing of a boundary between those within and those without imperial space was therefore accomplished via an act that also reconstructed the disparate parties within as subservient to unitary and unifying projects.[27]

Instead of, or alongside, such systems of corvée labor—I use the term advisedly, as it risks reducing institutions of enormous political importance to merely economic interest—many ancient states made elaborate claims to authority over market activities and monopolistic assertions to fiscal authority over their territories. But, as in other areas, so in respect of fiscality transregional states required the collaboration of extra-statal social institutions to actualize their claims. What is striking about comparative study of such systems is that no simple political or political-economic reading of them is possible. In some cases, it is elites who emerge as dependent on the transcendent power of the distant monarchy: as elites imbricated themselves into transregional structures of exchange, so they came to depend more and more on the empire to backstop their notionally legal claims to ownership and wealth extraction.[28] In other cases, the macro-regional state appears to have been reliant on local dynasts for tax collection, but the system rapidly evolved to a condition of mutual dependency and co-constitution.[29] The results in either case confound our desire for simple discrimination between strong and weak states and imperial and local infrastructural power.

* * *

I would like to thank both the Center for the Study of Ancient Religions and the Franke Institute for the Humanities at the University of Chicago for their support. The conversation within these pages was enriched by these institutions and by a number of colleagues who participated in the colloquium where drafts were first presented, notably Noel Lenski, Jim Scott, and Greg Woolf. I would also like to pay tribute to Lori Khatchadourian and Norman Yoffee, who were unable to contribute to the volume. To all of them, I offer my thanks.

Finally, this volume shares a number of contributors with another comparative volume of exceptional interest, *Cosmopolitanism and Empire: Universal Rulers, Local Elites, and Cultural Integration in the Ancient Near East and Mediterranean*, edited by Myles Lavan, Richard Payne, and John Weisweiler. In closing, I pay tribute to their endeavor and to the multiple forms of generosity that are required to sustain conversations of this kind across time, distance, and disciplines.

NOTES

1. Weber (1978, 54) ("A 'ruling organization' will be called 'political' insofar as its existence and order is continuously safeguarded within a given *territorial* area by the threat and application of physical force on the part of the administrative staff. A compulsory

political organization with continuous operations (*politischer Anstaltsbetrieb*) will be called a 'state' insofar as its administrative staff successfully upholds the claim to the *monopoly* of the *legitimate* use of physical force in the enforcement of its order" [italics in the original]), expanded at 901–4.

2. For an idiosyncratic effort to distinguish historical and sociological analysis in this domain, see Bourdieu 2014, 105–10.

3. Foucault 2007, 2008; Constable 1994; Brett 2011; Branch 2014. I observe but set aside without comment here the issue that ideals of state power (like all ideas) serve particular ideological and political functions. The ideal of some homeomorphy between state sovereignty and jurisdiction is a case in point, on which see, e.g., Resnik 2008.

4. Richardson 2012; Novak 2008; Mann 1984; and Scott 1998.

5. Up to a point, Yoffee 2015 is a valuable exception.

6. On empires, see Ando 2016. The prominence achieved by federations of poleis in peninsular Greece between the classical and late Hellenistic periods is an important exception to any too easy division of the premodern world into city-states and empires. On their history, see Mackil 2013; Beck and Funke 2015.

7. For further reflections on traditional scholarship on the emergence of the polis, see Emily Mackil's essay in this volume. On the notion of the agora as the only space where "politics" occurs, see Habermas 1989 (1962), 1–5; see also O'Neill 2003; Ando 2012; and Rosillo-López, forthcoming.

8. This unwillingness to examine the dominance exercised by poliadic elites—often called the dêmos—over populations in their hinterland is a recent phenomenon; it was an important theme in Rostovtzeff 1957 (1926), Jones 1940, and, to a point, Magie 1950. For a survey of earlier literature see Finley 1981, 3–23. There are, of course, some noteworthy exceptions to this generalization, which approach the issue from varied theoretical and political perspectives: see, e.g., Osborne 1985, Cohen 2000, and the essays edited by Christophe Chandezon and Christine Hamdoune in *Pallas* 64 (2004).

9. See Ando, this volume, as well as Ando 2012.

10. Reinfandt, Prochazka, and Tost 2015; Ando, forthcoming a.

11. Validity claims: Ando 2000. The role of law and procedure in the constitution of local social orders: Bryen 2012; Ando 2015.

12. My wording is indebted to Colin Gordon, "Afterword" to Foucault 1980, 257; the entire essay deserves consultation. On resistance, Scott 1985, 1990, and 2009, and Bourdieu 2014 may stand for a vast literature.

13. Kautsky 1982; Doyle 1986; Barfield 2001; Maier 2006; Burbank and Cooper 2010.

14. Ando, forthcoming b; many essays in Brooke, Anderson, and Strauss, forthcoming, bear on these themes.

15. This characterization of (ancient) empire is one that I have employed and explored in a number of publications, but I wish to acknowledge here the role played in my own thinking by the very clear exposition of these issues in Maier 2006, 19–77, esp. 31–33.

16. See, e.g., Ando 2000.

17. Important inspiration for such projects exists in postmodern theories of power, which understand it as distributed, as (often) created and conceded rather than (simply) wielded and imposed. More crucially, such theories urge that (state) power will tend to generate not simply social practices but especially forms of resistance that exist in mimetic relation to itself. Much the same might be said of historical anthropology, where an emphasis on power as practice, and politics as experiment, has been enormously revealing (Yoffee 2005; Wright 2006).

18. Monson and Scheidel 2015 is both a participant in this trend and also contains useful disclaimers about its interpretive utility.

19. Cf. Mann 1984.

20. Ando 2010.

21. Smith 2003; Smith 2011; Hartley, Yazicioglu, and Smith 2012.

22. Richardson, Mackil, this volume.

23. Shaw 1986, 74–75.

24. Covey and Wang, this volume.

25. Wang and Covey, this volume; MacCormack 2000.

26. Ando, this volume.

27. Payne, this volume.

28. Weisweiler, this volume.

29. Fernández, this volume.

BIBLIOGRAPHY

Ando, Clifford. 2000. *Imperial Ideology and Provincial Loyalty in the Roman Empire*. Berkeley: University of California Press.

———. 2010. "Imperial Identities." In *Local Knowledge and Microidentities in the Imperial Greek World*, edited by Tim Whitmarsh, 17–45. Cambridge: Cambridge University Press.

———. 2012. "Empire, State and Communicative action." In *Politische Kommunikation und öffentliche Meinung in der antiken Welt*, edited by Christine Kuhn, 219–29. Stuttgart: Steiner.

———. 2015. "*Exemplum*, Analogy and Precedent in Roman Law." In *Between Exemplarity and Singularity: Literature, Philosophy, Law*, edited by Michèle Lowrie and Susanne Lüdemann, 111–22. New York: Routledge.

———. 2016. "Colonialism, Colonization: Roman Perspectives." In *The Oxford Handbook of Literatures of the Roman Empire*, edited by Daniel L. Selden and Phiroze Vasunia. Oxford. Oxford Handbooks Online (published May 2016). DOI: 10.1093/oxfordhb/9780199699445.013.

———. Forthcoming a. "Petition and Response, Order and Obey: Contemporary Models of Roman Government." In *Land, Labour and the Relationships of Power: Governing Ancient Empires. Proceedings of the 3rd to 5th International Conferences of the Research*

Network Imperium and Officium, edited by Michael Jursa et al. Vienna: Verlag der Österreichischen Akademie der Wissenschaften, in production.

———. Forthcoming b. "Empire as State: The Roman Case." In *State Formations: Histories and Cultures of Statehood*, edited by John Brooke, Greg Anderson and Julia Strauss. Cambridge: Cambridge University Press.

Bang, Peter Fibiger, and Walter Scheidel, eds. 2013. *The Oxford Handbook of the State in the Ancient Near East and Mediterranean*. New York: Oxford University Press.

Barfield, T. J. 2001. "The Shadow Empires: Imperial State Formation along the Chinese-Nomad Frontier." In *Empires: Perspectives from Archaeology and History*, edited by Susan Alcock, T. N. D'Altroy, Kathleen D. Morrison, and Carla M. Sinopoli, 10–41. Cambridge: Cambridge University Press.

Beck, Hans, and Peter Funke, eds. 2015. *Federalism in Greek Antiquity*. Cambridge: Cambridge University Press.

Bourdieu, Pierre. 2014. *On the State: Lectures at the Collège de France 1989–1992*. Translated by David Fernbach. Cambridge: Polity.

Branch, Jordan. 2014. *The Cartographic State: Maps, Territory, and the Origins of Sovereignty*. Cambridge: Cambridge University Press.

Brett, Annabel S. 2011. *Changes of State: Nature and the Limits of the City in Early Modern Natural Law*. Princeton, N.J.: Princeton University Press.

Brooke, John, Greg Anderson, and Julia Strauss, eds. Forthcoming. *State Formations: Histories and Cultures of Statehood*. Cambridge: Cambridge University Press.

Bryen, Ari. 2012. "Judging Empire: Courts and Culture in Rome's Eastern Provinces." *Law and History Review* 30:771–811.

Burbank, J., and F. Cooper. 2010. *Empires in World History: Power and the Politics of Difference*. Princeton, N.J.: Princeton University Press.

Chandezon, Christophe and Christine Hamdoune, eds. 2004. *Les Hommes et la Terre dans la Méditeranée Gréco-Romaine. Pallas. Revue d'études antiques* 64. Toulouse: Presses Universitaires du Midi.

Cohen, Edward E. 2000. *The Athenian Nation*. Princeton, N.J.: Princeton University Press.

Constable, Marianne. 1994. *The Law of the Other: The Mixed Jury and Changing Conceptions of Citizenship, Law and Knowledge*. Chicago: University of Chicago Press.

Doyle, Michael W. 1986. *Empires*. Ithaca, N.Y.: Cornell University Press.

Finley, M. I. 1980. *Ancient Slavery and Modern Ideology*. New York: Penguin Books.

———. 1981. *Economy and Society in Ancient Greece*. Edited by Brent D. Shaw and Richard P. Saller. New York: Viking Press.

Foucault, Michel. 1980. *Power/Knowledge: Selected Interviews and Other Writings, 1972–1977*. Edited by Colin Gordon. Translated by Colin Gordon, Leo Marshall, John Mepham, and Kate Soper. New York: Pantheon Books.

———. 2007. *Security, Territory, Population: Lectures at the Collège de France, 1977–78*. Translated by Graham Burchell. New York: Palgrave MacMillan.

———. 2008. *The Birth of Biopolitics: Lectures at the Collège de France, 1978–79*. Translated by Graham Burchell. New York: Palgrave MacMillan.

Habermas, Jürgen. 1989 (1962). *The Structural Transformation of the Public Sphere: An Inquiry into a Category of Bourgeois Society*. Translated by Thomas Burger with the assistance of Frederick Lawrence. Cambridge, Mass.: MIT Press.

Hartley, Charles W., G. Bike Yazicioglu, and Adam T. Smith, eds. 2012. *The Archaeology of Power and Politics in Eurasia Regimes and Revolutions*. Cambridge: Cambridge University Press.

Jones, A. H. M. 1940. *The Greek City from Alexander to Justinian*. Oxford: Clarendon Press.

Kautsky, John H. 1982. *The Politics of Aristocratic Empires*. Chapel Hill: University of North Carolina Press.

Korolkov, Maxim. 2011. "Arguing About Law: Interrogation Procedure under the Qin and Former Han Dynasties." *Études chinoises* 30:37–71.

———. 2016. "Calculating Crime and Punishment: Unofficial Law Enforcement, Quantification, and Legitimacy in Early Imperial China." *The New Ancient Legal History: Critical Analysis of Law* 3 (1): 70–86.

Lavan, Myles, Richard Payne, and John Weisweiler, eds. 2016. *Cosmopolitanism and Empire: Universal Rulers, Local Elites, and Cultural Integration in the Ancient Near East and Mediterranean*. New York: Oxford University Press.

MacCormack, Sabine. 2000. "Processions for the Inca: Andean and Christian Ideas of Human Sacrifice, Communion and Embodiment in Early Colonial Peru." *Archiv für Religionsgeschichte* 2 (1): 110–40.

Mackil, Emily. 2013. *Creating a Common Polity: Religion, Economy, and Politics in the Making of the Greek Koinon*. Berkeley: University of California Press.

Magie, D. 1950. *Roman Rule in Asia Minor to the End of the Third Century after Christ*. Princeton, N.J.: Princeton University Press.

Maier, Charles. 2006. *Among Empires: American Ascendancy and Its Predecessors*. Cambridge, Mass.: Harvard University Press.

Mann, Michael. 1984. "The Autonomous Power of the State: Its Origins, Mechanisms and Results." *Archives européennes de sociologie* 25 (2): 185–213.

———. 1986–2013. *The Sources of Social Power*. 4 vols. Cambridge: Cambridge University Press.

Millar, Fergus. 1981. "The World of the Golden Ass." *Journal of Roman Studies* 71:63–75.

Monson, Andrew, and Walter Scheidel, eds. 2015. *Fiscal Regimes and the Political Economy of Premodern States*. Cambridge: Cambridge University Press.

Novak, William J. 2008. "The Myth of the 'Weak' American State." *American Historical Review* 113 (3): 752–72.

O'Neill, Peter. 2003. "Going Round in Circles: Popular Speech in Ancient Rome." *Classical Antiquity* 22 (1): 135–76.

Osborne, Robin. 1985. *Demos: The Discovery of Classical Attika*. Cambridge: Cambridge University Press.

Reinfandt, Lucian, Stephan Prochazka, and Sven Tost, eds. 2015. *Official Epistolography and the Languages of Power*. Vienna, n.p.

Resnik, Judith. 2008. "Law as Affiliation: 'Foreign' Law, Democratic Federalism, and the Sovereigntism of the Nation State." *I•CON* 6 (1): 33–66.

Richardson, Seth. 2012. "Early Mesopotamia: The Presumptive State." *Past and Present* 215 (1): 3–49.

Rosillo-López, Cristina. Forthcoming. *Public Opinion and Politics in the Late Roman Republic*. Cambridge: Cambridge University Press.

Rostovtzeff, M. 1957 (1926). *The Social and Economic History of the Roman Empire*. 2nd edition prepared by P. M. Fraser. Oxford, U.K.: Clarendon Press

Scheidel, Walter, ed. 2009. *Rome and China: Comparative Perspectives on Ancient World Empires*. New York: Oxford University Press.

———, ed. 2015. *State Power in Ancient China and Rome*. New York: Oxford University Press.

Scott, James C. 1985. *Weapons of the Weak: Everyday forms of Peasant Resistance*. New Haven, Conn.: Yale University Press.

———. 1990. *Domination and the Arts of Resistance: Hidden Transcripts*. New Haven, Conn.: Yale University Press.

———. 1998. *Seeing Like a State: How Certain Schemes to Improve the Human Condition Have Failed*. New Haven, Conn.: Yale University Press.

———. 2009. *The Art of Not Being Governed: An Anarchist History of Upland Southeast Asia*. New Haven, Conn.: Yale University Press.

Shaw, Brent. 1986. "Autonomy and Tribute: Mountain and Plain in Mauretania Tingitana." In *Desert et montagne au Maghreb: Hommage à Jean Dresch. Revue de l'Occident Musulman et de la Méditeranée*, edited by Pierre-Robert Baduel, 41–42:66–89.

Smith, Adam T. 2003. *The Political Landscape: Constellations of Authority in Early Complex Polities*. Berkeley: University of California Press.

———. 2011. "Archaeologies of Sovereignty." *Annual Review of Anthropology* 40:415–32.

Weber, M. 1978. *Economy and Society*. Edited by G. Roth and C. Wittich. Berkeley: University of California Press.

Wright, Henry T. 2006. "Early State Dynamics as Political Experiment." *Journal of Anthropological Research* 62 (3): 305–19.

Yoffee, Norman. 2005. *Myths of the Archaic State: Evolution of the Earliest Cities, States and Civilizations*. Cambridge: Cambridge University Press.

———, ed. 2015. *The Cambridge World History, Volume 3: Early Cities in Comparative Perspective, 4000 BCE–1200 CE*. Cambridge: Cambridge University Press.

CHAPTER I

Before Things Worked: A "Low-Power" Model of Early Mesopotamia

SETH RICHARDSON

Men Asking for Directions: A Programmatic Introduction

If infrastructural and despotic power are both ideal (or mythical) types, any historical investigation will have to qualify itself by degrees of extensivity or intensivity. But the two forms share an absolute dimension in a political sense, in that the relevant subjectivities they create are not originally grounded in subscription, but first in the belief that the state is preeminently (and perhaps exclusively) appropriate to and capable of exercising the powers it claims, in terms of domain and governance (or: authority and power). Subjects need not approve of or even know of a state's specific undertakings, wider policies, or even underlying legitimacy to remain entangled in the forms of power it wields; they need only to expect that the fields of action in which the state engages are natural and normal to it, more so than other institutions.

The state's authority and power, however, are most strongly exemplified by historical contexts in which its forms of persuasion are *least* in evidence—that is, when the state feels its claims need little reinforcement because they are beyond question or challenge. This comes when a consciousness of subjectivity, of its alternatives and particular history, has effectively been suppressed, through a suspension of disbelief, among elites and civil society. At that point, *claims* to power become less necessary. This creates a difficulty for the historian, because it means that the state generates the most evidence for its "powers" *as it is trying to usher them into being*, before it actually has them. We make a large error when we mistake evidence of persuasion to be evidence of capacity or audience belief.

Following this introduction, I will turn to some examples from Middle Bronze Age Babylonia (ca. 2000–1600 B.C., the Old Babylonian period in Mesopotamia)—partly as a way of giving more body to the "presumptive state" model,[1] especially as regards territoriality and law, but also to stake out three further points about ancient state societies: one is categorical and generic; one is historical; one concerns the sociology of our own study of the history of the state.

My first point is that infrastructural power is generated not only by the state's appropriation of various genres, but also by its deliberate confusion of the discourses or conceptual domains that lay behind them—by the blurring of their boundaries. Despotic and infrastructural powers need not be exclusively or reciprocally distributed: states make claims through both types of power simultaneously, motivating subscription to one type through an awareness of the other. This betokens not so much comprehensive power, or even coherent and deliberate state strategy, but a reinforcement of power's premises through its *strategic ambiguation*, without those powers necessarily being actionable.[2] We find not just individual instances of conceptual domains blurred within categories—for example, to imply that kingship had a *divine* nature; or that war could have a *legal* basis[3]—but a confusion across the two super-categories of power altogether. That is, repeated cross-referencing across domains meant that it was very difficult to distinguish clearly whether any particular field of action was ultimately undertaken by the state on the basis of its infrastructural *or* despotic powers. This forestalled the ability of subjects to interrogate the state even as the state proposed to interrogate them. Domain ambiguation was (and is) a principal mechanism enabling the kind of arena—a "space" in which "a state elite could manoeuvre"—which Michael Mann proposed for the autonomous state: its gnomic quality built resilience.[4]

Whereas those manipulations generated infrastructural power in synchronous time, my second thesis has to do with the diachronic life of power claims: infrastructural power also accrues through later historical misunderstandings about its reality or extent in earlier states. This is first of all an eventual consequence of the original foresight and imaginative power of states to articulate powers ahead of their capability.[5] All types of power are incipient and generated through rhetorical premises—in the pretense of the state to speak authoritatively in different spheres of action. But this presumption takes on a life of its own in the ability of state warrants to survive beyond their original interlocutors and later get readopted as historically "true," often on misunderstood or idealizing terms, as "invented traditions." Uniquely, the institutionalism of states has the power to generate and even amplify (if not always to control) governmental rationality across gaps and reformulations of social memory, especially through the preservation and reinterpretation of its monumental and canonical texts.[6] Presumptive powers were thus realized diachronically through *historical forgetting*, with subjectivity itself proving more durable than the historical states under which it formed. Infrastructural power can be enabled by fantasies about the past, not only through the "negative capability" of transcending the past's limitations, but also through a retrospective desire for and misapprehension of things as they never quite were. The analogy is to muscle tissue being rebuilt and expanded after sequences of damage, rest, and repair.

My third point has to do with our own scholarly attitudes about studying political dominance. One can't roll about in the literature about infrastructure, despotism, and empires for long without seeing that it is overwhelmingly male; the whole enterprise can seem depressingly close to "boys fetishizing power."[7] I worry not so much about the gendering of empire studies to that end, however, as I do about what remains thereby undertheorized: there is not so much one reads about how *weak* states work—what "low power" might look like as a political modus vivendi.

Incipience being all to the point about "presumptive states," it is valid to think of all polities as continuously and permanently mired in greater or lesser conditions of insufficiency and weakness. It is not too much to assume that most of humanity, for most of the history of states, lived under regimes we would not identify as "powerful." Indeed, it is even the case for the world today. Although the state form is about as strong as it has ever been, more than half of the world's population still lives under regimes in some stage of failure. At least 51 percent of all people alive today live in states which are "failed, weak, or fragile."[8]

This becomes particularly significant for Mesopotamian antiquity, when the state's significant others (for example, elites and civil society) were equally weak actors[9]—therefore, a balance of "low power." That being the case, I attempt a serious definition of how weakness works from the Mesopotamian case. This involves tracing the historical development of concepts of the public good in low-power contexts, so that are we speaking not so much of "boys fetishizing power" as we are about the culturally alien concept of "men asking for directions"—because early states had first to develop sovereignty, categorically, as a natural form, namely, a moral given, accepted by the subjects thereby created.

The Power(?) of Babylon

I will discuss these points through the historical case of the First Dynasty of Babylon (fl. 1900–1600 B.C.), and the relationship of its incomplete powers to the infrastructure of subsequent states. From certain points of view, Babylon appears the very picture of a mighty ancient kingdom:[10] under Hammurabi (r. 1792–1750 B.C.), Babylon became the most territorially coherent and militarily powerful state in more than 200 years, since the fall of the Third Dynasty of Ur in 2004. Its conquests stretched from Upper Mesopotamia to the Persian Gulf. The state possessed a monopoly of legitimate violence through legal codification, with statute law addressing civil and criminal processes.[11] Babylon regulated commercial practices, prices, and wages.[12] It held preeminent taxation authority.[13] It exercised powers of appointment not only over its own officers[14] but over local civil bodies and temple institutions.[15] Babylon set up a theological justification of power through the elevation of its city god, Marduk, to regional primacy, to whom the great gods had allegedly allotted "supreme power over all peoples."[16] The state intruded into elite scribal circles through revisions to curricula and practices;[17] into civil society through paternalist protections of the waif, the widow, and the indigent;[18] and into ethnicity through the styling of the king as a leader of "Amorites."[19] In all, Babylon appears to have been an infrastructurally powerful state that regulated elite and civil relations through a comprehensive package of social utilities: law, commerce, taxation, institutions, theology, knowledge, caretaking, and ethnic identity, all backstopped by a control of violence.

But everything I have just described is not really true. A point-by-point refutation is not practicable here and would keep me from my larger points, but I will try to illustrate some of the gaps between a maximalist and a minimalist perspective by addressing two aspects of infrastructural power central to Michael Mann's analytic: territoriality and law.

Babylon and Territoriality

The Shifting Ground

I will begin with territoriality, so central to Mann's formulation. Territory should comprise a convincing spatial demarcation externally, and a regular fabric of authority internally.[20] By these standards, Babylon fails on a number of levels.

For one thing, as with other political cultures addressed in this book, we are looking at one that did not rarefy the state terminologically. There was the king (*šarru*), the dynasty (*palû*), the land (*mātu*), the city (*ālu*), and the kingship (*šarrūtu*), but no differentiated term for kingdom or state.[21] Nor was the state the subject of any term for territorial extent: no word meaning "Babylonia" yet existed (though it would by about 1400 B.C. or so), and existing terms such as "Sumer and Akkad" and "the four quarters of the earth" were notional expressions of ethnicity[22] and cosmology, with no convincing references to national frontiers or borders.[23] There are clarifications worth making to those characterizations,[24] but they do not subtract from the fact that Mesopotamian political entities were not, at the basic level of denomination, realized in geographic terms in the Old Babylonian period.

If by "territory," however, we mean the extent of Babylon's geopolitical and military power on the ground, regardless of what it was called, we still come up short: Babylon's status and influence can only be defined by the negative characteristic of its elimination (rather than control) of rival states. Of Babylon's main competitors in the 150+ years after the 1760s, Mari was cashiered and emasculated; Ešnunna went permanently on the disabled list; Elam was driven from regional influence, not to reappear in Mesopotamian geopolitics until the Late Bronze Age; and Larsa was governed for only one generation before it rebelled and collapsed. The initial victories are not in dispute; but a deduction from them that Babylon controlled all the lands formerly held by those rivals by cession or conquest is not warranted.

Nor was Babylon demarcated externally, as part of a state system. In the first place, no contemporary conception of frontiers is attested. Instead we find a plethora of toponyms lacking areal definition—remote villages, trading posts, tribal camps, and "open country." The territorial extent of Babylonian power can thus only be vaguely guessed at by drawing lines around the outermost cities mentioned in Babylonian texts[25] and a few natural boundaries.

But this might be said of many ancient states. What is more salient is that Babylonian texts say virtually nothing about other major states after 1728[26]— not the kingdoms with which it had previously treated, nor even Aššur, Aleppo, or Qatna, though all three of those cities certainly survived down through the seventeenth century. Nor is Babylon mentioned in what few contemporary texts there are from other lands (for example, Tigunanum). It is as if a light switch had been flipped off: the world of warring and treating states so specifically and vividly documented ca. 1850–1750 B.C. simply disappeared from view in one generation, down to 1595 and beyond. Simultaneously, we find an uptick in references to enemies without any names at all—simply attackers called "the enemy." Hence, we are not only talking about an absence of frontiers, but of other states altogether—indeed, of an international system, a crucial criterion for state identity. We cannot, therefore, locate a kingdom of Babylon as a conventionally territorialized state among others in geographic space.

What about internal territoriality, about sovereignty as it was articulated *within* the spaces the state was understood to regulate? If anything, this kind of territorial power turns out to be even more difficult to verify. Strictly speaking, Hammurabi never styled himself as king of anything other than the city of Babylon—that is, *a* king, not *the* king. For each of the twenty-five other cities appearing in the prologue of the Laws of Hammurabi[27] (hereafter, LH), the king stakes his authority on his patronage and protection of temples and cities, as provider of plenty and builder of monuments, but not on any title (true for all of Hammurabi's successors as well). Hammurabi and his successors are nowhere even titled as kings over the core cities preexisting the conquest state that had been in hand since the infancy of the dynasty around 1900 B.C. (namely, Sippar, Kiš, or Dilbat). Having noted already that there was no categorical term for "kingdom" (that is, no "Kingdom of Babylonia"), it is therefore significant that neither were the kings of Babylon even kings of any other *city*.

Even the internal sovereignty implied by Hammurabi's epithets of patronage in the LH Prologue was inflated. This is not because it was mere overstatement (for example, his claims to have exercised "mercy" for Mari and Larsa, cities he had subjected to brutal attacks[28]), but by beefing up the list of cities under Hammurabi's "protection" with cities long in dormancy (Akkad,[29]

Lagaš, Eridu[30]), places his armies never even got close to (Aššur and Nineveh), and towns soon to be entirely depopulated (virtually the rest of the list).[31] Claims of power over south Babylonian cities in fact lost from control also show up in the dynasty's later debt-remission edicts.[32] In fact, these debt remissions express royal power not over cities or lands, but over people—specific *clients*—of four types: titled Crown officers; people holding concessions from the Crown (for example, fellmongers and herders); the peoples and corporate bodies of abandoned cities, mostly from the south, as diasporic or metic wards of the state;[33] and clients attached to the desmesne estates of the king of Babylon.[34] These were reliefs for specific people under obligations of clientage—not for "everyone"[35]—essentially to effect the tax-free status of elites—and not over places, let alone "everywhere."[36]

Hammurabi and his successors expressed their control over territory notionally, but it can hardly be the case that they exercised sovereignty over these lands. With fatuous claims suggesting that even empty or lost cities were local anchors, with open country[37] and tribal areas marbled throughout the state, and with no clear occupational control of those places as *terra nullius*, Hammurabi's kingdom was of the "swiss cheese" type:[38] centrality and peripherality were not inscribed geographically, but along lines of clientage and its absence.

What does all this mean for territoriality? It means that direct royal authority was limited to the Crown's domain lands that it held in ownership (for example, property called *ša* É.GAL, lit. "of the palace"). Elsewhere, its authority was mediated through institutional and even personal patronage or charter, rather than through any clear expression of state territoriality. This is as far as any territorial ecology of infrastructure extended. The Babylonian state exercised powers as a great (but not exclusive or preeminent) institution among other institutions (cities, temples, great households) that had isomorphic patron-and-client ties. This mixed basis of urban kingship, institutional patronage, and domain lordship had a diluting effect on what state spatial control there was. As such, the state focused more on the building and holding of clientele than it did on lands.

Finally, if one assumes that the hard edge of military might backstopped all these otherwise conditional expressions of territorial power—that is, that all this fine parsing of legal and geographic terms above ignores Babylon's operational military power on the ground—one would still be wrong. Babylonian conquests declined sharply after 1750, with little evidence for large deployments. Documents of the period describe units and fortresses staffed by not more than a hundred men, and often fewer—this after decades when tens of thousands of men had been mobilized at arms.[39] The idea that Babylon held sway over any patch of land by a preponderance of force is simply not in evidence.

Territorial Dreams

And yet paradoxically this state pretended so often to just such territorial integrity. The Babylonian kings spoke about giving "freedom for the country"[40] and "making their rule manifest in the mountain lands."[41] They gave models of "mountains and rivers" (another merism for the land) as votives,[42] called the country "obedient" to them,[43] and "provided just ways for the people of the land."[44] Though they demurred from specific, fixed, and local definitions of geographic control, they nevertheless played constantly and consistently at the largest possible terms of spatial power, but only in ways that could not be openly falsified. The framework hinted at cosmologies, ethnicity, and a landscape that naturalized royal power.

What is significant is not so much that the Crown did not control "everywhere," but that the term "the land" was used to *imply* it.[45] "Don't you know that the whole of the country (*mātum kalû*) belongs to Marduk and to Samsuiluna the king?" wrote one man to his brother. "The entire country (*mātum kalû*) has heard and rejoiced," wrote a Larsa king in another letter of the promulgation of his own debt remission.[46] The indistinction of the term "the entire land" was its chief advantage: to be king everywhere—but of no juridically or geographically specific place in particular—with an accumulation of highly specific patronage relations hinting at paramountcy, which suggested, by mixed metaphor, a total kingship that neither existed, nor was claimed, nor was locatable.

This is strategic ambiguation; what about historical forgetting? It is all to the point that Babylon's phantom territoriality nevertheless emerged as a substantial feature of the Kassite state in the following historical period. The change from the Old Babylonian to Kassite periods was a watershed, an intermission between historical acts. Between the two periods lies what is conventionally termed a "dark age."[47] Whether or not that intervening time was as thoroughly devoid of political organization and scribal activity as we think, the remission of Mesopotamian state society in that time was sufficient to form a barrier to social memory. Despite the absence of a political framework, enough cultural information was nevertheless transmitted across the gap that the memory-barrier sublimely transformed a fictional (and, to judge by revolts and state failure, a fairly unpopular) concept of territoriality into a belief that it was an objective historical fact.

Thus what emerged in the later Kassite period (after 1400 B.C.) was the first territorial nomenclature for Babylonia as a political unit (*māt Karduniaš*, "the land of the harbor of [the god] Duniaš");[48] an internal provincial system that territorialized city-states for tax-collection;[49] and internationally recognized external boundaries (*miṣru, taḫumu*) between Babylonia and its largest neighbors, Assyria and Elam, established through treaty relations.[50] The existence of these terms hardly implies their full effectiveness, but it does argue for a conceptual redevelopment of territoriality after the Old Babylonian period: even if they had not been fully workable forms, they were real and new ideas.

These three developments did not make any overt reference to Hammurabi's state. But since Babylon emerged not only as the dynastic seat of Kassite "Karduniaš" but as the region's exclusive and undisputed religious and political capital for the next 1200 years—and since it held the First Dynasty in historical esteem as the antecedent power from which its sovereignty was transferred[51]—it is likely that the sense of territorial centrality emerged from historical assumptions that Babylonia was a natural political unit, a "land" under the rule of the city of Babylon. Thus the millennial city of Late Bronze and Iron Age Babylon produced a more durable and accepted "state idea" than was warranted by any particular historical facts. Babylon's preeminence, hotly disputed by most Mesopotamians in the eighteenth century, had been naturalized by the fifteenth century, through historical fallowing, into an accepted truth, giving rise to one of what are sometimes called the ancient Near East's Late Bronze Age "national" states.

Territory and Political Membership

We expect the question of political membership to arise at the intersection of territory and law, as a consequence of jurisdiction (on which, see the following section). But for most of the history of Mesopotamian territorial and imperial states, personal status never escaped the frame of city identity—one was an Urukean or a Dilbatean or a Borsippean, a "son of City X," but not a "Babylonian" (except as a resident of Babylon). This held true juridically,[52] in the literary imagination,⁵³ and in the everyday business of letters,⁵⁴ with the state never developing membership categories, only vague terms such as *nīšū*, "[the] people." The terminology of political membership, unlike later developments for territorial identity and legal jurisdiction, thus never made the jump to express statewide relations, remaining stubbornly fixed on local affiliation.

But under even this apparently durable city identity lay an important change. After Old Babylonian times, the political status of individuals, groups, towns, and institutions began to be modified and articulated through charters and grants. These usually included negatively constructed entitlements (that is, "rights or privileges *from*")—exemptions from taxes, military service, or corvée work, legal immunities from state encroachment.⁵⁵ They could also, however, include positively-constructed entitlements ("rights or privileges *to*") such as prebends, incomes, compensation for damages, and legal process—rents and services conceded to individuals and communities by the state.⁵⁶ Both types of rights were endowed through *kiddinūtu*-status⁵⁷ and *narû*-endowments,⁵⁸ and reflected in literary texts.⁵⁹ The enumerated rights and privileges were limited—they would impress no Enlightenment *philosophes*—but the parties to whom they were extended expanded gradually over time from specific nobles to entire cities. Such privileges legally limited the reach of state power, and began to build lines of city-identity by enumerated rights, rather than clientage. This trajectory did not result in any finished, generalizable form, and it was a long way from citizenship;⁶⁰ but it later pushed in that direction by legally defining individuals and cities according to bundled entitlements determined by place.

Part of this development is attributable to a long-term trend of ruralization from the late third all the way into the first millennium.⁶¹ This process was well underway by Hammurabi's time, de-emphasizing the urban character that had marked Mesopotamian states since the Early Bronze Age.⁶² Babylonian royal power after 1750 was increasingly over rural areas:⁶³ the property and personnel under the direct command of the kings lay outside of cities, living on the kings' lands, in the towns they founded, the fortresses where their soldiers were billeted, and the tribes with whom they had treaty relations. These rural communities were the antecedents for what emerged in the Late Bronze Age as royal manors and feuds.

The king of Babylon's control over cities, meanwhile, became indirect across the seventeenth century, contingent on his role as protector and provider. This was a reversal of the distribution of power prevailing only a century before, as voiced in a south-Babylonian letter reading "those who live in Larsa belong to the king; those who live in the open country."[64] By the 1600s, Babylonian administration was being mediated through networks of merchants and local officials, actors who negotiated the collection of rents and conversion of staples into silver.[65] The types of charter concessions later granted to cities had their roots in this interface of negotiated authority. Thus, though Mesopotamian states had had a primarily urban character since Early Dynastic times, the waning of the Middle Bronze brought a new emphasis on kingship over lands rather than cities, and the realization of political membership based on domains and charters. Both were rooted in territorial identity, rather than clientage, an identity based on social relations. Thus the background demographic shift of ruralization came to deeply affect the character of the political as much as it did the patterns of landscape settlement.

One last historical problem of the Late Old Babylonian period illustrates how political membership was still in development and not yet a single category. Only one generation after Hammurabi's conquests, the Babylonian state became responsible for a number of loyalist refugees from the southern cities that had rebelled and become substantially depopulated between 1740 and 1720 B.C. The presence of these émigrés is known through post-1720 textual evidence from the north giving southern cultic titles, professions, and personal names there.[66]

Where this becomes relevant to the territory/membership question has to do with the position of those groups in the debt-remission edicts of the Babylonian kings mentioned above. The edicts included protections for the diasporic citizens (DUMU) and mercantile guilds (KAR) of southern cities lost to Babylon's control, now resident in northern Babylonia.[67] Their legal grouping with others created, at least on clay, administrative communities of state clients, brought into being by the edicts' having made them "legible" or "knowable" (in James Scott's terms) to the Crown. This we could call "documentary sovereignty." The direct authority of the Crown over this constituency was qualitatively different from the custodial discourse that bound the old temple-cities to the king. Thus not only a legal localism, city by city, but a distinction between the cities and the Crown domain, created irregular legal environments that worked away from a unified Babylonian political membership. These distinctions were also the basis for later historical (mis)understandings that cities held ancient communal privileges, while the king acted as he pleased in other places.

Prior to 1500 B.C., however, political membership was not, despite feints in that direction, based on state identity. We see irregular sovereignty environments, in both the Crown's direct (that is, "despotic") authority over royal domains and its negotiated authority in city-communes, as well as parallel infrastructural ethos of clientage and law. Such distinctions forestalled the development of any single common juridical category of citizenship, of unified subjectivity as part of the infrastructural package.

Babylon and the Discourse of Law

The Infrastructural Function of Law

An even more urgent project of the early Babylonian state was to generate infrastructural power in the domain of regulating civil, criminal, and commercial law. Yet the Crown's claims to juridical power ought not to be taken at face value, especially with respect to the gaps between statute and practice.[68] These gaps were not just partial and occasional, but wholesale and regular: virtually none of Hammurabi's "laws" found their way into the relevant contracts or legal processes where one might expect to find them, nor, conversely, is much of the contract language found in business documents discoverable in state laws.[69]

Much thought has already been poured into the problematic relationship of the law collections' broad discrepancy to both actual practice[70] and royal decrees.[71] These analyses need not be rehearsed here, except to note the wide variety of interpretations that have been offered: these range from, on the one end, a presumption of the laws' authority as so universal as not to require citation;[72] all the way down to the other, that they were not "positive law" at all, neither "authoritative [nor] enforceable."[73] The laws have been seen by some (especially in individual instances of application) as "basic rules" for the formation of more specific decisions; but by others as "decidedly *not legislative* . . . [they] must be viewed in the first instance as royal apologia and testaments."[74] The problem I examine is not why and how are the laws so infrequently seen in action, but—given that—why were they written in a statutory voice, or invoked statutorily at all? The answer has everything to do with the construction of legal discourse as a form of social power. Martha Roth has written: "Ultimately, such questions as Is there any concord between the formal law collections and the transactional contracts? or Is the daily operation of the law constrained by the rules of the formal law collections? are not really answerable and, moreover, miss the intimate connections between law and society. The many and varied manifestations of the law . . . are all evidence of the law as a function of social life."[75] This is undoubtedly correct (though one might add "political" as well as social life). But what kinds of functions might be meant? And what of their political dimension? My purpose lies not in chasing after such questions as Roth feels are unproductive, but in explicating what *kind* of infrastructural (that is, social and political) functionality those texts had for state and society.

Between Statute and Practice: Correspondences

Wherever along the spectrum of interpretations one's opinion lies about the laws' effectiveness, one must tangle with the unpleasant fact that there are a small number of citations of or allusions to Babylon's legal regulations, but also that many of those tend to be problematically inexact on close inspection. It may seem unnecessary to substantiate the paucity of correspondences between statute and practice, since that basic truth is well accepted. But a good deal of scholarly attention is still given to this small number of apparent equivalences, and this continues to give the impression that they attend to a historical norm. They do not. A properly comparative method ought to pay proportional attention to variances and deviations, which is in this case to say: a vastly superior amount of attention. Thus of necessity I will first detail the fact of this discrepancy, well known as it is, before I turn to the more important intervention, which is to ask the *why* of it: how is one to square the apparently enormous ideological importance of Babylonian law to Babylonian power, given the almost unbelievably low profile of the state's actual involvement in legal process?

As Roth has put it, two biases have characterized the history of Mesopotamian legal scholarship: first, that the relationship between statute and practice in this period might illustrate something called "Old Babylonian law"; second, that an evolutionary approach might identify that law as a "less sophisticated" antecedent to our own. She terms the second bias (of less concern to us here) outmoded, and the first one a "fiction," in these terms: "There is no reasonable reading of our sources that can lead us to assume there were *rules* that dictated the treatment by the Mesopotamian judicial bodies of relevant circumstances. There were, to be sure, *standards* that were applied to given situations . . . that allowed the authorities to use their experience, to evaluate the offenses and the offenders, and to apply equitable treatment."[76] This distinction between rules and standards points to the crucial role of analogy in the application of law-collection provisions, a function useful in the exegesis of the few letters and lawsuits in which correspondences between statute and practice seem apparent (see below). What Roth makes clear, however, is that any "assumption of generalizations over individual cases" is misguided; that not only law cases but even the law collections themselves are primarily "examples of successful practice"; and that a study of case law will be more informative about "the variety of legal and social experience"—all conclusions sound and true.[77]

What is much less clear is why, given that they were never used statutorily, the law-collections apparatus were as lengthy, specific, and complex as they were, or often seem to have been invoked as if they *were* rules; why standards not used as laws *sounded* like laws; and how their rhetorical presentation as such related to the social and political "group mores" Roth says they teach. These questions are important for three reasons. First, despite the fact that Roth's view reflects a *communis opinio* among scholars, there is, still and notwithstanding, broad deference to the idea that royal law was not only a preeminent and common standard, but even that it advanced rules that could be and sometimes were applied statutorily. The second reason is that the notion of preeminence has been bolstered by continued attention to a small minority of seeming correspondences rather than (what ought methodologically to be of greater importance) a supermajority of variances. And the third reason is that failure to attend to the law's nonnormative status has not developed any theory of the law collections' other values as rhetorical and political precepts; little attempt has been made to study the problem as a matter of law-as-literature. In these three respects, attention to the gaps between "statute" and practice take on a different importance: though the gaps have been generally acknowledged many times before, their specific differences have been primarily understood as the outcomes of analogistic procedure, and their underlying correspondence still asserted.

In fact, attention to specific differences reveals that the king's law, far from being a preeminent standard, was just one legal system among many; that law itself was only one conflict resolution system among many; and that the genre of royal law was a relative latecomer to the scene, more effective at generating infrastructural power presumptively than juridically (see Mackil, this volume).

State and private letters of the period provide our best opportunity to see how legal concepts played out in civil life.[78] Here, we may begin by looking at references to the king's "regulations" in the course of daily business.

A few Old Babylonian letters, though lacking important details, do seem to loosely correspond to the provisions found in LH, such as a case involving the restoration of a woman's dowry;[79] a boatman's liability to an owner for the value of a sunken boat;[80] and the mention of a stela (perhaps LH itself) establishing minimum wages.[81] Also suggestive are the many letters that appeal for justice to be rendered *kīma ṣimdatim*, "according to the regulations" (on which phrase, see below). Many of these, however, describe legal situations that are not found in, at significant variance with, or too vague to test against the provisions of LH. Yet a few do seem in keeping with the statutes. In the case of a man whose son and daughter-in-law had absconded with barley meant to seed a field, one might usefully interpret various provisions of LH governing investment losses as the basis for a verdict by analogy.[82] There is also an early loan foreclosure that claims that its collection would be *kīma ṣimdatim*; and there are indeed LH passages aplenty governing creditors' rights of collection for silver.[83] And a third letter involving responsibility for a dead ox at Nippur might bring into play the indemnification clauses of LH specific to ox-rentals.[84] Such cases might lend themselves to confidence that invocations of the law in a general way had specific statutes in mind.

But such correspondences, even with minor variances, are not the sort I wish to call into question. In many other cases, discrepancies between the king's laws and how cases were actually handled raise questions about why, how, and whether the law could be applied, even by analogy. I will review nine such cases that have either been discussed in the literature as pointing to an application of LH, or that themselves seem to appeal to the king's law.

In a first court document, a man swears that if he is ever caught bringing another man's bride-to-be out of the city gate, he may be punished as one would be for spiriting out a slave. This seems to allude to LH ¶ 15, which prescribes death for the latter infraction; but the letter does not specify a punishment, and is at most (*per analogiam*) the basis for taking a (voluntary) oath for a prospective—rather than past—infraction.[85] In a second case, a letter describing a man seized by "the enemy" finds Hammurabi arranging for the payment of his ransom by a temple, which possibility is raised by LH ¶ 32; but in that passage, the temple and the king are not responsible cooperatively or by command, as is the case here, but successively.[86] A third instance describes burglars caught red-handed, a situation described by LH ¶ 21; but they are put under guard, rather than put to death and hanged in the house, as the law prescribes.[87]

In a fourth case, a man is detained as a pledge against debt, and the creditor is warned by the letter writer against accepting liability for the detainee's well-being, since the distrained man is in state service.[88] The relevant provisions of the laws protecting distrainees for debt indeed caution that the original claim would be dismissed or compounded with a fine in the event of the distrainee's deliberate harm or unnatural death while in a distrainor's keeping (LH ¶ 115–116), and to this extent the law may apply. But the letter's concern for the legal condition of the distrainee's state servitude has no basis in LH: the relevant passages protect only the state *property* in such people's possession (LH ¶ 26–32, 35–41) and prohibit its exploitation by military superiors (LH ¶ 33–34); they do not protect their persons.

A fifth example has Hammurabi finding in favor of three sons who have come to claim the service field of their father, now occupied by an unrelated man acting as a squatter. This judgment would seemingly be supported by LH ¶ 28. But the fact that the father had fled, rather than been taken prisoner (as the statute stipulates, supporting POWs rather than AWOLs) actually puts it more in line with the conditions of LH ¶ 30—in which the squatter's rights are upheld, not the family's.[89] In a sixth case, Hammurabi orders the restoration of a runaway slavegirl to her owners, but neglects to mention any punishment for the man harboring her in his house, where LH ¶¶ 16 and 19 clearly call for his execution.[90]

Other letters are implausible as invocations of statute law, even when they specifically present their case "according to the regulations," *kīma ṣimdatim*.[91] Take a seventh example, a man who challenges another with "Do you not know that according to the regulations of my lord, a man should not be deprived of (even) one quart of barley (that he is entitled to) according to the wording of his sealed document (*ana pī kankišu*)?"[92] Yet nothing in LH backs this claim up, not even among the potentially relevant passages of ¶¶ 41–65. Or, eighth, consider the man who had given a mina of silver to a merchant "for safekeeping," but later found that, despite repeated requests, the merchant simply would not return the silver. The man then called for the seizure of the silver *per ṣimdatum*. But LH treats only the rules for repayment when merchants were creditors, not debtors (or guarantors, or trustees).[93] Or, ninth, take the innkeeper whose longtime servant abandoned him for another household, taking his entire staff with her. "Pronounce a verdict about her according to the regulations!" he demands. But since she was neither his wife nor daughter nor daughter nor slave, the law had nothing to say about any powers he might have over her, nor indeed the staff.[94] In such cases, the writers specifically appealed to the royal *ṣimdatum* despite the absence of relevant provisions.

These discrepancies are not so great that they require us to question the laws' *potential* statutory applicability, either specifically or as analogies, only to underscore how underwhelming the evidence is to conclude for the law's normativity. The cases that seem to illustrate the laws in practice are *never* quite as apposite as one might want—even in cases where appellants seem specifically to invoke them (on *kima ṣimdatim*, see further below). To reconstruct an environment of positive law by emphasizing a few imperfect equivalences between statute and practice—and ignoring the majority of cases running counter to that equivalency—cannot be an acceptable methodology. However correspondent the foregoing cases may or may not be to the law—and let us imagine for the sake of argument that they *are* correspondences or analogies, no matter how imperfect—they are still rare. What we have in superabundance are *disparities*, and these deserve an equally structured examination.

Between Statute and Practice: Disparities

What do we find when we give equal attention to differences? Among Old Babylonian letters describing legal matters, LH emerges only rarely as reference, analogy, or statute for contracts and disputes of the sort notionally governed under the law.[95] Out of some 2,800 Old Babylonian letters published in the series *Altbabylonische Briefe und Beiheft*,[96] only about twenty make convincing reference to the king's law as statute[97] (with a few more mentioning occasional decrees[98]), with many more revealing that the status of the law was complicated and tempered by location and the involvement of other authoritative bodies.

The most common phrases in letters appealing to some legal standard were, as mentioned above, variations of the phrase (*dinam*) *kīma ṣimdatim*, "(the law) according to the regulations." These were only occasionally specified as *royal* regulations (*kīma ṣimdat šarrim*, "of the king";[99] *šarrim* was commonly omitted), but there is no need to doubt that the unelaborated form usually meant the king's law. That we find more typically *kīma ṣimdat bēlī(ya)* ("of my lord"),[100] however, begins to point towards the primary force of *ṣimdatum* as administrative law, that is, the institutional rules of a lord for his clients and vassals, intramurally, and not of a king over all people.¹⁰¹

It is also evident that the king's legal powers were not exclusive of or prescriptive for other jurists or juridical bodies. Alongside the *ṣimdat šarrim*, "the regulations of the king," there were rules (*ṣimdatum*) and rulings (*dīnam*) of all kinds of officers and institutions, for example, of bosses (*dīnam šāpiri*), gods (*dīnam ša* DN, in juridical capacities), headmen (*ṣimdat ša* ENSÍ), local judges (*dīnam ša dayyanim ša* GN),¹⁰² and local notables (*ṣimdat awīlū*).¹⁰³ We also find traces of choice of law: in one case, a high administrator referred a case simultaneously, in parallel proceedings, to Hammurabi and to the headman of a local river district (a *šāpir nārim*);¹⁰⁴ in another, an official was told to choose adjudication by either the king's decree (*dīnam kīma ṣimdatim*) or through a legal process in the local temple: "Either you guarantee his lawsuit in accordance with the legal rules, or, if you want no lawsuit, see to it from the citizens of his city who go into the temple of Ea that you can grant him a process in accordance with the legal rules in the temple of Ea."¹⁰⁵

Other variances to the weight of the king's law are indicated by claims of exemption from it,¹⁰⁶ and complaints about unenumerated rights and unequal protection under the *ṣimdatum*.¹⁰⁷ Other appeals to the king make no mention of *ṣimdatum*, but ask him to render judgments on the basis of the terms of specific contracts.¹⁰⁸ One must also wonder about references to the way in which regulations were put into practice, that is, not just "according to the regulations," but as they were customarily applied *ša mahar*, "as they obtain (with),"¹⁰⁹ or *ina qāti*, "(as applied) by the hand of"¹¹⁰ various judges. The application of law as a process of justice is interpretive no matter what legal system might be under our lens; but statements like these anticipate local, customary, or even personal practices as regular and institutional variable applications, beyond the occasional, personal interpretive latitude of this or that judge in some particular case.

Just as significantly, the force of the king's law is proven—but also proven limited—by his acknowledgment of different jurisdictions, sometimes in the state's delegation or alienation of legal authority *away* from itself. Usually, the recognition of other jurisdictions involved resident aliens in the king's land,¹¹¹ or royal interests in tribal areas. In one instance combining the two circumstances, a free woman of the foreign land of Idamaraṣ, who had been deported in an Elamite invasion, wound up living in tribal Jamutbal, now notionally under Babylonian control.¹¹² In this instance, the king's law recognized and continued the force of a foreign law by legally reestablishing her free status by a Babylonian legal judgement (*dinam kīma ṣimdatim*).¹¹³ Sometimes, of course, cases remanded to one official or another were merely intra-jurisdictional, namely, the delegation (as against alienation) of legal authority to the king's subordinates.¹¹⁴ This was not much more than our determining, say, whether a case belonged in criminal court or family court, or should be tried in Virginia rather than Utah. Notwithstanding, this process sometimes involved such a tangle of overlapping authorities¹¹⁵ that the lack of clear jurisdiction was evidently itself the problem being solved.¹¹⁶

But in other cases, the Crown simply outsourced the administration of justice to other jurisdictions altogether.¹¹⁷ The recognition of alien jurisdiction is first of all implied by cases involving requests for extradition, as when the elders of one town wrote to an official to complain, "Is it customary to extradite free citizens on the basis of what a slave says?"¹¹⁸ In a second instance, Hammurabi asked that deserters from his own palace who had fled to tribal territory be tried there locally instead of returned to Babylon: "Grant them justice in accordance with the legal practice that is currently applied in Jamutbalum."¹¹⁹ Another letter finds two officials discussing the hazards of permitting a subject's residence in Jamutbal; if the man is "enrolled" there, he will be outside of the state's direct legal control: "Speak to Sin-ereš: Thus says Ubarum. May Šamaš keep you in good health for 3600 years! Concerning the honorable Adi-mati-ilī, he is written on my tablet. Do not *release* the gentleman *to* the tablet of the people of Jamūt-bālum. The matter is of great consequence to my lord. As to your bad feelings, about which you spoke to me, I want to insist that they provide judicial procedure (*dajānūtam lišāḫizu*); and should you enroll the gentleman (*awīlam tašaṭarma*), nobody will be able to take him (*laqiašu mamman*) as long as the sun . . . you."¹²⁰ The premise of local jurisdiction seems also enshrined by the broken passage of the Larsa letter quoted earlier ("Those who live in Larsa belong to the king"¹²¹). The king's deference to other, local legal bodies may have been a de facto acknowledgement of working reality, which required the recognition of alternate jurisdictions in practice, rather than royal ideal.

There were differences between statute and practice not only in civil and criminal but also in commercial law. In private letters, we see prices set at local,¹²² household,¹²³ and market¹²⁴ rates rather than the ones specified by the king's laws or edicts;¹²⁵ interest on loans discussed without reference to legal specifications;¹²⁶ wages paid on terms other than those specified in LH;¹²⁷ and a range of weights and measures, against LH's standard "small" and "large" units.¹²⁸ We find the private enforcement of costs and damages through personal persuasion,[129] shaming,[130] compensation,[131] and distraint or imprisonment[132] (though almost never through private violence[133]), rather than through state enforcement.

Thus, among the classes of non-correspondence between statute and practice, we find the application of the king's law structurally compromised by the recognition or alienation of other jurisdictions, exemptions and unequal protections, choice of law, variable application, other systems and standards (for example, contract terms), venue, and the *ṣimdatum* of other bodies. Under such circumstances, what was the point of making the king's law sound statutory?

Babylonian Law as Discourse: Legal "Voice"

The situation first of all reflects the social world we know from Mesopotamian proverbs, which cast doubt on the expectation of obtaining any real help from authorities in enforcement, and simply counsel the avoidance of all quarrels in the first place.[134] This dubiety is exemplified in a composition called "The Three Ox-Drivers from Adab," a cautionary tale about expectations of royal justice. It begins: "There were three friends, citizens of Adab, who fell into a dispute with each other, and sought justice. They deliberated the matter with many words, and went before the king." But the verdict—after the king seeks advice from a *nadītu*-priestess—engenders only further antagonism: "When the king came out from the cloistered lady's presence, each man's heart was dissatisfied," even though "with elaborate words, the case of the citizens of Adab was settled."[135] Just as state letters rarely made reference to legal process as a method of resolving disputes from the top down, private ones from below rarely voiced any expectation of law as a remedy, and literary references looked at the process of justice with a jaundiced—if longing—eye.[136]

It is the longing rather than the law that is the point. Even in disparities and shortfalls of application, one sees the growing purchase that law had on the public imagination, in a developing belief that law *could be* a remedy; a subscription marking the transformation of presumptive into infrastructural power. But the *actual* legal powers of the state largely did not yet exist, were not being exercised, and in fact were often not even claimed, only imputed and implied. By turns, the law as statute appears marginal, irrelevant, and subject to application by place and circumstance; but apparently it generated imaginative power nevertheless.

So let us consider the matter from a rhetorical and imaginative instead of a juridical perspective. A clear consensus has emerged that LH was primarily an "ideological" statement or guiding standard rather than something read for its statutory force. Yet less has been done to elaborate what ideology was being propagated beyond the presentation of the king as a paradigmatic just ruler. Why was statute law (so styled) the voice chosen to promote this idea? What would one find through a structured analysis of LH's juridical terms as a form of *rhetoric*?

Let us first think about the curious absence of the state in the text. What is particularly surprising is that not only is there a desideratum of the specifications one would need to apply the laws adjudicatively (which accords with their low incidence of use), but there is a shockingly low *topical* presence of king and crown in the text at all. Of 279 preserved laws in LH, only one reserves any specific powers to the king: the capacity to redeem the life of a male adulterer if his female partner has already been pardoned by her husband. Among all possible powers, this is not a particularly impressive intervention in civil affairs, and it really prescribes the king's responsibility to *do* something, rather than arrogating a power to him.[137]

In only five more laws is the jurisdiction of the palace as an institution specified. In two of these, the Crown is to prosecute fugitives from justice, but only if, first, the plaintiffs have dragged the accused to the palace authorities themselves.[138] Two more laws backed up standard rates of interest, but they name other royal edicts as their authoritative texts (that is, not the laws themselves), and the enforcement, as with the fugitives, is predicated on the plaintiff's self-help.[139] And the fifth provision in LH that specifies state involvement in a legal process is also telling: a soldier taken captive on a royal campaign should be ransomed by the palace—but only as third and last option, if the soldier's private household and then his city's temple are first demonstrably unable to do so.[140] This illustrates the Crown's basic desire to act as enforcer of last, not first, resort.

Thus Hammurabi's state defined its role in only 6 of 279 laws (=2 percent), and every single one of them either limits its responsibility to adjudicate, or shares it with other parties. The state is absent even from other cases in which royal property or service was at risk.[141] There *was* a presumption that the Crown would act or appear as an appellate judicial authority, available on application[142]—indeed, this role is the basis for many of the letters discussed above—and the intent of LH was to imply that the state should be credited with the effectiveness of the entire field of law. But this implication should not be mistaken for the actual exercise of these powers. The Crown rarely interested itself in disputes by originating or pursuing its authority through the law (administration, rather, was the domain in which power was exercised);[143] it entertained few actual appeals;[144] and, more to the point, it took care to severely limit its liability to do so by keeping itself out of statute law.

It is significant, then, that other institutional bodies have a similarly low profile in LH: only fourteen laws required oaths or proof before gods (that is, at temples);[145] eight involved judges;[146] three for city wards, two for assemblies, two for the city and *rabiānum* (paired), and one each for irrigation districts and merchants.[147] (Private households are the recognized authorities in eleven cases.)[148] Thus thirty-one laws assign juridical roles to institutions other than the state, but in no case do they entail exclusive or preeminent jurisdiction:[149] in every instance, other adjudicating authorities are involved.[150] In almost all of those cases, the institutions are only involved in the early phases of the legal process: discovery and trial; occasionally in judgment; almost never in sentencing or punishment.[151] The text does not only build a low profile for the king and the state, it categorically does not foreground institutions as infrastructurally powerful.[152] So even if we think of the laws as exemplary rather than statutory; and even if one looks here for the king-as-protagonist rather than the king-as-jurist; the composition makes little sense as a *depiction* of palace (or even institutional) legal authority.

Meanwhile, 164 laws of LH—more than half—are built on the premise of self-help through active verbal constructions: if something went wrong, it was the wronged party who was to go and arrange that justice be performed.[153] How that process was effected, and what authority might help a plaintiff, is never specified. Not unless that help is "they": forty-four more laws say that unnamed parties ("they") are to investigate, convict, and punish crime and delict.[154] Significantly, "they" are almost exclusively connected with violent punishments.[155] Further, the process and punishment for yet thirty-four more laws are only voiced as passive third-person constructions, that is, "(s)he shall *be* punished," with the agent again remaining unspecified.[156] Finally, twenty-two more laws are impunities and prohibitions (rather than violations) and also do not specify any enforcing agent, for example, LH ¶ 36, "The field, orchard, or house of a soldier, fisherman, or state tenant will not be sold."[157] This broad unspecificity of 100 laws as to enforcement can be contrasted to all sorts of practice documents, such as contracts and law cases, that obligated persons by unique, identifying patronyms, titles, professions, and/or sealings; or even to the very different kind of unspecificity of letters, where personal knowledge of identity rendered such identifications redundant. In such texts, liabilities and responsibilities were known or made known to all parties. LH's lack of specificity is of course generically formed to the extent that its laws strip away individualizing features of cases; but this cannot explain why they do not enumerate the regular duties of any civil officers in a general way.

Thus somewhere in the neighborhood of 264 passages of the Laws of Hammurabi have jurisdiction and enforcement neither prescribed nor made available, against 37 passages in which institutions are mentioned as *any* part of the legal process—a ratio of about 8:1 (and 48:1 for state control) within the text. Quite the opposite of emphasizing a monopoly of violence or state arbitration of order, *the text deliberately distances the state from creating docile bodies through the law*—this despite its implied intrusions into relations of family, household, property, commerce, cult, and sex.[158]

Reflecting that low impact, we may take note of what coercive power *was* used to back up the king's law. In letters describing cases that called on the Crown to effect the settlement of a legal dispute, we find a rather underwhelming mode of compulsion: one could have a king's soldier sent. That is, person A could come to the door of person B with one—*one*—soldier. "Hurry!" reads a typical letter. "Restore the field to its owner before the king's soldier can reach you, *please*!" The refrain is frequent.[159] In one strongly worded letter direct from Hammurabi's desk, the king takes the unusual step of sending *two* soldiers to get something done;[160] but in a low-power world, a single gendarme was usually quite enough to enforce the law.[161]

At this point, I return the reader to my specific argument. Any legal historian of Mesopotamia will and should object that a reading of LH as the "law of the land" misunderstands it from the start. It is by now widely held that LH (and other Mesopotamian law collections) are not statutes, but partly products of scribal scholarship, partly to be understood in the context of royal administration, and partly composed of ideological statements about the king as guarantor of order and his role in dispensing justice. These points have been made many times, and need not be reargued.[162]

But my question is not what kind of lousy jurisprudence is this; but what kind of lousy *propaganda* is it? Why should it be that the king, so visually prominent at the top of the law-code stela, is virtually absent from the laws themselves? Two of the minimal criteria for ideological messaging would seem to be that the content of propaganda has to satisfy an expectation of consonance (if not identity) with reality, and that it asserts the centrality of the propagandist.

Yet LH seems to do neither; the text keeps the reader guessing about its generic identity. The unconcern to write LH as a functional instrument is partly reflected in its asystematic construction. Like similar law collections, LH is an awkward pastiche of paradigmatic and exemplary decisions, traditional *nomoi* appropriated from civil society, and narrow commercial regulations, all written as casuistic statements meant to emulate the portentousness of omens (and perhaps also their strategic deployment of results-without-agents). The combined effect is one of domain ambiguation—in fact a wholesale destabilization of realistic expectations—that suggests a guiding intelligence behind and above the (mere) law.

Even the aggressive absence of the king from the laws achieves the perverse effect of his responsibility for them in their entirety, by way of implication. Topically, the prologue and epilogue of Hammurabi's laws that bookend the decisions are *entirely* focused on the person of the king, as Roth has pointed out.[163] Grammatically, the laws are framed as a temporal subjunctive clause to the prologue, introduced by the discourse marker *inūmišu* ("At that time"), which not only renders them pendant to the prologue's true subject ("I am Hammurabi"), but strategically unlinks them from mere events, because the serial uses of "at that time" in the text effectively mean "all the time."[164] These devices of the composition effectively subordinate the mundane practice of law, set in the middle, as a mere habitus of legal process within the king's larger field of justice. This field is created and sustained not through the king's record of everyday jurisprudence, but, as the prologue and epilogue assert, through divine authorization, the suprarational basis for Hammurabi's legal-rational rule.

Situated thusly, the king's legal powers need not have been paramount (jurisdictionally, hierarchically, or on appeal), because they were not mere rule-making. The king was categorically different: he was the entire domain generating the discourse of law in the first place, permitting it to exist. He was responsible for the order that made rule-making possible, a position that was, as it was with his claims to universal power and divine favor, unassailable partly because it was unfalsifiable. The sublimation accomplished by the text's tripartite structure is that despite saying almost nothing about the king as judge, it nevertheless claimed credit for the way in which justice was enacted through his law, much in the same way that the prologue implied territoriality through a patchwork of relationships with specific individual polities and control of all cosmographic space.

The corollary to the king's unverifiable preeminence produced an ideological double benefit: because neither did he statutorily oblige himself to the encumbrances of investigation, indictment, prosecution, and punishment.[165] The state appeared to provide justice, but avoided not only the fiscal and administrative costs associated with doing such work—the outlays of revenue necessary to consistently and credibly control legal process, personnel, and enforcement—but also avoided even greater political costs by eschewing responsibility and liability for the social conflicts and resentments that judgments inevitably produced.

We tend to think of the exercise of legal authority as an index or consequence of other types of power, political and military—that is, as an instrument indicating power and extending it further. But the law's intrusions into civil life and exactions on commercial affairs also create serious liabilities for the state in the form of political transaction costs.[166] Being seen as responsible for *all* legal decisions would first of all jeopardize elite settlements with other power-brokers by encroaching on their local authority (in the Mesopotamian case, the judges, assemblies, and elders of the individual Babylonian cities). But as much to the point, we must consider that negative political feedbacks are generated by every single legal decision, insofar as they always create at least one dissatisfied party (and even extended families or communities of dissatisfaction), because *someone always loses*. This was an especially acute liability given the king's role as judge-of-last-resort for capital cases.[167] From this point of view, the exercise of legal authority looks like a *losing* proposition for any institution: why would anyone in the business of creating and maintaining political clientele want to claim responsibility for an expensive process that created as many enemies as it did friends?

Babylon's adoption of a legal "voice," mumbling its specific powers and responsibilities, allowed it to extend the concept of law in political imagination while limiting specific costs and liabilities. The Laws of Hammurabi effected domain ambiguation by narratively subordinating the laws to two paeans to the king (and figurally to his image), despite, counterintuitively, his virtual absence from the statutes; through the text's broad unspecificity about every phase of legal process from investigation to punishment; and through its tacit acknowledgment (and practical recognition) of other jurisdictions in an environment of "choice-of-law." These elements all blurred the lines between the powers and responsibilities of royal authority, an ambiguation that exploited the subjective experience of the ruled.

It was a sublime piece of propaganda, in the end: the king enjoyed the benefits of an expanded legal discourse of governmentality while radically limiting his political transaction costs. The success of this strategy in discourse terms is reflected in the many letters in which complainants identified the king as the agent of justice they wanted to resolve their cases[168] and swore legal oaths by the king's name,[169] while the institution of the "palace" was perceived almost exclusively in fiscal terms, mentioned only in connection with taxes and expenditures. As Reuven Yaron has written, "though [the king and palace are] closely related [in the laws], they are by no means freely interchangeable, and their demarcation might be significant."[170] And as Ari Bryen has recently written of Roman law, its power lay not so much in its composition or use as a *ratio scripta*, but as one that worked as "one of the underlying narratives that made legal practice intelligible to ancient people *as legal practice* (rather than something else)."[171] The laws may have sounded authoritative; and people began to believe them to be so; but that was a consequence of its rhetorical strategies more than the state's actual juridical undertakings.

There is a historical dimension to this, too. The recursivity of belief and efficacy should also ask us to take stock of the reiterative power of legal discourse over time. Again we find a productive form of historical forgetting: on the one hand, as is well known, LH was received, copied, and celebrated in later times, with "dozens of duplicates and extracts" dating from the immediate successors of Hammurabi down to a thousand years later.[172] There is no question of the enduring influence of the text.

On the other hand, LH also sealed the end of the law collection tradition. Although LH had earlier generic foretexts in at least seven other Mesopotamian law collections, and was thus last in a long line of royal compositions with a legal "voice," it was not only the only one of them to survive into succeeding ages, but also the last one produced. LH alone was carried forward as the exclusive and paradigmatic statement on law, with no other codes copied, and no new text arose to replace, restate, or even emulate it for over a thousand years, not until at least ca. 700 B.C.E.[173] In the centuries after Hammurabi, the text stopped being thought of as *a* set of laws and started being thought of as *the* law (or, at least, *the* statement of justice), and law as an indispensible attribute of eternal king*ship*, rather than the historically contingent claim of one king. (As Michael Dietler said in our workshop, "the subjectivities of states were more durable than the states themselves.")

This is consistent with the notion that the law no longer had to be produced, or that kings and states needed to stake their authority through it, because the state's presumptive claim to legal authority had been effectively established.[174] When the laws stopped being generative *Vorlagen* and this particular text instead became the *Letztewort* (to coin a neologism), entering the stream of canonical texts, it marked the point at which law itself had become a natural (that is, moral) domain of the state because its roots did not require any further justification.

Toward a Theory of "Low Power"

There is more to be said about other Old Babylonian political claims that later came to be accepted fixtures in the repertoire of state power. For instance, the so-called Marduk theology that grounded Middle- and Neo-Babylonian ideas about kingship was constructed around royal paeans, prophecies, and historiolae about the restoration of Marduk to cosmic dominance after a period of self-exile (and thus of Babylon to world dominance).[175] But that "restoration" implied a kind of theological and political preeminence of Marduk in pre-Kassite times that never really existed. The Marduk of Old Babylonian times was a city-god like others, and a fairly new one at that. His career as a state god was rather modest, both in terms of the number and kinds of political claims made in his name (even by the Babylonian kings), and the types of interventions his cult and temple made in religious practice and economy. A specifically historical explanation of Marduk's dominion would belie its naturalness as state theology.

One might also say much about other infrastructural insufficiencies of Hammurabi's Babylonian state—in its officer corps,[176] taxation,[177] and ethnicity[178]—claims later mistaken for actual powers and then productive of later forms because they sounded presumptively true. If we pick away at the state's actual versus claimed influence over these areas of governance, we find a totally unsurprising shortfall in capability. This is much as "society-centered" theorists predict, and as probably any measurement of actual performance against voiced ideal would find any state's power wanting.

But what is further intriguing is the question of what states thought they were *doing* when they overstated their abilities in bombastic and misleading terms. We can first strip away language to show that the grandiosity and falsehoods were actually crafted quite carefully to avoid interrogation or falsification, as a defensive strategy. But beyond this, the claims created and held the ground of the conceptual domains in which they then aspired to act; that is, their first move was to create generic authority, to speak in its manifold voices. In the face of weakness in actuality, states were first interested in *developing the category of sovereignty itself*. This was accomplished by producing a moral claim to sovereignty, by advancing the "state idea"; for the state to feign a position, omnivorously and opportunistically, as the natural and unquestioned arbiter of as many types of activity as it could allocate to itself.

This brings me, finally, to "low power." States worked for centuries with powers that were largely prospective;[179] this was not a problem urgently needing a solution, as the despotic/infrastructural dyad seems to want.[180] But what constitutes "working" for a political landscape in which a discourse of governmentality had not yet developed? Let alone one in which sovereignty and the full portfolio of governance powers had not yet been established?

I see two necessary conditions for "low power": first, its assertion over an equally weak civil society, and elite cohorts still rooted in the politics of personal, face-to-face relations, neither with any territory-wide institutional or cultural apparatus. The gross labor and resource requirements for the state's business were simply not that great—as much as we might like to repeat their claims that they were, since it makes the states we study sound powerful—in consequence of which the political transaction costs necessary to effect them were simply not that high.[181]

The second condition was the developed ability to assert infrastructural powers by suggestion: to *plausibly* claim exclusive or preeminent authority to act in a full range of IEMP fields, irrespective of ability; to accomplish this by avoiding the falsifiability of claims, minimizing political transaction costs, and promoting the confusion of conceptual domains to move power out of traditional pathways; and finally to successfully transmit moral claims across time as natural facts. As Cliff Ando has said (personal communication), simple aggregations of reduplicated structures (in jurisdictions, in spatial representations) produce transformations in kind toward "an intensified governmentality and a new subjectivity."

From a pessimistic point of view, infrastructural power grew as states actively sought to destabilize the automaticity of tradition and localism. But, less cynically, it also grew when and as subjects came to see state governance as better than its alternatives (for example, tribalism, warlordism), even if (and sometimes because) it was weakly asserted. With some sympathy for weak kings, in fact, one could view the urgency of ideological expressions of state power, and subscriptions to it, as rather desperate responses to power's absence, to the insecurity of states, elites, and civil society bound in relations of multilateral weakness.

We write from a position of comfort and fantasy to imagine that the equitable and effective distribution of vast power was the chief problem that early states faced, rather than power's absence and its wanting. One can just as easily see a very cautious yearning in early societies that states might actually be able to *do* the jobs they claimed to do, to *become* what they pretended to be. Though tempered by long and disappointing experience, states and constituents shared an emerging presumption of one new thing: a public good—in security, in law, in membership—created out of nothing more substantial and nothing less powerful than desire, fear, and hope.

NOTES

This essay relies extensively on Babylonian letters identified by the abbreviation AbB (=*Altbabylonische Briefe in Umschrift und Übersetzung*, vols. I–XIV [Leiden: Brill, 1964–2005]); all unmarked citations refer to letters written under the jurisdiction of the King of Babylon; those with a ° symbol are from uncertain jurisdictions; those with a • are from jurisdictions of kingdoms certainly other than Babylon. In each case, a letter's non-Babylonian origin could potentially modify the point it supports. Other abbreviations include *BtM*=Benjamin R. Foster, *Before the Muses*, 2nd ed. (Bethesda, Md.: 1996); RIME 4=Douglas Frayne, *Old Babylonian Period (2003–1595 B.C.)*, The Royal Inscriptions of Mesopotamia, Early Periods, vol. 4 (Toronto: 1990); TLOB 1=Seth Richardson, *Texts from the Late Old Babylonian Period* (Boston: 2010); ETCSL=The Electronic Text Corpus of Sumerian Literature (http://etcsl.orinst.ox.ac.uk); all citations of the Laws of Hammurabi (LH) are from Roth 1995a. All other abbreviations follow the *Chicago Assyrian Dictionary*.

1. Richardson 2012a.
2. On strategic ambiguation, see Richardson 2014, 75–78.
3. Compare to Covey's discussion (this volume) of the Inca stylization of manpower levies as a cosmogonic form of "creating."
4. Mann 1986, 111.
5. Richardson 2012a, 44–45.
6. See Richardson 2014, 79–80, on historical forgetting, which builds on Norman Yoffee's comment in our workshop that the rationalization of subjectivity built not only state "legibility" but also a potential basis for its rejection or readoption on other terms.
7. A survey of the gender balance of authors in six recent volumes on empires and imperialism revealed that they were written by 66 men (74 percent) and 23 women (26 percent) (Hoyos 2013; Scheidel 2009; Mutschler and Mittag 2008; Areshian 2013; Bang and Kolodziejczyk 2012; Alcock et al. 2009 [with the highest proportion of female to male authors, 8:9]). This proportion manages to lag behind female faculty in U.S. history departments, where their 35 percent market share in turn runs behind female faculty in all humanities departments (51 percent): Townsend 2010.
8. Rice and Patrick 2008 surveyed 141 "developing countries" (already 73 percent of the world's 193 United Nations member states) and ranked them for economic, political, security, and social welfare issues. The analysis found 92 of them "failed, weak, or fragile."

Citing that study, and using U.S. Census world population estimates, Hanlon 2011 found that the population of those 92 states came to 50.7 percent of the world's population (3,425,197,205 of 6,758,572,329 people). This figure does not even account for the world's significant stateless populations, whom we may suppose by definition have already been failed by states. If we proceed from the axiomatic assumption that modern states already extend more power over more people than their premodern counterparts, the proposition about the low power of ancient states is supported.

9. As Wang, this volume, argues, our goal ought not to be the creation of typologies of power, but to track how and when states intrude into domains of civil society. Cf. Seri 2006, who saw local authorities as "the intermediaries between the state and the rest of society" (195); in focusing on local officers and institutions, she did not address "the rest of society" or social institutions as such (even 38–46).

10. Charpin 2003; Van De Mieroop 2004.

11. See nn. 72 and 73 of this chapter on "positive law."

12. See Richardson 2012a, 33–34, and nn. 87–90, with literature.

13. Ellis 1976; Kraus 1984; Pientka 1998, 567, with relevant entries s.v. "Abgabe"; Stol 2004, 747–76.

14. Harris 1976, esp. 53–57 ("royal officials"), enumerating nine titled officers with functions related to tax collection (the *šandabakku, mušaddinu, mākisu*, and perhaps the *tēr ekalli*), witnessing (the *sukkallu* and *rakbû*), and the royal household (the *abarakku* and *šabrû*); the function of the *mār ekalli* is unclear. Cf. Pientka 1998, 597–600, listing over a hundred titles and professional names; see n. 177, below.

15. Harris 1968.

16. Roth 1995a; 76 LH I 1–26; and (e.g.) RIME 4.3.6.7; cf. in this chapter on the later development of a "Marduk theology."

17. E.g., the copying of royal hymns for kings of Babylon (ETCSL 2.8, seventeen hymns), LH (e.g., RIME 4 3.6.10), and historical or epic texts (RIME 4 3.7.1, 3.9.2, 3.10.2); among regular practices, the insertion of oaths by the name of the king in contracts, and date formulae celebrating the achievements of the kings in every single dated text.

18. Foster 1995, 165–68 and 172, naming the true purpose of royal reforms to be the creation of "fresh opportunities for exploitation."

19. Charpin and Durand 1991; Charpin and Ziegler 2003; see below, n. 179.

20. For a discussion of territoriality, see Payne, this volume.

21. See Fleming 2004, 104–7.

22. "Sumer and Akkad" did not denote distinct areas or cultures any more than "Amorites and Akkadians" indicated specific ethnic identities; such terms were merisms meant to express the idea of "everyone," and had little independent meaning.

23. See Richardson 2007, 22–23, and Table 2.3.

24. Compare especially against the historically specific "national states" of Kassite and later times, using *mātu* (i.e., "the land of Karduniaš") as a rubric for the kingdom (similarly, *māt Aššur*, "the land of Aššur").

25. Often taken to include the Babylonian south that was only controlled for one generation (ca. 1760–1720); see below, n. 29, and Richardson 2005, 281.

26. I.e., after Samsu-iluna's twenty-eighth year, which mentions Šeḫna, Apum, and Susa.

27. I.e., LH i 50–iv 63, the closest thing we have to a description of the kingdom's extent.

28. Roth 1995a; LH Prologue ii 32–36 and iv 23–31.

29. Used mostly in its notional, areal sense (i.e., "the land of Akkad") rather than its local one; when used in the latter sense, descriptive of cults and offices original to the city (e.g., SANGA/GALA.MAḪ ᵈIštar of Akkad: see Richardson 2017), and not of the city itself.

30. A few eponymous personal names (e.g., Warad-Eridu, AbB VII 89 and BM 16603) testify to the survival of this city's political identity, if not to its continued occupation.

31. Especially Ur, Uruk, Isin, and Adab. On the abandonment sequence for southern Babylonia after 1720 B.C., see Gasche et al. 1998, 16–17, 25, and Richardson 2002, 5–8.

32. Including Isin, Kisurra, Larsa, and Uruk; see Richardson 2005, 280–82, and Richardson 2017, on the dynastic inheritance of these obligations.

33. But see now Richardson 2017, for a reinterpretation of "southerners" in the north.

34. I.e., the city of Babylon itself; royal foundations such as eponymous fortresses (compare with Covey's discussion of the creation of new units by the state); and the *libbu mātim*, the vaguely defined open country not belonging to other cities.

35. A letter from Samsuiluna's time (AbB XIV 130) has been used to suggest that the edicts were in force for an entire and general population of citizens, by relying on the translation of *muškēnu* as "common people" (see, e.g., Westbrook 2003, 364, that royal commands had general application). We admittedly have a less-than-perfect understanding of this problematic term; it derives from *šukênu*, CAD Š/III v. 2, "to submit oneself (before a person of higher authority)"; see also CAD M/II s.v. *muškēnu* s., with contradictory definitions as persons both "not liable" and "liable" for service. Notwithstanding, most Old Babylonian usage points toward those under *personal* obligation to the King (not a citizen's obligation to his state), and thereby exempt from additional duties. Thus I understand *muškēnu* as people in the status of clientage, i.e., those who have already submitted to the king as clients, distinguished from "citizens" or "the people of the land," or "everyone," as might be inferred from "common people." A remission discussed in AbB XII 172 has similarly suggested a general application by its use of *mātu*, "land," ll. 8'–10': "As my lord knows, the king has promulgated redress for the land (*mišar mātim*), has lifted up the golden torch for the land and has cleansed all of the land." But while this sounds like the debts of all people everywhere have been cleared, the rest of the letter concerns very specific administrative transactions of the Crown, not a statewide application.

36. Cf. Westbrook 2003, 364, in the logically awkward statement that "the debt-release decrees . . . applied in part to the whole citizen body, in part to all the citizens of particular cities."

37. Richardson 2007.

38. See Keightley 1980, 26, for the "swiss-cheese" state.

39. Joannès 2006, 18: Haradum was "un petite ville," about a hectare in size; TLOB 1 19, a monthly ration to a fortress that would support about 85 men; cf. TLOB 1 18. One

can compare to army sizes as high as 40,000 in Hammurabi's time (Richardson 2011, 35–37).

40. E.g., the year name Samsuiluna 2.

41. E.g., Samsuiluna 1b. See also RIME 4 3.6.2, the "levy of the army of my land" and 3.6.12, "who builds up the land."

42. E.g., Hammurabi 13, Samsuiluna 8, Ammiditana 15, and Ammiṣaduqa 14.

43. E.g., Samsuiluna 20.

44. LH xlviii 20–38.

45. In administrative contexts, a *mātum* designated specific arable lands, often attached to a city (*erṣet mātim* GN, "the arable fields of the land of GN") or in rural areas away from cities (*libbi mātim*, lit. "the heart of the land"). Its territorial distinction as a unit less than the entire country is indicated by the title *šāpir mātim*, "governor of the land," next to *šāpirū* of other places in the kingdom. The sense of *mātum* in legal and ideological contexts, however, was much less distinct; see Fleming 2004, 104–7, 110–12, 116–39.

46. AbB XIV 109 and XIII 53; similarly, XIV 140.

47. See Hunger and Pruzsinszky 2002; Gasche et al. 1998.

48. On "King of the Kassites," see Richardson 2016, nn. 13, 17–19; *BtM*, 113, for [ ]-itluḫ; and n. 54 below.

49. Slanski 2003, 488–89, at least twenty-one provinces "named after earlier countries, tribes, or a main city"; Oelsner et al. 2003, 917; see also ABC 21 I 22'.

50. See Altman 2012, 133–34.

51. See Richardson 2016 on reception histories and cultural memories of Hammurabi's age.

52. Westbrook 2003, 376; his proposal that the "lists of cities" in royal edicts "are synechdochic for the whole of Babylonia" cannot be sustained, since they are too few and heterogeneous; cf. the strictly local force of the Ḫaradum edict, Charpin 2010b. Cf. Slanski 2003, 496, that the Middle Babylonian designation *wilid māt Karduniaš*, "(native) born of Babylonia," documented only for slaves (Old Babylonian analogues only made this designation by city, not country), was not incompatible with citizenship principles; but the idea would be more convincing if it were also attached to non-slaves.

53. See the many references to people as "son of City GN" (*mār*[DUMU] ^{uru}GN) in Sumerian literature, e.g., of Uruk, Girsu, Akkad (the city), Ur, Nippur, Isin, and Adab (ETCSL 1.3.1, 1.8.1.4, 2.1.5, 2.4.2.04, 2.7.1.1, 3.1.19, and 5.6.5)—but only rarely of larger territorial entities (cf. ibid., 1.8.1.4, citizens of the notional Sumer and Akkad, or 2.4.02, of "Subir," a foreign barbarian land); in Akkadian literature, e.g., *BtM* III (late second millennium) .8 (Nippur and Babylon), .12e (Babylon); and IV (first-millennium) .12 (Sippar, Nippur, and Babylon), .23 (Nippur), .24 (Isin), .52 (Nineveh); cf. III.1, an Assyrian epic poem styling the Babylonian king as (merely) a tribal leader ("king of the Kassites"), where Assyrian kingship is said to be over "the land of Assur" (v 25'–26').

54. Old Babylonian letters also used *mār*(DUMU) ^{uru}GN to mark personal status (AbB I 14, 129 [negated]; II 10, 12, 31; III 1; V 130; VI 127, 138 [DUMU.MEŠ *ālišu*, "citizens of his city"]; VII 111; IX 52; X 3; XIV 108, 205); *mār māt* GN ("citizen of the land GN") is not found.

55. Slanski 2003, 486; Oelsner et al. 2003, 915.
56. Slanski 2003, 486; Oelsner et al. 2003, 913, 915.
57. CAD K s.v. *kidinnu* and *kidinnūtu*; Oelsner et al. 2003, 912–13.
58. See now Paulus 2014.
59. For protections of due process, limitations on punishment, and prohibitions against bribery, see especially the first-millennium literary texts "Advice to a Prince" and "The King of Justice" (*BtM* IV.12–.13).
60. Even the much-vaunted *mār banê* (lit. "son of a notable"), sometimes translated as "free citizen," was only the "functional equivalent" of the *awīlum* in the Old Babylonian period as a marker of class rather than a juridical category: Oelsner et al. 2003, 926; Slanski 2003, 497, properly treats *awīlum* under "class" instead of "citizenship."
61. Richardson 2007.
62. This trend culminated in the "national states" that identified themselves as "lands"; see above, n. 24.
63. Note the distinction of city lands as their *erṣet mātim*, the "territory" belonging to them; this term came into cadastral use in the time of Hammurabi, notably in LH ¶ 23 (Stol 1982; Simonetti 2014).
64. AbB XII 166; cf. Stol 2004, 840 and n. 1446.
65. This outsourcing of the state's fiscal governance through commercial mechanisms is the so-called "*Palastgeschäfte*."
66. On this evidence, see Richardson 2017, with literature.
67. Ibid.
68. Roth 2001, 244–48; Richardson 2012a.
69. E.g., whether or not LH's interest rates correspond to the "officially recognized variable interest rate" of loan documents (Skaist 1994, 125), it takes no interest in most other loan contract clauses, such as MÁŠ *mākālum* (the payment of interest by a meal), *šalmu-balṭu* (repayment on the restoration of the debtor to health), or even the important bearer-document clause *ana našî kanīkišu*. LH gives thorough attention to loans at interest (*ana ḫubullim*), but says nothing about emergency loans extended *ana ḫubuttatim* or *usātim*. See further Westbrook 2003, 403.
70. Among others, Petschow 1986; Westbrook 1989.
71. Most notably Veenhof 1997–2000; Charpin 1987 and 2000 (following Kraus 1958 and Finkelstein 1961).
72. Westbrook 2003, 17–20, that the laws are "direct statements of legal norms" (cf. Westbrook 1989, 222: the law codes are "not normative legislation") and "a canon of traditional problems" emerging from "a significant stream of juridical scholarship"; he cautions against arguments from silence for the apparent non-application of the laws, which anyway could not be specifically cited: as casuistic statements of specific cases, the "application of a rule could *only* be approximate" (emphasis mine). Similarly, if on different grounds, Charpin 2010a, 80–81; Veenhof 1997–2000, 53, 55, opines that there also must have been other royal regulations that simply have not yet been found. See esp. the very convincing counterargument of d'Alfonso 2008.

73. Veenhof 1997–2000, 79 and n. 141, with literature.

74. Veenhof 1997–2000 has "basic rules" as a possibility (cf. Yaron 1988, 12, who sees the Ešnunna code as not constituting "a systematic entity," yet still a "loose compilation of precedents and ordinances"); Finkelstein 1961, 103, on royal apologia.

75. Roth 1995a, 7; similarly 1995b, 13: "I now confess that I do not 'know' what the law collections . . . meant for the ancient scribes, for the judicial authorities, and for the contemporary and mostly illiterate populations."

76. Roth 2001, 244–45, 247–48, deems it "an open question" whether the situations described in legal processes and law collections were typical or atypical.

77. Roth 2001, 248–52, 281.

78. Veenhof 1997–2000, 54f.

79. The decision of the judges in AbB IX 25 corresponds partially to LH § 163, as Westbrook (in Veenhof 1997–2000, 73) pointed out, explaining the differences as the implementation of a "basic rule"; but Veenhof allows as how this may not sufficiently explain the gap. The case might also invoke to LH §§ 138, 142, or 149; but cf. §§ 141, 143, and 162, conditions not addressed in the letter.

80. Compare AbB XIII 6 and LH §§ 236–37; but note that LH indemnifies against the liability for lost cargo, while the letter calls only for the restoration of the boat, even though 1,500 liters of grain are said to have been lost.

81. See Roth 1995, 5–6, but listing triple the wages of LH § 274; also Charpin 2010a, 80; cf. AbB XI 26°, where a worker is paid only one shekel of silver for sixty-nine days of work; the stela (LH § 273) would dictate about twice that amount.

82. Compare AbB IX 268 (see also 269) to LH §§ 117 or 253–56. However, the protections for trustors in LH § 122–23 could just as easily nullify as validate the complaint (cf. the apparent statutory contradiction resolved by Westbrook 2007). Further, it is hard to believe that a father would choose to have his son's hand cut off, per LH §253; or that the wife's characterization as a "sorceress" (*kaššaptu*, twice) here would invoke the high-stakes provisions of LH §2 against witchcraft and false accusations thereof. See Petschow 1986, 36 n. 64, and Joannès 2000, 103.

83. Thus AbB XII 194° might find a statutory basis for a verdict anywhere in the eleven passages of LH gaps §§ a, t-cc (perhaps esp. gap §z), though one may note that only gap §a hints at the early recall of a loan ("[If] his merchant presses him for payment," *tamkāršu isiršuma*), as this seems to be.

84. Compare AbB XI 7 and LH §§ 245 and 249. The letter does not state, however, that the ox was rented.

85. Veenhof 1997–2000, 67 and n. 88.

86. AbB IX 32; cf. Charpin 2004, 292 n. 1538, who sees in this "un exemple concret de rachat."

87. AbB XIII 12. Of course, punishment could still be forthcoming; but since it has been held up as an example of the law's correspondence to practice (Charpin 1998, 340, with reservations; but subsequently and more confidently, 2004, 313, and 2010a 79–81), its imprecision is worth mentioning; see also Westbrook 2003, 367.

88. AbB XIII 125; see Charpin 1998, 342, and Joannès 2000, 99–100, esp. no. 56.

89. AbB XIV 98. Obviously the king would interpret and give preference to his own laws; but neither statute clearly corresponds to the facts of the case. Cf. Charpin 2010a, 79.

90. AbB XIII 18 vs. LII ¶¶ 16, 19; see the interpretation of this problem by Hirsch 1996, 137–39.

91. See also the cases discussed by Veenhof 1997–2000, 68–74.

92. AbB XI 183.

93. AbB XIII 27; cf. LH gap ¶ a, gap ¶ l through ¶ 107.

94. AbB XI 101 and LH ¶¶ 16 and 19, providing penalties for harboring fugitive slaves, and 108–9 and 111 (specific to women innkeepers, but with nothing to say on this situation). But the woman is only said to have "been answering to me for twenty years" (*ša ištu* MU 20.KAM *ippalānni*); she is not called a slave.

95. Roth 1995a, 5–6.

96. Jursa and Häckl 2016.

97. Letters marked with * in this note have significant caveats, however, discussed below: AbB I 120*; II 19; VI 80° and 138°*; VII 135*; IX 6, 19*, 25, and 268*; X 180; XI 78 and 183*; XII 194°*; XIII 10*, 27*, 38*, 47, and 176; and XIV 2 and 184°. For a discussion of other cases, see Veenhof 1997–2000 and Yaron 1988, 121–26.

98. E.g., AbB IV 56, wherein a field sale is said to be cancelled as a result of a debt-remission edict (also *ṣimdat šarrim*: "As you know, there is an edict of the King")—the money and land restored—even though the provisions of similar edicts only affect loans and sales of moveable goods and loans, not immoveables. One provision (§5) does cancel such sales if they are fraudulent, i.e., fictional sales masking loans and debts; but nothing in AbB IV 56 suggests this was the case; cf. Kraus 1984, 60.

99. E.g., AbB IX 268; but see especially Walters 1970 for a longer analysis of this case. On *kīma ṣimdat šarrim*, see Veenhof 1997–2000, 53f., and Yaron 1988, 121–26.

100. AbB IX 25, XI 78, XIV 184° (a case for which process documents are known: see the study of Wilcke 1997); cf. the unique *kīma ṣimdat Babili*[ki] ù [id]*Araḫtum* in X 180.

101. AbB XIII 45 addresses a purely administrative matter handled by an overseer, discussing men under his authority as being in his "jurisdiction" (*ša qātiya*, lit. "who are in my hand"; similarly XII 87; XIII 16, 24) and the carrying out of his orders as "justice" (*dīnam*); see also the interpretation of Charpin 1998, 341. Conversely, see AbB IX 192, in which Hammurabi says to a high official that any punishment for a group failing to deliver their taxes would be on that official's head; thus justice was both a responsibility and a tool of administration.

102. E.g., local judges (DI.KU₅[.MEŠ]) of Sippar-Amnānum and -Jaḫrurum (MHET I 68 and 69), Isin (AbB XIV 205), Larsa (AbB X 161°), Dilbat (RGTC 3 51), Uruk (ibid., 248), and Borsippa (ibid., 38); the judges of Nippur (e.g., AbB XI 162) enjoyed "special prestige," according to Westbrook 2003, 368). These were local judges, distinguishable from royal judges, DI.KU₅.LUGAL/.GAL/KÁ.DINGIR.RA.KI; and there were even temple judges (e.g., of the É [d]UTU, CT 8 28b).

103. AbB I 18, V 75 (a "trial of [i.e., before] the god," implying the use of canon or religious law; but cf. Westbrook 2003, 368), VI 75°, XI 7 and 101, respectively.

104. AbB IX 19 (in broken context); Westbrook 2003, 372, argues that convicted parties could appeal to the king, but that the decision of a lower court was not per se invalidated.

105. AbB VI 138°; see in this chapter on delegation/alienation.

106. AbB VII 85, a claim that a father's property is not subject to the king's ṣimdatum.

107. AbB VII 135 complains that the dinam kīma ṣimdatim says nothing about the writer's rights to enforce the terms of a specific contract; and AbB XIV 75 finds a man protesting: "Do different rules apply to me, as a special case?" ṣimdatum ana iašim aḫitam šaniāt, though the translator does not believe this refers to royal regulations. Cf. AbB XIII 27, 38, and 47, where the translator interpolates "(royal)" before "regulations" (though the second letter is, indeed, from Hammurabi).

108. AbB XII 2, in which the king will hear court testimony on the basis of tablets submitted to the court, but no ṣimdatum is mentioned; and XII 72 (ana pī riksatija, "in accordance with [my contract]"); see also XI 78.

109. Ša maḫar, lit. "as before (you)": AbB XI 78 (ša maḫar bēlija) and 101 (ša maḫrika ibaššû).

110. CAD D s.v. dīnu s. 2: YOS 8 1 and PBS I/2 10.

111. E.g., AbB III 1 (see Westbrook 2003, 377). The recognition of other jurisdictions is even acknowledged within the code itself at LH § 280–81, acknowledging the legitimacy of property rights established in foreign countries (see Charpin 1987).

112. AbB VI 80°.

113. Cf. the status of "foreigners" (aḫamma) in later Middle Babylonian times: Slanski 2003, 497.

114. E.g., AbB XII 65, an appeal to the Crown to intervene through a judge and a majordomo in a process of the local gentlemen (awīlū) of Sippar, who have detained one man and beaten another throughout a trial. Often, even administrative decisions were characterized as "justice" (dīnum), e.g., AbB XIII 26; see also XI 161, a royal delegation to the judges of Nippur; X 19 (see Westbrook 2003, 366); and XIII 10.

115. E.g., AbB IX 49°, a lawsuit to be settled by the combined jurisdictional authority of an entire tribe, "the authorities" (šūt têretim), the elders of the town (šībūt ālim), "the other gentlemen" (awīlim mādūtim), and two other unidentifiable persons (see Richardson 2012b, 631–34, 637). This tangle stands in stark contrast to the more hierarchical/nested/staged kinds of authority and subjectivity discussed by Payne (this volume) as "Chinese boxes," with major elites clearly acting over minor ones.

116. AbB IX 50° is a dispute about the custody of a runaway youth; the claimants are private individuals, two towns, and the palace (which must be "satisfied"). The dispute is adjudicated by authorities identified by title rather than name, as well as an assembly of "twenty elders of the town"; see also XI 62°.

117. Note similarly the delegation of trials from other regions to Sippar, the city seat of Šamaš, god of justice: Heimpel 2003, 249–50 and n. 6 (=ARM 26/194) and TLOB 1 95.

118. AbB XIV 144°.

119. AbB XIII 10: dīnam kīma dīnim ša inanna ina Emutbalum iddinnu šutešeršunuti; Charpin 2004, 324, and Joannès 2000, 86, see this as an outcome of the likelihood that

the deserters originally came from the kingdom of Larsa. Cf. the Jamutbal case discussed in XIII 38; and note also the jurisdictional questions raised by VI 80° and 138°, mentioned above, nn. 97, 105, and 112.

120. AbB XI 137; see similarly X 3, the case of a man of Ešnunna.

121. AbB XII 166• (its non-Babylonian origin is not relevant to the point here). The text also gives the puzzling "All the alluvial fields belong to the king, and who is there who does not hold any alluvial field?" Charpin 1993, 89, observed, "cela signifie qu'il n'y a pas de propriété privée de ces terrains, mais seulement des tenures attribuées par le roi," but this ignores that the letter itself is written to contest the abuse of that very claim.

122. AbB XII 95 and XIII 78 (KI.LAM *ālim*; see Charpin 1998, 340).

123. AbB X 195°.

124. AbB XI 3°–4° and XII 185° (*maḫīrat illaku*); XII 49 (*kārat illaku*); XIV 201 (*kārat ibaššû*). Variable market rates are already acknowledged by LH § 51, as well as by many contracts with similar repayment phrases such as KI.LAM *ibaššû* (see Skaist 1994, 192–95).

125. Hammurabi's laws, unlike most other law collections of its day (see Richardson 2012a, 40), do not set commodity prices. Such controls may simply have been out of reach.

126. In most cases, the crucial terms are simply not given in the letters: AbB XIV 201 cites a balance due of 3–1/5 shekels and 6 grains of silver on an original principal of 2–5/6 shekels; at 20 percent per annum, this would conform to LH gap §§ t–u—but only if one assumes the specific term of eight months, which is not stated. Similarly: AbB IX 231•, XI 185° and 190°, XII 51 (see Charpin 1993, 88), and XIV 221•, all of which mention some but not all of the terms necessary to compute the interest rate on the loan discussed.

127. E.g., AbB XIII 110 (see Stol 2004, 682, and Charpin 1998, 340, 342 on this odd text), and XIV 23 and 120, wages paid in grain, which is in contradiction to LH §§ 273–74, which stipulate silver. Cf. AbB XIV 54, 62•, and 110•, which might conceivably conform to LH §§ 257, 239, and 258 or 261, respectively.

128. Note the recognition of other measures in, e.g., AbB IX 161° and XII 57; cf. LH § gap x and 108.

129. Compare threats and suasion as modes of compulsion in, e.g., AbB IX 19 (*itti NN sarrātim atwûm* [see note b there, "to accuse NN of lies," lit. "to discuss dishonesty"]) versus 169 ("Have a nice conversation with the summoner").

130. AbB IX 49°, a woman fearing "humiliation" before Emutbalum, though von Soden 1982, 591, had doubts (but no alternative suggestions) about *ummuqum* as "demütigen." Still, other letters suggest shame and embarrassment as stigmata affecting disputes: AbB I 18, a discredited slavegirl (CAD Q s.v. *qalālu* v. 5); also VII 88, 187(?); XII 89; and XIV 166 and 217°.

131. See CAD N/2 s.v. *nēbeḫu* B, s., "compensation."

132. AbB IX 48° ("imprison him"), 169, 238• (with the pleasing cognate object construction, ll. 5–9, "let them distrain the distrainees"), and 245°; XI 22°, 79, 106, 129, and 130; XII 65; XIII 97; cf. LH § 114–16.

133. AbB IX 108°; XI 135• (a man "beat up his servants unlawfully," which may imply that some beatings were recognized as lawful); XII 65 and 166•; XIII 4; cf. the confusing

AbB XIV 208•, with references to literature. In fact, the law's only limitation on private violence draws the lines in the context of distraint.

134. On quarrels (Sum. (INIM) DU$_{14}$ "[words of] a quarrel," e.g., "The Instructions of Šuruppak" (ETCSL 5.6.1), ll. 22–27, 35, and 60; SP 1.170 and .196 (ETCSL 6.1.01); SP 3.18 (ETCSL 6.1.03); Nippur proverb N5225:2–3 (ETCSL 6.2.1); and Ur proverbs UET 6/2 276:1–2 and 334:1–2 (ETCSL 6.2.3). See also *BtM* 101 and 326–27.

135. ETCSL 5.6.5.

136. This is not to say that lamentations for the absence or perversion of justice meant that justice was not a desirable ideal—only that the results and expectations were ambivalent, and precepts of justice were not automatically associated with the state: see, e.g., proverbs SP 3.328, "When righteousness is cut off, injustice is increased" (ETCSL 6.1.03) and UET 6/2 256, "The expenses(?) of those who neglect justice are numerous" (ETCSL 6.2.3). See also AbB IX 231• and 238•, XI 5 and 7, and XIII 176, with expectations that legal process would right wrongs; of these, only one (XIII 176) associates justice with royal judges; two (XI 5 and 7) clearly indicate that a legal process itself has inflicted the wrong.

137. LH ¶ 129, a case of adultery.

138. ¶¶ 18 and 109, escaped slaves and "criminals" (*sarrūtum*, also "rebels").

139. Gap ¶ u and ¶ 51, *kīma ṣimdat šarrim*.

140. ¶ 32; cf. AbB IX 32 and n. 86, above.

141. E.g., LH ¶¶ 6, 8 15–16, 26–28, 33.

142. E.g., AbB IX 25: the judges "of Babylon" initiate proceedings against appellates "according to the regulations of our lord" (*kīma ṣimdat bēlini*; cf. "proceedings" in this text, *dinam*); but cf. LH ¶ 163, as Veenhof 1997–2000, 73, points out. See also AbB IX 49°; XI 82°; XII 65; cf. II 19 (*contra* Westbrook 2003, 370, who calls the king a "court of first instance").

143. AbB XIII 10, a rare example of the king apparently initiating a legal proceeding.

144. See esp. Roth 2002, who argues that LH's epilogue invites the "wronged man" not to bring his misjudged case to the king as a legal appeal, but to bring it before the stela to find "solace through prayer and by offering blessings to the king."

145. LH ¶¶ 9 (with the judges), 23 (with the city and the *rabiānum*), gap cc, 100, 103, 106, 107, 120, 126 (with the city ward), 131, 240, 249, 266, and 281. I do not include ordeal procedures here; divinely authorized though they were, the institutional authority behind them is unclear.

146. LH ¶¶ 9 (with the god), 13, 127, 168–69, 172 (with the household), 177; LH ¶ 5 limits the powers of judges rather than conferring powers upon them.

147. Wards: LH ¶¶ 126 (with the god), 142–43; assemblies: 5 (possibly implied) and 202; city and *rabiānum*: 23 (with the god) and 24 (see Seri 2005, 151, on LH ¶¶ 23–24, which hold the city and *rabiānum* responsible for prosecuting certain crimes, versus an absence of practice documents attesting to it); irrigation districts: 54; merchants: 116.

148. Ten laws confine jurisdiction to the family household, confirming the private space in which the state does not operate: LH ¶¶ 114–15, 165–67, 173–74, 178, 184; LH ¶ 172 identifies the household and the judges as the relevant authorities.

149. These clauses are also usually restricted to certain phases of procedure, e.g., finding of cause or evidence, collection of testimony, etc., without jurisdiction for the overall legal process.

150. Fourteen cases require or entail documents as supporting evidence or necessary grounds for legal action (LH ¶¶ 47–48, gaps a and v, 104–5, 123, 150–51, 165, 171, 178, 182, and 264); six cases require witnesses for similar purposes (LH ¶¶ 10–11, 13, gap z, 106, and 123). These requirements are not jurisdictional, but evidentiary—that is, their relevance and veracity was to be evaluated by their investigative authority—but only two of these nineteen passages even implies who was to do the evaluating (13: the judges? 106: the god?). Thus, this is not a legal environment in which "what the text/witness says" by itself determines legal process, but rather by an evaluating authority.

151. Punishment clauses even referring to institutional authorities are restricted to LH ¶¶ 127 (flogging before the judges), and 202 (flogging before the assembly). But neither here nor in most cases are the parties obligated to actually inflict violent punishment ever named: LH ¶¶ 153, 155, 157, 192–97, 200, 205, 210, 218, 226–27, 229–30, 253, and 256. The only exception is ¶ 282, in which the master of a slave is afforded the right to cut off the slave's ear (but for the law's political and metaphorical contexts, see n. 163 below); in ¶¶ 192–94 is it conceivable (though unlikely) that the offended parties are the punishers.

152. Cf. Seri 2006, who argues for the relative independence and efficacy of local institutions outside of the textual sphere.

153. I.e., "s/he shall": LH ¶¶ 12, 17, 29–32, 35, 37–44, 46–47, 49–53, 55–60, 62–65, gaps a, c, e, g–h, l, r, w–z, 101–2, 104–7, 111–12, 114, 116–22, 124–27, 131, 135, 138–42, 145–50, 156, 159–61, 164–65, 170–71, 178–82, 186, 189–91, 198–99, 201, 203–4, 206–9, 211–17, 219–25, 228, 231–43, 245–48, 251–52, 254–55, 257–61, 263–65, 267–82.

154. LH ¶¶ 18, 27, 42, 54, 61, gaps m, s, cc, 100, 108, 110, 113, 124, 127, 129–30, 133b, 137, 141–42, 144, 152–55, 157, 169, 176a–b, 192–97, 200, 205, 210, 218, 226–27, 230, 253, and 256. See the note to AbB IX 49 regarding *mādûtum*, "the many," but also "the others."

155. Of the nineteen anonymized violent punishments enumerated above in n. 151, only LH ¶ 229 does not use an active plural "they shall" (kill, cut, break) but a passive ("that builder shall be killed").

156. LH ¶¶ 1–4, 6–11, 13–16, 19–22, 25–26, 28, 33–34, gaps n, t–v, bb, 103, 109, 132, 158, 202, and 229.

157. LH ¶¶ 36, 45, 48, 115, 123, 128, 133a, 134, 136, 151, 162–63, 168, 175, 183, 185, 187–88, 244, 249–50, and 266.

158. The near-absence of specified enforcement is reminiscent of Emily Mackil's observation (this volume) about the absence of such agents in archaic Greek law collections.

159. AbB XI 147°. Similarly, III 71°; VII 20; VIII 17 (n.b., Michalowski 1983, 222, identifies this as a "school practice" text), 140°; IX 25, 27°, 33°, 40°, 42, 108°, 211•, 218•; XIII 6, 14, 19, 21, 31, 45, 63, 98°; XIV 4, 195°, 223°; cf. AbB XIII 77, "soldiers" (plural). Note the fragmentary Sumerian proverb SP 7.23, that a "soldier silences the argument" (ETCSL 6.1.07); Stol 2004, 738 and n. 676, sees the single soldier as effective. Note also CT 8 40a:6, PN AGA.UŠ *ša* DI.KU₅ *Bābili*, where a single soldier is attached to a royal judge.

160. AbB XIII 9; see also XIV 168°.

161. Westbrook 2003, 370, claims from AbB IX 268 and XI 158 that local courts also had the power to dispatch soldiers, but neither text actually mentions a soldier, only detention.

162. Roth 1995a, 4–7; and see nn. 48ff, above.

163. Roth 1995b, 15–19, identifying LH ¶¶ 1 and 282 (the first and last provisions, and thus the transitions for the prologue and epilogue) as addressing treason and rebellion, respectively.

164. LH i 50, though cf. i 1 and 27, introductory passages also introduced as *inu/inūmišu*. See Zadok 1996, 118, who identifies the temporal sentence in Old Babylonian royal inscriptions as occupying "the lion's share" of such texts; Cohen 2012, 135–36, on the "*inūma* strategy."

165. Cf. Yaron 1988, 104, who opined that for laws in which no sanction is specified, "it ought not to be taken for granted that these are all true *leges imperfectae*, which can be disregarded with impunity." This may yet be so, but what I emphasize is the rhetorical gimmick of the Crown's simultaneous *implication* of its right to punish in writing and its *reticence* to do so in fact; the Crown's power is imputed, but its liability is sidestepped.

166. Cf. Veenhof 1997–2000, 56, who sees that "a clear and binding rule, imposed by royal authority ... must have been welcome both to plaintiffs and judges." But as one analyst of political transaction costs explains it, "almost without exception, consolidation proposals ... trigger highly emotional debates and local protests, and centralized restructuring commonly incurs prohibitive political costs" (Sørensen 2006, 76).

167. E.g., AbB X 19. The documentable incidence of corporal punishment meted out by anyone (let alone the king) remains very low down into the Neo-Babylonian period, though fines and prison are well attested (Oelsner et al. 2003, 966–67).

168. AbB IX 92, 233•, and 262•; XI 62°, 83, 147°, and 161; XII 2 (after a hearing by the assembly, the judges and the "director" [GAL.UKKIN.NA]), 3, 7, 93 (a denunciation), 172; XIII 104 (see Charpin 1998, 342), 105 (ibid., 340–41), 121°, and 177; XIV 1 and 35.

169. Typically *nīš šarrim*: AbB III 55 and 82 (where the process is backstopped by five witnesses on a sealed tablet; see Moran 1980, 188); IV 121; X 81; XI 135• and 189; XIV 15°, 45, and 218. Note also the prominence of royal epithets based on justice in later periods, e.g., *šar mīšarum*, "king of justice": Oelsner et al. 2003, 915.

170. Cf. AbB X 19, the "palace" to inspect a verdict; Yaron 1988, 114.

171. Bryen 2014, 347 (my emphasis).

172. Roth 1995a, 74, and 1995b, 19–21.

173. Slanski 2003, 486; Oelsner et al. 2003, 912 ("a school text"), 915–16 (a "controversy" as to whether the text has an official or private character); Roth 1995a, 143–44.

174. Cf. Slanski 2003, 489, noting a few monumental inscriptions of Middle Babylonian kings pronouncing on specific cases; but, 490, that the royal appointment of judges has to be inferred. Cf. also Oelsner et al. 2003, 918–19, 953, on the curious absence of debt remissions and royal edicts in the first millennium, though royal judges and royal courts are explicitly attested. The clearest legal innovation of the post–Old Babylonian period

was the *narû*-monument, which attached rights and exemptions to tracts of territory, imbricating royal authority over territory with taxation, service, and land tenure.

175. Sommerfeld 1989, esp. 362–63, on the slim pre-Old Babylonian body of evidence for Marduk, though it does go as far back as Early Dynastic and Akkadian times; Oshima 2007; Marzahn 2008.

176. See n. 14 above on state officers. Seri 2006 decried a dominant "state-centered" approach to analyzing the Babylonian kingdom, but given that it seems possible to write an entire book about its local institutions (with a voluminous secondary literature cited, ibid., 46–49), while the known state apparatus can be outlined in twenty pages (as Harris 1976, 38–57, did, if obviously with less depth), the problem seems as much one in which the actual power of the state starts out by being poorly defined, poorly known, or (as I argue) very modest.

177. Space does not permit a real analysis of the extent and limits of Babylon's tax structure, a topic that is due for new attention (cf. Ellis 1976 and n. 13 above). There is a relative scarcity of tax collection as a subject of OB letters (though see generally AbB IX 2, 109, 192; XI 89; XII 2, 173°; XIII 138°; and XIV 13°, 68, 70, 87, 106, 124 [also p. 209 sub. *kasap zagmukkim*]), the exception being the many mentions of in-kind *biltu*-levies on productive land, e.g., AbB IV 17, 18, 23, 35, 39, etc. Three brief points worth making in the present context are the heavy use of gift and contract language in taxation terms (e.g., the *igisû*-"gift," AbB II 14, 68; V 275; XIV 87, 178), suggesting their notionally voluntary payment and personal nature; and, following Anthony Kaldellis's suggestions (this volume), both the wildly asymmetric structure of tax terms and categories generally, and the situation of Babylonian taxation-at-point (of use or production) and not at borders (i.e., at points of exchange).

178. Notably, the place of ethnic identity has again been under discussion for the Old Babylonian period, centered on J.-M. Durand's (2004) contention that Amorites of the time came to share a consciousness of a common heritage that rose to a full political identity for a brief time ca. 1900–1750 B.C., but subsequently receded into the background of cultural concerns thereafter (see de Boer 2014, 29–31, 112–14).

179. Richardson 2012a.

180. The serious and critical Assyriological literature on despotism as a form of political power is, unsurprisingly, mostly confined to the Soviet school; see esp. Diakonoff 1973.

181. See the argument in Richardson 2015.

BIBLIOGRAPHY

Alcock, Susan, T. N. D'Altroy, Kathleen D. Morrison, and Carla M. Sinopoli, eds. 2009. *Empires: Perspectives from Archaeology and History*. Cambridge: Cambridge University Press.

Altman, Amnon. 2012. *Tracing the Earliest Recorded Concepts of International Law: The Ancient Near East (2500–330 BCE)*. Leiden: Brill.

Areshian, Gregory E., ed. 2013. *Empires and Diversity: On the Crossroads of Archaeology, Anthropology, and History*. Los Angeles: Cotsen Institute of Archaeology Press.

Bang, Peter, and Dariusz Kolodziejczyk, eds. 2012. *Universal Empire: A Comparative Approach to Imperial Culture and Representation in Eurasian History*. Cambridge: Cambridge University Press.

Bryen, Ari. 2014. "Law in Many Pieces." *Classical Philology* 109 (4): 346–65.

Charpin, Dominique. 1987. "Les Décrets Royaux à l'Époque Paléo-Babylonienne, à Propos d'un Ouvrage Récent." *AfO* 34:36–44.

———. 1993. Review of W. H. van Soldt, AbB XII. *RA* 87:87–89.

———. 1998. Review of W. H. van Soldt, AbB XIII. *AfO* 44 (45): 339–43.

———. 2000. "Les prêteurs et le palais: Les édits de mîšarum des rois de Babylone et leurs traces dans les archives privées." In *Interdependency of Institutions and Private Entrepreneurs*, edited by A. C. V. M. Bongenaar, 185–212. MOS Studies 2. Leiden: Nederlands Instituut voor het Nabije Oosten Institut néerlandais du Proche-Orient.

———. 2003. *Hammu-rabi de Babylone*. Paris: Presses universitaires de France.

———. 2004. "Histoire Politique du Proche-Orient Amorrite (2002–1595)." In *Mesopotamien: Die altbabylonische Zeit*, edited by D. Charpin, D. O. Edzard, and M. Stol, 25–480. *Orbis Biblicus et Orientalis* (hereafter OBO) 160 (4). Fribourg: Academic Press.

———. 2010a. *Writing, Law, and Kingship in Old Babylonian Mesopotamia*. Chicago: University of Chicago Press.

———. 2010b. "Un èdit du roi Ammiditana de Babylone." In *Von Göttern und Menschen: Beiträge zu Literatur und Geschichte des Alten Orients. Festschrift für Brigitte Groneberg*, edited by D. Shehata, 17–46. Leiden: Brill.

Charpin, Dominique, and Jean-Marie Durand. 1991. "La suzeraineté de l'empereur (sukkalmah) d'Elam sur la Mesopotamie et le 'nationalisme' amorrite." In *Mésopotamie et Elam*, edited by L. De Meyer and H. Gasche, 59–66. Ghent: University of Ghent.

Charpin, Dominique, and Nele Ziegler. 2003. *Mari et le Proche-Orient à l'époque amorrite. Essai d'histoire politique*. Florilegium marianum V. Paris: SEPOA.

Cohen, Eran, 2012. *Conditional Structures in Mesopotamian Old Babylonian*. Winona Lake, Ind.: Eisenbrauns.

d'Alfonso, Lorenzo. 2008. "Le fonti normative del secondo millennio a.C.: confronto tra le culture della Mesopotamia e l'Anatolia ittita." In *I diritti del mondo cuneiforme*, edited by M. Liverani and C. Mora, 325–59. Pavia: Pavia University Press.

de Boer, Rients. 2014. *Amorites in the Early Old Babylonian Period*. PhD dissertation, University of Leiden.

Diakonoff, Igor M. 1973. "The Rise of the Despotic State in Ancient Mesopotamia." Translated by G. M. Sergheyev. In *Ancient Mesopotamia*, edited by I. M. Diakonoff, 173–203. Walluf bei Wiesbaden: Martin Sändig oHG.

Durand, J.-M. 2004. "Peuplement et sociétés a l'époque amorrite (I): Les clan bensim'alites." In *Amurru 3: Nomades et sédentaires dans le Proche-Orient ancien*, edited by C. Nicholle, 111–19. Paris: Éditions Recherche sur les civilisations.

Ellis, Maria De J. 1976. *Agriculture and the State in Ancient Mesopotamia: An Introduction to Problems of Land Tenure*. Occasional Publications of the Babylonian Fund 1. Philadelphia: University of Pennsylvania Museum.

Finkelstein, J. J. F. 1961. "Ammiṣaduqa's Edict and the Babylonian 'Law Codes.'" *Journal of Cuneiform Studies* 15 (3): 91–104.

Fleming, Daniel. 2004. *Democracy's Ancient Ancestors: Mari and Early Collective Governance*. Cambridge: Cambridge University Press.

Foster, Benjamin R. 1995. "Social Reform in Ancient Mesopotamia." In *Social Justice in the Ancient World*, edited by K. D. Irani and M. Silver, 165–78. Westport, Conn: Greenwood Press.

Gasche, Herman, et al., eds. 1998. *Dating the Fall of Babylon: A Reappraisal of Second-Millennium Chronology*. Chicago: Oriental Institute of the University of Chicago.

Hanlon, Querine. 2011. "State Actors in the 21st Century Security Environment." Washington, D.C.: National Strategy Information Center. http://www.strategycenter.org/wp-content/uploads/2011/07/State-Actors-21st-Century.pdf.

Harris, Rivkah. 1968. "Some Aspects of the Centralization of the Realm Under Hammurapi and His Successors." *JAOS* 88 (4): 727–32.

———. 1976. *Ancient Sippar: A Demographic Study of an Old-Babylonian city (1894–1595 B.C.)*. Publications de l'Institut historique-archéologique néerlandais de Stamboul (PIHANS) 36. Leiden: Nederlands Instituut voor het Nabije Oosten Institut néerlandais du Proche-Orient.

Hirsch, Hans. 1996. "An den Rand geschrieben I [including review of AbB XIII]." *AfO* 42–43:122–44.

Hoyos, Dexter, ed. 2013. *A Companion to Roman Imperialism*. Leiden: Brill.

Hunger, Hermann, and Regine Pruzsinszky, eds. 2004. *Mesopotamian Dark Age Revisited*. Vienna: Austrian Academy of Sciences Press.

Joannès, Francis. 2000. *Rendre la Justice en Mesopotamia*. Paris: Presses Universitaires de Vincennes.

———. 2006. *Haradum II: les textes de la période paléo-babylonienne*. Paris: Presses Universitaires de Vincennes.

Jursa, Michel and Johannes Häckl. 2016. "Rhetorics, Politeness, Persuasion and Argumentation in Late Babylonian Epistolography: The Contrast Between Official Correspondence and Private Letters." In *Official Epistolography and the Language(s) of Power*, edited by S. Procházka et al., 141–56. Vienna: Austrian Academy of Sciences Press.

Keightley, D. 1980. "The Shang State as Seen in the Oracle-Bone Inscriptions." *Early China* 5:25–34.

Kraus, F. R. 1958. *Ein Edikt des Königs Ammi-ṣaduqa von Babylon*. Leiden: Brill.

———. 1984. *Königliche Verfügungen in altbabylonischer Zeit*. Leiden: Brill.

Mann, Michael. 1986. "The Autonomous Power of the State: Its Origins, Mechanisms and Results." In *States in History*, edited by J. A. Hall, 109–36. Reprint of 1984. Oxford: Basil Blackwell.

Marzahn, J. 2008. "Marduk—Der Eine und die Vielen." In *Babylon, Mythos und Wahrheit: eine Ausstellung des Vorderasiatischen Museums Staatliche Museen zu Berlin*, edited by J. Marzahn et al., 172–73. München: Hirmer.

Michalowski, Piotr. 1983. Review of AbB VIII. *Journal of Cuneiform Studies* 35:221–28.

Moran, William. 1980. Review of AbB III. *Journal of the American Oriental Society* 100:186–89.

Mutschler, Fritz-Heiner, and Achim Mittag, eds. 2008. *Conceiving the Empire: China and Rome compared*. Oxford: Oxford University Press.

Oelsner, Joachim, et al. 2003. "Neo-Babylonian Period." In *A History of Ancient Near Eastern Law*, edited by R. Westbrook, 911–74. Handbuch der Orientalistik I:72. Leiden: Brill.

Oshima, Takayoshi. 2007. "The Babylonian God Marduk." In *The Babylonian World*, edited by G. Leick, 348–60. Oxford: Routledge.

Paulus, Susanne. 2014. *Die babylonischen Kudurru-Inschriften von der kassitischen bis zur frühneubabylonischen Zeit: Untersucht unter besonderer Berücksichtigung gesellschafts- und rechtshistorischer Fragestellungen. Alter Orient und Altes Testament* (hereafter AOAT) 51. Münster: Ugarit-Verlag.

Petschow, H. P. H. 1986. "Beiträge zum Codex Hammurapi." *Zeitschrift für Assyriologie* 76:17–75.

Pientka, Rosel. 1998. *Die spätaltbabylonische Zeit*. Münster: Rhema Verlag.

Rice, Susan E., and Stewart Patrick. 2008. *Index of State Weakness in the Developing World*. Washington, D.C.: Brookings Insitution. https://www.brookings.edu/wp-content/uploads/2016/06/02_weak_states_index.pdf.

Richardson, Seth. 2002. *The Collapse of a Complex State*. PhD dissertation, Columbia University.

———. 2005. "Trouble in the Countryside, ana tarṣi Samsuditana: Militarism, Kassites, and the Fall of Babylon I." In *Ethnicity in Mesopotamia*, edited by W. H. van Soldt, 273–89. Leiden: Brill.

———. 2007. "The World of the Babylonian Countrysides." In *The Babylonian World*, edited by G. Leick, 13–38. Oxford: Routledge.

———. 2011. "Mesopotamia and the 'New' Military History." In *Recent Directions in the Military History of the Ancient World*, edited L. Brice and J. T. Roberts, 11–51. Publications of the Association of Ancient Historians 10. Claremont, Calif.: Regina Books.

———. 2012a. "Early Mesopotamia: The Presumptive State." *Past & Present* 215 (1): 3–49.

———. 2012b. "'The Crowns of Their *bābtum*': On Wives, Wards, and Witnesses." *Journal of the American Oriental Society* 132 (4): 623–39.

———. 2014. "Mesopotamian Political History: The Perversities." *Journal of Ancient Near Eastern History* 1 (1): 61–93.

———. 2015. "Building Larsa: Labor-Value, Scale, and Scope-of-Economy in Ancient Mesopotamia." In *Labor in the Pre-Classical Old World*, edited by P. Steinkeller, 237–328. Dresden: ISLET.

———. 2016. "The Many Falls of Babylon and the Shape of Forgetting." In *Envisioning the Past through Memories*, edited by D. Nadali. Cultural Memory and History in Antiquity. London: Bloomsbury.

———. 2017. "Sumer and Stereotype: Re-forging 'Sumerian' Kingship in the Late Old Babylonian Period." In *Conceptualizing Past, Present and Future*, edited by S. Fink and R. Rollinger. Melammu Symposia 9. Münster: Ugarit-Verlag.

Roth, Martha. 1995a. *Law Collections from Mesopotamia and Asia Minor*. 2nd ed. Atlanta: Society of Biblical Literature.

———. 1995b. "Mesopotamian Legal Traditions and the Laws of Hammurabi." In *Symposium on Ancient Law, Economics & Society Part II*, edited by J. Lindgren, L. Magali, and G. P. Miller. *Chicago-Kent Law Review* 71 (1): 13–39.

———. 2001. "Reading Mesopotamian Law Cases PBS 5 100: A Question of Filiation." *JESHO* 44–43:243–92.

———. 2002. "Hammurabi's Wronged Man." *Journal of the American Oriental Society* 122 (1): 38–45.

Scheidel, Walter, ed. 2009. *Rome and China: Comparative Perspectives on Ancient World Empires*. Oxford: Oxford University Press.

Seri, Andrea. 2006. *Local Power in Old Babylonian Mesopotamia*. London: Equinox.

Simonetti, Cristina. 2014. "Peace after War: Ḫammurapi in Larsa." In *Krieg und Frieden im Alten Voderasien*, edited by H. Neumann et al., 735–42. AOAT 401. Münster: Ugarit-Verlag.

Skaist, Aaron. 1994. *The Old Babylonian Loan Contract*. Ramat Gan: Bar-Ilan University Press.

Slanski, Kathryn. 2003. "Middle Babylonian Period." In *A History of Ancient Near Eastern Law*, edited by R. Westbrook, 485–520. Handbuch der Orientalistik 1:72. Leiden: Brill.

Sommerfeld, Walther. 1989. "Marduk. A. Philologisch I. In Mesopotamien." *Reallexikon der Assyriologie* 7 (5–6): 360–70.

Sørensen, Rune. 2006. "Local Government Consolidations: The Impact of Political Transaction Costs." *Public Choice* 127 (1–2): 75–95.

Stol, Marten. 1982. "A Cadastral Innovation by Hammurabi." In *Assyriological Studies Presented to F. R. Kraus on the Occasion of his 70th birthday*, edited by G. van Driel, 351–58. Leiden: Brill.

———. 2004. "Wirtschaft und Gesellschaft in altbabylonischer Zeit." In D. Charpin, D. O. Edzard, and M. Stol, *Mesopotamien: Die altbabylonische Zeit*, 643–975. OBO 160 (4). Fribourg: Academic Press.

Townsend, Robert B. 2010. "What the Data Reveals About Women Historians." *Perspectives on History* 48 (5). https://www.historians.org/publications-and-directories/perspectives-on-history/may-2010/what-the-data-reveals-about-women-historians.

Van De Mieroop, Marc. 2004. *King Hammurabi of Babylon: A Biography*. London: Wiley-Blackwell.

Veenhof, K. R. 1997–2000. "The Relation Between Royal Decrees and 'Law Codes' of the Old Babylonian Period." *Jaarbericht "Ex Oriente Lux"* 35–36:49–83.

Walters, Stanley D. 1970. "The Sorceress and Her Apprentice: A Case Study of an Accusation." *Journal of Near Eastern Studies* 23 (2): 27–38.

Westbrook, Raymond. 1989. "Cuneiform Law Codes and the Origins of Legislation." *Zeitschrift für Assyriologie* 79:201–22.

———. 2003. "The Character of Ancient Near Eastern Law" and "Old Babylonian Period." In *A History of Ancient Near Eastern Law*, edited by R. Westbrook, 1–92, 361–430. Handbuch der Orientalistik 1:72. Leiden: Brill.

———. 2007. "LH 7 and 123—A Contradiction?" *NABU* 2007/2 (27).

Wilcke, Claus. 1997. "Nanāja-šamḫats Rechtsstreit um ihre Freiheit." In *Ana šadî Labnāni lū allik (FS W. Röllig)*, edited by B. Pongratz-Leisten et al., 413–27. AOAT 247. Kevelaer: Butzon & Bercker.

Yaron, Reuven. 1988. *The Laws of Eshnunna*. Jerusalem: Magnes Press.

Zadok, Tikva. 1996. "The Distribution of the Temporal Sentences in the Old Babylonian Royal Inscriptions." *Journal of the Ancient Near Eastern Society* 24:111–19.

CHAPTER 2

Property Claims and State Formation in the Archaic Greek World

EMILY MACKIL

In a comparative light, the oddity of ancient Greek city-states, poleis, is striking.[1] Power was conspicuously decentralized; the more or less legitimate use of violence was so widespread throughout each state's population that it has been possible to argue that the Greek polis does not meet the Weberian standards for statehood and should instead be deemed a stateless community.[2] This skeptical position has been rejected by most historians, who see the poleis of ancient Greece as states in a meaningful sense, but concede that these were states whose institutions, norms, and acts were deeply embedded in Greek society.[3] Greek poleis look weak—almost unlike states at all—not only because there was no centralized, exclusive claim to the legitimate use of violence in the Weberian sense, but also because virtually every action they took required negotiation with some part of civil society; indeed, the integral role played by community members in the day-to-day functioning of the state is a distinctive feature of Greek political institutions. Legislation, adjudication, the enforcement of rules, the creation and empowerment of large numbers of officials, negotiation with other communities, and the management of economic and religious practices as an autonomous entity were all generated, and evolved over time, through negotiation between community members. This conundrum—was the Greek polis a state? If so, what kind?—stems at least in part from the fact that historians utilize, whether explicitly or implicitly, different definitions of state power.[4] Michael Mann's distinction between despotic and infrastructural power may offer a perspective from which to see with greater clarity the ways in which Greek states developed, articulated, and promulgated their distinctive form of power.

Despotic power in Mann's sense—"the range of actions which the state elite is empowered to undertake without routine, institutionalized negotiation with civil society groups"—was virtually nonexistent in Greece.[5] This is true in part because the legitimate use of force was not carefully protected in the hands of a small group or a single institution like a police force or a standing army, despite a general opposition to the bearing of arms within a city during times of peace, and a relatively well-established set of rules determining a boundary between acceptable and unacceptable forms of violence within civic life.[6] We can, however, see that every Greek polis was strong in the infrastructural sense, having the "capacity . . . to actually penetrate civil society, and to implement logistically political decisions throughout the realm."[7]

Now, not all Greek states were poleis, and not all were city-states, but they were all quite small, particularly in comparison to many of the imperial states discussed in this volume, ranging in area from a few hundred to a few thousand square kilometers; nevertheless, at this small scale, the states of ancient Greece were strikingly strong in the infrastructural sense.[8] To ask how this situation came about is to ask how states as autonomous entities developed in the Archaic Greek world, the period about 800–500 B.C.E., when the eastern Mediterranean experienced rapid and widespread demographic and economic growth, as communities regenerated after the collapse at the end of the Bronze Age.[9] Mann isolates three components as essential to the development of autonomous state power in the infrastructural sense: property, legislation, and territoriality. In order to explore the applicability of the infrastructural power model for ancient Greek states I shall explore the interrelationship of these three phenomena.

Yet by putting property at the heart of an analysis of state power in the Greek world, I am staking an unusual claim (for a working definition of "property," see below). To analyze the emergence of infrastructural power is to consider a particular facet of state formation. For the Greek world, most studies of state formation proceed on the basis of archaeological evidence, which is far more abundant than literary or epigraphic evidence, and it has accumulated to tell a fairly consistent story from one polis to the next. Explorations of Archaic cities have revealed the early demarcation of public spaces in the urban center, as for example at Megara Hyblaia in eastern Sicily in the eighth and seventh centuries and at Azoria in eastern Crete. The construction of border sanctuaries and evidence for rural settlement and the exploitation of the hinterland have provided indications of the territorial extent of early Greek poleis.[10] The picture we gain is of small communities—ranging in most Archaic poleis from a few hundred to a few thousand souls—staking out spaces for public meetings and the veneration of the gods and in so doing creating the distinctive Greek state formed by the voluntary association of a community into a public entity that we can readily recognize as a microstate. Yet this evidence tells us nothing about the nature or efficacy of the authority exerted by a particular community over the territory it staked out for itself, and by treating "domestic space" as a matter for the history or urbanism or family life this approach systematically ignores the question of the relationship between claims made by individuals to particular plots of land, the creation of a territory, and the development of state power. Private property has entered into such studies only in cases where the evident regularity of plot sizes points to the possibility of an equitable distribution of land in new foundations.[11] Property is, in other words, interpreted as a function of actions taken by an already efficacious (if tiny) state.

This interpretation of the archaeological evidence is rooted in an implicit acceptance of the claim that the creation of political communities in the Greek world was grounded in the complete and deliberate isolation of the free political process from the material basis of human existence. This claim can, of course, be traced back as far as Aristotle's assertion that the household exists for the sake of subsistence, while the polis exists for the sake of the self-sufficiency of the community and the good life; this distinction, as Pocock has pointed out, is made possible by the labor of women and slaves, which effectively emancipated male citizens from material concerns in order to devote themselves to political deliberation and activity.[12] Aristotle was writing in, and was very much the product of, the fourth century, when property qualifications for public office and military service had, in much of the Greek world and certainly in Athens, become de facto inoperative. Yet even there, the material conditions for political activity remained a vivid part of political memory, such that oligarchic movements tended to reinstate these Archaic arrangements. The identification of purely public spaces as signs of state formation is, in other words, an anachronistic retrojection of the results of several centuries of political experiments, revolutions, and reforms. Such accounts also tend to leave to one side the very real problem of how private property claims relate to a state's territoriality, insofar as public spaces never made up more than a tiny fraction of a single state's territory.

This chapter, then, has two interrelated aims, one methodological and one substantive. First, I hope to show that Mann's model of infrastructural power, in which property relations, territoriality, and legislation are central, offers a valuable approach to thinking about state power in the Greek world. Second, I attempt to begin to complement the archaeological understanding of Greek state formation as a phenomenon of urbanization and the demarcation of public space by considering the intersection of private property claims, the emergence of autonomous state power, and the development of territoriality. I use the term property relations in the sociological sense, to refer to rules governing relations between people with regard to things.[13] The property claims of my title cut two ways: I am interested in how individuals' need to have their property claims supported and the incipient state's claim to meet that need together contributed to the development of two vital aspects of autonomous state power: legislation and territoriality. I shall discuss the importance of legislative activity and property relations from both historical and theoretical perspectives, and will then consider a series of Archaic laws on property to suggest that the construction of property as a jural relation catalyzed and strengthened the legal apparatus of the state and contributed directly to the territorialization of emergent state power.

One effect of this argument will be to propose that liberal concerns over the role of private property in the creation of states—most prominent in the work of Locke and Kant—have been misleadingly sidelined in the implicitly republican understanding of the classical past, with its emphasis on public institutions, public space, the exercise of citizen rights, and the performance of citizen obligations, all of which are taken to be radically separated from the material basis of individual self-sufficiency and prosperity.

The Power of Law and Literacy

Written law emerged in Archaic Greece in an environment of strong custom and oral law, with judicial processes that involved hearings by local notables. The Homeric poems famously describe scenes of judgment, and reflect the view that all civilized societies have laws; the community of Cyclopes is defined by the absence of laws.[14] Hesiod's *Works and Days*, a poem composed toward the end of the eighth century B.C.E. and framed around a dispute between brothers over their inheritance, depicts a small community relying for conflict resolution on local elites whose judicial function appears to be only one facet of their social power. The earliest surviving written law, inscribed on stone and erected in a temple in the Cretan community of Dreros, dates to the mid-seventh century B.C.E.[15] The practice of inscribing laws and erecting them for display in public—and often sacred—spaces becomes widespread quickly thereafter, though many communities continued to rely, in part or in whole, on oral law and custom.[16]

The significance of written law in Archaic Greece is highly controversial. Many Greek historians, following the view of fifth and fourth-century democratic authors, have seen the emergence of written law as an essential condition for the development of democracy insofar as it made a community's rules accessible to all who could read.[17] But this postulate, at least superficially reasonable, has been called into question. If high degrees of literacy were not widespread, the inscribed laws will not have been consulted by the masses. Furthermore, accessibility may not have been the aim of those who chose to publish them. The monumental nature and awkward display of many written laws in this period rather gives the impression that the inscription of laws was an assertion of power by the scribal elite, designed to impress if not to overawe the illiterate and unfree members of society.[18]

Each of these interpretations of the evidence proceeds on the basis of two assumptions that are never articulated. The first is that written law is an assertion of power by the body that enacts it, and bestows power upon the body that utilizes it. The second is that legislation itself played an important role in state formation, regardless of whether those states were oligarchic or democratic. There is no doubt that a widespread transition from orally transmitted norms to written prescriptions enacted as a result of some deliberative process within a community occurred contemporaneously with the emergence of states that performed multiple functions over a more or less clearly delimited territory, that is, states that had at least some form of infrastructural power. This is surely no accident. Mann, building on an observation by Anthony Giddens, suggests that literacy is a major logistical technique for the growth of infrastructural power above all because it facilitates the codification and storage of rules and legal responsibilities.[19] But Giddens's original observation may be a little closer to the mark in ways that will prove important at least for the Greek case: for him, storage capacity is a means of generating power, which is considerably less anodyne than the mere storage of rules. Written law was "an indispensable and creative source of expanding economic and political power" in the Greek world as in other historical contexts, because it stamped the power of the enacting authority with the imprimatur of both popular and divine will, and gave the appearance of neutralizing that power by making it law.[20] The production and display of written laws was, in Richardson's terms, an act of strategic ambiguation that contributed significantly to the emergence of autonomous state power.[21]

From this perspective, the writing down of laws can be seen not as an expression of power or a simple mechanism for communication and access to information, as is frequently asserted or implied, but rather as a means of generating power itself.[22] The earliest Greek laws do not read as descriptions of rules backed by a power capable of or especially committed to enforcing them, but rather as normative statements about the achievement of social order and justice. In this respect there is a striking similarity to early Mesopotamian laws, which can be read as ideological statements of royal power and vehicles for persuading people that the king actually had a power to which in reality he only aspired.[23] Exposing the gap between promulgated laws and actual judicial practice has been productive in the Mesopotamian case; although we lack the evidence to test for a similar gap in the Archaic Greek world, the tendency of plaintiffs in Classical Athens to argue their cases on moral grounds that go beyond the statutes they cite in their own support suggests that law continued to function as an expression of political ideology.[24]

Yet statutes were cited in court, and by the Classical period it is evident that citizens regularly and fully utilized the legal apparatus of the Greek state, showing knowledge of and appealing to the laws, and using both arbitration and the courts to resolve disputes. And if Greek laws originated in aspirations to power by an elite in the name of a community that was still becoming political, by the Classical period they had become mechanisms for the maintenance of social order through the authority of an autonomous state. As has recently been shown for the case of early modern England, broad participation in the legal apparatus of a state that provided an effective forum for the resolution of conflict was a vital part of the process of state formation and a crucial arena for the acquisition of political legitimacy.[25] All of these perspectives suggest that jurisgeneration in Archaic Greece played a crucial role in the formation of Greek states, not only as autonomous agents per se but as specific historic entities. To elucidate the latter point we need to consider not the means but the matter of these laws, the problems they addressed, and the solutions they posed.

The Problem of Property

Laws were established in the Archaic Greek world to regulate a wide array of issues and practices, including what we would call both public and private laws. Laws detailing political and judicial procedures are often cited as evidence for the existence of developed poleis. Yet prominent among the concerns reflected in these legislative activities is the issue of property, and I should like to suggest that these laws allow us to glimpse not only the outcome but also the process of state formation.[26] In a recent collection of Archaic inscriptions recording laws and regulating social life, which is representative if not comprehensive, more than one third are dedicated to regulating property.[27] From Massalia (modern Marseilles) to Cyprus and from the Black Sea to Crete, these texts suggest that emergent states throughout Archaic Greece felt urgently the need to regulate property relations. The geographic spread of these texts is important to bear in mind, for just over half of them come from Crete, and in particular from the polis of Gortyn. The number and complexity of the texts we have from Gortyn make it possible to analyze the laws and their political import in greater detail than we can for any other state in Archaic Greece, but there are enough documents from other places reflecting similar concerns and strategies to suggest that the Cretan laws should be understood as more or less representative.[28]

The background to these laws is difficult to discern with any certainty. Property claims, inscribed on physical objects, are common among early inscriptions, which may suggest a relatively high degree of property insecurity.[29] This took three primary forms in the Archaic Mediterranean.[30] First, indebtedness and confiscation: we know that by the early sixth century in Athens, land was frequently pledged as collateral for loans and confiscated by creditors in the event that debtors defaulted on their loan agreements. Indebtedness and its attendant forms of servitude were part of the crisis in early sixth-century Athens that Solon's reforms attempted to ameliorate. Solon's poetic report of his own legislative activity is controversial, but it seems to indicate that he enacted a cancellation of some debts and a prohibition on the practice of debt slavery, which would have liberated some individuals and transformed others working as tenants into small landowners.[31] The second principal form of property insecurity was the apparently age-old custom of seizing goods as a means of redress, whether temporary or permanent, for some other wrong; seizure would obviously have affected moveable property—and bodies—more than land, but these too were highly valuable. Two letters inscribed on lead sheets at the end of the sixth century attest to the vulnerability of traders venturing beyond the legal protections afforded by their own cities, experiencing the seizure of their property by the creditors of their associates.[32] In the same period, a contract for the office of public scribe and "remembrancer" from a small polis in central Crete provides the magistrate with protection from seizure of both person and property.[33] Finally, the prevalence of legislation on inheritance in the Archaic period suggests that property disputes within families were commonplace, creating another context in which individuals worried about the security of their claims to ownership. Lack of evidence hampers attempts to flesh out other ways in which individuals struggled against property insecurity, but these hints alone accord well with the concerns reflected in the earliest property laws: pledge, seizure, and inheritance.

The laws from Gortyn derive from two contexts: the so-called Pythion laws, a set of laws inscribed in the first half of the sixth century on the walls of the slightly earlier Temple of Apollo Pythios; and the famous "Great Code" from the mid-fifth century.[34] The inscription of the Pythion laws occurred during the period in which the aggregation of several settlements into one had been largely completed: it was finished after the construction of a monumental temple for the community, and before archaeological indications of a peak in urban activity at the end of the sixth century. Despite some important differences in developmental trajectories and chronologies from site to site, the late seventh and early sixth century was also the period when poleis emerged and developed across central Crete, as systematic study of the archaeological evidence has shown.[35] In a study of the Pythion laws, Paula Perlman remarks that "if anything emerges as a central concern of these laws and so of Archaic Gortynian society, it is the protection and disposal of property."[36] In a more general study of the laws from Gortyn, John Davies has observed that they reflect "a system of protecting privilege, of safeguarding the ownership and transmission of property . . . and of ensuring the continuance of male lineages."[37] Perlman and Davies are noticing the same concern, but where they interpret it in social terms, I would like to suggest that these laws, and others like them from other parts of the Greek world, tell us much about how these incipient states created their own infrastructural power by responding to the needs of individuals, asserting their role as caretakers of citizens and their material interests. The emergent state thus presents itself as an autonomous entity that paternalistically protects the interests of the most privileged members of society, who will be further empowered as its magistrates.

If writing served as a technique for the creation and propagation of infrastructural power by enabling the recording, publication, and codification of laws, what were the conditions under which this general technique of social power was appropriated by incipient states? Mann observes that three factors enable this appropriation: the necessity of the state, the state's multiplicity of functions, and the state's territorialized centrality. The first two, on his account, relate directly to concerns over property, but the third is predicated upon at least putative control over land, the most important form of property in Archaic Greece, and arguably the only politically significant form. Let me take these in turn.

The state arises out of the need for long-term order, which can be effected only by establishing rules; norms, while they play a role, are not usually adequate, especially for property. Mann puts it thus: "Most societies seem to have required that some rules, *particularly those relevant to the protection of life and property*, be set monopolistically, and this has been the province of the state."[38] Because the state can assume multiple functions, of which the protection of property relations is just one, it acquires the ability to play interest groups off one another for its own interest, thereby acquiring a unique cross-cutting authority. The Greeks, by creating a convergence between landowners, decision-makers, and warriors, were able both to create a stable military force and a basis for revenues that would support the state. Mann argues that territorialized centrality is "the most important precondition of state power," but this is an ex post analytical assertion, and causes trouble for historians attempting to understand in clear terms the *process* by which that state power developed.[39] It seems to me that in the act of creating property rights—of offering to protect claims made by community members particularly in reference to land—we can see the foundation, if not the full realization, of centralized territorial control. The juridical formation of property is, in other words, a necessary but not a sufficient condition for the formation of autonomous state power.

Let me define a little more carefully what I mean by property. I glossed it above as "rules governing relations between people with regard to things," and in doing so I am consciously eschewing the perspective of the Roman legal tradition, which holds that property—*dominium*—is the rule of an individual over a thing. Despite the frequency with which historians of Greek law explicitly or implicitly adopt this anachronistic framework, there is no evidence to suggest that it would have made sense to the Greeks.[40] The Greek laws themselves are remarkably indifferent to the "things," with only a few notable exceptions; instead, they reflect the concern to regulate relations between people as they arise over things, from land to houses to moveable goods. Yet even the Roman legal definition obscures the role that property plays in the construction of both society and state. While the Roman legal tradition defines property as a series of rights with regard to a thing, including, most importantly, usufruct and alienation (whether by sale, gift, or bequest), each of these rights is actually a description of the relationship between the owner and other people with regard to the object owned. Usufruct means that the owner has the right to exclude all others from using the property in question—cultivating the land, renting out to another party, and so on. The right to alienate property amounts to the sole right to determine who else may acquire some or all exclusive rights to the property in question.

These rights are a significant source of power over others particularly when they apply to land in an agricultural society, as Morris Cohen, an early theorist of legal sociology, showed.[41] And they can be bestowed, as laws, only by a state. Cohen's concern was to show that the state was "implicated . . . directly in the legal-political structuring of the market" and thereby to dispel the myth of laissez-faire capitalism. This, of course, is what captures William Novak's interest.[42] But Cohen's core observations can also help us to understand the process of state formation itself. For if property ownership is seen not in a Lockean light (that is, as an innocent, natural condition that a benevolent state seeks to protect), but rather as the product of a legal intervention in a field of almost endless dispute, we can begin to see that legislation about property plays no small part in creating both public and private power, and ensuring that the two are closely interwoven.[43]

Making Property, Making States

From these rather abstract points it is necessary to turn to a consideration of some of the most important and detailed laws about property promulgated by several emergent states of Archaic Greece, to suggest that the formulation of these laws not only created specific property regimes, but also contributed significantly to the development of autonomous state power. The earliest surviving laws on property were promulgated in central Crete at the city of Gortyn in the late seventh and early sixth centuries, precisely the period when changes in funerary practices, the use of sacred sites, and settlement patterns appear as a set of interlocking phenomena pointing to the development of poleis across the island.[44] Inscribed on the walls of the temple of Apollo Pythios, the stones are too fragmentary to yield continuous sense in most cases. But we learn that in this very early period—when the citizen group at Gortyn was recognized and receiving legal definition, and when Gortyn and nearby Dreros were both working out important details of their political institutions, like limitations on the iteration of public offices—laws were promulgated at Gortyn regulating property in a number of ways.[45] If the possession of property by individuals had previously been recognized and protected by any collectivity, it must have been in accordance with informal norms that we cannot recover.

The inscribed laws from the Pythion appear to be the earliest attempts of this emergent state to enact formal laws and, in the process, to create its own jurisdiction. We have fragments prohibiting purchase and exchange in an uncertain context, while another recognizes and regulates the practice of debt bondage.[46] We have a reference to redistribution in a fragment that also mentions a building; given that the word for redistribution is followed by a penalty clause, it may have been a law putting some kind of restriction on the redistribution of property, but its precise import is wholly obscure.[47] Two texts from the mid-sixth century at Gortyn contain regulations on adoption that impinge on property. One is quite fragmentary, but preserves distinctions between legitimate and either illegitimate or adoptive children, and between maternal and paternal property. (Women, in other words, were property owners in their own right at Gortyn, which was not uniformly true across the Greek world.) The same law suggests that property was divisible at least for the purposes of inheritance.[48] The second law, less fragmentary but still containing several uncertain passages, addresses disputes over inherited property between an adopted child and another party, perhaps the biological child or children of the adoptive father. The law makes it abundantly clear, however, that adopted children could in fact inherit property from their adoptive fathers.[49]

Cumulatively, the laws on property from the late seventh and sixth centuries at Gortyn give the impression of an early state attempting to create a stable ownership regime, limiting the ways in which land and other kinds of property could be transferred but allowing the bequest of such goods to adopted children by adoptive fathers. By the late sixth century, the Gortynian state had public land to give to benefactors, which could become private property and come with citizen rights attached, or could be granted for use rather than ownership.[50]

In the first half of the fifth century, the Gortynians began to strengthen laws governing property relations within the city. They established procedures for the resolution of boundary disputes between neighbors, made exceptions to the apparently general prohibition on trespassing, and established penalties for water damage done to a neighbor's property due to negligence.[51] We can safely infer from two laws prohibiting the sale or pledge of land under special circumstances that in general land was alienable and therefore constituted private property in Gortyn in this period.[52]

In the mid-fifth century, the Gortynians inscribed the massive collection of laws known as the "Great Code" (**G72**), which tells us a great deal about how this state regulated inheritance. As has recently been shown, the overall import of the laws on property in the Great Code is to prevent property from leaving male households or, put another way, to maximize the property of male citizens.[53] This broad aim is accomplished by a series of detailed measures. A divorced woman is allowed to take the property that she brought with her into the marriage, but only half of the produce from her own property, and half of what she has woven in her former husband's house.[54] A widow *with children* may remarry, holding her own property and whatever her former husband gave her, but she is liable to a lawsuit if she takes away anything that belongs to the children.[55] Her role is clearly to preserve the husband's estate for his children. It is not surprising, of course, to find that daughters receive half the share of sons when an estate is divided for inheritance, a measure taken with the same goal of maximizing the property of the male household, for the female heiress will take her property with her upon her marriage.[56] But that marriage is likewise determined by the desire to keep patrimony intact: she is to be married to her oldest paternal uncle; failing that, to her oldest patriline cousin; and, if that too fails, "she is to be married to whomsoever she wishes of those who ask from the tribe (*pyla*)."[57] The law also determines the path for inheritance: when a man or a woman dies, the property is to go first to children, grandchildren, and great-grandchildren. Failing that, it is to go to any brothers of the deceased and their children; next, to the sisters of the deceased and their children. But if there are no kinsmen, the law states that "those of the household who are the *klaros* are to have the property."[58] This has been plausibly taken to mean that the serfs who lived on and worked the estate would inherit the property of the deceased and become free persons, perhaps belonging to the lower-status group of *apetairoi*, people not belonging to a social group known as a *hetaireia*.[59]

Restrictions placed on sale and gift are equally revealing. No son may sell or mortgage property given to him by his father until the father is dead, whereas he is free to sell or mortgage at will any property he has acquired himself.[60] No father may sell or mortgage the property of his children, whether they have acquired or inherited it.[61] And as a final means of preserving the property of male households, the law allows sons to give to mothers, and husbands to give to wives, no more than 100 staters, while fathers face limits on what they can give to married daughters.[62]

Now all this sounds like it pertains to private law and is irrelevant for the study of the state. That is certainly the way historians of Greek law have approached this material. Yet the ultimate goal toward which all these regulations work—the maximization of property in the hands of citizen male households—is of vital interest to the incipient state. When Morris Cohen observed the interrelationship of public and private power in property relations, he was noting the way in which the possession of property by private individuals gives them power over others that is necessarily social and often political in nature.[63] From a historical perspective it is productive to view this dynamic from the other side: at Gortyn it appears that establishing regulations on the use and distribution of private property contributed directly to the establishment of state power.

To understand why, we need to see how these regulations, which seem to belong so fully to the realm of private law, in fact contribute to the infrastructural power of the state. For the concern is not only to preserve the property of each citizen household, including a male and his extended biological family, but also to prevent it from being transferred out of larger public groupings within the polis. This concern shines forth with particular clarity from the regulations that require an heiress who does not have any eligible kinsmen to marry a member of her *pyla*, her tribe.[64] Now the tribes in Gortyn provided, in rotation on an annual basis, the *kosmoi*, the board of officials who were de facto the leaders of the polis during their term in office.[65] Similarity of nomenclature in one instance seems to tie the *pyla* to another citizen group at Gortyn, the *startos*, which has recently been interpreted as a military unit although it only appears in civilian contexts of governance.[66] The legal commitment to ensuring that an heiress will marry within her tribe if she has no kinsmen who can or will marry her suggests a concern, in the first instance, to protect patrimony, and in the second instance, to protect the resource base of the larger civic groups that constitute both the rulers and—probably—the warriors of the state. The law that allows "those of the household who are the *klaros*" to inherit property in the event that there are no kinsmen might work in the same direction; if this phrase in fact refers to serfs, who would thereby become free property owners, possibly of a lower status (*apetairoi*), it might suggest a desire to retain the connection between a plot of land and a citizen family that could perform military service.

This is a highly particular property regime, the product of an aspiring state that simultaneously responded to what must have been a real need for the protection of property claims and the delineation of inheritance rules, created its own military and ruling class, and effectively made itself into a territorial entity. The state thereby claimed jurisdiction over all the land belonging to the citizens who sought its protection, while also claiming some land as public, which it could distribute to benefactors at will, and from which it may well have derived revenues. The strategy was to map the distribution of political power onto the distribution of property.

There is no doubt that Gortyn in the Archaic and Early Classical periods was in many ways a singular place, but its strategy of using law to establish a property regime that would simultaneously meet the needs of individuals and contribute to the creation of autonomous state power by establishing the emergent state's territory and jurisdiction was not unique in this historical context. Several documents from other parts of the Greek world suggest that the establishment of rules governing property relations played a crucial role in state formation beyond Crete.

One class of important documents in this connection are those that record the establishment of new settlements and enact rules for participation. A fourth-century decree of Cyrene in North Africa contains what is purported to be the original agreement of the terms upon which citizens of Thera, a small polis in the Cyclades, participated in the settlement of Cyrene in the seventh century.[67] There is no way to determine whether the original agreement is quoted verbatim from some other written source, but it accords relatively well with the written account of the settlement by Herodotus, and nothing about its provisions is seriously anachronistic.[68] And this text exposes clearly the central role of property in the creation of a new state: settlers are to receive citizenship and an allotment of land, and the same is to be made available to Theraeans who wish to join them at a later date, which is the clause that was of interest to the Theraeans of the fourth century who were resident in Cyrene and were actively seeking citizenship there.

Two more documents establishing the rules for new settlements, and the states that arose from them, come from Ozolian Lokris in central Greece, a small region north of Attica that is rather like Crete in being legally precocious but poorly represented in ancient literary sources. An inscribed bronze tablet from the last quarter of the sixth century contains a record of regulations about rights to property on two plains, which are clearly intended for both agricultural and pastoral use.[69] The issuing authority is something of a mystery; we know very little about Lokrian political organization in the late sixth century. This community sent out settlers to two territories, the plains of Hyla and Liskara, which they divided into lots, some for private use (τόν ἀπότομον) and some for public (τόν δαμοσίον). Individuals received some form of property right with respect to the former class of lots; the Greek word, ἐπινομία, may mean either the right of pasturage or simple property. Whatever the character of that right, it was heritable in ways that are quite familiar from Gortyn: first to sons, then to daughters, and as a last resort to the brothers of the owner. Agitation of any kind to alter the original division of lots is strictly prohibited; offenders are to be accursed and punished with the confiscation of their property and demolition of their house. The only exception is the case in which circumstances warrant the introduction of 200 "men worthy of battle" as additional settlers, presumably to swell the defensive capacity of the community; it is anticipated that such a move would trigger a sanctioned re-division of the land.[70] The law does not mention the right to alienate the property thus distributed and created, though it does explicitly allow for the exchange (ἀλλαγὰ) of lots, provided it is performed before a magistrate. There is no sign that these settlers will constitute a new state; their citizenship does not change, but they are agents in the expansion of the state's territoriality, and their secure possession of land in the new area is critical to their success.

The preservation of patrimony is an important feature of another Lokrian law, a well-known text on the establishment of a settlement—an ἀποικία—at Naupaktos, on the Gulf of Corinth not far at all from Lokris.[71] This law, dating to the second quarter of the fifth century and so virtually contemporary with the Great Code from Gortyn, clearly envisions the creation of a new city-state at Naupaktos with its own laws (ll. 19, 28), and seeks to ensure its stability by prohibiting the abandonment of the land by settlers, who are given permission to return to Eastern Lokris only if they leave a son or brother in their place in Naupaktos (ll. 7–10). The Lokrian state also, however, ensures that those who participate in the new settlement will not lose their right to inherit property from their fathers and brothers who remain in Lokris (ll. 29–31, 35–37). At first glance a benevolent measure to protect settlers' interests, the law also protects the state's interests by ensuring that citizen landholdings remain intact, presumably to prevent them from losing their property qualification for citizenship and, with it, military service.

The Public Nature of Private Property

These examples should suffice to make the general point that the emergent states of Archaic Greece promulgated laws about property to root people to land within the state's territory, a strategy for establishing territorial power, jurisdiction, and a delineation of citizenship that seems to have responded to the needs of individuals. It is striking that so few historians have commented on the rather limited nature of the property rights thus created: the detailed regulations prescribing the line of inheritance, and the frequent restrictions on sale and mortgaging, all worked in the interests of the state to maximize the number of citizens who would meet property qualifications, which we know determined military service and the right to hold public offices in many Archaic Greek states.[72] Furthermore, the same states that sought to ensure the long-term integrity of the property of its citizen households regularly used confiscation as a penalty for violations of its decisions.

The threat of confiscation is present alongside many of the most detailed property regulations that survive. Any citizen of Thera who is asked to go as a settler to Cyrene but refuses will be executed and his property will be made public, that is, it will be confiscated by the state.[73] When the Ozolian Lokrian state expanded its territory to include the plains of Hyla and Liskara, it prescribed the confiscation of property and demolition of any houses as the penalty for agitating for a redistribution of the new land, and noted that this was the same penalty prescribed by the law for homicide.[74] When the Lokrians established their new settlement at Naupaktos, they warned that anyone who violated the decisions set forth in the decree would be stripped of his rights as a citizen and would have his property confiscated.[75]

Other, less extreme, forms of expropriation were common too and attest to the state's role in creating private property to establish its own power. At Gortyn, as we have seen, some restrictions were placed on pledging property (**G72** 6.2–46), but it was generally accepted that goods offered as legal pledges would in fact be seized in the event of default. We learn of several interesting exceptions: creditors could not seize agricultural implements or the property that a head of household was providing for his *andreion*, dining clubs to which all citizens belonged. Now Aristotle reports that the Cretan dining clubs were provisioned by the produce of public lands, and it has recently been suggested that this law proves he was wrong; a compulsory levy on the produce of land owned by citizens provided the food for these citizen clubs.[76] In one sense, however, Aristotle was right: the private property of the Gortynians (and, *a fortiori*, many other Greek states) was essentially public, in several respects. First, it was recognized and protected by the state as a crucial step in the process of creating—and then of maintaining—autonomous state power. Second, it could be used not only to determine political rights and military obligations, but also as a source of revenue for the state. Despite frequent protestations to the contrary, Greek states were not averse to levying direct taxes, especially on land and produce, but they preferred in this period to raise those taxes in kind and to use them for redistributive, community-building purposes like mandatory common meals for the citizen-soldiers, as happened at Gortyn and Sparta alike, or much later to sell grain, collected as a tax from foreign grain-producing regions controlled by imperial Greek states, at low prices to the citizens, as happened in fourth-century Athens.[77]

Conclusion

I have tried to show that the emergence of written law, and its prominent preoccupation with issues of property, contributed vitally to the development of autonomous, infrastructural power among the emergent microstates of Archaic Greece. By asserting a willingness to protect the property claims made by individuals, the agents of these early states—who are so difficult to detect with precision—created a group, whom we might recognize as the ruling elite, in whom property, political authority, and military obligation overlapped and commingled. They crafted laws to protect the integrity of this group and its subdivisions, simultaneously creating and protecting the political and military basis of the state, and protecting the property of individuals. Insofar as we can suppose that these laws were passed by, or at the initiative of, the elites themselves, we should not see the state as a disinterested third party in origin.[78]

Yet their decision to elaborate laws of private property to protect their own interests ultimately led to the transformation of ownership into governance by establishing a state territory where previously there was only possession by individuals, as the Kantian understanding of the relationship between property and territorial rights suggests.[79] It was only by publicly imposing the right to property that they were able to establish a set of rights and duties relative to property that was binding on everyone. In so doing they created both the state's *territorial jurisdiction*, the geographical boundaries within which its laws were recognized as binding, and its *metajurisdictional authority*, the exclusive authority of the state to alter its own jurisdiction, by claiming new land as territory whether by settlement, annexation, or war.[80]

I have not attempted to sketch a systematic application of Mann's model of infrastructural power onto the states of the ancient Greek world. Instead, I have explored the complex interrelationship of property claims, written law, and territoriality in the historical process of the emergence and development of infrastructural power in this world, phenomena that are all important components of his model. The need for monopolistic regulation of property relations is, along with the protection of life, part of the need for order that makes states necessary in the original sense. Meanwhile, the state's active protection of existing property relations, alongside its provision of military force, the maintenance of communications infrastructure, and redistributive economic activities, contributes to the multiplicity of state functions that lends it autonomous power.[81] Literacy was a crucial "logistical technique" that promoted the growth of infrastructural power in Archaic Greek states, both because it made it possible to record and store legal responsibilities, and to publicize those rules to the group that was bound by them. I have suggested that the concern with property reflected in inscribed laws of the Archaic period was both a response to the needs of individual possessors for the maintenance of the existing social order and a mechanism by which the emergent state could begin to establish and enforce its territorial jurisdiction, a crucial component of infrastructural state power. There is much in Mann's model that I have not touched on at all, some of it less productively applicable to the Greek world than these components. But Mann's emphasis on the roles of property, literacy, and territoriality in establishing infrastructural state power accord very well with the Greek evidence, and encourages historians to contemplate an alternative model for state formation that incorporates the role of private material interests and acknowledges the deep imbrication of state and civil society in Greek antiquity.

NOTES

I should like to thank Clifford Ando and Seth Richardson for their invitation to participate in this volume. Clifford Ando, Seth Richardson, Eric Driscoll, and the anonymous reviewer for the press gave me suggestions that have made this a better chapter.

1. I am grateful to Paula Perlman for sharing with me, in advance of publication, her monumental work, coauthored with Michael Gagarin, on the inscribed laws of Archaic and Classical Crete (2016), a splendid new collection of the texts with full commentary and references to other publications of the texts (including *Inscriptiones Creticae,* van Effenterre and Ruzé 1994–1995 and Koerner and Hallof 1993). All references below to Cretan inscriptions that begin with a letter and number in bold are to the documents in this work.

2. The skeptical position is most forcefully stated by Berent 2000, 2004.

3. Rebuttals of different kinds are offered by Hansen 2002, Herman 2006, 227–29, and Anderson 2009.

4. For a similar observation about American history, see Novak 2008.

5. Despotic power: Mann 1986, 113. Not even the so-called tyrannical regimes of the seventh century are likely to meet this description: Anderson 2005.

6. On the shift away from bearing arms during the Archaic period and its association with state formation, see van Wees 1998. On violence in the civic context of fourth-century Athens, see Riess 2012.

7. Mann 1986, 113.

8. Regional states, comprised of multiple communities inhabiting a single territory and united by some sense of shared identity, emerged in Greece in the Archaic period and remained a feature through the Classical; see Morgan 2003. Many of these became federal states, incorporating multiple poleis; see Mackil 2013.

9. Morris 2006 gives a general overview.

10. Megara Hyblaia: De Angelis 2003, and Gras, Tréziny, and Broise 2004. Azoria: Haggis et al. 2007, 2011. Border sanctuaries: de Polignac 1994. Evidence for exploitation of the hinterland ranges from grain silos (seventh-century Megara Hyblaia: De Angelis 2002) to metal working (eighth-century Pithekoussai: Ridgway 1992, 91–100), but in general archaeological evidence for activity in the eighth- and seventh-century countryside is quite sparse (Osborne 2007, 283–84).

11. E.g., Di Vita 1990; Tréziny 1999, with the cautionary remarks of De Angelis 2003, 51.

12. Arist. *Pol.* 1252b16–1253a18; Pocock 1992.

13. This sociological definition of property was first articulated by Hohfeld 1913; for a recent critical discussion see Hann 1998, 1–47.

14. Cyclopes: Hom. *Od.* 9.105–15. Cf. Hdt. 4.106 on cannibals who "pay no regard to justice nor make use of any established laws."

15. Gagarin and Perlman 2016, 200–207, **Dr1** (Meiggs and Lewis 1988, no. 2; van Effenterre and Ruzé 1994–1995, I.81).

16. Thomas 1996, suggesting, in particular, that written law was a means of establishing innovative procedures while oral law and custom promulgated traditional norms.

17. Gagarin 1986, 146; Robb 1994, 74–96; Detienne 1994; Gagarin 2008, 39–92.

18. Whitley 1997, focusing on Crete and differentiating literacy and legislation there (i.e., finding a high degree of scribal literacy, but little evidence for even widespread functional literacy) from what occurs in Athens (a high degree of functional literacy suggested by *dipinti* and graffiti; and late and low levels of written law). Awkward display: Papakonstantinou 2009. Eder 1986 has suggested that laws were written down to enshrine the powers of the elite before they could be eroded by incipient revolutionary demands.

19. Mann 1986, 117. Giddens 1981, 5–6 and passim. Codification in the modern (indeed even the Roman) sense is rarely, if ever, applicable for the Greek world; the "Gortyn Code" could be seen as an exception (Gagarin 1982), but even that seemingly unitary and wide-ranging set of legal documents was clearly amended (*IC* IV 72 cols. XI.24–end), and the "code" is in places highly disorganized (e.g., *IC* IV 72 col. II.2–45), as Davies 1996 has shown.

20. Novak 2008: 767–68 on American law. We find appeal to popular will in the first line of the mid-seventh-century Dreros law (Gagarin and Perlman 2016, 200-207,

Dr1; Meiggs and Lewis 1988, no. 2; van Effenterre and Ruzé 1994–1995, I.81): πόλι ἔϝαδε, preceded immediately by an invocation to the divine (θιός), which was inscribed below line 1 as a result of scribal error and/or the challenge of inscribing on an undressed block of stone (Gagarin and Perlman 2016, 200–202, with discussion of alternative interpretations of this out-of-place word). For early laws as decisions of the people see e.g., van Effenterre and Ruzé 1994–1995, I.78 (*AE* 1975: 105–203) from Tiryns (late 7C or early 6C): ℎό|πυι κα δοκεῖ τοῖ δάμοι ἁλιαιίαν, "as it is resolved by the people in an assembly"; van Effenterre and Ruzé 1994–1995, I.62 from Chios (early to mid 6C): δήμο | ῥήτρας; Gagarin and Perlman 2016, 486–92, **Lyktos1A** (van Effenterre and Ruzé 1994–1995, I.12) from Lyktos (late 6C) ἔϝ]αδε Λυκτίοισι, etc, "resolved by the people of Lyktos."

21. Richardson, this volume.

22. For a recent example of this assumption see Coldstream 2013, 341–42.

23. Yoffee 2005, 100–112; Richardson 2012: 32–44; Richardson, this volume.

24. Yunis 2005.

25. Hindle 2005.

26. Gagarin (1986, 2006, 2008) has continued to argue that early Greek law was primarily concerned with procedure, but can do so only by ignoring or distorting much of the evidence (Wallace and Westbrook 1989).

27. Van Effenterre and Ruzé 1994–1995, vol. II.

28. In the collection of van Effenterre and Ruzé 1994–1995, vol. II, 37 of 99 texts regulate property broadly construed. Of these 37 laws, 19 (56 percent) come from Crete; all but one of those 19 texts comes from Gortyn. Cretan laws represent 64.64 percent of the total corpus (64/99). So the Cretan poleis do not appear uniquely concerned about property. Laws from other places and contexts will support this hypothesis (see below in this chapter).

29. E.g., Nestor's Cup (Meiggs and Lewis 1988, no. 1), with Pavese 1996 and Faraone 1996, including references to other owners' inscriptions (*CEG* 447, 450, 452, 460; 443a=893; 454a=897; 642a=902).

30. For an exploration of the limits of property security in the Classical period, see Mackil, forthcoming.

31. Note the cancellation of debts by removing from the land *horoi*, boundary stones that probably demarcated and publicized land pledged as collateral for a loan (Solon frag. 36.5–7). Interpretation of this passage is fraught, but I am inclined to agree with Murray 1980, 189–94; Osborne 2009, 208–13; see also Ober 1995, 2006. Harris's claim (2006) that this amounted to a resolution of civil strife by abolishing a system of pay for protection and the maintenance of internal order is imaginative but not persuasive.

32. The Berezan lead letter: van Effenterre and Ruzé 1994–1995, II.72; the Olbia lead letter: *SEG* 54.694.

33. The "Spensithios decree": Gagarin and Perlman 2016, **Da1B** 6–11 and pp. 194–95 (ed. pr. Jeffrey and Morpurgo-Davies 1970); Bravo 1980, 767–69; Koerner 1981, 187–88.

34. Perlman 2002; Gagarin and Perlman 2016, 263.

35. Gortyn: Gagarin and Perlman 2016, 23–24. The broader picture: Kotsonas 2002; Coldstream 2013; Perlman and Gagarin 2016, 28. Excavations at the site of Azoria in north-

eastern Crete have produced (inter alia) details that support the general picture: Haggis et al. 2007, 2011.

36. Perlman 2002, 205.

37. Davies 2005b, 327.

38. Mann 1986, 120 (my italics).

39. Mann 1986, 122.

40. Garnsey 2007, 177–82. The *Corpus Civilis Iuris* does not contain a definition of property; this definition of *dominium* stems from the Napoleonic code, written very much under the influence of the ancient Roman codes. Johnston 1999, 53–76, organizes his discussion of the Roman law on property by distinguishing ownership itself from relations with neighbors arising over claims to ownership. Discussions of Greek laws on property frequently adopt the assumptions implicit in Roman law; see e.g., Todd 1993 whose chapter (12) on the topic is revealingly entitled "Relations between Persons and Things."

41. Cohen 1927. For ownership as power see also Purcell 2012 and Purcell's "Venal Histories" Sather lectures given at Berkeley in 2012.

42. Novak 2008: 770.

43. Locke, *Second Treatise of Government*, §§25-51 (property in state of nature), §§124–26 (property-related needs met by the state). See Simmons 2001, 222–306; Miller 2011.

44. Kotsonas 2002; Haggis et al. 2007, 2011; Coldstream 2013. See also S. Wallace 2010, 327–49.

45. Citizen group at Gortyn: **G13**. Public office: **G14** (Gortyn, c. 600–525), 200–207 **Dr1** (Dreros, c. 650).

46. **G4** with Gagarin and Perlman 2016, 100–101, for cautionary remarks (prohibition on purchase and exchange); **G30** (debt bondage).

47. **G5**; Gagarin and Perlman (2016) leave open the possibility that the fine is related to a (permanent) interruption to the flow of a river; to my mind that is hard to reconcile with the language of redistribution (ἀνδάζαθαι) earlier in the line.

48. **G20**.

49. **G21**; *SEG* 52.857.

50. Public land given as gift, along with citizen rights: **G64**, c. 525–500; grant of usufruct of public land: **G43**Ba.3-7, 500–450.

51. Boundary disputes: **G42** B2; trespassing: **G46** B7–9; water damage: **G52**; cf. the slightly later **G73**A.

52. The traditional view that land was inalienable, which is heavily influenced by the problematic Aristotelian account of "the Cretan order" (regarding land, Arist. *Pol.* 1272a1–22), is still current, e.g., Brixhe and Bile 1999, 108–15; Chaniotis 2005, 183. But it is difficult to reconcile this claim with **G43**Ba.3-7, which prohibits the sale or pledge of public land over which a benefactor is given usufruct by a decree of the polis, and **G72** 6, which lists conditions under which family property may not be sold or pledged. For the view that land was both alienable and divisible, see Link 1994, 80–82; Mandalaki 2000; Maffi 2003, 175–80; Davies 2005a, 160–61; Gagarin and Perlman 2016, 100–103.

53. A similar argument is made in a different way by Davies 2005a.

54. **G72** 2.45–52. The mention of produce (*karpos*) clearly indicates that women could own land. The restriction on what she is to take from the marriage is still true if the husband is the cause of the divorce, but in this case the woman also receives five staters in damages.

55. **G72** 3.17–24.

56. **G72** 4.39–43.

57. **G72** 7.27–52; cf. **G72** 8.8–33 (on unmarried and married heiresses). Anxiety about heiresses also appears in Megara in the latter half of the sixth century: Theognis 183–92.

58. **G72** 5.9–28.

59. For this interpretation of the law on inheritance see Gagarin and Perlman 2016, 376, contra Maffi 1997, 59–61. That the *apetairoi* were a lower status group is demonstrated by the law on rape (**G72** 2.5), which sets the penalty for raping an *apetairos* at one-tenth the penalty set for raping a free man or woman. On the *apetairoi* generally see Gagarin and Perlman 2016, 92.

60. **G72** 6.2–9; cf. **G72** 9.40–43.

61. **G72** 6.7–9; cf. 6.31–36.

62. Sons to mothers, husbands to wives: **G72**.10.14–17; fathers to daughters: G72 4.48–54.

63. Cohen 1927, 14.

64. **G72** 7.50–52.

65. **G72** 5.5–6.

66. The *startos Aithaleus* appears as the group providing the *kosmoi* at one time in fifth-century Gortyn (**G72** 5.5–6); *Aithaleis* appear as a group serving the same capacity in three Hellenistic decrees from Gortyn (*IC* IV 167.3, IV 184.1, IV 259.1). The *startos Aithaleus* and the *Aithaleis* appear to be a single tribe within Gortyn the name of which changed over time (Gagarin and Perlman 2016, 66). The *startos* as a military unit: Kristensen 2002, 71–74; Chaniotis 2005, 180–81.

67. Meiggs and Lewis 1988, no. 5; van Effenterre and Ruzé 1994–1995, I.41; *SEG* 9.3.

68. On this issue see Graham 1960, 1983. At the very least we can say that the document "preserves the memory of the representation that the founders had made of their collective future" (Létoublon 1989, 112). See also Helmis 2005, 128–31.

69. *IG* IX 1² 3.609; Meiggs and Lewis 1988, no. 13; van Effenterre and Ruzé 1994–1995, I.44. The text is called a τεθμός (l. A1). Pastoral use is suggested by ἐπινομία and related verbs (ll. A3–6). Agricultural use is demonstrated by the provision that whatever is planted on these lots is to be ἄσυλος (ll. A 6–7).

70. ll. A 7–9.

71. Meiggs and Lewis 1988, no. 20; van Effenterre and Ruzé 1994–1995, I.44.

72. Two rather different examples will suffice to make the broader point. In Solonian Athens the property classes determined both military service and office holding; see Foxhall 1997. In sixth-century Thessaly, if the reforms of Aleuas the Red are indeed historical, the territory of the city of Larisa at least was divided into sections (*kleroi*) upon which military recruitment quotas were imposed (Arist. frag. 498 Rose); see Helly 1995,

150–75. Whereas we have the impression that Athenian properties had been acquired gradually over time by individuals, with the emergent state simply imposing obligations on people that depended on the size and productivity of their holdings, the sixth-century Thessalian reforms seem to have been intended to expand the size of the military by establishing a basis for recruitment in the obligation of landholders.

73. Meiggs and Lewis 1988, no. 5 37–38.

74. Ibid., no. 13 ll. 9–14.

75. Ibid., no. 20 ll. 40–41, and 43–45 stipulate confiscation of the property of any magistrate who fails to provide a trial for the man who accuses another of violating the decisions.

76. The exceptions are spelled out in **G75** B. Arist. *Pol.* 1272a16–21, accepted by Willetts 1955: 252, inter alii. The importance of the passage is highlighted by Davies 2005a. On the Cretan *andreion*, see Gagarin and Perlman 2016, 93–95.

77. Stroud 1998. For an overview of taxation practices see Bresson 2016, 102–10, 293–99.

78. While elite competition undoubtedly played a role in the formation of states in Archaic Greece, recent scholarship has tended to focus on this dynamic to the exclusion of almost everything else; see, e.g., Foxhall 1997, 119, and Morris 2007, 238.

79. Kant, *Metaphysics of Morals* 6: 260–70, with Miller 2011.

80. I am building here on the helpful distinction between jurisdictional and meta-jurisdictional authority drawn by Anna Stilz in her lucid analysis of Kant's theory of property rights and their relationship to the territorial rights of states (Stilz 2009, esp. 201–10). On the different methods by which states could legitimately acquire territory in the Greek world, see Chaniotis 2004.

81. Mann 1986, 120.

BIBLIOGRAPHY

Anderson, G. 2005. "Before *Turannoi* Were Tyrants: Rethinking a Chapter of Early Greek History." *Classical Antiquity* 24 (2): 173–222.

———. 2009. "The Personality of the Greek State." *Journal of Hellenic Studies* 129: 1–22.

Berent, M. 2000. "Anthropology and the Classics: War, Violence, and the Stateless *Polis*." *Classical Quarterly* 50 (1): 257–89.

———. 2004. "In Search of the Greek State: A Rejoinder to M. H. Hansen." *Polis* 21 (1–2): 107–46.

Bravo, B. 1980. "Sulan: Représailles et justice privée contre des étrangers dans les cités grecques." *Annali della Scuola Normale Superiore di Pisa* 10:675–988.

Bresson, A. 2016. *The Making of the Ancient Greek Economy: Institutions, Markets, and Growth in the City-States*. Princeton, N.J.: Princeton University Press.

Brixhe, C., and M. Bile. 1999. "La circulation des biens dans les lois de Gortyne." In *Des dialectes grecs aux Lois de Gortyne*, edited by C. Dobias-Lalou, 75–116. Paris: Boccard.

Chaniotis, A. 2004. "Justifying Territorial Claims in Classical and Hellenistic Greece: The Beginnings of International Law." In *The Law and the Courts in Ancient Greece*, edited by E. M. Harris and L. Rubinstein, 185–228. London: Duckworth.

———. 2005. "The Common Institutions of the Cretans." In *La Grande Iscrizione di Gortyna: Centoventi anni dopo la scoperta*, edited by E. Greco and M. Lombardo, eds., 175–94. Athens: Italian Archaeological School of Athens.

Cohen, M. 1927. "Property and Sovereignty." *Cornell Law Quarterly* 13: 8–30.

Coldstream, J. N. 2013. "Geometric and Archaic Crete: A Hunt for the Elusive Polis." In *Kreta in der geometrischen und archaischen Zeit. Akten des Internationalen Kolloquiums am Deutschen Archäologischen Institut, Abteilung Athen, 27.–29. Januar 2006*, edited by W.-D. Niemeier, O. Pilz, and I. Kaiser, 341–53. Munich: Hirmer.

Davies, J. K. 1996. "Deconstructing Gortyn: When Is a Code a Code?" In *Greek Law in Its Political Setting: Justifications Not Justice*, edited by L. Foxhall and A. D. E. Lewis, 33–56. Oxford: Oxford University Press.

———. 2005a. "Gortyn Within the Economy of Archaic and Classical Crete," In *La Grande Iscrizione di Gortyne: Centoventi anni dopo la scoperta*, edited by E. Greco and M. Lombardo, 153–74. Athens: Italian Archaeological School of Athens.

———. 2005b. "The Gortyn Laws." In *The Cambridge Companion to Greek Law*, edited by M. Gagarin and D. Cohen, 305–327. Cambridge: Cambridge University Press.

De Angelis, F. 2002. "Trade and Agriculture at Megara Hyblaia." *Oxford Journal of Archaeology* 21 (3): 299–310.

———. 2003. *Megara Hyblaia and Selinous: The Development of Two Greek City-States in Archaic Sicily*. Oxford: Oxford University Press.

de Polignac, F. 1994. "Mediation, Competition, and Sovereignty: The Evolution of Rural Sanctuaries in Geometric Greece." In *Placing the Gods. Sanctuaries and Sacred Space in Ancient Greece*, edited by S. E. Alcock and R. Osborne, 3–18. Oxford: Clarendon Press.

Detienne, M. 1994. "L'éspace de la publicité: ses opérateurs intellectuels dans la cité." In *Les savoirs de l'écriture en Grèce ancienne*, edited by M. Detienne, 29–81. Lille: Presses universitaires de Lille.

Di Vita, A. 1990. "Town Planning in the Greek Colonies of Sicily from the Time of the Foundation to the Punic Wars." In *Greek Colonists and Native Populations*, edited by J.-P. Descouedres, 343–63. Oxford: Oxford University Press.

Eder, W. 1986. "The Political Significance of the Codification of Law in Archaic Societies: An Unconventional Hypothesis." In *Social Struggles in Archaic Rome: New Perspectives on the Conflict of the Orders*, edited by K. Raaflaub, 262–300. Berkeley: University of California Press.

Faraone, C. A. 1996. "Taking 'The Nestor's Cup Inscription' Seriously: Erotic Magic and Conditional Curses in the Earliest Inscribed Hexameters." *Classical Antiquity* 15 (1): 77–112.

Foxhall, L. 1997. "A View from the Top: Evaluating the Solonian Property Classes." In *The Development of the Polis in Archaic Greece*, edited by L. Mitchell and P. J. Rhodes, 113–36. London: Routledge.

Gagarin, M. 1982. "The Organization of the Gortyn Law Code." *Greek, Roman, and Byzantine Studies* 23 (2): 129–46.

———. 1986. *Early Greek Law*. Berkeley: University of California Press.

———. 2006. "Early Greek Law." In *The Cambridge Companion to Ancient Greek Law*, edited by M. Gagarin and D. Cohen, 82–96. Cambridge: Cambridge University Press.

———. 2008. *Writing Greek Law*. Cambridge: Cambridge University Press.

———. 2010. "Slaves and Serfs at Gortyn." *Zeitschrift für Savigny-Stiftung* 127:14–31.

Gagarin, M., and P. Perlman. 2016. *The Laws of Ancient Crete, c. 650–400 BCE*. Oxford: Oxford University Press.

Garnsey, P. 2007. *Thinking About Property: From Antiquity to the Age of Revolution*. Cambridge: Cambridge University Press.

Giddens, A. 1981. *A Contemporary Critique of Historical Materialism. Volume I: Power, Property, and the State*. London: Macmillan.

Graham, A. J. 1960. "The Authenticity of the ΟΡΚΙΟΝ ΤΩΝ ΟΙΚΙΣΤΗΡΩΝ of Cyrene." *Journal of Hellenic Studies* 80:94–111.

———. 1983. *Colony and Mother City in Ancient Greece*. 2nd ed. Chicago: Ares.

Gras, M., H. Tréziny, and H. Broise. 2004. *Mégara Hyblaea 5: L'espace urbain d'une cité grecque de Sicile orientale*. Rome: École française de Rome.

Haggis, D. C., et al. 2007. "Excavations at Azoria, 2003–2004, Part 1: The Archaic Civic Complex." *Hesperia* 76 (2): 243–321.

———. 2011. "Excavations in the Archaic Civic Buildings at Azoria in 2005–2006." *Hesperia* 80 (1): 1–70.

Hann, C. M. 1998. "Introduction: The Embeddedness of Property." In *Property Relations: Renewing the Anthropological Tradition*, edited by C. M. Hann, 1–47. Cambridge: Cambridge University Press.

Hansen, M. H. 2002. "Was the *Polis* a State or a Stateless Society?" In *Even More Studies in the Greek Polis*, edited by T. Heine Nielsen, 17–47. Stuttgart: Franz Steiner Verlag.

Harris, E. M. 2006. "Solon and the Spirit of the Law in Archaic and Classical Greece." In *Solon of Athens: New Historical and Philological Approaches*, edited by J. Blok and A. Lardinois, 290–318. Leiden: Brill.

Helly, B. 1995. *L'état thessalien: Aleuas le roux, les tétrades et les tagoi*. Lyon: Maison de l'Orient Mediterranean.

Helmis, A. 2005. "Le 'degré zéro de l'écriture' du droit: à propos des décrets de fondation des cités coloniales." In *Le législateur et la loi dans l'Antiquité: Hommage à Françoise Ruzé*, edited by P. Sineux, 127–37. Caen: Presses universitaires de Caen.

Herman, G. 2006. *Morality and Behaviour in Democratic Athens: A Social History*. Cambridge: Cambridge University Press.

Hindle, S. 2005. "Law, Law Enforcement, and State Formation in Early Modern England." In *Staatsbildung als kultureller Prozess: Strukturwandel und Legitimation von Herrschaft in der Frühen Neuzeit*, edited by R. G. Asch and D. Freist, 209–34. Cologne: Böhlau.

Hohfeld, W. N. 1913. "Some Fundamental Legal Conceptions as Applied in Judicial Reasoning." *Yale Law Journal* 23 (1): 16–59.
Jeffery, L. H., and A. Morpurgo-Davies. 1970. "Poinikastas and Poinikazen: BM 1969.4-2.1. A New Archaic Inscription from Krete." *Kadmos* 9:118–54.
Johnston, D. 1999. *Roman Law in Context*. Cambridge: Cambridge University Press.
Koerner, R. 1981. "Vier frühe Verträge zwischen Gemeinwesen und Privatleuten auf griechischen Inschriften." *Klio* 63:179–206.
Koerner, R., and K. Hallof. 1993. *Inschriftliche Gesetzestexte der frühen griechischen Polis. Aus dem Nachlaß von Reinhard Koerner*. Cologne: Böhlau.
Kotsonas, A. 2002. "The Rise of the Polis in Central Crete." *Eulimene* 3:37–74.
Kristensen, K. R. 2002. "On the Gortynian Πυλά and Σταρτός of the 5th Century BC." *Classica et Mediaevalia* 53:65–80.
Létoublon, F. 1989. "Le serment fondateur." *Métis* 4:101–15.
Link, S. 1994. *Das griechische Kreta: Untersuchungen zu seiner staatlichen und gesellschaftlichen Entwicklung vom 6. bis zum 4. Jahrhundert v. Chr.* Stuttgart: Franz Steiner Verlag.
Mackil, E. 2013. *Creating a Common Polity: Religion, Economy, and Politics in the Making of the Greek Koinon*. Berkeley: University of California Press.
———. Forthcoming. "Property Security and its Limits in Classical Greece." In *Ancient Greek History and Contemporary Social Science*, edited by M. Canevaro, A. Erskine, B. Gray, and J. Ober. Edinburgh: Edinburgh University Press.
Maffi, A. 1997. *Il diritto di famiglia nel Codice di Gortina*. Milan: CUEM.
———. 2003. "Studi recenti sul Codice di Gortina." *Dike* 6:161–226.
Mandalaki, A. 2000. "Ο κλᾶρος στὴ μεγάλη δωδεκάδελτο ἐπιγραφή τῆς Γόρτυνος." *Tekmeria* 5:71–86.
Mann, M. 1986. "The Autonomous Power of the State: Its Origins, Mechanisms and Results." In *States in History*, edited by J. A. Hall, 109–36. Oxford: Blackwell.
Meiggs, R., and D. M. Lewis. 1988. *A Selection of Greek Historical Inscriptions to the End of the Fifth Century B.C.* Revised edition. Oxford: Clarendon Press.
Miller, D. 2011. "Property and Territory: Locke, Kant, and Steiner." *Journal of Political Philosophy* 19 (1): 90–109.
Morgan, C. 2003. *Early Greek States beyond the Polis*. London: Routledge.
Morris, I. 2006. "The Collapse and Regeneration of Complex Society in Greece, 1500–500 BC." In *After Collapse: The Regenration of Complex Societies*, edited by G. M. Schwartz and J. J. Nichols, 72–84. Tucson: University of Arizona Press.
———. 2007. "Early Iron Age Greece." In *The Cambridge Economic History of the Greco-Roman World*, edited by W. Scheidel, I. Morris, and R. Saller, 211–41. Cambridge: Cambridge University Press.
Murray, O. 1980. *Early Greece*. Stanford, Calif.: Stanford University Press.
Novak, W. J. 2008. "The Myth of the 'Weak' American State." *American Historical Review* 113 (3): 752–72.
Ober, J. 1995. "Greek Horoi: Artifactual Texts and the Contingency of Meaning." In *Methods in the Mediterranean: Historical and Archaeological Views on Texts and Archaeology*, edited by D. B. Small, 91–123. Leiden: Brill.

———. 2006. "Solon and the Horoi: Facts on the Ground in Archaic Athens." In *Solon: New Historical and Philological Perspectives*, edited by J. Blok and A. Lardinois, 441–56. Leiden: Brill.

Osborne, R. 2007. "Archaic Greece." In *The Cambridge Economic History of the Greco-Roman World*, edited by W. Scheidel, I. Morris, and R. Saller, 277–301. Cambridge: Cambridge University Press.

———. 2009. *Greece in the Making, 1200–479 B.C.*, 2nd edition. London: Routledge.

Papakonstantinou, Z. 2009. "Review of Michael Gagarin, Writing Greek Law." *Bryn Mawr Classical Review.* http://bmcr.brynmawr.edu/2009/2009-06-49.html.

Pavese, C. O. 1996. "La iscrizione sulla kotyle di Nestor da Pithekoussai." *Zeitschrift für Papyrologie und Epigraphik* 114:1–23.

Perlman, P. J. 2002. "Gortyn. The First Seven Hundred Years. Part II: The Laws from the Temple of Apollo Pythios." In *Even More Studies in the Ancient Greek Polis*, edited by T. Heine Nielsen, 187–227. Stuttgart: Franz Steiner Verlag.

Pocock, J. G. A. 1992. "The Ideal of Citizenship Since Classical Times." *Queen's Quarterly* 99:33–55.

Purcell, N. 2012. "*Quod enim alterius fuit, id ut fiat meum, necesse est aliquid intercedere* (Varro). The Anthropology of Buying and Selling in Ancient Greece and Rome: an Introductory Sketch." In *Anthropologie de l'antiquité*, edited by P. Payen and É. Scheid-Tissinier, 81–98. Turnhout: Brepols.

Richardson, S. 2012. "Early Mesopotamia: The Presumptive State." *Past and Present* 215 (1): 3–49.

Ridgway, D. 1992. *The First Western Greeks.* Cambridge: Cambridge University Press.

Riess, W. 2012. *Performing Interpersonal Violence: Court, Curse, and Comedy in Fourth-Century Athens.* Berlin: de Gruyter.

Robb, K. 1994. *Literacy and Paideia in Ancient Greece.* New York: Oxford University Press.

Simmons, A. J. 2001. "On the Territorial Rights of States." *Philosophical Issues* 11 (1): 300–326.

Stilz, A. 2009. "Why Do States Have Territorial Rights?" *International Theory* 1 (2): 185–213.

Stroud, R. S. 1998. *The Athenian Grain-Tax Law of 374/3 B.C.* Hesperia Supplement 29. Princeton: American School of Classical Studies at Athens.

Thomas, R. 1996. "Written in Stone? Liberty, Equality, Orality, and the Codification of Law." In *Greek Law in Its Political Setting: Justification not Justice*, edited by L. Foxhall and A. D. E. Lewis, 9–32. Oxford: Clarendon Press.

Todd, S. C. 1993. *The Shape of Athenian Law.* Oxford: Clarendon Press.

Tréziny, R. 1999. "Lots et îlots à Mégara Hyblaea. Questions de métrologie." In *La colonisation grecque en méditerranée occidentale: actes de la rencontre scientifique en hommage à Georges Vallet*, 141–83. Rome: École française de Rome.

van Effenterre, H., and F. Ruzé. 1994–1995. *Nomima. Recueil d'inscriptions politiques et juridiques de l'archaïsme grec.* Rome: École française de Rome.

van Wees, J. 1998. "Greeks Bearing Arms: The State, the Leisure Class, and the Display of Weapons in Archaic Greece." In *Archaic Greece: New Approaches and New Evidence*, edited by N. Fisher and H. van Wees, 333–78. London: Duckworth.

Wallace, R. W., and R. Westbrook. 1989. "Review of *Early Greek Law* by Michael Gagarin." *American Journal of Philology* 110:362–67.

Wallace, S. 2010. *Ancient Crete: From Successful Collapse to Democracy's Alternatives, Twelfth to Fifth Centuries BC*. Cambridge: Cambridge University Press.

Whitley, J. 1997. "Cretan Laws and Cretan Literacy." *American Journal of Archaeology* 101 (4): 635–61.

Willetts, R. F. 1955. *Aristocratic Society in Ancient Crete*. London: Routledge and Kegan Paul.

Yoffee, N. 2005. *Myths of the Archaic State: Evolution of the Earliest Cities, States, and Civilizations*. Cambridge: Cambridge University Press.

Yunis, H. 2005. "The Rhetoric of Law in Fourth-Century Athens." In *The Cambridge Companion to Ancient Greek Law*, edited by M. Gagarin and D. Cohen, 191–210. Cambridge: Cambridge University Press.

CHAPTER 3

Western Zhou Despotism

WANG HAICHENG

One central argument of Seth Richardson's article "The Presumptive State" (2012) is that in the formation of early states, political competition for constituencies was much more crucial than territorial competition for land.[1] There was no shortage of land, but manpower was always in short supply. Early states repeatedly waged small wars to conquer villages close to their urban centers, and they insistently used royal rhetoric to persuade "people settled outside the cities" that it would be safer and more comfortable to live on the king's land. But they lacked effective means to get hold of people scattered over nonurban areas. Without a solid infrastructure they could not control the countryside. Echoing Benedict Anderson's definition of the modern nation-state, Richardson says that the ancient state too imagined itself as a well-defined territory under the rule of one person or assembly, but that it never fully realized what it imagined.

Richardson's insistence on viewing people as the ultimate source of wealth for the early state resonates with James Scott's 2009 book, *The Art of Not Being Governed*.[2] I fully agree with both of them, and I have made a similar argument elsewhere.[3] But I would add that arable land was also crucial to the economies of all ancient states. As the distinguished Assyriologist Nicholas Postgate puts it, "in an agricultural environment, land is carefully monitored. Each farmer knows his fields, each village knows its boundaries."[4] The sense of territorial right is an inevitable consequence of settled agriculture. The question for modern historians is what the ancient countryside looked like and how early states controlled it or failed to control it. To Max Weber and Michael

Mann, state formation was an ongoing process of establishing and keeping a legitimate monopoly of force and taxation *within a certain territory*.

In this chapter I want to examine an early Chinese state—how it made its claims to land and people, and how it went about achieving dominion over them. My example is not a city-state like those of Old Babylonian Mesopotamia but a colonial empire called Zhou. The Zhou empire ruled from the eleventh to the eighth century B.C.E., a time historians call the Western Zhou period. It overlaps in time with the Assyrian empire of the Middle Assyrian (1500–1000 B.C.E.) and Neo-Assyrian periods (1000–600 B.C.E.), and the two actually have many features in common.

For Assyria, Postgate wrote a classic paper called "The Land of Assur and the Yoke of Assur."[5] This chapter is inspired by his, but much narrower in scope, because the textual and archaeological evidence at my disposal would strike him as pathetically lean. He has memoranda, lists, monitoring documents, periodical accounts, expenditure or consumption accounts, predictive and prescriptive texts, debt notes, receipts, receipts for customs dues, ratified documents, seal-impressions, temples, palaces with spectacular reliefs, and numerous settlements with distinctive assemblages of Assyrian ceramics.[6] Enjoying the richest source material for the practice of government that the ancient world has left us, he has dealt with Assyria's royal ideology, ethos of government, army, home provinces, urban-rural relations, land tenure, taxation, and much more.[7]

Western Zhou texts, by contrast, belong almost exclusively to the genre of commemorative inscriptions. Not a single administrative text has survived. Archaeological evidence is limited mainly to cemeteries in metropolitan areas and colonies. Little is known about the distribution of small settlements. There is no revealing anatomy of any kind of settlement. Given the poverty of the sources, comparative study is more than usually urgent. It offers the possibility of extracting new insights from familiar materials and of attempting at least a broad overview of despotic and infrastructural power in Zhou China. Let me begin with the self-representation of the Zhou state.

Claiming Land and People Through the National God

Like Assyria, which was named after its original capital Assur, the Zhou empire got its name from an urban center, a place called Zhou, located near modern Xi'an in the Wei River valley (map 3.1). The valley is a flat plain lying

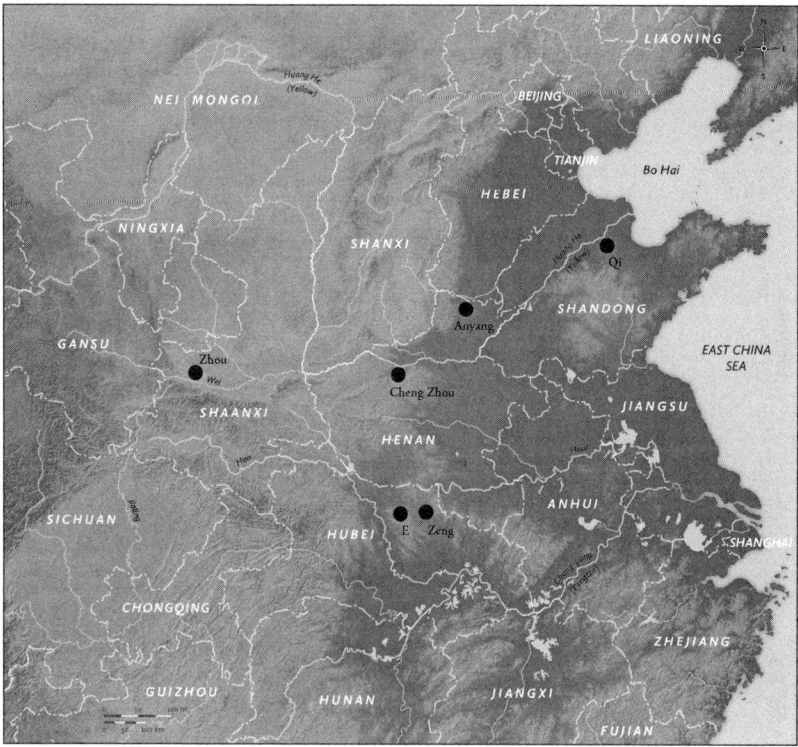

Map 3.1. Chinese sites mentioned in the text. Map by Kyle Steinke.

between high mountain ranges in the south and the Loess Highland in the north. It is a classic state space, well suited to nurture an agrarian kingdom. The Zhou kingdom gained the upper hand here in the eleventh century in a game of monopoly that must have been going on for centuries.[8]

But the Zhou state arose in the shadow of a more powerful state located farther east, a state known as Shang. Shang had its capital at modern Anyang (map 3.1), source of the famous inscribed divination bones.[9] We do not know the exact relationship between Shang and Zhou, but Shang was a hegemonic power ruling a loose confederation of polities in the eastern plain, and it is possible that Zhou was one of its clients.[10] Western Zhou sources maintain that during the reign of the last Shang king, a Zhou ruler later referred to as King Wen received a great command or mandate from a deity called Tian, normally translated as Heaven. The mandate, we are told, enabled him both to overthrow the Shang and to receive rule over the four quarters and their people. This looks like Zhou propaganda meant to supply either a pretext for a war of conquest or an after-the-fact justification for it.[11] But the sources say that it was not King Wen who finished off the Shang, but his son King Wu who led a confederation of western powers, marched to the east, and captured the Shang capital. Wen, "cultured, gentle," and Wu, "martial," are evidently posthumous names conferred on them by their respective successors to codify their roles in the change of dynasty.[12]

King Wu died shortly after the conquest, but apparently left his son and advisors a blueprint for empire building. A speech that purports to have been given by his son and successor, King Cheng, quotes from his will. We know of the speech because it was in turn quoted in a commemorative inscription cast inside a bronze ritual vessel (figure 3.1). This formidable object was commissioned by a member of the audience, a certain Mr. He, probably a minor prince from the Zhou royal lineage. Here is an English translation:

> [1] It was when the king first moved (his) court to Cheng Zhou, (when) he returned from making the *guan* offering to King Wu at the (Chamber of) Heaven.[13] In the fourth month, *bingxu* (day 23), the king addressed the ancestral young princes in the Capital Chamber, saying, "Formerly, with your deceased fathers, the elders were capable of assisting King Wen. And so King Wen received this great mandate. It was after King Wu had conquered the Great City Shang that (he) respectfully reported to Heaven, saying, 'I shall inhabit this central quarter (and) from it govern the people.' *Wuhu*! Although you are but young princes without experience, look upon the elders' meritorious service to Heaven, and carry out the commands and reverently make offerings! Help the king make firm his virtue, so that Heaven may look favorably upon our indolence." The king completed the address. He [the maker of the vessel] was awarded cowries, thirty strands, and herewith makes for Duke Mo (this treasured sacrificial vessel). It is the king's fifth ritual cycle.[14]

To judge from the inscription, King Wu planned for his new empire to have a new capital located at the center of the realm, and his son carried out his plan by building a city that he called Cheng Zhou, adding a prefix to the name of the old capital Zhou.[15] Cheng Zhou perhaps means "Victorious Zhou," or "Zhou Completed." The new Zhou was also sometimes called the "New City" or "New Great City."

 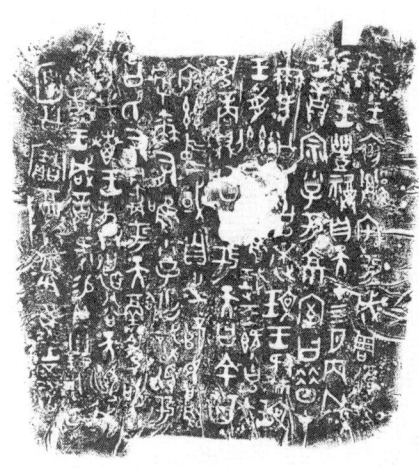

Figure 3.1. *He zun*, bronze wine vessel, with a rubbing of the cast inscription on the interior. Early Western Zhou, late eleventh century B.C.E. Height 38.5 cm. Photograph by Wu Zhenlong. Rubbing after *JC*, vol. II, no. 6014.

Cheng Zhou was indeed located between the old Zhou domain in the west and the old Shang domain in the east, and between the northern and southern regions that had already been or were soon to be incorporated into the empire (map 3.1). Throughout the Western Zhou period, it was the secondary capital from which the eastern half of the empire was administered, while the old capital Zhou remained the home of many old families as well as an active political arena.[16] The Zhou kings shuttled between the two capitals.[17] Armies were stationed in both capitals and were sometimes combined for major campaigns (see below).

Inscription [1] and another that is slightly earlier, that of the *Tian Wang gui*, show that the Zhou king had a temple in which he made sacrifices to the god Heaven and to the two dynastic founders, Kings Wen and Wu. The second inscription states that representatives from the northern, eastern, and southern quarters were summoned to witness the sacrifices.[18] Since the Zhou king himself represented the western quarter, all four quarters were thus symbolically united in the temple of Heaven. Some scholars have argued that this temple was on top of the highest mountain near Cheng Zhou.[19] Whether or not this is correct, it seems clear that Heaven was treated as a universal god and as the patron deity of the new empire, which Zhou inscriptions refer to as Zhou Bang, "the Zhou State."

Assyria too had a patron deity. The Assyrians called their state the "Land of Assur," a name that "reflects the ideological centrality of the city of Assur, and [of] the city-god, henceforth also the national god, who bears the same name."[20] Postgate tells us that the Assyrian kings made a very clear distinction between two forms of domination. The Land of Assur was a politically uniform territory divided into provinces and directly administered by the state. Client states by contrast were "areas acknowledging Assyrian domination but retaining some form of autonomy." To belong to the Land of Assur meant to join in the worship of the god Assur, and the membership dues were food provisions for the daily operation of the Temple of Assur. Temple archives tell us that the responsibility for maintaining deliveries was divided among the provinces according to a fixed rota.[21] Outside the Land of Assur were the client states, which were said to "bear the yoke of Assur." They paid annual tribute, but not to the Assur Temple. Instead their tribute went to the Assyrian king and his relatives and high-ranking officials. The tribute symbolized a secular relationship between the hegemonic state and the client. The god Assur had no particular power over the client states.

How the Zhou conceived their empire is less clear. The Zhou king was called "the Son of Heaven," so, rhetorically at least, he ruled all four quarters under Heaven's authority, and Zhou kingship evidently was understood to mean governing both people and land. But what the term "Zhou State" meant is uncertain. It occurs several times in the corpus of bronze inscriptions, from early to late Western Zhou, but never in a context that gives us a clear sense of what belonging to "the Zhou State" meant. Did one have to contribute offerings to the cult of Heaven to be considered part of the Zhou State? Unfortunately we do not possess any Zhou administrative texts to confirm or rule out this parallel with Assyrian practice.

Client States

However, the Zhou do seem to have had a concept of territory, and they did acknowledge the existence of semi-autonomous states:

[2] The king set out to inspect the land which King Wen and King Wu had with great effort gained. Fu Zi of the southern quarter had dared to seize and to occupy our land. The king led a fierce campaign against it, attacked and destroyed its capital city. Fu Zi then sent middlemen to seek peace with the king.[22] The Southern Yi and the Eastern Yi all assembled in audience, twenty-six states altogether.

May august Di[23] above and the hundred spirits preserve me, this young son, and may my plans meet with unfailing success. As the successor of the former kings who served august Heaven I have cast this precious bell of Zong Zhou. Let it ring, let it chime, let it welcome down my glorious grandfather and father kings. May the former kings look down from above and send great blessings down upon me, gracing me, their obedient grandson, with ten thousand years' long life, that I may firmly protect the four quarters.[24]

This inscription is cast on a bronze bell that was probably commissioned by a late Western Zhou king. From it we learn that the king led his army in person to attack the capital city of an enemy state called Fu Zi because Fu Zi "had dared to seize and to occupy" Zhou territory.[25] Hard-pressed by the Zhou forces, Fu Zi employed intermediaries to negotiate a peace, and apparently it induced twenty-six small states of the so-called Yi barbarians from the eastern and southern quarters to join in the agreement.

Several related inscriptions show that Fu Zi and other Yi barbarians paid tribute to the Zhou. Evidently the Zhou government sent officials to collect tribute from each of its client states and to deposit it in the secondary capital Cheng Zhou. One such inscription is partly translated here:

[3] The King charged Jia, "Administer the piles of grain and fodder at Cheng Zhou (that are collected) from the four quarters, even to the lands of the Southern Huai Yi. Formerly, the Huai Yi submitted to us silk, and served us as subjects. They shall not dare fail to offer up silk, grain, and fodder. When they submit people, they shall not dare fail to come to the army camps; when they submit grain and fodder, they shall not dare fail to come to the *shi* (market?). If they disobey, you shall strike at them in punishment. As for our various lords and lineage heads, their grain and fodder must also be brought

to the *shi*. They shall not dare receive grain and fodder from the Man peoples; if they do, they too shall be punished."[26]

The Zhou exacted not only light and high-value commodities like silk but also bulky foodstuffs like grain and fodder. They also demanded people as tribute; from other inscriptions we know that such foreigners were used as soldiers and domestic servants.[27] The inscription above gives the impression that the Zhou had established formal, ongoing tributary arrangements with these southern states, and that the southerners were being punished for failing to meet their obligations. Postgate suggests that the Assyrians treated their client states in the same way, agreements to pay tribute being "reinforced by oaths and solemnized by religious sanctions, especially being witnessed by Assur and the local gods. To have broken such an agreement then constituted gross sin against Assur, and was seen as justification for punitive action on the part of the Assyrian ruler." He also suggests that "the exact level of annual contribution would be fixed, and failure to make it would be construed as a political statement."[28] The Zhou likewise construed failure to pay as rebellion and said so in their inscriptions.[29] Richardson has edited a volume on rebellion and periphery in which he argues that rebellions are indicators of the incompleteness of the state,[30] but I am not sure if his argument applies to the relationship between an overlord and its clients. Neither Assyria nor Western Zhou seems to have treated its client states as part of its territory.

The Zhou Conception of Territory

If the Zhou state did have a concept of territory, how did it define and maintain that territory? In his study of the Babylonian countryside, Richardson argues that the conceptual map of the Akkadian empire "incorporated no landscapes beyond the city walls."[31] Postgate, on the other hand, insists that the Assyrian territory proper was like an "oil-stain," perceived by the Assyrian king as a spread of land, not as a network of cities.[32] If both are correct, then these two Mesopotamian empires had drastically different ideas about territory. Which is closer to the Western Zhou conception? The bronze inscriptions are not as informative as the cuneiform record, but a few clues hint that Western Zhou was closer to the Assyrian end of the spectrum, though not quite the same. The last two sentences of inscription [3] make it clear that it was not only southerners who were required to deliver grain and fodder to Cheng

Zhou; the same was expected from "our various lords and lineage heads." Clearly these people were not considered to be foreign, because the king says "*our* lords and lineage heads." But who were they? The interpretation of the term "lineage head" is controversial and too complicated to discuss here, but most historians agree about the "various lords": they were regional governors installed by the Zhou kings in the territories Zhou acquired when it overthrew Shang.

The strategy of the Zhou royal house was to found colonies both within and beyond the former Shang territory.[33] Fortified settlements were established all across north and central China within a few generations. The lands the Zhou moved into were occupied already by people who may well have outnumbered the colonists, meaning that colonization had to be backed up by military force. Colonizing expeditions seem to have been ordered by the Zhou king and led by his relatives and commanders. One inscription shows us how the king gave the order:

> [4] It was the fourth month, the *chen* was on *dingwei* (day 44), <the king> inspected the map of King Wu and King Cheng's attack on Shang, [then] went to inspect the map of the eastern quarter. The king stood in the Yi ancestral temple, facing south. The king commanded Lord Ze of Yu, saying: "Move to be lord at Yi. [I] award *sao*-fragrant wine 1 *you* jar, 1 Shang wine vessel . . . 1 red-lacquered bow and 100 red-lacquered arrows, 10 traveling bows and 1,000 traveling arrows; award land: its acreage 300 . . . its . . . 100 and . . . its . . . villages 35, its . . . 140; [I] award you King's men (who live) at Yi . . . and 7 wards, award 7 subjugated elders and captives . . . and 50 men, award Yi common men 600 and . . . (and) 6 men." Lord Ze of Yi extols the king's beneficence, making (for) Father Ding, the Duke of Yu, (this) sacrificial vessel.[34]

This inscription records the king's transfer of Lord Ze from his original domain at Yu to a new territory called Yi. Presumably to decide on the details of the orders he would give, the king inspected maps before ordering the move. Apparently he or his advisers already had the information they needed about the land and people of Yi. The appointment of Lord Ze was made by the king in person at Yi, so Yi must already have been conquered and surveyed by the Zhou army. If it had not, how would the king know the area of the land he was awarding, the number of villages that already existed, and the number of the local population? Any organized migration needs intelligence about the destination before the migrants actually move, information obtained before conquest by scouts or afterwards by occupying troops.

These colonies seem quite similar to the provinces of the Assyrian empire. The Zhou governors were usually members of the royal lineage or of other old aristocratic lineages from the capital at Zhou, just as the Assyrian governors were "usually (if not always) 're-deployed' members of the old families of Assur."[35] They were appointed ceremoniously by the king, and they carried out military campaigns and economic exploitation on behalf of the king. Inscription [3] indicates that Zhou colonies were obligated to deliver foodstuffs (but not labor) to the eastern capital. It also hints that these regional governors in the seized lands had direct contact with the client states beyond them when it says that the governors were prohibited from receiving tribute from barbarians. The colonies were established on contested peripheries. Their main function was to fend off potential encroachment into Zhou territory and to help the central government procure such key resources as labor, metal, and salt.[36]

By establishing colonies on contested frontiers, the Zhou state in effect sketched out its borders: inside the ring of defensive colonies was the Zhou territory proper. Li Feng maintains that the Western Zhou state "did not exist as an integral geographic whole clearly demarcated by linear borders," but in inscription [2], the king seems to have a clear idea of his borders when he says that Fu Zi attacked and occupied "our land."[37] It might have been left to each colony to decide its own borders, but to judge from inscription [4], the Zhou king knew each colony's landscape right down to its villages.[38] Another appointment inscription shows the king similarly well-informed about the size and classification of the population he orders to move. Land survey and population census of some kind thus seem to have preceded at least some parts of the Zhou military colonization.[39]

There are some interesting differences in the way Zhou colonies and Assyrian provinces operated. Postgate says that in the Middle Assyrian period "provincial governorships were sometimes, but not always, passed on within the family."[40] Other scholars have stated that in the Neo-Assyrian period many of the governors were eunuchs.[41] The numerous letters between the king and the governors suggest that the Assyrian king had very tight control over the provinces. In the Western Zhou state, on the other hand, most of the governorships went to branches of the royal lineage, and they were normally passed on within the family. Others went either to trusted commanders of the first few kings or to local dynasts reemployed by the early kings, but they too passed their rights on to their descendants. They also very often had marriage relationships with the royal house.

Center-Periphery Relationships

The delicate relationship between Zhou colonies and the central government can be illustrated by recent archaeological discoveries in the southern quarter of the Zhou realm. In the middle Yangzi region archaeologists have recently discovered two cemeteries about twenty kilometers apart (map 3.1). The bronze vessels from the two are very similar, and they are familiar enough as types to be easily dated to the first two or three generations of the Western Zhou period. Many are inscribed with the names of their owners. The one in figure 3.2 belonged to a lord of Zeng, the one in figure 3.3 to a lord of E. Though the excavations are yet to be published in full, it is clear that the cemeteries belonged to two ruling families holding governorships of adjacent Zhou colonies called E and Zeng. Related inscriptions make it clear that the family ruling at Zeng came from a prominent aristocratic lineage in the Zhou homeland. The ruling family at E may instead have been a local dynast reemployed by the Zhou state at an early stage in its empire building.[42] What is interesting to us here is that lengthy inscriptions recording events from later in the history of the two colonies exist on a few bronze vessels not found by archaeologists.

According to one such inscription, a lord of E married off his daughter to the Zhou royal house.[43] Another inscription records a Zhou king's appointment of a commander for the armies stationed at E and Zeng. This would seem to mean that the Zhou king had direct control of the colonial army.[44] Yet another inscription tells us that the king, returning from a campaign in the south (possibly the one mentioned in inscription [2]), stopped at a place where the Lord of E gave him a bronze vessel and assisted him in a ritual. The king then hosted a banquet and an archery contest and awarded the lord many gifts.[45] So far so good. But very soon the same lord of E would ally himself with the southern client states he was supposed to be managing for the Zhou king and rebel against Zhou:

[5] Yu said, "Illustrious and great august ancestor Duke Mu was capable of standing beside and assisting the prior kings and settling the four quarters. And so Duke Wu could not forget my sagely grandfather and deceased father Youda Shu and Yi Shu, commanding Yu

Figure 3.2. Bronze cooking vessel of the type *fangding* from the Zeng colony at Suizhou Yejiashan in northern Hubei. Early Western Zhou, late eleventh or early tenth century B.C.E. Height 49 cm. The inscription, cast on the interior wall, says "The Lord of Zeng made for Father Yi this precious vessel." Photographs courtesy of Zhang Changping.

to continue my grandfather and deceased father's governance at the Jing state. And so Yu also does not dare be disordered and myopic in supporting my ruler's command. *Wuhu*! Oh woe! Since Heaven has sent down great destruction on the lower quarter, Lord Yufang of E has led the Southern Huai Yi and the Eastern Yi to attack our southern quarter and eastern quarter as far as Li and Rui. The king commanded the Western Six Armies and the Yin Eight Armies, saying, "Attack and destroy Lord Yufang of E; do not leave either old or young." But the armies feared and trembled, and did not succeed in attacking E. And so Duke Wu then dispatched Yu to lead one hundred of the duke's war chariots, two hundred charioteers, and one thousand infantry, saying, "In rescuing my resolute plan, assist the Western Six Armies and the Yin Eight Armies to attack Lord Yufang of E. Do not leave either old

Figure 3.3. Bronze cooking vessel of the type *fangding* from a tomb of the E colony at Suizhou Yangzishan in northern Hubei. Early Western Zhou, late eleventh or early tenth century B.C.E. Height 35.4 cm. The cast inscription, which reads "Zhong of E made this precious vessel," is inside the lid. Inscriptions on other bronzes from the same tomb name the Lord of E as their maker, so Zhong was probably the lord's personal name. Photographs courtesy of Zhang Changping.

or young." When Yu took Duke Wu's infantry and chariotry and advanced as far as E, ramming and attacking E, he was victorious, capturing their leader Yufang. And so, Yu, having had success, dares in response to extol Duke Wu's dazzling glory, herewith making (this) great treasured cauldron. May Yu for ten thousand years (have) sons' sons and grandsons' grandsons to treasure and use it.[46]

This is a notable inscription for several reasons. One is the king's order to attack E and kill all its inhabitants, young and old. We do not know how faithfully the order was carried out, but the goals of the war sound like recapture of lost territory and extermination of rebellious subjects.[47] The king's order does not mention how E's allies should be punished.

Another interesting feature of the inscription is the information it contains about the Zhou military hierarchy. This is a complicated issue crucial to Mann's argument about the sources of social power. I do not have space to discuss this here, but I would like to suggest that the Western Six Armies stationed in the western capital and the Yin Eight Armies stationed in the eastern capital are comparable to the "royal cohort" of the Neo-Assyrian empire discussed by Postgate, while the armies stationed in E and Zeng are comparable to the "king's troops" at the disposal of provincial governors in the Neo-Assyrian empire.[48] The monopoly of violence was an indispensable component of despotic power.

According to the Mandate of Heaven ideology, as glimpsed in Western Zhou bronze inscriptions and filled out from later sources, Heaven gave the Zhou king his right to rule, but Heaven could also take it away, and Heaven's approval was contingent on something in the king's conduct.[49] This ideology sustained the king's power but also restrained it; Western Zhou despotism had a Catch-22: the author of inscription [5] laments that "Heaven has sent down great destruction," but does not say why Heaven did so. Did he privately blame the king for the disaster? Who did the king blame? What did the rebels say? We may never know the details, but Scott has taught us that subordinate groups never really buy the ruling ideology: people have the imaginative capacity to reverse or negate the elite's propaganda, and rulers are well aware of this.[50] Richardson's study has shown us that in the early state there were plenty of people who were not susceptible to the persuasions of ideology. The Western Zhou example makes it plain that when persuasion fails, despotic power relies on violence.

The Zhou Countryside

Within the royal domains around the western and eastern capitals, the Zhou state's control over land and people was stronger than in the colonies, and stronger than what Richardson describes for Hammurabi's Babylon in this volume. There is no mention of rebellions in the royal domains. A few bronze inscriptions hint instead at bureaucratic control of the countryside. To understand its mechanisms, we need first understand what Zhou countryside looked like.

Recent research in archaeology and epigraphy has suggested that the royal domains consisted of two basic landed units: estates belonging to the aristocratic lineages big or small, including estates of members of the royal house, and properties controlled by the state.⁵¹ The largest aristocratic estate found so far belonged to the Duke of Zhou, brother of King Wu, and a celebrated culture hero in later Chinese imagination. It was located to the west of the old Zhou capital and covered an area of about three square kilometers, with seven cemeteries surrounding it and about forty large building foundations, as well as the remains of non-elite residences dispersed throughout the settlement. Ceramic and bronze workshops have also been found in the estate.⁵² Within a radius of about five kilometers, archaeologists have identified at least ten smaller sites that were in all likelihood subordinate to the main estate, but whose residents could afford to bury bronzes in their own tombs and hence belonged to the elite. Similar estates with subordinate settlements have been found elsewhere in the western royal domain; the distance between estates is often around ten kilometers.⁵³

We do not know the average size of the subordinate settlements, but archaeological survey in the eastern royal domain suggests that they could have been from one to eight hectares.⁵⁴ Establishing the size of any site from surface survey is a thorny problem in archaeology, but in light of other regional surveys of the same period, it has been estimated that subordinate settlements ranged from a few thousand square meters to thirty thousand (that is, at most three hectares).⁵⁵ Bronze inscriptions tell us that such a Zhou village would have had a few dozen farming families:

> [6] It was the eighth month, first auspiciousness, *gengchen* (day 17). The lineage lady ordered the steward Fu to award Zi Ji Ji the farmers of Kongmu, consisting of the family of chief Ding and the 25 families of his relatives. (She) [further] awarded (Zi Ji Ji) their land and livestock: horses 10 plus X, cattle 69, sheep/goat 385, and 2 granaries of grain. In response (Zi Ji Ji) extols the beneficence of her august mother. Wherefore was cast this precious vessel. May sons and grandsons treasure it forever.⁵⁶

This vessel is said to have been found in an elite tomb near the eastern capital at Luoyang and can be dated to the tenth century B.C.E. The place Kongmu was probably a village inhabited by twenty-six nuclear families who were related by blood and who shared livestock and grain. Since male lineage heads often served as officials in the Zhou government and very likely maintained separate residences in the capital cities, it was probably customary for their wives to manage their estates, as this and a few other inscriptions suggest. Even the king's own estate was overseen by his queen.[57] The lady in inscription [6] had the power to reassign lineage properties to her daughter. In other cases the senior lady of a lineage dictated the division of lineage properties when a junior branch was separated from the main branch.[58] But for a great estate like that of the Duke of Zhou, which no doubt had many subordinate villages, the lineage lady obviously needed intermediaries to relay her orders. The steward Fu in inscription [6] is an example. The intermediaries were appointed by the lineage head:

> [7] It was in the king's first year, first month, first auspiciousness, *dinghai* (day 24). The words of Elder Hefu were, "Master Hui! Your father and grandfather served my family with great merit. Although you are but a youth, I order you to serve my house unto death, and to supervise the charioteers, the hundred craftsmen, the herders, and the servants of the eastern and western countryside (of my estate), managing affairs both internal and external. Dare not fail to act well. I award you a decorated lance, fifteen red horse headplates, a set of bells, and five copper ingots. Be assiduous day and night." Hui bowed prostrate and dared in response to extol the beneficence of his august ruler. Wherefore I [Hui] cast this *gui* for my cultured father Yi Zhong. May my descendants treasure it forever.[59]

The speech of appointment quoted here is similar to speeches quoted in bronze inscriptions that record appointments of government officials.[60] Like official posts, the posts to which stewards were appointed were often hereditary; a family of stewards might serve the same aristocratic lineage for as many as six generations.[61]

Stewards supervised village chiefs like Ding in inscription [6]. One bronze cast by such a chief to commemorate his appointment is known.[62] Villages consisted of a few dozen peasant families who had communal property, including livestock and grain, and were likely to be related. The chief of a village was presumably chosen from among the villagers. Two poems possibly written in late Western Zhou hint that the peasants cultivated both land allocated for their own subsistence (literally "private fields") and the master's land ("public fields"), in a loose parallel to the tenements and demesne of the medieval European manorial system.[63] The peasants were not slaves but neither were they totally free, since they could be transferred from one master to another, as in inscriptions [4] and [6]. In inscriptions that mention such transfers, it is not always clear whether the peasants were relocated to another place or stayed where they were. If they moved, kinship ties might be broken; if they did not, the transfer meant only that they worked for new masters. Either way, the transfer created a need to keep track of the people involved, and a few inscriptions explicitly mention registers of labor forces in the service of aristocratic estates.[64] In the royal domains, as many scholars have noted, land ownership became increasingly fragmented because of the Zhou king's granting of land to aristocrats, the branching of sublineages, and economic transactions that used land as collateral. Land surveys were correspondingly crucial, and they are frequently mentioned in bronze inscriptions that concern a land transaction or a dispute. Land registers, possibly including cadastral maps delineating field boundaries, were kept by the lineages.[65] The people who carried out the land surveys and kept rosters of peasants were precisely the village chiefs at the bottom of the three-tiered management hierarchy of aristocratic estates sketched above.

The Zhou state controlled its countryside through a similar chain of command, probably inspired by the management of aristocratic estates that preceded the founding of the state. The king, at the top, appointed officials to take charge of economically or militarily important regions within the royal domains:

> [8] It was the first month, first auspiciousness, *dingchou* (day 14). At dawn, the King was in Zong Zhou. He arrived at the Grand Chamber. Lian Shu accompanied Ling at his right and stood at the center of the court. The Chief Scribe gave Ling a written command, awarding him jingles, ordering him to be the magistrate of Zheng and to be in charge of judicial proceedings, [with a salary equivalent to] five measures of copper. Ling in response extols the beneficence of the king. Wherefore I [Ling] cast this precious *gui* for my cultured ancestor Feng Zhong. May sons and grandsons treasure it forever.[66]

In the bronze inscriptions, Zheng figures as a region where forest and pasture land crucial to the state economy were located. It also had many aristocratic estates. There is another inscription recording the appointment of a magistrate of Zheng, but the two magistrates were not from the same family, and the inscriptions do not say that the position was hereditary, as appointment inscriptions typically do. It is also unusual that they were given official salaries of so-and-so many measures of copper (or the equivalent in, for example, grain),[67] suggesting that they were appointed as administrators rather than granted an aristocratic estate.

Below the magistrate of Zheng were other officials with more specific charges. They too were appointed by the king. One was in charge of the forest, wild beasts, and pasture land "of the countryside of Zheng." Another, also obviously outside the urban center of Zheng, was in charge of raising horses.[68] As for the villages that did not belong to any aristocratic estate, the king would appoint an official to supervise their village chiefs.[69] There are even inscriptions that seem to suggest that villages around the western capital were grouped in fives, each group supervised by an official appointed by the king.[70] Such groups, if this reading of the inscriptions is correct, would remind us immediately of the communes (*xiang*) of the Warring States and Han periods (fifth century B.C.E. to second century C.E.), which carried out population census and cadastral surveys for the state.[71]

This particular interpretation may go too far, but the bronze inscriptions discussed above leave no room for doubt that multi-tiered bureaucratic control of the countryside, traditionally thought to have originated in the Warring States period, was already present half a millennium earlier. The Zhou state had personnel sufficient to penetrate part of the countryside directly, without the intervention of aristocratic families. In this part of the state, the king's claim to rule the land and people matched reality.

But this was only a fraction of the state. As we have seen, Zhou control over its colonies relied on governors, many of whom had blood and marriage ties with the royal house. To paraphrase Mann, in the provinces the state's infrastructure was the provincial aristocracy,[72] and it was a fragile one. Blood and marriage ties loosened with the passage of time, but the distance and difficult terrain between the empire's capitals and its colonies left the Zhou no choice but to delegate power, making it "territorially federal," like other ancient empires.[73] Eventually, in the eighth century, the empire collapsed and the colonies became de facto independent states. Several centuries would pass before the states were united in another, larger empire that achieved the deepest infrastructural penetration into people and land of any ancient administration.

NOTES

As a committed comparativist, I want to thank Cliff Ando for inviting me to a conference with an explicitly comparative agenda. Robert Bagley routinely provided penetrating comments on drafts. I would like to thank Seth Richardson and two anonymous reviewers for valuable suggestions. Kyle Steinke kindly made the map; Cao Dazhi and Zhang Changping, for whose help I am most grateful, unfailingly obtained the photos. The abbreviation *JC* in this chapter refers to the work *Yin Zhou jinwen jicheng* (1984–1994).

1. Richardson 2012.
2. Scott 2009, 64–97.
3. Wang 2014, 176.
4. Postgate 1992, 256.
5. Ibid.
6. Postgate 2013, 337, 414–24.
7. Postgate 2007 and 2013.
8. For an illuminating model that imagines state formation as a game (in the game theorist's sense of the word), see Kemp 2006, 73–78. For a succinct history of predynastic Zhou, see Rawson 1999, 375–82. An up-to-date account in Chinese is Lei 2010, which includes some of the latest archaeological findings.
9. For Anyang and its divination records, see Wang 2015.
10. On the Shang state as the overlord of a confederation, see Lin 1981. Li Zongkun has recently proposed a new interpretation of a key character used in Lin's argument, but this does not seem to invalidate the argument; see Li 2007, 128–33. The murky relationship between Shang and predynastic Zhou is made even murkier by Dong Shan, who argues that the Zhou people mentioned in Shang oracle bone inscriptions was not the same group that later overthrew Shang; see Dong 2013.
11. On the Mandate of Heaven doctrine in early Chinese history, see Wang 2014, 44–52. The contents of King Wen's mandate are inferred from transmitted texts that might have been based on Western Zhou documents; see Wang 2003, 82–83.
12. Du 2002.
13. For the reading of this sentence, I follow Tu 2010.
14. *JC*, no. 6014. English translation modified from Shaughnessy 1997, 77–78.
15. When "Zhou" is mentioned in inscriptions, it can be unclear which city is referred to (the problem is not quite as bad as with "Alexandria"). See Chen 2011b, 162–65.
16. On the importance of Cheng Zhou, see Zhu 2006, 10–11.
17. Li 2006, 65.
18. This is my reading of the inscription on the *Tian Wang gui* (*JC* no. 4261), based on interpretations by Lin Yun 1993, Li Xueqin 2009, and Wang Ziyang 2011.
19. E.g., Lin 1993.
20. Postgate 1992, 251.
21. Ibid.; Postgate 2013, 98, 103.
22. For the reading of this sentence, I follow Zhu 2013, 5.
23. Di was a deity worshiped by both the Shang and the Zhou, but the Zhou seem to have conflated it with Heaven.
24. The inscription is on the so-called *Hu zhong* or *Zong Zhou zhong*, *JC* no. 260. English translation after Eno 2010, no. 100, with modifications.

25. The inscription does not mention the capture of people by either side.

26. The inscription is on the *Xi Jia pan*, *JC* no. 10174. English translation after Eno 2010, no. 124, modifications mainly based on Zhu 2013, 12 n. 3, and Lin 2005.

27. Qiu 2012, 107–20.

28. Postgate 1992, 254–55.

29. Li 2008, 266.

30. Richardson 2010, xxv.

31. Richardson 2007, 22.

32. Postgate 1992, 256.

33. Li 2006, Appendix 1; Wang 2014, 188–93.

34. *JC* no. 4320. The inscription was sadly damaged after its chance discovery, leaving room for numerous interpretations, conveniently collated in Zhou 2007, 1–201. My translation here is slightly different from a previous one given in Wang 2014, 188, Text 4.7. The modifications benefited from Qiu 2012, 188.

35. Postgate 1992, 252.

36. Zhu 2013, 12–13; 2014, 272–75.

37. His argument (Li 2008, 297) is that "there were empty spaces existing within the state's conceived 'territory'" and "there were also overlaps between the perceived 'territories' of the regional states [i.e. the colonies]." But he is describing only the uneven distribution of Zhou armies and the variable reach of Zhou civil administration. This is not really an argument against a territorial state, a state that the Zhou king imagined in territorial terms. Any state is necessarily a network of settlements. As Postgate 1992, 255, puts it, "all territorial control must take such a configuration since people cannot be evenly distributed across a landscape and communications must be maintained between the groups." John Baines (2014, 100) eloquently defines a territorial state as a state "in which a single culture predominates and fills its territory, defining itself to a great extent by its boundaries." Zhu (2013) makes a convincing argument that the Zhou had a clear distinction between the "southern land" and the "southern quarter." Only the southern land was considered part of Zhou territory proper.

38. I am therefore puzzled by Richardson's statement that "a cartographic conception of the world was anachronistic to ancient Mesopotamia, as it was to most times and places in world history" (2010, xxvii). On the use of maps in Zhou China, see Wang 2014, 195–98.

39. Wang 2014, 189–90.

40. Postgate 1992, 252; see also Postgate 2013, 332.

41. Radner 2011, 359.

42. See the special sections in the journals *Wenwu* 2011, no. 11, 64–77, and *Jianghan kaogu* 2014, no. 4, 52–60. For pictures of bronzes from the two cemeteries, see Hubeisheng Bowuguan et al. 2013, and Suizhoushi Bowuguan 2009.

43. *JC* no. 3930.

44. The inscription is on the *Jing fangding* in the Idemitsu Bijutsukan in Tokyo, see Li 1999, 76–78, for a full transcription. A similar appointment was made by a Zhou king

for the armies in the Qi colony on the Shandong peninsula (map 3.1), as recorded on the *Yin gui* recently excavated from an early to middle Western Zhou cemetery in Shandong; see Li 2011, 371–75.

45. *JC* no. 2810; Eno 2010, no. 95.

46. The inscription is on the *Yu ding*, *JC* nos. 2833–34. English translation after Shaughnessy 1997, 82–83, slightly modified; cf. Eno 2010, no. 104.

47. The recent discovery of a Chunqiu-period (the period after the Western Zhou) cemetery belonging to various lords of E at Henan Nanyang suggests that, after the suppression of Yufang's rebellion, the E colony was relocated, but there are too many unanswered questions and the preliminary report is too sketchy to be helpful; see Zhu 2013, 10 n. 2, for reference to the preliminary report.

48. Postgate 2007, 345–49.

49. Wang 2014, 50–51.

50. Scott 1990, 77–82.

51. Li Feng further divides the latter into royal properties and state-maintained land (2008, 151ff.), but the royal properties were in fact akin to lineage estates, only bigger.

52. Lei 2010, 266–75.

53. Zhang 2013, 54.

54. Chen et al. 2003, 189–90.

55. Chen 2011b, 112.

56. My translation based on Chen 2011b, 116–23.

57. See the *Cai gui* (*JC* no. 4340), English translation in Li Feng 2008, 69.

58. Most revealingly, in a set of bronzes commissioned by Zhousheng, head of the junior branch of the Shao lineage. See Chen 2011a, whose interpretation is very different from Eno's (2010, nos. 121 and 122).

59. *Shi Hui gui*; *JC* no. 4311; Eno 2010, no. 111, greatly modified according to Chen Jie's reading (Chen 2011b, 132).

60. Wang 2014, 184–88; Li 2008, 103–11.

61. Chen 2011b, 133.

62. *JC* no. 2755; Chen 2011b, 133.

63. Zhu 2004, 413–15; Wang 2014, 193. Li Feng 2003 explicitly rejected a parallel with the feudalism of medieval Europe, but his discussion does not touch on the manorial system, which preceded and outlived vassalage; see Sarris 2004 and Bloch 1961, vol. 1, 241–54.

64. *JC* nos. 4293 and 4465; Chen 2011b, 146.

65. Wang 2014, 193–99.

66. My translation is based on Zhu 2007 and Chen 2011b, 137–39.

67. In the second inscription, the sum is twice that in the first inscription; see Chen 2011b, 138.

68. Ibid., 140–42.

69. *JC* 4246–49, 4279–82; Chen 2011b, 142–45. Appointment inscriptions like these for some reason do not mention salaries.

70. Chen 2011b, 159–66.
71. Hsing I-tien 2011, 209–340; Wang 2014, 211–37, passim.
72. Mann 2012, 170.
73. Ibid.

BIBLIOGRAPHY

Baines, John. 2014. "Civilizations and Empires: A Perspective on Erligang from Early Egypt." In *Art and Archaeology of the Erligang Civilization*, edited by Kyle Steinke, 99–119. Princeton, N.J.: Princeton University Press.

Bloch, Marc. 1961. *Feudal Society*. Translated by L. A. Manyon. Chicago: University of Chicago Press.

Chen Xingcan et al. 2003. "Zhongguo wenming fudi de shehui fuzahua jincheng." *Kaogu xuebao* 2:161–218.

Chen, Jie. 2011a. "Zhousheng zhuqi mingwen zonghe yanjiu." In *Xinchu jinwen yu Xi Zhou lishi*, edited by Zhu Fenghan, 82–105. Shanghai: Shanghai Guji Chubanshe.

———. 2011b. "Zhoudai nongcun jiceng juluo chutan: yi Xi Zhou jinwen ziliao wei zhongxin de kaocha." In *Xinchu jinwen yu Xi Zhou lishi*, edited by Zhu Fenghan, 106–67. Shanghai: Shanghai Guji Chubanshe.

Dong, Shan. 2013. "Shilun Yinxu buci zhi Zhou wei jinwen zhong de Yunxing zhi Zhou." *Zhongguo guojia bowuguan guankan* 7:48–63.

Du, Yong. 2002. "Jinwen 'sheng cheng shi' xinjie." *Lishi yanjiu* 3:3–12.

Eno, R. 2010. "Inscriptional Records of the Western Zhou." http://www.indiana.edu/~g380/3.10-WZhou_Bronzes-2010.pdf. Last accessed August 29, 2014.

Hsing I-tien (Xing Yitian). 2011. *Zhiguo anbang: fazhi, xingzheng yu junshi*. Beijing: Zhonghua Shuju.

Hubeisheng Bowuguan et al. 2013. *Suizhou Yejiashan*. Beijing: Wenwu Chubanshe.

Kemp, B. J. 2006. *Ancient Egypt: Anatomy of a Civilization*. London: Routledge.

Lei, Xingshan. 2010. *Xian Zhou wenhua tansuo* (*Study on the Proto-Zhou Culture*). Beijing: Kexue Chubanshe.

Li, Feng. 2003. "'Feudalism' and Western Zhou China: A Criticism." *Harvard Journal of Asiatic Studies* 63 (1): 115–44.

———. 2006. *Landscape and Power in Early China: The Crisis and Fall of the Western Zhou 1045–771 BC*. Cambridge: Cambridge University Press.

———. 2008. *Bureaucracy and the State in Early China: Governing the Western Zhou*. Cambridge: Cambridge University Press.

Li, Ling. 2011. "Du Chenzhuang yizhi chutu de qingtongqi mingwen." *Haidai kaogu* 4:37–377.

Li, Xueqin. 1999. *Xia Shang Zhou niandaixue zhaji*. Shenyang: Liaoning Daxue Chubanshe.

———. 2009. "'Tian Wang gui' shishi ji youguan tuice." *Zhongguoshi yanjiu* 4:5–8.

Li, Zongkun. 2007. "Buci zhong de Wang Cheng." In *Guwenzi yu gudaishi*, vol. 1, edited by Chen Zhaorong, 117–38. Taipei: Academia Sinica.

Lin, Yun. 1981. "Jiaguwen zhong de Shangdai fangguo lianmeng." *Guwenzi yanjiu* 6:67–92. Reprinted in Lin Yun 1998, 69–84.

———. 1993. "*Tian Wang gui* 'wang si yu tianshi' xinjie." *Shixue jikan* 3:24–29. Reprinted in Lin Yun 1998, 166–73.

———. 1998. *Lin Yun xueshu wenji*. Beijing: Zhongguo Dabaike Quanshu Chubanshe.

———. 2005. "*Baixing* guyi xinjie." *Jilin Daxue shehui kexue xuebao* 4:193–200.

Mann, Michael. 2012. *The Sources of Social Power*, vol. 1. Cambridge: Cambridge University Press.

Postgate, J. N. 1992. "The Land of Assur and the Yoke of Assur." *World Archaeology* 23 (3): 247–63. Reprinted in Postgate 2007, 199–215.

———. 2007. *The Land of Assur and the Yoke of Assur. Studies on Assyria: 1971–2005*. Oxford: Oxbow.

———. 2013. *Bronze Age Bureaucracy: Writing and the Practice of Government in Assyria*. Cambridge: Cambridge University Press.

Qiu, Xigui. 2012. *Qiu Xigui xushu wenji*, vol. 5. Shanghai: Fadan Daxue Chubanshe.

Radner, K. 2011. "Royal Decision-Making: Kings, Magnates, and Scholars." In *The Oxford Handbook of Cuneiform Culture*, edited by K. Radner and E. Robson, 358–79. Oxford: Oxford University Press.

Rawson, J. 1999. "Western Zhou Archaeology." In *The Cambridge History of Ancient China: From the Origins of Civilization to 221 B.C.*, edited by M. Loewe and E. Shaughnessy, 352–449. Cambridge: Cambridge University Press.

Richardson, S. 2007. "The World of Babylonian Countrysides." In *The Babylonian World*, edited by G. Leick, 13–38. London: Routledge.

———. 2012. "Early Mesopotamia: The Presumptive State." *Past and Present* 215 (1): 3–49.

———, ed. 2010. *Rebellions and Peripheries in the Cuneiform World*. New Haven, Conn.: American Oriental Society.

Sarris, Peter. 2004. "The Origins of the Manorial Economy: New Insights from Late Antiquity." *English Historical Review* 119 (481): 279–311.

Scott, J. C. 1990. *Domination and the Arts of Resistance: Hidden Transcripts*. New Haven, Conn.: Yale University Press.

———. 2009. *The Art of Not Being Governed: An Anarchist History of Upland Southeast Asia*. New Haven, Conn.: Yale University Press.

Shaughnessy, E. L. 1997. "Western Zhou Bronze Inscriptions." In *New Sources of Early Chinese History: An Introduction to the Reading of Inscriptions and Manuscripts*, edited by E. L. Shaughnessy, 57–84. Berkeley, Calif.: The Society for the Study of Early China and the Institute of East Asian Studies.

Suizhoushi Bowuguan. 2009. *Suizhou chutu wenwu jingcui*. Beijing: Wenwu Chubanshe.

Tu, Baikui. 2010. "Shuo *He zun* de fu . . . zi tian ji xiangguan wenti." *Kaogu yu wenwu* 1:91–94.

Wang, Haicheng. 2014. *Writing and the Ancient State: Early China in Comparative Perspective*. Cambridge: Cambridge University Press.

———. 2015. "Writing and the City in Early China." In *The Cambridge World History, Volume 3: Early Cities in Comparative Perspective, 4000 BCE–CE 1200*, edited by N. Yoffee, 131–57. Cambridge: Cambridge University Press.

Wang, Hui. 2003. *Guwenzi yu Shang Zhou shi xinzheng*. Beijing: Zhonghua Shuju.

Wang, Ziyang. 2011. "Jiaguwen jiushi 'fan' zhi zi jueda duoshuo dang shiwei 'tong'—jiantan 'fan' 'tong' zhibie." http://www.gwz.fudan.edu.cn/SrcShow.asp?Src_ID=1588. Last accessed August 28, 2014.

Yin Zhou jinwen jicheng. 1984–1994. 18 vols. Beijing: Zhonghua Shuju. Abbreviated as JC in this chapter.

Zhang Tian'en. 2013. "Xizhou shehui jiegou de kaoguxue guancha." *Kaogu yu wenwu* 5:53–62.

Zhou, Baohong. 2007. *Xizhou qingtong zhongqi mingwen jishi*. Tianjin: Tianjin Guji Chubanshe.

Zhu, Fenghan. 2004. *Shang Zhou jiazu xingtai yanjiu*, rev. ed. Tianjin: Tianjin Guji Chubanshe.

———. 2006. "*Shaogao, Luogao, He zun* yu Cheng Zhou." *Lishi yanjiu* 1:3–14.

———. 2007. "Xizhou jinwen zhong de 'quduan' yu xiangguan zhu wenti." In *Guwenzi yu gudaishi*, vol. 1, edited by Chen Zhaorong, 191–211. Taipei: Academia Sinica.

———. 2013. "Lun Xizhou shiqi de nanguo." *Lishi yanjiu* 4:4–15.

———. 2014. "Guanyu Xi Zhou fengguo junzhu chengwei de jidian renshi." In *Liang Zhou fengguo lunheng*, edited by Wang Weilin et al., 272–85. Shanghai: Shanghai Guji Chubanshe.

CHAPTER 4

The Ambitions of Government: Territoriality and Infrastructural Power in Ancient Rome

CLIFFORD ANDO

How strong were ancient states? In particular, how well—how deeply, how uniformly—did the state power of ancient empires penetrate the territories and populations over which they claimed sovereignty? These questions demand attention all the more insistently as one observes that perhaps 85 percent of the population of the Roman empire dwelled in villages or scattered in the countryside, and some unknown number sustained largely pastoralist lifestyles. Such people(s) did not meaningfully figure in the cultural productions of ancient elites, even when they imagined the countryside. Theirs, however, was the labor that sustained those elites and built their cities; they manned the army and fed its appetites. As regards this bulk of the population, did it matter what power exercised macroregional hegemony, or was everyday dominance in the ancient world always a purely local affair? And what forms did such dominance take?

For just over a generation, the answer to these questions in regards to the Roman empire was simple. Largely in response to the work of Fergus Millar but also, to a point, Keith Hopkins, scholars understood Roman government as minimalist in its ambitions (Ando, forthcoming). According to this tradition, the actions of Roman government were reactionary rather than proactive; there is little or no evidence for the design and implementation of policy; a substantial majority of government outlays were devoted to the military. This interpretive claim about the empire's minimalist ambitions was later seconded by scholars of the Roman provinces in the age of postcolonialism, who wished to assign agency for the changes they charted—largely confined to aspects of material culture—to indigenous victims rather than Roman overlords and who therefore received and echoed the minimalist orthodoxy with gratitude.[1] In these scholarly traditions, state power was military power; its primary tool was spectacular violence; its influence, minimal.

Two further theoretical and historiographic traditions converged to enhance the cogency of these claims (even if the ancient history community has largely conducted itself without explicitly engaging literatures beyond its own). The first "tradition" is perhaps better identified as plural: I refer to all those sociologically oriented histories and theories of modernity that posit profound changes in the technologies of communication and knowledge production as causing or marking the break between the modern and whatever came before, by Benedict Anderson, James C. Scott, Michel Foucault, Jürgen Habermas, Reinhart Koselleck, and Michael Mann.[2] In their theories, changes in technology give rise to profoundly new ambitions on the part of government, which in turn prompts the development of new forms of knowledge and new self-interpretations. The economy, modern domesticity, the public sphere, political subjectivity, propaganda, and even ideology in some narrow sense issue from these transformations. The knock-on effect of these convergent intellectual currents was to imply the deficiency or absence of all such effects and social fields in the premodern world.

The second tradition burnishing the luster of the minimalist school of ancient government originates in modern empire studies and has, of all this work, the greatest claim to empirical validity and interpretive utility (Maier 2006; see also Doyle 1986). Students of modern empire commonly differentiate modern empires from ancient ones as follows: modern empires have commercial ambitions at their core and civilizing missions as their pretext. Their operation is understood, not incorrectly, as intended to issue in the incorporation of subaltern regions into unified and universalizing metropolitan networks, whether of commerce, culture, law, development, politics, or what have you. Ancient empires, by contrast, operated through the cultivation and management of difference. Being wholly unable to govern their territories directly and, indeed, largely uninterested in doing so, ancient empires delivered the control of territories into the hands of local elites, who facilitated the extraction of wealth by the center in exchange for material and ideological support of their own continuance. Far from imposing universalizing norms, ancient

		Infrastructural co-ordination	
		low	*high*
Despotic power	*low*	feudal	bureaucratic
	high	imperial	authoritarian

Figure 4.1. Two dimensions of state power, according to Michael Mann. Figure adapted from Michael Mann, "The Autonomous Power of the State: Its Origins, Mechanisms and results," *Archives européennes de sociologie* 25 (1984): 191.

empires developed institutional and communicative structures that rived subaltern communities one from the other and encouraged each to have purely bilateral relations with the metropole (Ando 2015a offers a recent statement of this perspective). Ideally, they would come to compete with each other in a culture of loyalism, each subunit celebrating its culture in rivalry with others, with whom relations of solidarity might be formed exclusively around the norms of empire.

This chapter seeks to call into question many of the distinctions drawn in the literature that I have so far evoked, distinctions often drawn, I might add, by way of supposition and rarely subjected to empirical verification. Along the way, I shall employ as an heuristic a theoretical distinction drawn by Michael Mann in his historical sociology of the 1980s, that between infrastructural and despotic power. Infrastructural power he defines as "the capacity of the state actually to penetrate civil society, and to implement logistically political decisions throughout the realm" (Mann 1984, 189); despotic power is "the range of actions that the [state] elite is empowered to undertake without routine, institutionalized negotiation with civil society groups" (188). Three further aspects of his theory deserve emphasis. First, he describes these as "analytically autonomous dimensions of power." Second, Mann also believes that these are usefully studied in their varied implications; and he himself suggests a loose typology of states based on such an analysis (191). Third and last, Mann generally understands the movement from left to right across his chart as a movement through time: bureaucratic liberal democracies and totalitarian, authoritarian regimes are modern phenomena; empires and feudal states are premodern (see figure 4.1).

Infrastructural power, or what Mann here labels "infrastructural coordination," obviously performs some of the same work effected by (communicative) technological development in the theories of modernity that I cited earlier. That is to say, it provides an apparently quantifiable and nonsubjective index of historical change, against which to index—and by which to explain—qualitative changes in style of power and sociopolitical change in the nature of subjectivity. That said, the concept of infrastructural power embraces a fuller range of instruments, including both static and dynamic materiel (for example, monumentalized urban spaces as well as transport systems) and also personnel. Up to a point, it therefore escapes the fetishization of temporality implicit when one emphasizes the speed of communication as a distinctive variable in the conduct of politics and formation of subjects.[3]

As regards empire studies and contemporary theories of modernity, a focus on infrastructural power achieves one further end that deserves emphasis here. It allows one contingently to bracket the division between metropolitan and local or indigenous structures and institutions. (One might observe as a corollary that a notable feature of Bill Novak's invocation of Mann's theory, in his renowned study "The Myth of the Weak American State" [2008], is precisely that Novak elides as ideological the distinction between federal, state, and local governments in his pseudo-quantification of state power in American federalism.) If we treat the metropolitan cooptation of local elites as a mechanism for the overcoming of material constraints on metropolitan power—as clearly we should—then we likewise need a theory of imperial power that allows us to embrace the instrumentalization of local government and indigenous institutions and the cooptation of non-statal forms of social dependency within a broader history of governmentality (Ando 2015b). To achieve this end, one must to a point bracket normative and theoretical questions regarding the politics of cultural autonomy or ethnic self-determination, and this should be done cautiously. There are, however, good reasons to hesitate before attributing historical and cross-cultural universality to such ideologies, and in any event I have employed the term governmentality knowingly.[4] My own focus lies instead with an effort to understand the effects of power on the formation of political subjectivities, and to this end one must understand the ways in which notionally autonomous and semi-autonomous social fields constituted and legitimated each other. (More on this below and in the Conclusion.) And of course, if such a history can be written of antiquity, this would have implications for the status of normative theorizing derived from the empirical work of Foucault, Habermas, Koselleck and the others that I named above.

With regard to the present chapter, I hope in the end also to show that despotic and infrastructural power themselves coexist in mutually constitutive ways. More importantly, as regards not least Mann's own periodization of state power, I will argue that imperial despotic power was instrumental in shaping and promoting the infrastructural capacity of subaltern communities within the Roman empire, which capacity was then coopted to Roman ends. (Additionally, one might say, following Seth Richardson, that claims-making on the part of the empire was instrumental in both bringing into being and monopolizing the very powers that it claimed, and efficacy in this regard both legitimated the initial act of claims-making and enabled further claims to be made.) What is more, these developments in subaltern communities (unsurprisingly) took place through processes of mimetic reduplication, such that *both* the institutional and material structures of subordinate communities *as well as* the principles of legitimation operative in respect to public powers specifically and social differentiation more generally came to exhibit deep homologies with Roman ones. It was, however, crucial to the long-term vitality of Roman politics that these communities remained notionally autonomous. They thus came to function as a constitutive outside to the central power, and, in echoing back Roman principles of legitimation regarding the functions of government, they collaborated with empire in creating and sustaining a single and singular imperial social order.

If this analysis is correct, then in the Roman case, at least, no simple division between the metropolitan and the local or between the imperial and the indigenous can long be sustained, nor can any strict accounting of the limits of the infrastructural power of the central state based on such a division be accepted. As a related matter, a strong distinction between ancient and modern empires organized around some ancient surrender of autonomy to local elites, based on a calculus of pure extraction (whatever its ideological justification), will necessarily collapse. Finally, the theorizing of states as weak—transregional imperial states and (colonial) city states alike, each in their way—fails to account for their synergized power. Their mutual constitution did more than provide ideological support in claims making, whether to rights of dispute resolution, fiscal sovereignty, or the legitimation of the exercise of force. Rather, local institutions enabled dramatic extension in the reach of imperial techniques of knowledge production and the effective interpellation of individuals as subjects of government; while the existence of a superordinate state—an empire—undergirded and backstopped the dominance of poliadic elites over their hinterlands. Indeed, those hinterlands were likely often larger, and city-state elites therefore richer, precisely in consequence of a mutuality of interest between civic and imperial elites.

This chapter pursues these larger theoretical aims through the study of two institutions, one underexplored, the other unexciting. The first is the practice of *adtributio*, whence English "attribution," which is to say, the administrative subordination of populations to cities. Though quite substantial communities dwelling in monumentalized conurbations might be subordinated to other, similar populations for administrative convenience or narrowly political motives, I concern myself here with cases that involved populations deemed to deserve such subordination because they were nonurban. Was their attribution an administrative convenience, a case simply of a premodern state ruling through cities? Or did Rome have other objectives in mind? And, bracketing the question of intent, what was the effect of such attributions?

The second institution is the road, an instrument of infrastructural power par excellence. Although I will allude to the variety of aperçus that Roman roads offer the historian, I will focus on the response generated in local communities by the requirement imposed by Rome that communities located along roads take charge of their maintenance. This will permit as well a brief survey of other such functions that local governments were betimes required by the metropole to fulfill.

Attribution

The long-standing uninterest of classical historians in the administrative subordination of rural populations to city-based elites has a number of likely causes, two of which merit some reflection in this context.[5] The first is a simple uninterest in unurbanized populations. In part this is a matter of self-regard: populations dwelling in villages or living by transhumance have not been understood as constituents of that classical world that we identify as having given birth to ourselves or, one might say, they did not contribute in any way deemed important to those forms of cultural production that we esteem as part of our own past. In so judging, we are heirs to an imbricated series of willful blind spots that commenced already in antiquity, according to which cities and not villages were centers of culture (hence *urbs*, "city," urban, urbane); cities and not villages sustained intersubjective relations worthy of the name "politics" (*polis—politeia—politikos—politeusthai*); and so forth. As a related matter, the sciences that we have developed and the locations where we have deployed them in our archaeologies of the classical past have focused overwhelmingly on civic, which is to say, city life.[6]

The second cause for contemporary neglect of the administrative subordination of nonurban populations is the challenges of the evidentiary regime. No general regulations governing such relations survive. Rather, the evidence consists of occasional remarks in technical literatures (including, most importantly, several asides in the corpus of Roman land-surveying manuals), as well as references to such relations in official records and legal instruments. As regards the latter documents, these do not survive in toto, nor in the form in which they circulated in antiquity. Versions, representations, and excerpts were transcribed to permanent media, often after having been translated; these texts were then posted by interested parties, to achieve specific ends; and the stone surfaces and bronze tablets that carried those texts, having suffered two thousand years of neglect, abuse, reuse, and fragmentation, constitute the bulk of the evidence. Even beyond problems of reconstruction and translation, there lie the essential problems that such instruments were sometimes written (and in any event have often been read) as if applicable only to the situation at hand; in consequence, the case for their utility in establishing a normative practice must be made and not assumed. What is more, like many such occasional texts, they could easily be written without reference to the conceptual and institutional structures that enabled their operation. As in many fields in ancient history, the evidence for the governance of nonurbanized populations presents profound challenges of aggregation.

These features of the evidence have naturally played a role in the historiographic and interpretive debates described above: the contingent particularities that generated any given text may naturally (if not persuasively) be read quite narrowly, such that what we know about the contribution of villages and farmsteads in the hinterland of Oenoanda to festivals in that city, say, is not generalized to other such cities. The questions of when and how we are entitled to reconstruct weak or strong institutional contexts to explain the pragmatics of such texts is obviously at the heart of the debate in which this project intervenes.[7] The evidence for the building and repair of roads, the subject of the next section of this chapter, is relevant here. In that context, epigraphic records of particular actions often assign agency at a material level to local officials, while assigning authority and motivation to the emperor himself. The complex imbrication of (imperial, global) authority and (local) action is there made clear.[8]

In this section, I will discuss a few documents only, ones that speak to the ways in which social relations and cultural change followed upon (and were in my view intended to follow upon) the attribution of unurbanized populations to city centers. Let me, however, gesture at the range of relations cited in the documentary record. Just as Oenoanda in Lycia wrested contributions of sacrificial animals from villages and farmsteads in its hinterland, so the city of Nacoleia required towns in its hinterland to contribute to its ritual life, a fact cited by the Christians of one such town in their petition to the emperor Constantine for the status of autonomous municipality. Cities are likewise on record as responsible for collecting taxes from villages and other populations in their catchment: in an inscribed schedule from Roman Sparta, in literary texts from Roman Judaea, in remarks on Italy by a Roman land surveyor, and in records from Roman Carthage. Civic elites might also impose financial burdens (in the form of so-called liturgies) quite narrowly on village elites: this occurred in Roman Egypt and high imperial Syria, as well as Trieste, where the civic elite sought to preempt any effort to seek autonomy by its subordinate communities by coopting their elites into its municipal council. Very occasionally, even as civic elites gave money to their cities in support of some building project or even as tax relief, so very rarely individuals are on record as paying the share also of villages subordinated to their city. Finally, cities were responsible to levy troops not simply from their own populations but also from any residents of the territories assigned to them. (The phrases "responsible for," "assigned to them," and the like are not intended to convey any judgment on the question of whether cities distributed burdens of taxation, etc., fairly; I note, however, that on occasion cities were punished by emperors by being deprived of administrative autonomy and attributed to their neighbors and such subordination was very occasionally glossed as a form of slavery.)

To begin, we might consider the range of terminology employed to describe relations of administrative subordination; though the terms are lexically diverse, they mostly point to access to law as their common reference. In the middle of the first century c.e., a massively experienced Roman official named Pliny composed a natural history of the Roman world. It opens with a three-book geography, which is now widely recognized to have been based very largely on Roman administrative surveys (Shaw 1981): the world is divided into provinces, assize districts, cities, subordinated towns and peoples, etc. I quote some representative language regarding the situation of Roman cities in wider provincial landscapes (with very minor changes, I employ the translation of the Loeb Classical Library edition) (see table 4.1).

Table 4.1. The Function of Cities in the Roman Imagination: The Language of Pliny the Elder

3.25	*Carthaginem **conveniunt** populi LXV exceptis insularum incolis...*	At Cartagena sixty-five peoples **come together/assemble**, not including inhabitants of islands...
3.26	*In Cluniensem **conventum** Varduli ducunt populos XIV, ex quibus Alabanenses tantum nominare libeat, Turmogidi IV, in quibus Segisamonenses et Segisamaiulienses.*	To the assize (lit: "coming-together) at Corunna the Varduli bring 14 peoples, among whom we would mention only the Alabanenses, and the Turmogidi bring 4, among whom are the Segisamonenses and the Segisamaiulienses.
3.37	*oppida vero ignobilia XIX sicut XXIV Nemausensibus **adtributa**.*	There are also 24 unimportant towns, as well as 24 **administratively subordinated** to Nîmes.
3.134	*verso deinde in Italiam pectore Alpium Latini iuris Euganeae gentes... ex his Triumpilini... dein Camunni conpluresque similes finitimis **adtributi** municipiis.*	On the side of the Alps facing Italy are the Eugaenean peoples, who have the Latin right. Among these are the Triumpilini... and then the Camunni and many similar peoples **administratively subordinated** to neighboring municipalities.
3.142	***petunt** in eam [coloniam] **iura** viribus discriptis in decurias CCCXLII Delmataei...*	The Delmataei **seek laws** in that colony, their forces being divided into 342 tithings...
5.109	*Praeterea sunt Thydonos... Alabanda libera quae conventum eum cognominavit... longinquiores **eodem foro** disceptant Orthronienses, Alidienses...*	There are also Thydonos [and] Alabanda, the free town that gives its name to this assize... More distant places settling their disputes **in the same forum** are the Orthronienses, the Alidienses...

In two examples (3.37, 3.134), Pliny both employs the technical term for administrative subordination and likewise indicates his own impatience with populations not worthy of metropolitan attention: hence, after all, their subordination. (In all fairness, if Pliny had in fact attempted to list all persons and things known to Roman government, he would never have completed the geographical books, let alone the thirty-one books that follow.) But Pliny also employs language that implicitly singles out access to law as a preeminent justification for subordination: *conventus*, "assize" (3.26), derives from *convenire*, "to come together, assemble" (3.25). Hence in the latter passage one might more accurately translate, "At Cartagena sixty-five peoples come together [to settle their disputes]." The same understanding of the ties that bind nonurbanized populations to cities is explicit in the phrase *petunt . . . iura*, here rendered "seek laws" (3.142).

Finally, Pliny employs the term *forum* in synecdochic relation to the city whose public core it is and simultaneously as a metonym for *conventus*, a "coming together" (which was itself a metonym referring to the purpose for which people come together, namely, the holding of an assize). In other words, the naming of a Roman-style monumentalized urban core can stand—by virtue of the assumption that all properly ordered cities will have one—for the functioning of depersonalized, communal institutions of dispute resolution and rights redemption, which are understood to have such a *forum* as their necessary context. Pliny can thus employ *forum* in synecdoche for city because it suffices—as no other part of the city would—to identify the function of Roman-style conurbations as nodal points for the intrusion of Roman institutions into landscapes of peoples not articulated along Roman lines.

Although the documentation is (as always) scattered, let me add that there exists very considerable evidence *both* of a normative kind (identifying assize centers) *and* regarding specific cases, to suggest that individuals as well as public and private corporate bodies did in fact make the journey to assize centers to have their cases heard before Roman tribunals (even when it was not required that they use a Roman court), and that the mechanics of the court often required them to revisit the *forum* of adjudication, not least because decisions were posted there (see, for example, *AÉ* 2008, 1349 = *SEG* 58, 1536).

In addition, please observe that Pliny elides public law distinctions between communities that were obliged to observe Roman private law and autonomous ones, which is to say, communities that used their own laws. This is true even of so-called free cities, despite the fact that public law instruments typically explain the implications of their so-called freedom by saying that they were "removed from" or "lay outside the schedule of the province" (Reynolds 1988; Ando 2010, 35). In other words, free cities and their citizens went notionally unrecorded in administrative mappings that counted persons or sources of revenue. Pliny's elision of such distinctions suggests that, in the perspective of the metrople, it was nonetheless possible to view all these communities as governed, and their populations and territory as accounted for. Free cities, too, might be instrumentalized in the service of imperial epistemics and metropolitan power.

In my view, it should ultimately be possible to vindicate two further claims—first, that the Romans intended such relations of attribution to promote specific forms of development among the populations so subordinated, and, second, that they conceived dispute resolution according to law as fundamental to that process. Certainly in the most famous narrative of the most conspicuous failure of Romanization to be preserved from antiquity, the Roman historian Velleius Paterculus attributes to the Germans an awareness of the Roman conceit that they bring law to uncivilized peoples. Indeed, in his narrative that conceit is their undoing, and it is articulated as a confusion between the one (German, unurbanized) context and another (urban, Roman) one (Velleius 2.118.1):

> *At illi, quod nisi expertus vix credat, in summa feritate versutissimi natumque mendacio genus, simulantes fictas litium series et nunc provocantes alter alterum in iurgia, nunc agentes gratias, quod ea Romana iustitia finiret feritasque sua novitate incognitae disciplinae mitesceret et solita armis discerni iure terminarentur, in summam socordiam perduxere Quintilium, usque eo,* **ut se praetorem urbanum in foro ius dicere***, non in mediis Germaniae finibus exercitui praeesse crederet.*

But the Germans, in a fashion scarcely credible to one who has no experience of them, are extraordinarily crafty and terribly savage all at once—a race born to lying. By feigning a series of made-up lawsuits, now summoning each other to disputes, now giving thanks that Roman justice was settling them and that their savagery was being rendered mild by this unknown and novel discipline and that quarrels which were customarily settled by arms were now being settled by law, they brought Quintilius to such a degree of negligence that he came to think of himself as though he were the urban praetor administering justice in the forum and not as commanding an army in the middle of Germany.

That said, this chapter is not the place to vindicate such claims. Instead, let me turn to two case studies of cultural and social change prompted by relations of proximity and, in part, of administrative subordination. I take these in chronological order of the source that attests them.

On the Ides of March in the year 46 C.E., the emperor Claudius issued an edict resolving a set of legal problems that had first been reported to the imperial court under the emperor Tiberius, but which lingered unresolved at his death and likewise at the death of his successor, Caligula. One of these concerned the status of three Alpine peoples in the neighborhood of Tridentum (modern Trento). A copy of the edict, inscribed on a sheet of bronze, was found near Trento (*ILS* 206; translation after R. K. Sherk):

> *Quod ad condicionem Anaunorum et Tulliassium et Sindunorum pertinet, quorum partem delator adtributam Tridentinis, partem ne adtributam quidem arguisse dicitur, tametsi animadverto non nimium firmam id genus hominum habere civitatis Romanae originem: tamen, cum longa usurpatione in possessionem eius fuisse dicatur et ita permixtum cum Tridentinis, ut diduci ab is sine gravi splendidi municipii iniuria non possit, patior eos in eo iure, in quo esse se existimaverunt, permanere benificio meo, eo quidem libentius quod plerique ex eo genere hominum etiam militare in praetorio meo dicuntur, quidam vero ordines quoque duxisse, non nulli allecti in decurias Romae res iudicare.*
>
> *quod benificium is ita tribuo, ut quaecumque tanquam cives Romani gesserunt egeruntque, aut inter se aut cum Tridentinis alisve, rata esse iubeam, nominaque ea, quae habuerunt antea tanquam cives Romani, ita habere is permittam.*

As concerns the status of the Anauni and Tulliassi and Sinduni, some of whom an informant is said to have proved are attributed to the Tridentini but some are not: Although I realize that this class of people does not have a very strong case for Roman citizenship, nevertheless, since by long arrogation they are said to be in possession of it and are so intermingled with the Tridentini that they cannot be withdrawn without serious harm to that splendid municipality, I permit them by my favor to remain in the legal status in which they believed themselves to be. I do this all the more freely because many from this class of human beings are said to be serving in my Praetorian Guard, indeed, some are commanders of units, and not a few have been enrolled in jury panels to judge cases at Rome.

I so grant this benefit to them that whatever they have done or transacted as if they were Roman citizens, either among themselves or with the Tridentini or with others, those things I order to be legally valid, and the names which they have previously had as if they were Roman citizens, I permit them to retain.

As it happens, the Tridentini were themselves a Gallic tribe raised to prominence over their neighbors by Julius Caesar, who (re)founded their capital city, Tridentum, on a Roman plan, high in the foothills of the Alps in the valley of the Adige. Claudius makes no mention of this fact. But the situation that he is called upon to address is therefore the historical product of the proximity and intermingling of *juridically* Roman and non-Roman populations, one of which is Roman only by virtue of an earlier incorporation of a non-Roman people into the Roman state (whatever that process entailed). It has henceforth played a metropolitan role in similar processes involving its neighbors. What is more, as regards the specificities of the situation under Claudius, some of the populations in question were in fact legally subordinated to the Tridentini; others were not. Nevertheless, they had all come to regard themselves as like unto the Tridentini and, what is more, they so mimicked their self-fashioning as Roman that they were able to pass as Roman in two of the most crucial duties of citizenship, service in the legions and as member of juries. Indeed, they had done so at Rome. Observe, too, Claudius's concern that the restoration of legal propriety would damage the Tridentini: the taking up of non-citizens into the community is understood to have benefitted a citizen population in ways the government did not wish to undo, the ideological charge of usurping metropolitan status notwithstanding.

Nearly two centuries before Caesar founded Tridentum as a Roman(izing) city, the Romans had begun their expansion across the Apennines into the Po Valley with the foundation of two colonies, Cremona and Placentia, both in 218 B.C.E. (modern Cremona and Piacenza). This occurred on the eve of the Hannibalic invasion, and though they suffered greatly in the disastrous first years of that war, when Hannibal allied with Gauls and ranged at will in Italy, they stayed loyal to Rome and figure prominently in narratives of Roman action in the north in the first decades of the second century B.C.E. In 69 C.E., Cremona became embroiled in the civil wars that erupted after the death of Nero, being held first by troops of Vitellius against those of Otho. Later, troops loyal to Vespasian occupied the city and, motivated by greed and spite, turned on the populace; the entire urban fabric of public and private buildings was destroyed (Tacitus, *Histories* 3.26–33). "Cremona sufficed them for four days; when all its buildings, sacred and profane, settled into flame, the temple of

Mefitis alone remained, before the walls, protected either by its location or the god" (Tacitus, *Histories* 3.33.2).

> This was the end of Cremona, in the 286th year since its founding. It was founded when Tiberius Sempronius and Publius Cornelius were consuls, as Hannibal was entering into Italy, as a bulwark against Gauls acting across the Po (*propugnaculum aduersus Gallos trans Padum agentes*) and if some other force should cross the Alps. Thereafter, thanks to the number of colonists, the convenience of the rivers, the richness of its fields and association and intermarriage with indigenous peoples (*adnexu conubiisque gentium*), it grew rich and flourished, untouched by foreign wars but unlucky in civil ones. (Tacitus *Histories* 3.34.1)

By the time Tacitus wrote, Gaul south of the Alps had long since been reclassified as a region of Italy. Nonetheless, Tacitus preserves an awareness of Cremona's status as a bulwark of empire against non-Italians across the Po, and so his conjoining of "association and intermarriage with indigenous peoples" alongside other factors as causal in the flourishing of the colony speaks volumes—indeed, these were presumably the very indigenous peoples against whom the colony had been founded in the first place.

To the two cases of Tridentini and Cremona we might compare briefly the history of the Tricastini and Arausio (modern Orange). This was one of the Celtic tribes in Gallia Narbonensis (southern France) whose land was expropriated around 36 B.C.E. for the foundation of a colony of Roman veterans; the official name of the colony was "The Loyal Julian Colony of Veterans of the Second Legion, Arausio." Seventy years earlier the site had witnessed a monumental Roman defeat, and the seizure of land and implantation of a colony of Roman veterans presumably allowed for the material elision and erasure from public memory of the site's pre-colonial past. We possess today fragments of a cadastral map from Arausio, and though it was inscribed in the 70s C.E., it appears still to distinguish land assigned to veterans, land assigned to other colonists, and land left to the Tricastini (Piganiol 1962).

Notwithstanding the incorporation of the Tricastini as defective non-members of the colony or, one might say, as aliens in its landscape, to which they of course were native, their own "intermingling" with Roman veteran colonists issued in a similar transformation to that at once imposed upon and undertaken by the Tridentini. Perhaps a generation after the foundation of

Arausio, a subordinate village of the Tricastini was awarded autonomous status by the emperor Augustus and named *Augusta Tricastinorum* (Pliny *Nat.* 3.36). A half century or more on, that town was granted the status of a Roman colony under the Flavians, under the name *Colonia Flavia Tricastinorum*, "The Flavian Colony of the Tricastini" (HD016699=*AE* 1962, 143). Not only are its residents granted Roman citizenship, the fiction is implicitly entertained that they had been Romans all along who emigrated to a colony in subject lands. But their true history abides, preserved in their new Roman name.

In all these cases, social and juridical transformations were causally connected with the material transformation of colonial landscapes, with the result that, in the perspective of the imperial center at least, non-poliadic (or non-urbanized), indigenous populations were ultimately reclassified as metropolitan, with all that entailed. Furthermore, it was the extension of state infrastructure into the territories of nonmetropolitan peoples, and their performance on that stage, that rendered them recognizable to the center, whence they assumed the status of metropolitans vis-à-vis further non-Roman populations who were henceforth attributed to them.

Bureaus of Roads

Roman roads have since antiquity been a symbol of Roman power and aspects of their history have long been studied; this is especially true of their routes, construction technique, and dates of building and repairs.[9] In consequence of the evidence (on which more in a moment), some attention has also be paid to the organization and maintaining of the so-called imperial post (Kolb 2000). Nonetheless, the importance of roads for promoting but also channeling the mobility of persons and goods and thus directing flows of social energy and culture change remains underexplored or, perhaps one might say, undercharted. I adopt the latter term because this is an area where appropriate graphic representation could clarify the importance of transportation infrastructure to human mobility most fundamentally and culture change in consequence of that, but that opportunity has often not been seized. Let me discuss two such missed opportunities here. The first concerns the "mapping" of the epigraphic habit in Roman Gaul, in a map from Greg Woolf's *Becoming Roman* (1998), a justly celebrated book in the field. Here is an adaption of Woolf's map (map 4.1) displaying the distribution of clusters of inscriptions according to the gross number at any given site.

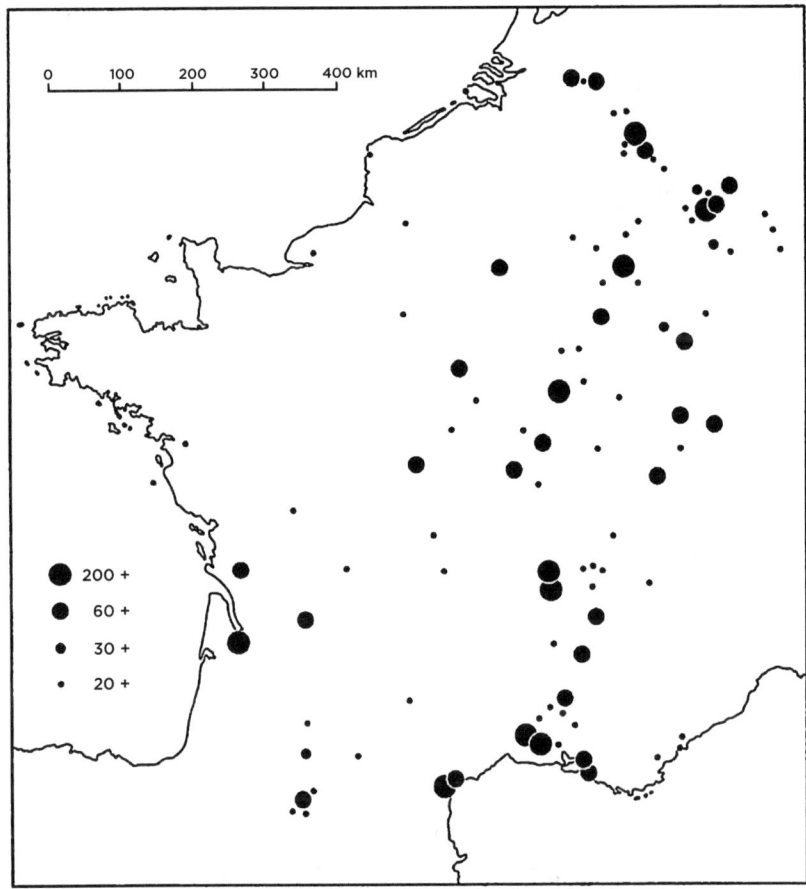

Map 4.1. Clusters of inscriptions, the size of the circle being proportionate to the number of inscriptions. Adapted from Greg Woolf, *Becoming Roman: The Origins of Provincial Civilization in Gaul* (Cambridge: Cambridge University Press, 1998), figure 4.5, p. 87.

Woolf does provide a map of major roads, but on another page (and not a facing one) (redrawn here as map 4.2).

The importance of the road system to the spread of the Roman epigraphic habit is left unillustrated. As a related matter, the map of clusters of inscriptions does not name the cities or identify their type (for example, Roman colony or native settlement), which information would also seem to be essential—certainly Jonathan Edmondson's splendid investigation of names and epithets in the region of Augusta Emerita suggests that colonies functioned

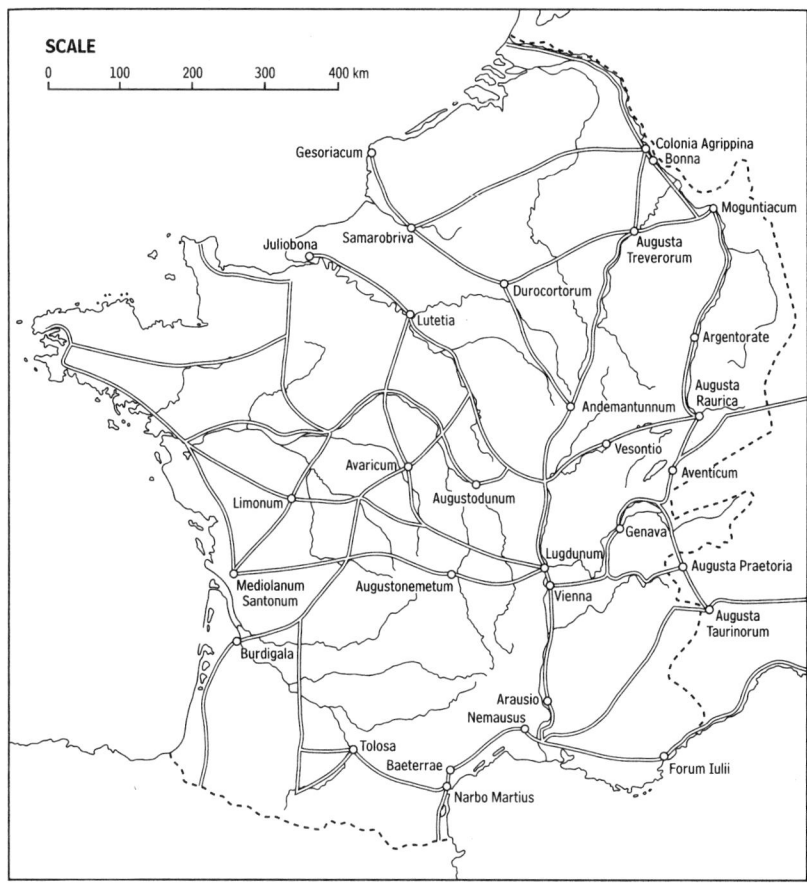

Map 4.2. Major roads of Roman Gaul. Adapted from Woolf, *Becoming Roman*, figure 4.6, p. 89.

as nodal points for the transmission of metropolitan trends to the provinces in which they were located (Edmondson 2009). But one can nevertheless understand a great deal more about the role of roads in culture transfer if one simply overlays Woolf's maps on one another (see map 4.3).

I could multiply examples of this kind: Christian Goudineau's contribution to the multivolume history of the city in France contains many maps, none of which displays the road system in addition to the various phenomena it charts. Mark Humphries's fine essay, "Trading Gods in Northern Italy," signals "the location of Jewish and Christian communities by the early fourth

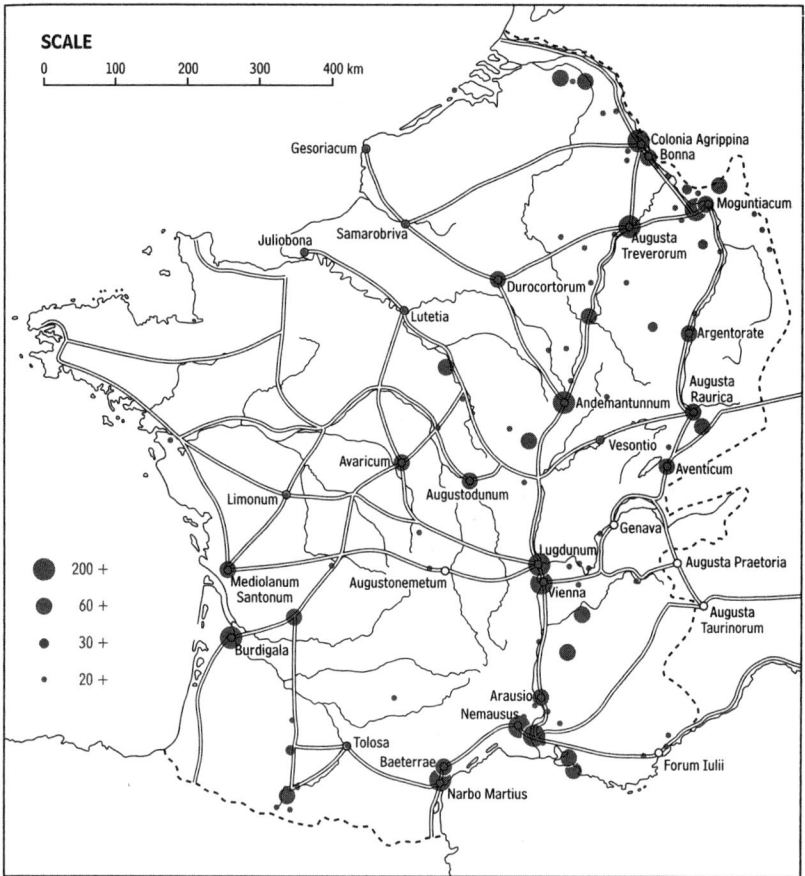

Map 4.3. Clusters of inscriptions in Roman Gaul, overlaid on the road system. Prepared from Woolf, *Becoming Roman*, figures 4.5 and 4.6.

century," but it offers no insight as to why such communities flourished in these cities first (see map 4.4).

In fact, one would need to find a map of the Po Valley in the imperial period on one's own in order to see that all these cities lay on paved Roman highways (see map 4.5). I emphasize "paved" to draw attention to the fact that the road systems of the Roman empire were complex and included paved roads of many kinds and varying quality as well as unpaved ones. (The Roman state concerned itself directly with the maintenance of the major arteries that it had itself built, which it denominated public roads—meaning, roads of the Roman people—but it understood all roads to be public goods and laid down

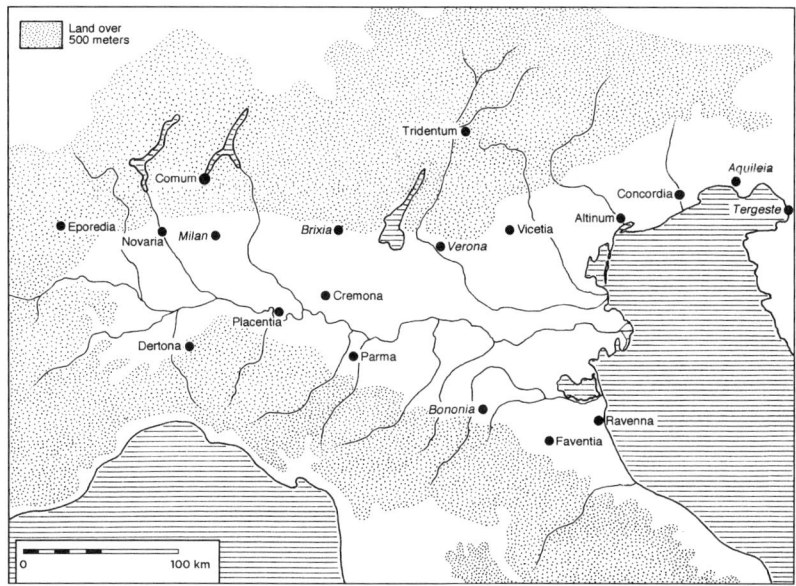

Map 4.4. Map of northern Italian sites with Jewish or Christian communities by the early fourth century. Adapted from Mark Humphries, "Trading Gods in Northern Italy," in *Trade, Traders and the Ancient City*, ed. Helen Parkins and Christopher Smith (London: Routledge, 1998), figure 10.2, p. 211.

various injunctions for their upkeep.) Simply put, those religions that spread did so along axes of human mobility; and in the premodern Mediterranean, humans and goods, as well as gods and ideologies, moved most easily and rapidly on sea, then up rivers, then along paved roads, and finally into the countryside. Not for naught does the term "pagan" originate in a word with no religious significance, meaning merely "dweller in the countryside." They were the last to get the word.

In sum, one would expect phenomena like those studied by Woolf, Goudineau, or Humphries over the *longue durée* to move first along major shipping lines, then from major ports to minor ones by cabotage; perhaps simultaneously to move from major ports inland along navigable rivers and paved highways; and only much later to penetrate the countryside. This is of course a wholly uncontroversial point. (Indeed, many Roman policies, not least as concerns taxation, were structured around just this expectation.) I wish only to emphasize that it has rarely been cashed out graphically. The most suggestive

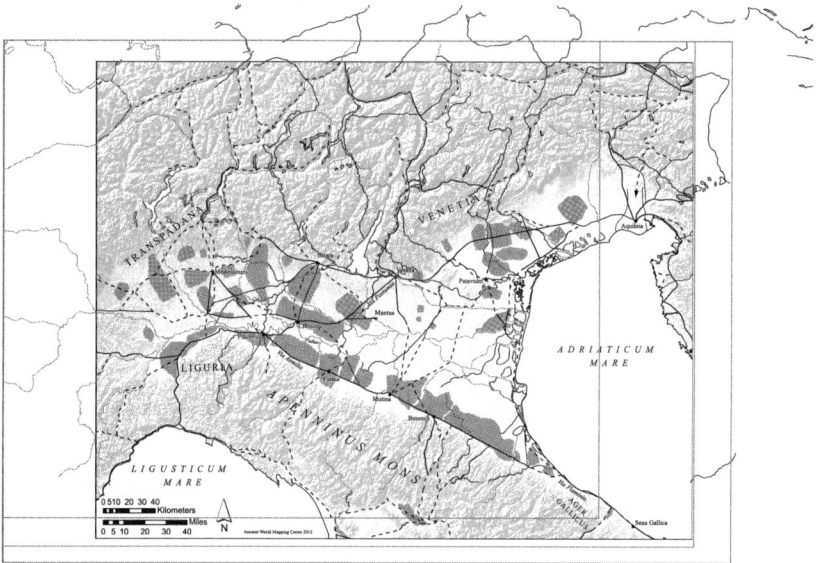

Map 4.5. Cisalpine Gaul. Hatch marks indicate areas of centuriation. Ancient World Mapping Center © 2012 (www.unc.edu/awmc).

example known to me is that produced by Michel Malaise to accompany his "Preliminary Inventory" of texts attesting Egyptian cults in Italy (see map 4.6). Alas, for all its many virtues, Malaise's map provides a guide neither to the temporality of the distribution nor to its intensity, while later maps in his volume, for example, that of "Sites Isiaques assures et probables," do not trace the road system.

In what follows, I focus on the role played by roads in mediating relations both between subaltern communities and Rome and between the subaltern communities themselves. Along with the roads themselves, negotiation about roads, I will argue, spurred institutional and cultural change. To put the matter briefly, Rome required communities located along roadways to contribute to the maintenance of the road; when the roads in question served the *cursus publicus*, the imperial post, those communities were obliged to supply materiel to the imperial post as well. (The term "post" is slightly misleading, as the system moved not only messengers but officials of a certain rank, too, as well as anyone outfitted with appropriate letters of transit.) But when one received a memorandum from the Roman bureau of roads and transport, it was best to have a bureau of roads and transport to write the reply.

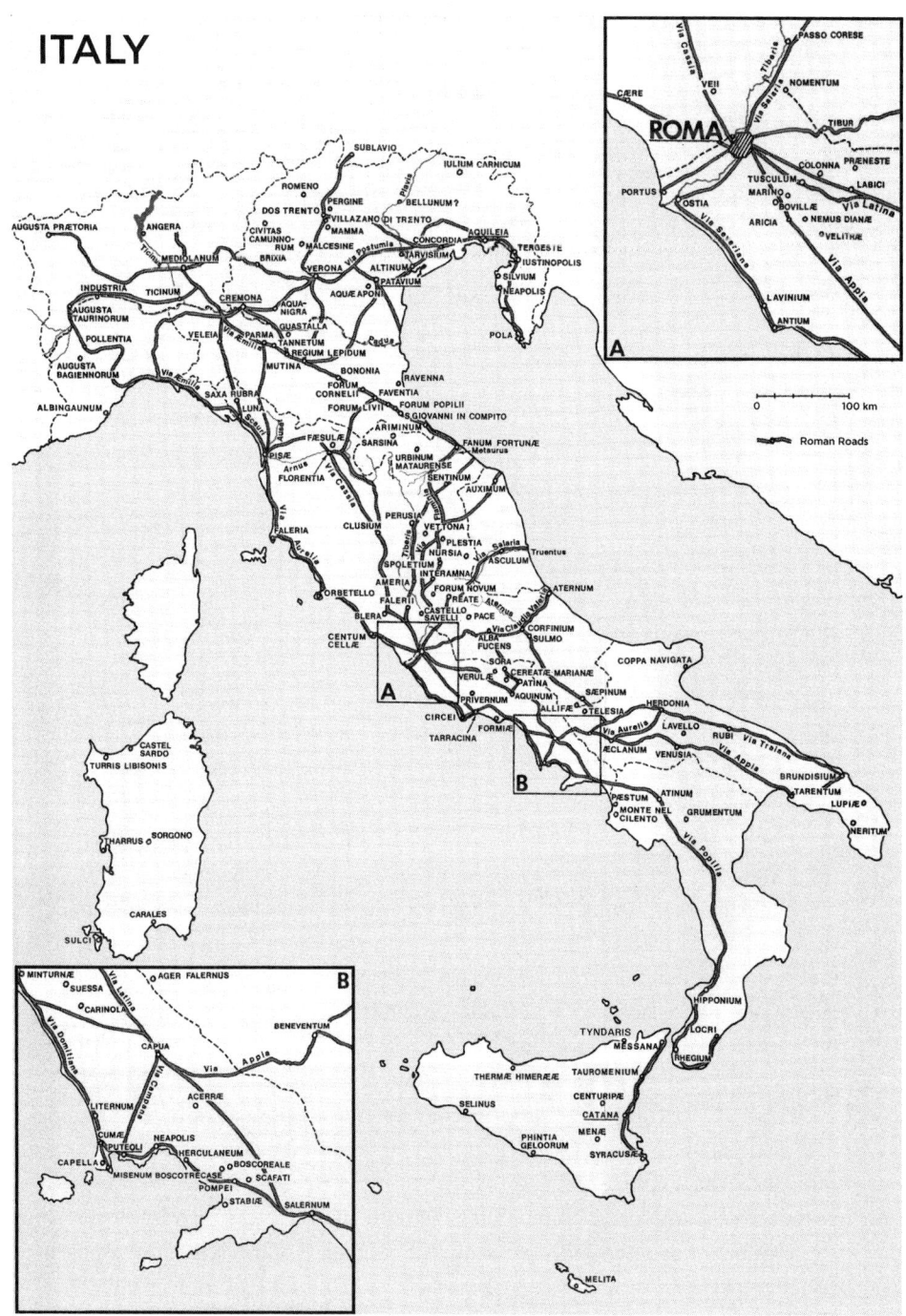

Map 4.6. Sites mentioned in Michel Malaise's catalog of texts relating to Egyptian cults in Italy. Adapted from Michel Malaise, *Inventaire préliminaire des documents égyptiens découverts en Italie* (Leiden: Brill, 1972), map 1.

As with administrative subordination of communities, so in the case of roads, a significant portion of surviving evidence for the burdens levied on neighboring landowners and communities consists of occasional documents. In particular, we possess numerous inscribed records of protests and petitions from local communities, to the effect that they have been subjected to excessive or inappropriate demands. Sometimes the party protests against illegal exactions on the part of Roman officials; at others, a party urges that a neighboring community, namely, one that exists in parallel relation to it in public law, or a city in administrative supervision over it, has attempted to shift its burden onto them. When such petitions obtained a favorable response, the recipients often transcribed relevant portions to permanent media for public display, in the hope of warding off bad conduct in the future. Such were often also the instructions of the imperial officials who wrote the response. Again, this pattern, to wit, that our evidence consists largely of responses, might be taken as indicative of some underlying feature of Roman government. It is not. The pattern is rather a function of the interests that determined which documents would be transferred to permanent media, as well as contingencies that affected the survival of any given inscribed document from antiquity to today. That the surviving documentation consists largely of responses to petitions should not be taken to indicate that Rome created and administered its roads and messenger network reactively rather than proactively, in response to communications from below. The pattern affirms merely local interest and investment in the permanent display of documents that offered them privileges or protection.

I take as a case study the inscribed record of a dispute brought before a succession of imperial procurators by two villages in Phrygia, Anossa and Antimacheia, whose public affairs were to a point overshadowed by (and whose territory may have lain wholly inside) a great imperial estate (*SEG* 16, 754; editio princeps and still valuable: Frend 1956; translation: Levick 2000, 63–64). The location of the villages has still not been securely established, but the terrain of the territory, including sites of ancient cities and the major roads, can be drawn with reasonable accuracy (see map 4.7).

The dispute stretched from before 213—it may have started as early as 200—to at least 237 C.E. The fragmentary text preserves the records of proceedings before three procurators, as well as two letters addressed to the councils of the villages in question, written by a procurator's assistant seeking to enforce the decision. (I term the text fragmentary because the left edge of the stone is broken off; depending on the area of the stone, perhaps twenty to

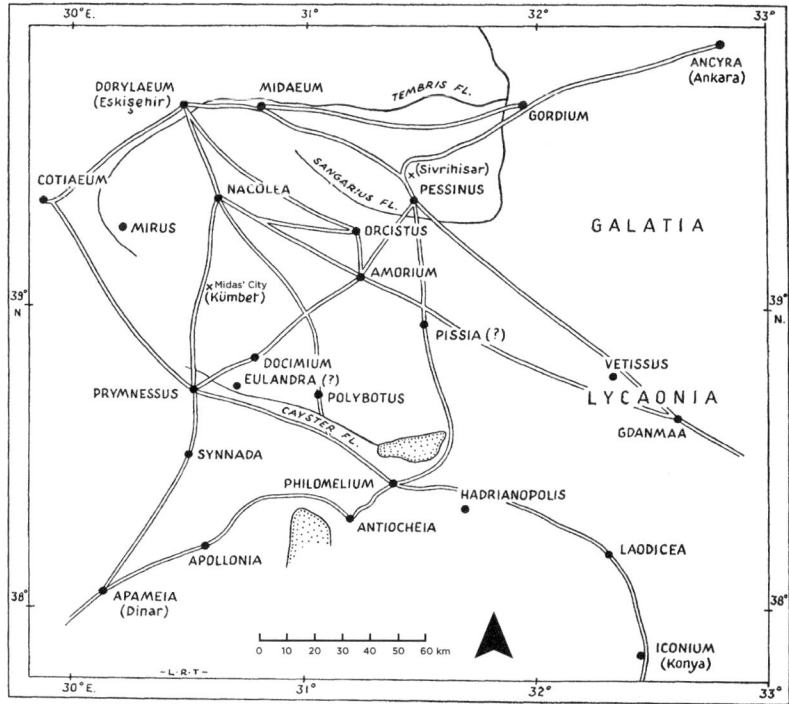

Map 4.7. Cities and Roman roads in Phrygia in the region of Anossa and Antimacheia. Adapted from W. H. C. Frend, "A Third-Century Inscription Relating to Angareia in Phrygia," *Journal of Roman Studies* 46 (1956), figure 8, p. 50.

twenty-five characters are missing from the left of each line.) One formal aspect of the inscription bears on its interpretation: within the records of proceedings (as opposed to the letters), the protocols—namely, the dating formulae, the names of the speakers, etc.—are in Latin, while the text of the speeches is in Greek.

The dispute concerns an obligation placed on communities along so-called public roads, to wit, to supply animals and occasionally carts for transport for the imperial post. It is clear that the obligation placed on the villages is assessed in two units: a distance along the road or roads that pass through their territory (described by reference to milestones: "for those coming from Synnada, from the fifth mile" [line 5]), and cash, a contribution very likely made in kind but assessed in cash, that was apparently directly proportional to the village's overall tax liability ("according to a proportion of the [tax] liability," [line 11]). The dispute arises between two villages, but the procurator clearly feels the heart of the issue at this moment to be that one village does not wish to meet its obligation, and he seeks to discover why the village feels it can no longer provide in the future the contribution it has always made in the past. And on it goes.

A number of aspects of the dispute, the behavior of the principals, and the text deserve our attention. First, the villagers are fully aware that the structure of Roman administration, and the administration's procedures, allowed nearly any decision to be appealed and nearly every question to be reopened. In the first hearing, the spokesman for Anossa, the poorer village, one Panas, evidently sensed the conversation turning against him and threatened an appeal over the procurator's head (ll. 11–12). Though the procurator asked a rhetorical question, "What more would you say there than you have said here?" and obviously considered the matter closed, we of course know that the case did in fact continue. It continued both because one party appealed, and because the people of Anossa complained that the people of Antimacheia had not been acting in accord with some aspect of the earlier judgment. For the present argument, interested as we are in the culture of government, the essential point to emerge from the villagers' explicit references to an appeals process and to lower- and higher-ranked officials is that the villagers understood themselves to be engaging a hierarchical bureaucracy and furthermore that they were savvy in manipulating it. In this case, therefore, and also in many others, the form taken by *resistance* to power existed in mimetic relation to the form taken by power itself.

A second aspect of the text that deserves comment here concerns the form taken by its bilingualism. The text from Phrygia is one of a number of inscriptions and papyri that preserve in Latin either the formal protocols that indicate imperial authorship (for example, the first-person notation in Latin "I have signed") or the protocols that locate the origin of the text or some part thereof in a (Roman) record of proceedings. On my reading, the format of these documents attests a faith, however motivated or strong, in the social efficacy of the procedures of Roman government. A similar faith might be said to inhere in the act of inscription itself, which can only have been undertaken in the hope that the very display of a text would induce obedience to its content. The format of the inscriptions also attests a conviction that others will recognize and esteem Roman documents by virtue of their formal aspects: their use of Latin, their dating formulae, and other characteristics specific to particular genres, whether the record of proceedings or the rescript.[10]

A third consideration follows on the second. Reading the dispute between Anossa and Antimacheia, a modern reader might well be struck by the very high level of the debate, as well as the high level of agreement among the participants over what the terms of the debate should be. In the first hearing, everyone knows, and no one contests, the formula that defines the burden for each community. What is at issue are the facts that one should plug into the formula. Here, the procurator's global knowledge of practice in past and present plays an essential role. But overall, what merits observations is the conduct of the villagers and its implications. When the dispute began, they were aliens in respect to the metropole and almost undoubtedly regulated their private social and economic affairs according to their own laws. Nonetheless, the pragmatics of Roman government shaped their lives, and it seems to have been wholly legible to them.

Villages in Phrygia thus contributed essentially to sustaining the infrastructural power of the central state. To do so, they must have organized considerable aspects of their day-to-day existence around the need as a community to provide quite specific materiel upon demand. They had also come to possess, because the structures of empire made it essential to do so, knowledge of the second-order institutional structures that regulated that provision. Furthermore, their relations with each other were mediated by formulae controlled, and justice dispensed, by Roman officials. Even at the level of village-to-village microregional relations, the superordinate structures of empire played a role. The same was true at an even more profound level of the legal, economic, and cultic ties between villages and cities.[11]

The lives of these villagers were thus shaped by, even as their mutual relations revolved around, one of the great material facts of empire, its roads. The road systems of Asia Minor antedated the arrival of Roman power, of course. But it would be nearly impossible to overstate the material and symbolic importance of the roads in uniting the local, regional, and imperial in the Roman period. What is more, Roman agents had long recognized this importance on both levels, material and symbolic: they devoted enormous resources to building and maintaining roads, and mobilized and therefore shaped the social and economic energy of alien communities in those projects. They also exploited fully the opportunities afforded by road systems to address their users (as, occasionally, did locals: the milestone erected in Lycia in honor of Claudius being a most prominent example). In the discursive system so established, roads were a gift of imperial power, and the road system was described as uniting the local, provincial, and imperial into a single whole. The Romanness of this ideological apparatus, and even of the conception of physical space that underlay its use, is visible even in this text in the casual use by all parties of the Latin loanword "mile" in Greek.

Allow me to offer a brief comparandum in the census (for bibliography and historical considerations see Ando 2000, 350–59). The ideological and cultural importance of the Roman census can scarcely be overstated, and certain aspects of its history have of course received important scrutiny. But three aspects of its conduct have hardly been sufficiently emphasized and deserve mention here. First, it was in many regions a wholly novel undertaking. Second, before the reign of Augustus, the Roman census had counted exactly the same objects as every other institution of its kind, namely, Romans. Under Augustus, the Roman census began to count alien subjects of rule. Third, the Roman state did not have the personnel to conduct this count on its own. Despite the provision of high-level supervision, especially in its early iterations, the actual count must have been performed by local governments. This was revolutionary.

In a number of contexts, direct attestation of the mandating of local cooperation in the conduct of the census survives, none more explicit than a law of the mid-first century B.C.E. from Heraclea, a Greek city of southern Italy. The law in question is a mad pastiche of Roman laws directed at others and Roman laws concerned with life at Rome itself. This heterogeneity suggests that the text was not produced as a unity in Rome and imposed on the cities of Italy. Rather, the text attests an extraordinary effort on the part of one city to refashion its internal self-governance in response to the political and juridical realities of the Roman state, in the years immediately following its incorporation. The clauses on the census, however, do appear to have a general status in respect to the polities of Italy. They run as follows (*Roman Statutes* no. 24, ll. 142–48):

> Whatever *municipia*, colonies, or prefectures of Roman citizens are or shall be in Italy, whoever in these *municipia*, colonies or prefectures shall there hold the highest magistracy or highest office, at the time when a censor or any other magistrate shall conduct the census of the people at Rome, within the sixty days after he learns that the census is being conducted at Rome, he is to conduct a census of all his fellow *municipes* and colonists and those who shall be of that prefecture, who shall be Roman citizens; and he is to receive from them under oath their *nomina*, their *praenomina*, their fathers or patrons,

their tribes, their *cognomina*, and how many years old each of them shall be and an account of their property, according to the schedule of the census, which shall have been published at Rome by whoever is then about to conduct the census of the people; and he is to see that all this is entered into the public records of the *municipium*, <and send the information on to Rome . . . > and he is to receive from them under oath their *nomina*, their *praenomina*, their fathers or *patrons*, their tribes, their *cognomina*, and how many years old each of them shall be and an account of their property (*rationem pecuniae*), according to the schedule of the census (*ex formula census*), which shall have been published at Rome by whoever is then about to conduct the census of the people.

Note the seemingly principled noninterference in the structures of local self-governance: no uniform constitution or charter being imposed by Rome, and the title of the highest magistracy or office is not specified. That said, not only is frequent communication between center and periphery supposed (no provision being here made to inform localities that a census is being conducted), but a synchronicity between Roman municipal and local municipal governance is perforce required, a product of despotic power.

As for the information required, the census of the high empire demanded a list of all persons resident in any given household, including slaves, a register of significant moveable and immoveable goods, an account of one's liquidity (cash and debts), and a full accounting of real estate holdings:

It is provided in the schedule for the census that land should be recorded in the census in this way: the name of the property to which it belongs, and in what civic community and in what district it belongs, its nearest two neighbors; the extent of the land on the property under cultivation over the last ten years, measured in *jugera*; how many vines in its vineyards; how many *jugera* of olives under cultivation and how many trees; how many *jugera* of pasture have been mowed [to produce hay] over the last ten years; how many *jugera* of pastureland there seems to be; likewise, how much of forest. (Ulpian *De censibus* bk. 3 fr. 22 Lenel = *Dig.* 50.15.4.*pr.*).

On one level, this amounted to an extraordinary act of interpellation—individual subjects of empire becoming known, person by person, to the metropole. What is more, their self-knowledge will inevitably have been shaped by the range and import of the facts deemed salient *as knowledge* in the eye of the center: families and households are constituted as Roman *familia*; persons are fixed in space in relation to others similarly interpellated, each naming the other to the center; economic wealth and productivity are elevated in importance beyond any factor of purely intersubjective interest—such are the interests of the state, the reduction of wealth to money and quantification being related acts of simplification and abstraction in the history of government. By similar means, persons are aggregated into populations, and the messy clutter and dynamism of the world is reduced to a list of stuff susceptible of counting. The emergence of these facts to salience in relations of power must have affected understandings of self and other in purely local and affective matters, too.

This was so not least because, as we have seen, the census was in many places a local affair. Local infrastructural power was mobilized through mandate, but local it remained. The act of interpellation accomplished by the census was thus not narrowly bilateral, center to subject. It was a more complicated act, requiring local authorities, created through local institutions and produced and esteemed through local systems of social differentiation, to be the eyes of center. It was they who elicited self-descriptions from members of their communities that conformed to the epistemics of empire. The result was a new and distinctive form of political subjectivity.

Like the maintenance of roads and the imperial post, the census thus served as an aperçu through which relations between indigenous populations, and between individuals and public powers within subaltern communities, were radically reconfigured. In large measure, this occurred not through some direct exercise of state infrastructural power on the part of the imperial center. On the contrary, it was precisely the limits of metropolitan power that called forth the system that I have described, which rested upon the capacity of the center to summon into being and betimes to reshape local institutions.

Conclusion

The Roman empire poses a series of interpretive challenges to a historian of government. The civilian bureaucracy of the Roman state had fewer personnel than a modern research university has employees, and the empire declared a policy of noninterference in the structures of social, legal, and religious life of alien subalterns. What is more, the technological, financial, and manpower limitations on its power were substantial. Nonetheless, the Mediterranean world of the high Roman empire was vastly more interconnected, greatly more urbanized, and culturally and linguistically more homogeneous than it had ever been before, and its urban centers exhibited a uniformity of style that remains striking.

This chapter has argued that the implication of local communities in infrastructure projects (like road maintenance) not only bound them to the macro-regional and imperial economies; it also served to bring into being within local communities institutional structures that responded, and indeed, corresponded to the supervisory and regulatory structures of the imperial state. A bureau of roads was required to talk to a bureau of roads.

It has made this case by reference to two organizing thematics. "Attribution" studied the administrative subordination of nonurban populations to city-states denominated centers of metropolitan authority by the empire. The intrusion of metropolitan populations in the form of colonies, and the development of depersonalized state institutions in preexisting city-states, advanced claims for the superordinate legitimacy of metropolitan powers, over dispute resolution and markets above all. This appears to have set in motion dynamics of mobility and exchange that led to intermarriage and cultural transfer on a wide scale.[12] The subsequent recognition and public law elevation of nearby, formerly subordinated populations set in motion the furtherance of these processes in respect of populations at still further remove.

"Bureaux of Roads," by contrast, focused on processes of mimesis in the domain of governmental and political culture, as nonurban populations were required to further the infrastructural projects of the center. The cooptation of local resources was of course a principal means toward the extension of metropolitan infrastructural power. On my argument, it had the further effect of producing, or, one might say, inducing, local institutional change. Power being what it is, these changes also engendered social and cultural change, as those on the top of local systems of social differentiation claimed authority over new state functions, in consequence of which those same local systems of social differentiation came to echo the principles that organized authority within the superordinate social, political, and institutional structures of empire.

In the Roman case, at least, the distinction between ancient empire and modern state therefore has diminishing value over time. The intrusion of quite limited material infrastructure into provincial landscapes emerges as instrumental in the reconstitution of even extra-urban populations in fractal reduplication of the metropole, such that they appear homeomorphic as regards the structures of government and homologous in its responsibilities and principles of legitimation.

The argument of this chapter has also unfolded in relation to three strands in the analysis of state power: one is internal to historiography on the Roman empire and concerns the ambitions of the Roman state; another derives from post-Weberian social theory and embraces Benedict Anderson, Michael Mann, and James C. Scott, and other, more disparate figures in various continental traditions—these differentiate modern government and politics and the subjectivities that they generate from varied conceptions of the premodern; and a third seeks to distinguish ancient from early modern empires. In seeking to break down the distinction between despotic and infrastructural power—or, perhaps, highlight their mutuality at the level of practice—this chapter also suggests revision to many of the distinctions and assumptions inherent in those analyses. On my reckoning, the independent weakness of the despotism and infrastructure of the Roman state and its largely autonomous constituents can scarcely account for their synergized power. To bring my own language into alignment with that of Seth Richardson (2012; see also 2014), the coming-to-be of institutional homeomorphies and homologies of principle in respect of the ambitions of government, both imperial and local, reflects a gradual sharing by local and imperial elites of kindred perceptions, beliefs, and fantasies about the state. The power of those conceptualizations and commitments—those desires—over social ideologies amounted to a power of its own sort.[13] What is more, this power was purely ideological, which is why it has so often escaped the percipience of the materialist traditions in the study of state power that have held such extensive sway in recent scholarship.

NOTES

This chapter has benefitted immensely from a critical reading by Seth Richardson, whose language at a crucial juncture I have attempted to adapt.

1. This orthodoxy is well captured in the claim that, "whatever its purposes, the government could do no more than encourage a process which, with no system of public education, it lacked the means to impose. Provincials Romanized themselves" (Brunt 1990 [1976], 268). Brunt focused on indigenous agency in the first instance because, in his view, Rome lacked the institutions to promote cultural change. His language has been taken by many. Millett 1990 provides an excellent survey of the problematic and a case study. An excellent recent essay in this tradition is Sinner 2015. For a recent survey of these themes see Ando 2016a.

2. Anderson 1991; Foucault 2004 may stand for a body of extraordinary work; Habermas 1989 (1962); Koselleck 1988 (1959); Mann 1986–2003, esp. vol. 1; Scott 1998. Among many splendid overviews of some of this material, I have a special affection for Honneth 1991. See also below (n. 3) on Rosa 2013.

3. Regarding the importance of temporality and speed of communication in particular to cashing out, both theoretically and empirically, theories of modernity, Rosa 2013 seems to me without peer.

4. Ando 2016a.

5. An important exception is Laffi 1966; see also the bibliography in Ando 2016b.

6. The dispreferral of nonurban populations in ancient and modern systems of political, moral, and aesthetic evaluation scarcely requires documentation. What does merit some reflection is the lack thereby created of historiographic models for writing histories of nonurban populations in Roman antiquity. To a lamentable degree, the great works in the field exist in splendid isolation: one thinks immediately of Tchalenko 1953, Leveau 1984, Tate 1992, and Dossey 2010, but other studies might be cited. A review of this literature and its achievement is a major desideratum. As a further matter, the emergence of ecologically and demographically marginal areas to prominence in cultural history—in the rise of the late ancient holy man—may stand as a demonstration of my point *ex negativo*.

7. On problems of aggregation in ancient history see Ando 2006, 192; idem, forthcoming. For an attempt to situate political economic relations between Oenoanda and its hinterland within a wider consideration of city-village relations, see Ando 2016b.

8. Ando, forthcoming, discussing texts of the form *Imp. Vespasianus . . . iussit . . . agente curam L. Valerio Ummidio Vasso*, "The Emperor Vespasian ordered . . . with Lucius Valerius Ummidius Vassus taking care [sc. to act on that order in this instance]" (*AE* 1963, 197).

9. Pekáry 1968 provides an overview. The literature is vast. For surveys of documentary evidence, see Meijer and Van Nijf 1992; Llewelyn 1994, 58–92.

10. Ando 2000, 128–30, 364–65, 379–80.

11. For further literature, see Mitchell 1993, 1: 165–97; Ando 2016b.

12. Edmondson 2009, a truly superb essay, advances similar claims in very different language and with different theoretical ambitions.

13. Cf. Richardson 2014, 75: "The political issues we think of as prehistoric were still being worked out long into the historic period. Ancient states were not legally and spatially integrated; they were networks of local and professional actors with closely circumscribed goals and interests. In practice, Mesopotamian states had discontinuous powers—yet routinely claimed authority over spheres of action in which they could not effect or even did not want to accept actual problem-solving responsibility. This may seem counter-intuitive to us until we think of the claims themselves as conceptually real desires of the state—that they wished they could exercise such powers. In this sense political rhetoric was more erotic than documentary. But one still must account for eros: at the point when the desire for power was more potent than its actual exercise, wants influenced the course of political history more than abilities. The state was important as a developing form;

but to fetishize it as the finished form par excellence is to have acquired, by purchase, a bridge of great dimension."

BIBLIOGRAPHY

Anderson, Benedict. 1991. *Imagined Communities*. New York: Verso.
Ando, Clifford. 2000. *Imperial Ideology and Provincial Loyalty in the Roman Empire*. Berkeley: University of California Press.
———. 2006. "The Administration of the Provinces." In *The Blackwell Companion to the Roman Empire*, edited by D. S. Potter, 177–92. Oxford: Wiley.
———. 2010. "Imperial identities." In *Local knowledge and Microidentities in the Imperial Greek World*, edited by Tim Whitmarsh, 17–45. Cambridge: Cambridge University Press.
———. 2015a."La forme canonique de l'empire antique: le cas de l'empire romain." *Ius Politicum* 14. http://juspoliticum.com/La-forme-canonique-de-l-empire.html.
———. 2015b. "Three Revolutions in Government." In *Official Epistolography and the Languages of Power*, edited by Lucian Reinfandt, Stephan Prochazka, and Sven Tost, 163–72. Vienna: Verlag der Österreichischen Akademie der Wissenschaften.
———. 2016a. "Colonialism, Colonization: Roman Perspectives." In *The Oxford Handbook of Literatures of the Roman Empire*, edited by D.L. Selden and P. Vasunia. Oxford Handbooks Online (published May 2016). DOI: 10.1093/oxfordhb/9780199 699445.013.4.
———. 2016b. "City, Village, Sacrifice: The Political Economy of Teligion in the Early Roman Empire." In *Mass and Elite in the Greek and Roman World: From Sparta to Late Antiquity*, edited by Richard Evans. New York: Routledge.
———. Forthcoming. "Petition and Response, Order and Obey: Contemporary Models of Roman Government." In *Land, Labour and the Relationships of Power: Governing Ancient Empires*, edited by Michael Jursa et al. *Proceedings of the 3rd to 5th International Conferences of the Research Network Imperium and Officium*. Vienna: Verlag der Österreichischen Akademie der Wissenschaften.
Brunt, P. A. (1990 [1976]). "The Romanization of the Local Ruling Classes in the Roman Empire." In *Roman Imperial Themes*, edited by Brunt, P. A., 267–81. Oxford: Clarendon Press.
Dossey, L. 2010. *Peasant and Empire in Christian North Africa*. Berkeley: University of California Press.
Doyle, M. W. 1986. *Empires*. Ithaca, N.Y.: Cornell University Press.
Edmondson, Jonathan 2009. "The Virginity of the Soldier Zosimus and Other Family Myths: Terms of Affection Within and Beyond the Family at Augusta Emerita." In *Lusitânia Romana entre o mito e a realidade*, edited by J.-G. Gorges, J. d'Encarnação, T. Nogales Basarrate, and A. Carvalho, 249–79. Cascais: Camera Municipal.
Foucault, M. 2004. *Sécurité, territoire, population. Cours au Collège de France (1977–1978)*. Edited by M. Senellart. Paris: Gallimard.

Frend, W. H. C. 1956. "A Third-Century Inscription Relating to *Angareia* in Phrygia." *Journal of Roman Studies* 46:46–56.
Habermas, J. 1989 (1962). *The Structural Transformation of the Public Sphere: An Inquiry into a Category of Bourgeois Society*. Translated by T. Burger with the assistance of F. Lawrence. Cambridge, Mass.: MIT Press.
Honneth, A. 1991. *The Critique of Power: Reflective Stages in a Critical Social Theory*. Translated by K. Baynes. Cambridge, Mass.: MIT Press.
Humphries, M. 1998. "Trading Gods in Northern Italy." In *Trade, Traders and the Ancient City*, edited by H. Parkins and C. Smith, 203–24. London: Routledge.
Kolb, A. 2000. *Transport und Nachrichtentransfer im römischen Reich*. Berlin: Akademie Verlag.
Koselleck, R. 1988 (1959). *Critique and Crisis: Enlightenment and the Pathogenesis of Modern Society*. Cambridge, Mass.: MIT Press.
Laffi, U. 1966. *Adtributio e contributio. Problemi del sistema politico-administrativo dello stato romano*. Pisa: Nistri-Lischi.
Leveau, P. 1984. *Caesarea de Maurétanie. Une ville romaine et ses campagnes*. Rome: École française de Rome.
Levick, B. 2000. *The Government of the Roman Empire: A Sourcebook*. New York: Routledge.
Llewelyn, S. R., ed. 1994. *New Documents Illustrating Early Christianity*. Vol. 7. North Ryde, N.S.W.: Ancient History Documentary Research Centre.
Maier, C. S. 2006. *Among Empires: American Ascendancy and Its Predecessors*. Cambridge, Mass.: Harvard University Press.
Malaise, M. 1972. *Inventaire préliminaire des documents égyptiens découverts en Italie*. Leiden: Brill.
Mann, M. 1984. "The Autonomous Power of the State: Its Origins, Mechanisms and Results." *Archives européennes de sociologie* 25 (2): 185–213.
———. 1986–2013. *The Sources of Social Power*. 4 vols. Cambridge: Cambridge University Press.
Meijer, F., and O. van Nijf. 1992. *Trade, Transport, and Society in the Ancient World: A Sourcebook*. London: Routledge.
Millett, M. 1990. *The Romanization of Britain. An Essay in Archaeological Interpretation*. Cambridge: Cambridge University Press.
Mitchell, S. 1993. *Anatolia: Land, Men, and Gods in Asia Minor*. 2 vols. Oxford: Oxford University Press.
Novak, W. J. 2008. "The Myth of the 'Weak' American State." *American Historical Review* 113 (3): 752–72.
Pekáry, T. 1968. *Untersuchungen zu den römischen Reichsstrassen*. Bonn: Habelt.
Piganiol, A. 1962. *Les documents cadastraux de la colonie romaine d'Orange*. Gallia supplement 16. Paris: CNRS.
Reynolds, J. 1988. "Cities." In *The Administration of the Roman Empire 241 B.C.–A.D. 193*, edited by David Braund, 15–51. Exeter: Exeter University Press.
Richardson, S. 2012. "Early Mesopotamia: The Presumptive State." *Past and Present* 215 (1): 3–49.

———. 2014. "Mesopotamian Political History: The Perversities." *Journal of Ancient Near Eastern History* 1 (1): 61–93.

Rosa, H. 2013 (2005). *Social Acceleration: A New Theory of Modernity*. Translated by J. Trejo-Mathys. New York: Columbia University Press.

Scott, J. C. 1998. *Seeing like a State: How Certain Schemes to Improve the Human Condition Have Failed*. New Haven, Conn.: Yale University Press.

Shaw, B. 1981. "The Elder Pliny's African Geography." *Historia* 30 (4): 424–71.

Sinner, A. G. 2015. "Cultural Contacts and Identity Construction: A Colonial Context in NE Spain (2nd—Early 1st c. B.C.)." *Journal of Roman Archaeology* 28:7–37.

Tate, G. 1992. *Les campagnes de la Syrie du Nord du IIe au VIIe siècle: un exemple d'expansion démographique et économique dans les campagnes à la fin de l'antiquité*. Paris.

Tchalenko, G. 1953. *Villages antiques de la Syrie du Nord: le massif du Bélus à l'époque romaine*. 3 vols. Paris: P. Geuthner.

Woolf, G. 1998. *Becoming Roman: The Origins of Provincial Civilization in Gaul*. Cambridge: Cambridge University Press.

CHAPTER 5

Populist Despotism and Infrastructural Power in the Later Roman Empire

JOHN WEISWEILER

In Rome around the year 390 C.E., Ammianus Marcellinus, a former senior officer of the imperial army, published a thirty-one–book history of the Roman Empire.[1] Ammianus knew when the decline of the empire had started. In 284, the Pannonian officer Diocletian had been proclaimed by the Roman army as emperor. Ammianus believed that it was this man (who had risen from simple origins to the rulership over the world) who had introduced a new style of imperial ceremonial into the Roman Empire. Henceforth, members of the imperial aristocracy would greet their ruler no longer with a kiss on his mouth. Instead, they were expected to perform *adoratio,* prostrate their full body, and kiss the border of his robe:[2] "For the emperor Diocletian was the first of all rulers who according to foreign custom and despotic practice wished to receive *adoratio.* Earlier emperors (I read) were greeted in the same way as provincial governors."

Ammianus's claim that Diocletian had introduced Oriental forms of ceremonial in the Roman Empire was mistaken. As Andreas Alföldi has long ago shown in a groundbreaking paper, already in the second century C.E. emperors had sometimes been greeted in this way.[3] Nor should the suggestion be accepted that *adoratio* was an Iranian import; as Matthew Canepa has recently pointed out, this ritual never formed part of Sasanian court ceremonial.[4] Even so, Ammianus's claim that Diocletian imported this "foreign custom" *(extero ritu)* and "despotic practice" *(regio more)* into the Roman Empire is unanimously repeated by the entire Greek and Latin historiographical tradition.[5] The popularity of this interpretation highlights the ways in which the late antique transformations in government were perceived by leading members of the governing elite of the Roman Empire. They believed that Roman emperors had become successors of the Achaemenian Kings of old—Oriental despots who ruled over their subjects like masters over slaves.[6]

Men such as Ammianus were convinced that the adoption of this style of rulership not only revealed a regrettable lack of self-control amongst the rulers of the Late Roman world. They also believed that the unconstrained power of the emperor had destructive effects on the behavior of the governing class of the empire. Knowing that any unpredictable change in the constellation of power at court might lead to their immediate removal or annihilation, senior administrators used their periods in high office to line their pockets with the fortunes of their subjects. In Ammianus's evocative phrase, members of the governing class of the later Roman Empire were like wild beasts, whose mouths were fed by emperors with the "vital organs of the provincials."[7] Such views of the socially corrosive effects of unconstrained monarchical power have long shaped our understanding of Late Roman history. In Edward Gibbon's *History of the Decline and Fall of the Roman Empire*, Rome's transformation from a constitutional monarchy into an "Oriental despotism" was one of the main reasons why the Roman governing class lost the independence and virtue by which it had procured rulership over the world.[8] The same interpretation of the later Roman Empire as an "Oriental despotism" was adopted by leading figures of nineteenth and twentieth century scholarship, such as Theodor Mommsen and Mikhail Rostovtzeff, and remained popular amongst many late antique historians until the 1970s. For them, it seemed clear that the abandonment by late antique emperors of the more restrained forms of monarchy developed by Augustus and his successors eroded the stable functioning of state institutions and was both a symptom and a contributing cause of political, economic, and cultural decline.[9]

Such views are now decidedly out of fashion. The last decades of late antique scholarship have convincingly shown that the late third and fourth centuries were a period of political success and economic growth. After the military crises of the preceding period, and before the onset of the invasions that would lead to a disintegration of the empire in Europe and North Africa, emperors built a state infrastructure (to quote John Matthews) "unmatched in Graeco-Roman history in its scale and complexity of organisation and its physical incidence on society."[10] Nor did the later Roman Empire go through an economic depression. As the archaeological evidence shows ever more clearly, the expansion of state power did not lead to an impoverishment of the provinces, or disrupt Mediterranean trade networks, but, on the contrary, served as a strong stimulus for wealth creation and interregional exchange. Several regions of the empire would only in the early modern period once again obtain the same levels of prosperity and population density as in late antiquity.[11] Far from leading to a decline in infrastructural capacity, the formation of the Late Roman state inaugurated a period of resurgent economic growth and political stability, which lasted in the western half of the Mediterranean for 125 years and in the eastern half for 325 years. Mercifully, in recent historiography, there is no more talk of the Roman Empire as a self-destructive Oriental despotism.[12]

And yet, there is a price to be paid for this rejection of traditional paradigms. A gap opens up between our own accounts of political change in the later Roman Empire and those put forward by contemporary observers. Were fourth-century writers really mistaken when they believed that the introduction of new styles of monarchical ceremonial was an important development which says something significant about the ways in which power was exercised and conceptualized in late antiquity? In other words, what precisely was the relationship between ceremonial change (the transformation of the emperor into what contemporaries perceived as an Oriental despot) and infrastructural change (the late antique expansion of the reach of the state institutions)? The objective of this chapter is to explore the reasons for the parallel intensification of despotic and infrastructural power in the later Roman Empire.

Recent literature in the field of institutional economics claims that limiting the arbitrary power exercised by state elites is the crucial prerequisite for building successful infrastructures of governance. Daron Acemoğlu and James A. Robinson cite the later Roman Empire as an example of how an accumulation of authority in the hands of autocrats and their followers corroded the functioning of state institutions: "Rome's increasingly extractive political and economic institutions generated its demise because they caused infighting and civil war."[13] Such views of the detrimental effects of despotism are reminiscent of claims by republican theorists that the flourishing of free polities chiefly requires the energetic defence of the political and economic rights of propertied citizens against encroachments by absolutist rulers.[14] It is one of the many merits of Mann's paper on the autonomous power of the state that it rejects such simplistic views of an inevitable opposition between monarchical power and the formation of efficacious institutions: "If compulsory co-operation is successful, it increases both the despotic and the infrastructural power of the state."[15] According to Mann, the growth of infrastructural power in early polities (the ability of the state elite to "actually to penetrate civil society and to implement logistically important decisions throughout the realm") is often inextricably intertwined with the growth of "despotic power" (the ability of ruling groups to push through its demands "without routine institutionalized negotiation with civil society groups").[16]

In this chapter, I argue that Mann's idea of a link between infrastructural and despotic power is helpful for understanding processes of state formation in Late Antiquity. I propose that the new theories of unlimited monarchy developed at late antique courts did not inhibit the formation of successful institutions in the Roman Empire (as analysts from Ammianus to Acemoğlu have argued), but, on the contrary, made a crucial contribution to the growth of state infrastructural power. In order to understand why that was the case, we need to look more closely at the distinctive cultural shape of the late Roman monarchy. If Gibbon, Mommsen, and Rostovtzeff depicted the later Roman state as an Oriental despotism, they correctly identified a significant shift in the ways in which monarchs represented their power. What their interpretations do not properly bring into focus, however, is the meaning of these new tactics of self-representation. The purpose of the sophisticated forms of ceremonial developed at late antique courts was not simply to celebrate power itself—the raw ability of a ruler to terrify, to punish and to subdue. Rather, the new theories of monarchy entailed distinct normative commitments.

By emphasizing their links with the divine sphere, emperors laid claim to forms of charisma that transcended loyalties of class, ethnicity, and geography. They fashioned themselves as populist monarchs whose care extended not merely to privileged groups of imperial citizens but to *all* their subjects. Of course, these claims never were fully put into practice: in late antiquity, wealth and honor in the Roman Empire remained distributed in a brutally unequal way. Even so, the adoption by emperors of new ideologies of populist despotism had material consequences. By presenting themselves as divinely ordained protectors of the entire human species, emperors established coalitions with social groups who previously had been excluded from the benefits of state infrastructural power, and contained the power of the predatory elites who had been fantastically enriched in earlier centuries of imperial rule.

Imperial Crisis and Recovery

In order to understand the meaning of the late antique transformations in imperial power, it is useful to look more closely at the distinctive sociocultural shape of the early Roman monarchy. I begin with a portrait head of the emperor Vespasian, which is kept in the Ny-Carlsberg Glypothek in Copenhagen (figure 5.1). It belonged to a statue that was produced during the reign of the emperor between 69 and 79 C.E. The ruler of the world here appears as a bald old man. The uncompromisingly realistic form of representation communicates an important message. Vespasian is not a divine king but the first citizen of a restored republic.[17] The same image of the Roman ruler as a republican monarch is communicated by the inscriptions commissioned for emperors in the first two centuries C.E. On public buildings paid for by the imperial government, and on the bases of honorific statues of rulers, the power of the emperor was described by the republican offices to which he had formally been elected by senate and people of Rome: he was *consul* (highest magistrate of the Roman state), *pontifex maximus* (supreme priest of the state cult), and holder of the tribunician powers (wielding the legal authorities of tribunes, the ancient defenders of the Roman plebs). These titles asserted that the power of the emperor derived not from divine election, but from legal acts by the traditional institutions of the Roman city-state. They staked out a claim that the emperor was not a god but the leader of a restored republic.[18]

Usually, we take the self-fashioning of early Roman emperors as republican monarchs not quite seriously. Since the early second-century senator Tacitus, historians have become accustomed to disregarding the political culture of the early Empire as mere theater—empty words without broader social consequences.[19] There have been good reasons for such an attitude. Unlike in the constitutional monarchies of early modern Europe, there were no legal limitations to the power of the emperor: "the emperor is not subject to the laws" (*princeps legibus solutus est*), as it was put by the early third century jurist Ulpian.[20] The assertion that the emperor was elected by senate and people of Rome was a fiction too—of course, in reality, the choice of a new monarch was decided by a small circle of high officers and senior officials.[21] Still, I would like to suggest that the self-presentation of Roman emperors as legal rulers had important consequences.[22] By presenting themselves as republican magistrates, elected by senate and people of Rome, rulers such as Vespasian staked out a claim that they would preserve the power of the most ancient institutions of the Roman state. In other words, they promised that the imposition of monarchy would not disrupt, but instead preserve the unequal social order created by the Roman conquest of the Mediterranean. By fashioning themselves as leaders of a restored republican empire, emperors appealed above all to two social groups: the senate and the Roman citizenry.

Figure 5.1. Statue of the emperor Vespasian. Ny-Carlsberg-Glyptothek, Copenhagen. Photograph: Wikimedia Commons.

The primary addresses of new ideology were no doubt senators, the 600 former and current officeholders who formed the traditional ruling class of the Roman state. By fashioning himself as republican magistrate, the emperor guaranteed senators that he would treat them not as his subjects but as his friends.[23] The ideology of friendship between emperor and imperial aristocracy had far-reaching material consequences. Senators enjoyed constant access to the emperor's presence. As permanent guests at his dinner parties and morning receptions, they were the most important brokers of patronage in the Roman Empire.[24] Senators also maintained traditional monopolies on the most powerful and remunerative government posts in the Roman Empire.[25] To be sure, some emperors made attempts to break the exclusive hold of senatorial officeholders on imperial patronage. In particular, several rulers of the Julio-Claudian dynasty (14–68 C.E.) employed ex-slaves of the imperial family in powerful positions at court. Interestingly however, this experiment did not prove successful. The subjection of senators to men of servile descent was incompatible with the ideals of republican monarchy enunciated by emperors in their official statements. By the end of the first century C.E., all key positions at the imperial court were held by senators and equestrians (members of the second-highest status group in the Roman Empire).[26]

The inability of emperors to create a palatial organisation more independent from the influence of the traditional ruling classes of the empire is indicative of the extent to which the ideology of republican monarchy shaped the distribution of power in the early Roman Empire. The highly idiosyncratic political culture developed by early emperors gave the aristocracy manifold opportunities to impose their wishes on the imperial monarchs. The profits derived by Roman families from this configuration can be seen from the enormous wealth accumulated by them. Under the early empire, senators not only became richer than they had been in the republic,[27] their fortunes were also considerably larger than those of contemporary Chinese aristocrats.[28] This attests to the enormous benefits accrued to senators by their patronage, power, and political offices. They were not the victims but the primary beneficiaries of the system of government introduced by the first emperors.

By showing respect to the institutions of the Roman Republic, emperors shored up the power not only of senators but also of the Roman citizen population at large. In this context, ancient and modern historians of the Roman Empire tend to think of the constant provisioning by emperors of food distributions and spectacles in the city of Rome.[29] But I would like to suggest that equally important to the maintenance of consensus with the inhabitants of the capital was the personal relationship entertained by emperors with city notables dispersed across the provinces of the empire. These notables normally had Roman citizenship.[30] In Latin-speaking regions, the constitutions of municipalities were explicitly modelled on those of Rome. They were governed by local senates, made up of former officeholders, who upon their election automatically became full Roman citizens.[31]

The power of these provincial citizen elites was massively strengthened in the early Roman Empire. Firstly, the possession of Roman citizenship ensured that they would receive privileged judicial treatment by Roman governors.[32] Secondly, the fact that city-councils enjoyed complete fiscal autonomy gave their members considerable opportunities for enrichment.[33] Thirdly, as Leslie Dossey has shown, the Roman provincial administration systematically disbanded previously self-governing villages and distributed their lands to neighboring cities.[34] This combination of judicial discrimination, fiscal autonomy, and the reassertion of urban rulership over the countryside offered city-based aristocracies manifold opportunities for profit-making.[35] Again, the rise in private wealth is a useful index for the benefits accrued to civic elites from the social configuration of republican monarchy. Under the carapace of the Roman state, local notables became considerably richer than they had been in previous periods of history.[36]

On this reading, what was significant about the self-presentation of early Roman emperors as legal rulers was not that it entailed a commitment to the maintenance of correct procedure. As we have seen above, even in legal theory, emperors explicitly stood above the law, and could always breach formal regulations if it suited their interests.[37] In this sense, senatorial writers were right if they insisted that already in the early empire every emperor was a *dominus*, a despot, whose power was not constrained by any legal limitations.[38] What mattered about the legal titles adopted by the emperor was, rather, that they expressed the shape of the class coalition on which the power of emperors rested. By fashioning themselves as republican magistrates, emperors articulated their unbending loyalty to the members of the imperial aristocracy in Rome and urban elites across the empire, both of whom equally benefited from the distinctive style of city-based imperialism pursued by the Roman imperial government.

Late Roman Despotism

But in the late second and early third centuries, this splendid coalition came under pressure. Already in 168 a group of invaders had reached the gates of

Aquileia in Northern Italy. In the early third century, the pace of incursions accelerated. The Rhine and Danube frontiers became porous, and Gaul and the Balkans were ravaged by foreign armies. Meanwhile, in the East, the formation of the Sasanian Empire threatened the Euphrates frontier. In 253 or 256, Antioch, the third largest city in the empire, was plundered by an Iranian army. In 260, the great king Shapur I captured the Roman emperor Valerian. For the next one and half centuries, Roman emperors would frequently be involved in wars on two fronts against Central European and Iranian enemies. At the same time, the recurrent losses against foreign enemies faced by third-century emperors undermined their legitimacy. Since the end of the Severan dynasty, usurpations became frequent events. Most strikingly, after the emperor Valerian fell into Persian captivity, armies in different regions of the empire proclaimed four different emperors simultaneously. For a short period of time, it seemed as if Rome would disintegrate under the weight of civil war and external invasions.[39]

But then, emperors were slowly able to reassert their authority over the Mediterranean World. The reign of the emperor Aurelian (270–275) was the turning point. Invading groups now began to be decisively repelled and the most dangerous usurpers defeated.[40] Under the so-called Tetrarchy—the reign of Diocletian and his three corulers (284–305)—new administrative, fiscal, and economic structures were established that would shape the course of Roman history for the next centuries.[41] Diocletian's reforms were consolidated and deepened by the emperor Constantine (306–337), the first Christian ruler in the Roman Empire. By the time of his death, the onset of crisis had been reversed, and the empire was the wealthiest and most powerful state in the world. Under his successors and until the end of the fourth century, the empire entered a prolonged period of stability and growth.

And yet the newly strengthened Roman state of the fourth century looked significantly different than it had in the first two centuries C.E. The urgent need to secure the loyalty of imperial armies forced emperors to raise new revenues, and these revenues most likely came from the senators and municipal elites who had profited so greatly from the constellation of power in the early Empire. As Greg Woolf observes, "Given the vast inequalities of wealth in the Roman Empire, the emperors could only really afford to let the rich off lightly when times were good."[42] The ideals of civility and equality which had defined modes of interaction between ruler and imperial aristocracy in the first two centuries broke down. Instead, emperors now explicitly asserted their superiority over the empire's property-owning elites.

A fourth-century statue that was found in Aphrodisias (in Caria in southwestern Turkey) and is housed today in the Archaeological Museum in Istanbul visualizes the late antique ideal of rulership (figure 5.2).[43] An important difference to Vespasian's first-century portrait is immediately apparent. The emperor now wears a pearl diadem, an unambiguous symbol of monarchical power, deliberately avoided by all before Constantine. The ruler of the Roman world was no longer conceived of as first citizen but as a divinely ordained king. Other features further highlighted the emperor's special relationship to the divine sphere. His large eyes and youth communicate notions of divine calm and imperial omniscience. To which ruler does the statue belong? It was discovered next to a group of bases that were put up in the years 388 and 392 and which presumably belonged to a group of monuments representing the ruling emperors Valentinian II, Theodosius (whose base is missing), Honorius, and Arcadius. Most likely, the statue represents Valentinian II, but it could also conceivably belong to one of the other rulers. The fact that the best experts do not agree on the emperor's identity is significant. Early imperial portraits are so highly individualized that they can almost always be unambiguously ascribed to one ruler. By contrast, portraits of late antique emperors closely resemble each other. As R. R. R. Smith points out, this "highly unified and consistent image" communicates a new conception of the emperor's authority. Emperors are no longer seen as human beings, endowed with idiosyncratic personal characteristics (such as Vespasian's bald head), but as unchanging embodiments of divine energy. Late antique portraits do not celebrate the emperor as an *individual*, but as earthly instantiation of an ageless *ideal* of rulership.[44]

The same transformation of the emperor from a republican ruler into a divine king is also visible from the inscriptions carved on the bases of honorific monuments put up for Roman emperors. From the mid-third to the mid-fourth centuries, the legal titles and republican magistracies that previously had described the power of the emperor disappeared from Latin inscriptions. Instead, commissioners celebrated the emperor's superhuman abilities in a new religious language. He was "born for the good of the human species" (*bono generis humani nato*),[45] "liberator of the earth" (*liberatori orbis*)[46] or "restorer of the world" (*restitutori orbis terrarum*).[47] Significantly, a new word is now regularly used, which had always been carefully avoided in inscriptions from the early Empire: *dominus*, "master."[48] In the fourth century, the new titulature becomes predominant, and the old legal titles of the emperor disappeared from inscriptions. The imperial monarch was conceptualized no longer as a

Figure 5.2. Statue from Aphrodisias of a late fourth-century emperor, attributed to Valentinian. Photograph: Wikimedia Commons.

republican magistrate whose power derived from legal acts by the institutions of the Roman state, but as a divine defender of imperial civilization whose power was an earthly emanation of the power of the gods.[49]

Protectors of the World

Late Roman writers like Ammianus emphasized the deplorable effects of the abandonment by emperors of their old image as legal rulers. But the purpose of the sacralisation of the emperor's person was not simply the celebration of despotic power. It also articulated a new vision of a just political order.[50] The self-fashioning of early emperors as republican monarchs communicated an important message about their ethnic affiliation. In their uncompromising realism, early imperial statues resembled not idealized Hellenistic ruler portraits, but the veristic style common amongst representations of leading generals and officeholders of the late republic.[51] In this way, they highlighted the emperor's Roman identity. The message of the statues was reinforced by the texts carved on their bases. As *consul, pontifex maximus*, and holder of the powers of a tribune of the plebs, the emperor was not a successor of the local rulers replaced by Roman conquest, but rather a delegate of the *Roman* senate and the *Roman* people. These references to the titles and institutions of the Roman city-state were a permanent reminder that Rome was not a nation-state, in which all citizens enjoy equal rights and responsibilities, but an empire, in which an imperial aristocracy and an imperial people ruled over a heterogeneous variety of subject communities.[52]

By contrast, late antique inscriptions efface the inequalities of empire. The pearl-jewelled diadem, since the reign of Constantine part of the imperial insignia, was an allusion to the ideologies of universal rulership first popularized at the court of Alexander the Great.[53] Also the inscriptions carved on the bases of imperial statues emphasize the role of Roman emperors as global rulers. He is "born for the good of the human species" (*bono generis humani nato*)[54] or "liberator of the earth" (*liberatori orbis*).[55] This exalted religious language implies a different image of monarchical power than the monotonous succession of legal titles that described the power of the emperor in the early Roman Empire. Late antique emperors were seen as rulers whose care extended not merely to a privileged group of imperial masters, but to all human beings in their realm. Significantly, these expressions have their closest parallels not amongst earlier Roman rulers, but the royal titulatures of Hellenistic kings.[56]

Like the portraits, so also the texts carved on the bases of honorific statues derive not from a Roman political tradition but draw on a pan-Mediterranean vocabulary of monarchical representation. They no longer present Rome as an empire, riven by inequalities of ethnicity, class, and culture, but as a world-state, in which one ruler governs a unified citizen population.[57]

By openly rejecting the institutions of empire as the primary sources of the monarch's legitimacy, the new imperial ideology changed the horizon of what was politically thinkable and doable. Of course, emperors still faced staggering obstacles in the implementation of their will. As the second-millennium B.C.E. polities whose functioning Seth Richardson has so incisively illuminated for us, so also Roman emperors always and inevitably fell short of their far-reaching governmental ambitions: like early Mesopotamian city-states, so also global empire envisaged by the commissioners of late antique honorific monuments was "much more fully imagined than established."[58] Yet the new language of monarchical authority enabled the emperors to mobilize new social groups for the realisation of their aims. The propagation of the idea of the emperor as a provider of public goods for all of his subjects enabled him to forge new coalitions between private and public authority, which promoted a significant expansion of the infrastructural reach of the state.[59] In the next section, I will trace the social effects of the late antique expansion of state power in three fields: fiscality, law, and governance.

Building an Infrastructural State

Fiscality

Significantly, in the same years in which emperors adopted a new image as rulers of a unified world state, they also abolished many of the fiscal privileges enjoyed by the traditional governing classes of the empire. On the one hand, late antique emperors removed many of the fiscal privileges enjoyed by the old governing classes of the empire. Not coincidentally, Diocletian, the populist despot par excellence, was responsible for the most radical reforms. For the first time in more than 400 years, Diocletian and his corulers subjected the inhabitants of the imperial homeland of Italy to taxation.[60] His example was followed by his successors. Since the reign of Constantine, senators were forced to pay a variety of new levies. Not only did the emperor introduce a new senatorial land-tax, the *gleba*, but it was probably also in his reign that *aurum oblaticium*, "voluntary gold" was regularized, a levy raised on the occasion of imperial anniversaries, and the senatorial equivalent of the *aurum coronarium* paid on these occasions by ordinary provincials.[61] The creation of these new taxes is indicative of a significant shift in Roman conceptions of governance. Italians and senators were no longer seen as masters of the empire who could justly expect to be exempted from the expenses involved in the running of conquered territories, but as two of several groups of subjects, each of which had to make a contribution to the defence of the Roman world against barbarian invasions.

Also in other ways, Late Antique emperors sought to ensure a more equal distribution of the tax burden. As seen above, in the early Roman Empire, the central state had not been involved in the extraction of taxes. Instead, the collection of revenues had been devolved onto the hands of the thousands of autonomous city-states through which the empire was governed.[62] Under Diocletian and his corulers, the fiscal autonomy of municipalities was abolished. All lands across the empire were assessed according to unified measures of account, the *caput* and *iugum*.[63] The introduction of the system of *capitatio-iugatio* meant that all lands in the empire for the first time were assessed according to the same rates. This had two important consequences. On the one hand, municipal lands lost their tax exemptions. Previously, local notables had leased these lands at artificially low rents. In late antiquity, this source of profit was removed. As Gilles Bransbourg has observed, as a result, the revenues of municipal elites declined.[64] On the other hand, the greater involvement of the central state in tax collection offered benefits for previously disenfranchised groups. In particular, rural taxpayers may have profited from the new dispensation. As Campbell Grey has suggested, the fiscal apparatus of the Roman state could be used by peasants to enforce the contractual obligations of their landlords, or to resolve local conflicts in their own favor.[65]

Other fiscal reorganizations further promoted rural prosperity. In the first three centuries C.E., state-owned lands had normally been leased out on limited-term contracts. In late antiquity, they were generally given out on permanent leases (*emphyteusis*). As long as they paid their rents, tenants enjoyed security of ownership on their plots.[66] This provided a strong incentive to invest in expensive hardware. The results of this change in policy can clearly be seen in the archaeological record. As Anne Leone and David Mattingly have shown, the fourth century witnessed a rise in the number of olive presses discovered in the African countryside.[67] There are other signs that some inhabitants of the countryside managed to turn the new fiscal constellation to their own advantage. As Leslie Dossey has observed in her important new study on the north African peasantry in late antiquity, villagers in the fourth and fifth centuries C.E. for the first time obtained access to high-quality ceramics, urban clothing, and that ultimate symbol of Roman-style sophistication, the bathhouse.[68] This is powerful evidence that the fiscal reforms introduced by late antique emperors not only offered new opportunities for graft to well-connected members of the imperial administration (although no doubt there were many such opportunities too), but also provided benefits to a wider group of taxpayers. In particular, the top stratum of the peasantry seems to have profited from the introduction of a more equitable fiscal system. The adoption by emperors of a new image as global rulers enabled them not only to reduce the fiscal privileges of traditionally favored groups, it also made it possible for them to offer the chief public good provided by the Roman state—protection of ownership—to a wider group of imperial subjects.

Law

A second tool in the implementation of new ideals of populist despotism was imperial law. Significantly, it was again under the emperor Diocletian that two legal advisers of the emperor, Aurelius Hermogenianus and Gregorianus, for the first time compiled wide-ranging collections of imperial legislation: the *Codex Hermogenianus* and the *Codex Gregorianus*. It is not clear whether these collections were intended to serve as authoritative law codes in the modern sense, with universal application throughout the empire. More likely, they were the products of private initiatives, undertaken with the emperors' encouragement.[69] On this reading, the purpose of Hermogenianus's and Gregorius's collections was to enhance the predictability of judicial decisions by widely advertising imperial decisions on a great variety of legal questions. In this sense, the publication of collections of imperial law by private lawyers employed by the emperor should be seen not as a weakening, but as an expansion of the infrastructural reach of the Roman state. In line with the new universalist bent in imperial ideology, imperial models of decision making were made more broadly accessible to the general population of the empire than ever before. Nor were these efforts entirely unsuccessful. As Liselot Huchthausen and Serena Connolly have demonstrated in their studies of the *Codex Hermogenianus*, the social range of the people who made use of the imperial system of conflict resolution was remarkably broad. They included not only elites, but also many members of middling strata of society: artisans, small landowners, and soldiers. Significantly too, 26 percent of petitioners were women, and 6 percent were slaves.[70]

Later emperors continued these efforts to use the law as a tool to enhance state infrastructural power, and curb the influence of competing local power brokers. As John Dillon has shown in an important new study, the legislation of Constantine (306–337) is deliberately designed to project an image of the emperor as a heroic protector of the people against the depredations of elites: "he is a firebrand, a populist autocrat, more terrible than majestic, who in one breath proclaims his devotion to the welfare of his subjects and his wariness of the officials he appoints to govern them."[71] Even more radical was the emperor Valentinian I (364–375). As Sebastian Schmidt-Hofner has demonstrated, much of this emperor's extant legislation did not serve a legal, but a communicative purpose—it was carefully calculated to advertise the emperor's fatherly concern for different groups of the imperial population.[72] The high point in these populist attempts by emperors to show themselves as protectors of *all their subjects* was the publication in 438, under the reign of the emperor Theodosius II, of the first authoritative collection of imperial laws: "This code shall permit no order, no ambiguities; it shall be called by our name and shall show what must be followed and what must be avoided by all . . . it shall exclude every contradiction of the law and shall undertake the guidance of life."[73] This *Codex Theodosianus* was now explicitly designed to serve as a universal norm of human life in the empire (*magisterium vitae*). The storage of imperial laws in new authoritative collections, explicitly designed to govern the conduct of the entire population of the empire, is suggestive of the infrastructural effects of the new despotic universalism. As the embodiment of divine justice on earth, the emperor was responsible to bring the law to all of the world's inhabitants. Like the reorganization of fiscality, so also the codification of imperial law is indicative of the ways in which the new ideologies of communal welfare summoned new social groups into collaboration with the imperial state.

Governance

A third field in which the infrastructural impact of the new universal bent in imperial ideology can be traced is imperial governance. In the first three centuries C.E., probably no more than 10,000 officials were directly employed by the central government. In late antiquity, according to an often-cited estimate by A. H. M. Jones, the number of imperial bureaucrats tripled to more than 30,000, and this figure is probably still too low.[74] Not only the size, but also the internal structure of the administration changed. Previously, access to government had been predominantly regulated through informal networks of friendship and patronage. In late antiquity, posts and services in the imperial administration were officially sold. At first sight, this privatization of government functions could be seen as a symptom of state weakness. But as William Novak has demonstrated in his paper on the "myth of the weak American state," which provides one of the conceptual underpinnings of this volume, infrastructural strength cannot exclusively be measured by the size of the resources that stand under direct control of public institutions. Rather, states derive much of their power from co-opting civil-society groups for their own purposes. Such "public-private" partnerships often play a crucial part in expanding the role played by the state in the settlement of conflicts and in the redistribution of resources.[75] It is in this context that the marketization of government functions in the later Roman Empire may most profitably be understood. As Christopher Kelly points out, the sale of public posts and public services should not be seen as corrosive of state authority, but on the contrary made the imperial administration more independent from the demands of aristocratic networks of patronage and friendship. Of course, most imperial administrators were recruited from local notables. Manifold ties of obligation connected them to their peers and relatives in provincial city-councils. Still, the fact that imperial administrators had purchased their posts—and thus no longer exclusively owed their preeminence to the recommendations of leading families in the regions in which they governed—meant that they were more independent from outside influence than they had been in previous centuries: "access to Roman government was made possible without the necessity of entanglement in a web of endless reciprocal obligations."[76]

Like the sale of public of offices, the extraction of fees for governmental services also expanded the reach of the Roman state. Kelly shows that fees for the resolution of a court case at one of the newly created imperial courts of late antiquity cost 121 bushels of wheat, the approximate equivalent of the yearly subsistence needs of a peasant family. Under such conditions, most inhabitants of the empire did not employ the newly expanded imperial administration for the resolution of conflicts.[77] But for urban artisans and the wealthiest stratum of the peasantry, the expansion of the reach of the state was a beneficial development. They were no longer quite as dependent on the power of local landowners and urban elites as they had been in previous centuries.

From this perspective, like the sale of office, the sale of government services was a symptom not of a weakening, but of a strengthening of state capacity. More inhabitants of the empire than ever before made use of the mechanisms for conflict resolution provided by the institutions of the Roman state.

But equally important was the impact of these developments on the self-understandings of the imperial population. As Clifford Ando observes, the administrative institutions of the Roman state—based on expectations of predictability, repetitiveness, and equal treatment—engendered a distinctive form of rationality amongst the governed. By using the imperial judicial system, litigants came to see themselves as subjects of a state—of an impersonal set of institutions from which they could reasonably expect equitable treatment and some minimal form of judicial protection.[78] The expansion of the state administration spread this imperial subjectivity amongst larger sections of the population. This change in self-understandings had concrete material effects. As Leslie Dossey notes, if late antique peasants were less willing than their early imperial predecessors to accept traditional practices of exploitation such as usury and debt slavery, this was not only due to the diffusion of Christian ideals of justice, but also the product of the penetration of state institutions into the provincial countryside. The exposure to the normative texts of the Roman state made peasants less willing to put up with blatant disregard of law by their superiors.[79]

Similarly, the open sale of offices and services by the imperial government contributed to eroding traditional social distinctions. The fact that access to state institutions depended no longer exclusively on rank and patronage power, but was open to everybody who was able and willing ready to pay the requisite sums of money, reconfigured expectations of justice amongst wider sections of the population. The late fourth-century orator Libanius was shocked to find that when the inhabitants of the Syrian countryside were unhappy with the performance of their traditional patrons—members of the city-council of Antioch—they simply bought new ones amongst ex-officers of the imperial army stationed in the region.[80] Of course, Libanius was one of the landowners affected by this decision; his denunciation of the ways in which the late antique expansion of state power upended traditional hierarchies cannot be taken as accurate representation of actual events.[81] Still, his account is suggestive of the wider effects of the late antique expansion of state infrastructure. The expansion of the imperial administration not only increased the control of emperors over the resources produced by their subjects. It also changed the self-understandings of the inhabitants of the Roman Empire. New expectations of rationality, based on market exchange and the normative force of written documents, gained ground over older forms of interaction, based on gift giving and the authority of custom.

Like the new taxation system and publication of new universalizing law codes, so also the expansion of the imperial administration made a real contribution to realize some of the equalizing aspirations of late antique imperial ideology. As wider sections of the population were accepted as equal participants in imperial law courts and self-directed economic actors, it became harder for elites to enforce traditional expectations of deference and obsequiousness amongst their inferiors. In this sense, the self-presentation of Diocletian and his successors as populist despots who defended the entire citizenry of the empire against depredations by the state elite was not an empty boast. The reforms introduced by late antique emperors gave wider sections of the imperial population than ever before access to the benefits of infrastructural power.

Infrastructural Power and Its Discontents

In highlighting the infrastructural achievements of the Roman state, this chapter has drawn on a rich harvest of scholarly work that in the last decades has reconfigured our understanding of late imperial governance. In the light of this work, we are now able to see that the later Roman Empire was in important senses the culmination of millennia-old processes of state formation in western Eurasia, whose timid beginnings Seth Richardson has analyzed, and whose continuations in archaic Greece is the subject of Emily Mackil's contribution to this volume. But precisely because the later Roman state was so successful in the building of institutions that harnessed the energies of its subjects for its own purposes, it also enables us to see with particular clarity the price paid for such intensification of infrastructural power.

It was still an exceedingly small part of the population of the empire which profited from the new infrastructural capacities acquired by the late antique state. The villagers who had sufficient wealth and political connections to invest their proceeds into olive presses and permanent leases of imperial lands, and managed to exploit the taxation system created by late antique emperors for their own purposes, needed to have significant material resources at their disposal. Similarly, the litigants who profited from the monetized judicial system, the universalist objectives of which have been analyzed by Dillon and Schmidt-Hofner, constituted only a small part of the inhabitants of the late Roman countryside. Finally, those who could afford to buy the services of (or a position in) the privatized imperial administration, whose workings have been elucidated by Kelly, must have constituted an even tinier stratum of the population of the Roman Empire. The great majority of the inhabitants of the Mediterranean world continued to be excluded from the state infrastructure built up by late antique emperors. On the contrary, for the largest section of the population, the fact that the coercive and fiscal apparatus of the Roman state reached more deeply into the Roman countryside may have increased the intensity of exploitation. On this reading, the new wealth to which inhabitants of the countryside obtained access in late antiquity may reflect not only a distribution of resources from city dwellers to peasants, but also greater levels of inequality between peasants.

Here we must not forget the ubiquity of slavery in the later roman countryside, highlighted in an important recent study by Kyle Harper. He suggests that the robust networks of private and public cooperation created by the late Roman state significantly served the purpose to keep in check a massive slave population.[82] From this perspective, the acceptance by large sections of the Roman populace of an emperor who fashioned himself as *dominus*, "master," over the population of the empire takes on a different meaning. For the urban elites and wealthy peasants, who formed the backbone of the new social coalition on which the stability of the later Roman Empire was based, subjecting themselves to the rule of a despot may have been a small price to pay for the maintenance of their own rule over the human cattle kept on their lands and in their houses. Both on the highest and on the lowest rungs of the social ladder, at the court of the emperor and in a provincial slave household, despotic and infrastructural power may have looked deceptively alike.

NOTES

1. On the circumstances of composition and literary texture of Ammianus's history, see the masterful accounts of Matthews 1989, Barnes 1998, and G. Kelly 2008.

2. Ammianus Marcellinus, *Res Gestae* 15.5.18 (ed. W. Seyfarth) *Diocletianus enim Augustus omnium primus externo et regio more* (thus Traube, Novák, Heraeus and Seyfarth, but the reading in G is *extero ritu et regio more) instituit adorari, cum semper antea ad similitudinem iudicum salutatos principes legerimus*.

3. Alföldi 1934.

4. Canepa 2009, 149–53.

5. See Aurelius Victor, *De Caesaribus* 29.2–4; Eutropius, *Breviarium* 9.26; Hieronymus, *Chronicon* 226c (ed. Helm); Leon Grammaticus, *Chronicon* (ed. Bonn) 82. The sources are translated and analysed by Kolb 2001, 171–75.

6. The link between despotism and Orientalism in classical conceptions of monarchy is traced by Alföldi 1934, 9–25, and is a recurrent theme of Isaac 2004, especially 316–17. The reception of this tradition in early modern Europe is analysed by Anderson 1974, 398–401, and Nyquist 2013.

7. 16.8.12 *medullis provinciarum*. Other denunciations of the relationship between despotism and elite rapacity include Lactantius, *De mortibus persecutorum* 31; Anonymous, *De Rebus Bellicis* 2; and *Panegyrici Latini* 3(11).20. The transformations in monetary and fiscal systems which provided powerful incentives for such rapacity are explored by Banaji 2007.

8. Gibbon's views on the reasons for the decline of Roman virtue are masterfully explored by Ando 2008b and situated in the wider context of Enlightenment historiography in the groundbreaking studies of Pocock 1999 and 2005.

9. Mommsen 1893, especially 351, and the final chapter of Rostovtzeff 1957. The history of scholarship on late Roman governance is incisively analysed by Meier 2003, Rebenich 2008, and Wiemer 2006.

10. Matthews 1989, 253. Other important contributions to the reassessment of late Roman governance include Brown 1992 and C. M. Kelly 2004.

11. Excellent summaries of archaeological research are provided by Kingsley and Decker 2001, Bowden, Lavan, and Machado 2004, and Wickham 2005.

12. The new consensus is elegantly expressed in the recent narratives of late Roman political history provided by Wickham 2009, Harries 2012, and Pfeilschifter 2014.

13. Acemoğlu and Robinson 2012, 157–76, cited at 168.

14. Pocock (1975) masterfully narrates the history of republican thought; Ando (2011, 81–114) incisively dissects the problematic use made by some contemporary strands of this tradition of Roman political theory.

15. Mann 1986, 125–32, cited at 129.

16. Ibid., 113–15, cited at 113.

17. Daltrop, Hausmann, and Wegner 1966, Plate 3. Classic analyses of the ideology that animated early imperial portraiture include Hannestad 1986 and Zanker 1988, 80–100. An outstanding corpus is provided by Fittschen and Zanker 1994.

18. The structure and meaning of the early imperial titulature is elucidated by Kienast 1990, 1–57; Witschel 2011; and Cooley 2012, 488–509.

19. The most powerful analysis of the role played by theatricality in the literature and self-understandings of the early imperial elite is Bartsch 1994.

20. *Digestae* 1.3.31. Brunt 1977 convincingly demonstrates that the exemption of emperors from the law was not a recent innovation, but was already present in the *Lex de imperio Vespasiani*, issued in 69 C.E., and can be traced back to the early first century.

21. Flaig 1992 offers an outstanding sociology of imperial succession in the early Roman Empire.

22. In seeking to revive some aspects of Mommsen's idea of the Principate of a dyarchy between emperor and senate, I am inspired by the work of Winterling 2001 and 2005. What I seek to offer here is a materialist complement to the systems-theoretical approach outlined in those papers.

23. The personal relationships that senators entertained with early emperors is analysed by Wallace-Hadrill 1996 and Winterling 1999.

24. Saller 1982, 75–77 and 169, explores the role played by senators as "brokers" of patronage who connected the emperor with lower-ranking petitioners.

25. Hopkins and Burton 1985 and Eck 2000 magisterially map the workings of the senatorial office-holding system.

26. Winterling 1999, 83–116, brilliantly traces the emancipation of the imperial court from the slave household of the emperor. For an in-depth study of the prosopography and institutional structure of the imperial monarch's servile staff, see Weaver 1972.

27. As clearly emerges from a comparison of the data on early imperial senatorial wealth assembled by Duncan-Jones (1982, 343–44), with the republican fortunes discussed by Shatzman 1975.

28. Lewis 2007, 115, observes that the properties owned by the largest landlords in Han China were ten times smaller than the biggest estates known from the Roman Empire.

29. Yavetz 1969 and Veyne 1976, 477–696 map the relationship of the emperor to the urban population of Rome.

30. Sherwin-White 1973, 221–90.

31. The paradoxical effects of this arrangement are explored by Ando 2016.

32. Garnsey 1970 and Meyer-Zwiffelhoffer 2002, 143–71.

33. Liebenam 1900; Lo Cascio 1999; and Garnsey and Saller 1987, 32–34.

34. Dossey 2010, 103–14.

35. Bang 2008, especially 93–110.

36. Zuiderhoek 2009 shows that under Roman rule, civic elites were richer and invested considerably higher sums in munificence than in the Hellenistic period.

37. See n. 20 above.

38. Roller 2001, 213–88, and Lavan 2011 explore the crucial role played by slavery in making sense of the relationship between emperor and senators.

39. Excellent recent accounts of the socio-political history of the third century are provided by Carrié and Rousselle 1999 and Ando 2012. The dynamics of the Roman frontier are masterfully analysed by Whittaker 1994 and Heather 2009.

40. The groundbreaking study of Peachin 1990 establishes a firm basis for the chronology of the period. Imperial self-presentation in the third century is mapped by Potter 2004, 215–98, and Manders 2012.

41. Kolb 1987; Rees 2004; Leadbetter 2009.

42. Woolf 2012, 192.

43. Stichel 1982, Plate VIII.

44. Smith 1985, 219–21, cited at 219, provides the most incisive discussion of the meaning of late antique portraiture. A brilliant diachronic account of the development of the late imperial image is provided by MacCormack 1981, especially 17–92.

45. See, e.g., *CIL* VII 995=*ILS* 4727; *CIL* VI 32326; *CIL* II 3413=*ILS* 485.

46. See, e.g., *AE* 1963, 140b; *CIL* III 13304=*CIL* XVII 376=*IIulian* 64; *CIL* VI 1193=*CIL* VI 36889.

47. See, e.g., *CIL* VIII 10222=*ILS* 742=*MiliariXIRegio 15*; *CIL* III 3207; *CIL* III 3207=*IIulian* 63.

48. The rise of the term is traced by Noreña 2011, 227–28 and 284–97. On the use of the word as honorific address in private correspondence between aristocrats, and between emperor and aristocrats, see Dickey 2002, 77–99.

49. On the late imperial titulature, see Chastagnol 1988, Rösch 1978, and Weisweiler 2012, 327–28.

50. I explore the political implications of the new ecumenical language in greater detail in Weisweiler 2016, which offers a longer version of the argument articulated in this section.

51. Hölscher 1978; Tanner 2000.

52. The tessellated shape of early imperial sovereignty is analysed by Ando 2011.

53. On the Hellenistic royal image, see Smith 1988 and Hölscher 2009. The adoption of this image by Constantine is brilliantly traced by Bardill 2011.

54. See, e.g., *CIL* VII 995=*ILS* 4727; *CIL* VI 32326; *CIL* II 3413=*ILS* 485.

55. See, e.g., *AE* 1963, 140b; *CIL* III 13304=*CIL* XVII 376=*IIulian* 64; *CIL* VI 1193=*CIL* VI 36889.

56. On ecumenical rhetoric amongst Hellenistic kings, see Ma 1999, 187–88.

57. The problem of how to theorize the political shape of the Roman Empire after the *constitutio Antoniniana* is explored by Ando 2008a.

58. Richardson 2012, cited at 45.

59. On the role played by moral goods in the expansion of infrastructural power, see also the remarks of Richardson and Mackil in this volume.

60. Giardina 1986.

61. The senatorial tax regime in late antiquity is analysed by Gera and Giglio 1984 (direct taxes) and Giglio 2007 (euergetism).

62. See n. 33 in this chapter.

63. Carrié 1994.

64. Bransbourg 2008.

65. Grey 2011, 178–225.

66. Vera 1986.

67. Mattingly and Leone 2004.

68. Dossey 2010, 62–100.

69. Corcoran 1996, 25–42. On the newly discovered fragments of the *Gregorianus*, see Corcoran and Salway 2010.

70. Huchthausen 1974 and 1976, as well as Connolly 2010, 67–82, explore the social composition of petitioners in the *Codex Hermogenianus*.

71. Dillon 2012, 258.

72. Schmidt-Hofner 2014.

73. *Codex Theodosianus* 1.1.5 . . . *qui nullum errorem, nullas patietur ambages, qui nostro nomine nuncupatus sequenda omnibus vitandaque monstrabit*. . . . *praetermissa inanem*

verborum copiam recusabit, alter omni iuris diversitate exclusa magisterium vitae suscipiet . . . On the motives behind the publication of the Code, see Matthews 2000, 1–9 and 168–99, and Sirks 2007, 36–53.

74. Jones 1964, 3.341–42, and Bagnall 1993, 66. For problems with this low estimate, see C. M. Kelly 2004, n. 10, 268, and Wickham 2005, 73.

75. Novak 2008.

76. C. M. Kelly 2004, 107–85, cited at 112.

77. Ibid., 139–42.

78. Ando 2000.

79. Dossey 2010, 173–94.

80. Libanius, *Oratio* 47.

81. Carrié 1976.

82. Harper 2011.

BIBLIOGRAPHY

Alföldi, A. 1934. "Die Ausgestaltung des monarchischen Zeremoniells am römischen Kaiserhof." *Mitteilungen des deutschen archäologischen Instituts. Römische Abteilung* 49:3–118 (=A. Alföldi [1970]. *Die monarchische Repräsentation im römischen Kaiserreiche*, 1–120. Darmstadt: Wissenschaftliche Buchgesellschaft.

Acemoğlu, D., and Robinson, J. A. 2012. *Why Nations Fail: The Origins of Power, Prosperity and Poverty.* New York: Crown Publishers.

Anderson, P. 1974. *Lineages of the Absolutist State.* London: Verso.

Ando, C. 2000. *Imperial Ideology and Provincial Loyalty in the Roman Empire.* Berkeley: University of California Press.

———. 2008a. "Aliens, Ambassadors, and the Integrity of the Empire." *Law and History Review* 26 (3): 491–519.

———. 2008b. "Narrating Decline and Fall." In *A Companion to Late Antiquity*, edited by P. Rousseau, 59–76. Oxford: Blackwell.

———. 2011. *Law, Language and Empire in the Roman Tradition.* Philadelphia: University of Pennsylvania Press.

———. 2012. *Imperial Rome AD 193 to 284: The Critical Century.* Edinburgh: Edinburgh University Press.

———. 2016. "Making Romans: Democracy and Social Differentiation under Rome." In *Cosmopolitanism and Empire: Universal Rulers, Local Elites, and Cultural Integration in the Ancient Near East and Mediterranean*, edited by M. Lavan, R. Payne, and J. Weisweiler, 169–86. New York: Oxford University Press.

Bagnall, R. S. 1993. *Egypt in Late Antiquity.* Princeton, N.J.: Princeton University Press.

Banaji, J. 2007. *Agrarian Change in Late Antiquity: Gold, Labour, and Aristocratic Dominance.* Oxford: Oxford University Press.

Bang, P. F. 2008. *The Roman Bazaar: A Comparative Study of Trade and Markets in a Tributary Empire.* Cambridge: Cambridge University Press.

Bardill, J. 2011. *Constantine, Divine Emperor of the Christian Golden Age.* Cambridge: Cambridge University Press.

Barnes, T. D. 1998. *Ammianus Marcellinus and the Representation of Historical Reality.* Ithaca, N.Y.: Cornell University Press.

Bartsch, S. 1994. *Actors in the Audience: Theatricality and Doublespeak from Nero to Hadrian.* Cambridge, Mass.: Harvard University Press.

Bowden, W., L. Lavan, and C. Machado 2004. *Recent Research on the Late Antique Countryside.* Leiden: Brill.

Bransbourg, G. 2008. "Fiscalité impériale et finances municipales au IVe siècle." *Antiquité Tardive* 16:255–96.

Brown, P. R. L. 1992. *Power and Persuasion in Late Antiquity: Towards a Christian Empire.* Madison: University of Wisconsin Press.

Brunt, P. A. 1977. "Lex de Imperio Vespasiani." *Journal of Roman Studies* 67:95–116.

Canepa, M. P. 2009. *The Two Eyes of the Earth: Art and Ritual of Kingship between Rome and Sasanian Iran.* Berkeley: University of California Press.

Carrié, J.-M. 1976. "Patronage et propriété militaires au IVe siècle: objet rhétorique et objet réel du discours 'sur les patronages' de Libanius." *Bulletin de Correspondance Hellénique* 100:159–79.

———. 1994. "Dioclétien et la fiscalité." *Antiquité Tardive* 2:33–64.

Carrié, J.-M., and A. Rousselle. 1999. *L'Empire romain en mutation.* Paris: Éditions du Seuil.

Chastagnol, A. 1988. "Le formulaire de l'epigraphie latine officielle dans l'antiquite tardive." In *La terza età dell'epigrafia: Colloquio AIEGL-Borghesi 86 (Bologna, ottobre 1986),* edited by A. Donati, 11–65. Faenza: Lega.

Connolly, S. 2010. *Lives Behind the Laws: The World of the Codex Hermogenianus.* Bloomington: Indiana University Press.

Cooley, A. E. 2012. *The Cambridge Manual of Latin Epigraphy.* Cambridge: Cambridge University Press.

Corcoran, S. 1996. *The Empire of the Tetrarchs: Imperial Pronouncements and Government, AD 284–324.* Oxford: Oxford University Press.

Corcoran, S., and B. Salway. 2010. "A Lost Law-Code Rediscovered? The Fragmenta Londiniensia Anteiustiniana." *Zeitschrift der Savigny Stiftung für Rechtsgeschichte: romanistische Abteilung* 127:677–78.

Daltrop, G., U. Hausmann, and M. Wegner. 1966. *Die Flavier: Vespasian, Titus, Domitian, Nerva, Julia Titi, Domitilla, Domitia.* Berlin: Gebrüder Mann.

Dickey, E. 2002. *Latin Forms of Address: From Plautus to Apuleius.* Oxford: Oxford University Press.

Dillon, J. N. 2012. *The Justice of Constantine: Law, Communication and Control.* Ann Arbor: University of Michigan Press.

Dossey, L. 2010. *Peasant and Empire in Christian North Africa.* Berkeley: University of California Press.

Duncan-Jones, R. 1982, *The Economy of the Roman Empire: Quantitative Studies.* Cambridge: Cambridge University Press.

Eck, W. 2000. "Emperor, Senate and Magistrates." In *The Cambridge Ancient History Volume XI: The High Empire, AD 170–192*, edited by A.K. Bowman, P. Garnsey, and D. Rathbone, 214–37. Cambridge: Cambridge University Press.

Fittschen, K., and P. Zanker. 1994. *Katalog der römischen Portraits in den Capitolinischen Museen und den anderen kommunalen Sammlungen der Stadt Rom Band 1: Kaiser und Prinzenbildnisse*. Mainz: Philipp von Zabern.

Flaig, E. 1992. *Den Kaiser herausfordern: Die Usurpation im Römischen Reich*. Frankfurt: Campus Verlag.

Garnsey, P. 1970. *Social Status and Legal Privilege in the Roman Empire*. Oxford: Clarendon Press.

Garnsey, P., and R. P. Saller. 1987. *The Roman Empire: Economy, Society and Culture*. Berkeley: University of California Press.

Gera, G., and S. Giglio. 1984. *La tassazione dei senatori nel tardo impero romano*. Rome: Bulzoni.

Giardina, A. 1986. "Le due Italie nella forma tarda dell'impero." In *Società romana e impero tardoantico 1: Istituzioni, ceti, economie*, edited by Giardina, A., 1–36. Bari: Laterza.

Giglio, S. 2007. "Il 'munus' della pretura a Roma e Costantinopoli nel tardo impero romano." *Antiquité Tardive* 15:65–88.

Grey, C. 2011. *Constructing Communities in the Late Roman Countryside*. Cambridge: Cambridge University Press.

Hannestad, N. 1986. *Roman Art and Imperial Policy*. Aarhus: Aarhus University Press.

Harper, K. 2011. *Slavery in the Late Roman World, AD 275–425*. Cambridge: Cambridge University Press.

Harries, J. 2012. *Imperial Rome AD 284 to 363: The New Empire*. Edinburgh: Edinburgh University Press.

Heather, P. 2009. *Empires and Barbarians: Migration, Development and the Birth of Europe*. London: Macmillan.

Hölscher, T. 1978. "Die Anfänge römischer Repräsentationskunst." *Mitteilungen des deutschen archäologischen Instituts. Römische Abteilung* 85:315–57.

———. 2009. *Herrschaft und Lebensalter: Alexander der Grosse: politisches Image und anthropologisches Modell*. Basel: Schwabe.

Hopkins, K.H., and G. Burton 1985. "Ambition and Withdrawal: The Senatorial Aristocracy under the Emperors." In *Death and Renewal*, edited by K. Hopkins, 120–200. Cambridge: Cambridge University Press.

Huchthausen, L. 1974. "Kaiserliche Rechtsauskünfte an Sklaven und in ihrer Freiheit angefochtene Personen aus dem Codex Iustinianus." *Wissenschaftliche Zeitschrift der Wilhelm-Pieck-Universität Rostock* 23:251–57.

———. 1976. "Zu kaiserlichen Reskripten an weibliche Adressaten aus der Zeit Diokletians (284–305 u. Z.)." *Klio* 58:55–85.

Isaac, B. H. 2004. *The Invention of Racism in Classical Antiquity*. Princeton, N.J.: Princeton University Press.

Jones, A. H. M. 1964. *The Later Roman Empire 284–602: A Social, Economic, and Administrative Survey.* Oxford: Blackwell.
Kelly, C. M. 2004. *Ruling the Later Roman Empire.* Cambridge, Mass.: Harvard University Press.
Kelly, G. 2008. *Ammianus Marcellinus: The Allusive Historian.* Cambridge: Cambridge University Press.
Kienast, D. 1990. *Römische Kaisertabelle: Grundzüge einer römischen Kaiserchronologie.* Darmstadt: Wissenschaftliche Buchgesellschaft.
Kingsley, S. A., and M. Decker, eds. 2001. *Economy and Exchange in the East Mediterranean during Late Antiquity.* Oxford: Oxbow.
Kolb, F. 1987. *Diocletian und die erste Tetrarchie: Improvisation oder Experiment in der Organisation monarchischer Herrschaft?* Berlin: Walter de Gruyter.
———. 2001. *Herrscherideologie in der Spätantike.* Berlin: Akademie Verlag.
Lavan, M. 2011. "Slavishness in Britain and Rome in Tacitus' *Agricola.*" *Classical Quarterly* 61 (1): 294–305.
Leadbetter, B. 2009. *Galerius and the will of Diocletian.* London: Routledge.
Lewis, M. E. 2007. *The Early Chinese Empires: Qin and Han.* Cambridge, Mass.: Harvard University Press.
Liebenam, W. 1900. *Städteverwaltung im römischen Kaiserreiche.* Leipzig: Duncker & Humblot.
Lo Cascio, E. 1999. "*Census* provinciale, imposizione fiscale e amministrazioni cittadine nel Principato." In *Lokale Autonomie und römische Ordnungsmacht in den kaiserzeitlichen Provinzen vom 1. bis 3. Jahrhundert*, edited by W. Eck and E. Müller-Luckner, 197–211. Munich.
Ma, J. 1999. *Antiochos III and the Cities of Western Asia Minor.* Oxford: Oxford University Press.
MacCormack, S. 1981. *Art and Ceremony in Late Antiquity.* Berkeley: University of California Press.
Manders, E. 2012. *Coining Images of Power: Patterns in the Representation of Roman Emperors on Imperial Coinage, A.D. 193–284.* Leiden: Brill.
Mann, M. 1986. "The Autonomous Power of the State: Its Origins, Mechanisms and Results." In *States in History*, edited by J.A. Hall, 109–136. Oxford: Blackwell. Originally published 1984. *Archives européennes de sociologie* 25:185–213.
Matthews, J. F. 1989. *The Roman Empire of Ammianus.* London: Duckworth.
———. 2000. *Laying Down the Law: A Study of the Theodosian Code.* New Haven, Conn.: Yale University Press.
Mattingly, D., and A. Leone. 2004. "Vandal, Byzantine and Arab Rural Landscapes in North Africa." In *Landscapes of Change: The Evolution of the Countryside in Late Antiquity and the Early Middle Ages*, edited by N. Christie, 135–65. Aldershot, Hants: Ashgate.
Meier, M. 2003. "Das späte Römische Kaiserreich ein 'Zwangsstaat'? Anmerkungen zu einer Forschungskontroverse." In *Freedom and its Limits in the Ancient World: Proceedings*

of a Colloquium Held at the Jagiellonian University Kraków, edited by D. Brodka, J. Janik, and S. Sprawski, 193–213. Kraków: Jagiellonian University Press.

Meyer-Zwiffelhoffer, E. 2002. *Politikos archein: zum Regierungsstil der senatorischen Statthalter in den kaiserzeitlichen griechischen Provinzen*. Stuttgart: Franz Steiner.

Mommsen, T. 1893. *Abriss des römischen Staatsrechts*. Leipzig: Duncker & Humblot.

Noreña, C. F. 2011. *Imperial Ideals in the Roman West: Representation, Circulation, Power*. Cambridge: Cambridge University Press.

Novak, W. J. 2008. "The Myth of the 'Weak' American State." *American Historical Review* 113 (3): 752–72.

Nyquist, M. 2013. *Arbitrary Rule: Slavery, Tyranny, and the Power of Life and Death*. Chicago: University of Chicago Press.

Peachin, M. 1990. *Roman Imperial Titulature and Chronology: AD 235–284*. Amsterdam: Gieben.

Pfeilschifter, R. 2014. *Die Spätantike: der eine Gott und die vielen Herrscher*. Munich: C. H. Beck.

Pocock, J. G. A. 1975. *The Machiavellian Moment: Florentine Political Thought and the Atlantic Republican Tradition*. Princeton, N.J.: Princeton University Press.

———. 1999. *Barbarism and Religion Volume Two: Narratives of Civil Government*. Cambridge: Cambridge University Press.

———. 2005. *Barbarism and Religion Volume Three: The First Decline and Fall*. Cambridge: Cambridge University Press.

Potter, D. S. 2004. *The Roman Empire at Bay, AD 180–395*. London: Routledge.

Rebenich, S. 2008. "Late Antiquity in Modern Eyes." In *A Companion to Late Antiquity*, edited by P. Rousseau, 77–92. Oxford: Oxford University Press.

Rees, R. 2004. *Diocletian and the Tetrarchy*. Edinburgh: Edinburgh University Press.

Richardson, S. 2012. "Early Mesopotamia: The Presumptive State." *Past and Present* 215 (1): 3–49.

Roller, M. B. 2001. *Constructing Autocracy: Aristocrats and Emperors in Julio-Claudian Rome*. Princeton, N.J.: Princeton University Press.

Rösch, G. 1978. *Onoma basileias: Studien zum offiziellen Gebrauch der Kaisertitel in spätantiker und frühbyzantinischer Zeit*. Vienna: Verlag der Österreichischen Akademie der Wissenschaften.

Rostovtzeff, M. I. 1957. *The Social and Economic History of the Roman empire*. Oxford: Clarendon Press.

Saller, R. P. 1982. *Personal Patronage under the Early Empire*. Cambridge: Cambridge University Press.

Schmidt-Hofner, S. 2014. "Ostentatious Legislation: Law and Dynastic Change, AD 364–365." In *Contested Monarchy: Integrating the Roman Empire in the Fourth Century AD*, edited by J. Wienand, 67–99. Oxford: Oxford University Press.

Shatzman, I. 1975. *Senatorial Wealth and Roman Politics*. Brussels: Latomus.

Sherwin-White, A. N. 1973. *The Roman Citizenship*. Oxford: Clarendon Press.

Sirks, B. 2007. *The Theodosian Code: A Study*. Friedrichsdorf: Éditions Tortuga.

Smith, R. R. R. 1985. "Roman Portraits: Honours, Empresses, and Late Emperors." *Journal of Roman Studies* 75:209–21.

———. 1988. *Hellenistic Royal Portraits.* Oxford: Oxford University Press.

Stichel, R. H. W. 1982. *Die römische Kaiserstatue am Ausgang der Antike: Untersuchungen zum plastischen Kaiserporträt seit Valentinian I. (364–375 v. Chr.)* Rome: Bretschneider Editore.

Tanner, J. 2000. "Portraits, Power and Patronage in the Late Roman Republic." *Journal of Roman Studies* 90:18–50.

Vera, D. 1986. "Enfiteusi, colonato e trasformazioni agrarie nell'Africa Proconsolare del tardo impero." *Africa Romana* 4:287–93.

Veyne, P. 1976. *Le pain et le cirque: sociologie historique d'un pluralisme politique.* Paris: Éditions du Seuil.

Wallace-Hadrill, A. 1996. "The Imperial Court." In *The Cambridge Ancient History Volume X: The Augustan Empire, 43 BC–AD 69*, edited by A. K. Bowman, E. Champlin, and A. Lintott, eds., 283–308. Cambridge: Cambridge University Press.

Weaver, P. R. C. 1972. *Familia Caesaris: A Social Study of the Emperor's Freedmen and Slaves.* Cambridge: Cambridge University Press.

Weisweiler, J. 2012. "From Equality to Asymmetry: Honorific Statues, Imperial Power and Senatorial Identity in Late-Antique Rome." *Journal of Roman Archaeology* 25:319–350.

———. 2016. "From Empire to World-State: Ecumenical Language and Cosmopolitan Consciousness in the Later Roman Aristocracy." In *Cosmopolitanism and Empire: Universal Rulers, Local Elites, and Cultural Integration in the Ancient Near East and Mediterranean*, edited by M. Lavan, R. Payne, and J. Weisweiler, 187–208. New York: Oxford University Press.

Whittaker, C. R. 1994. *Frontiers of the Roman Empire: A Social and Economic Study.* Baltimore, Md.: Johns Hopkins University Press.

Wickham, C. 2005. *Framing the Early Middle Ages: Europe and the Mediterranean 400–800.* Oxford: Oxford University Press.

———. 2009. *The Inheritance of Rome: A History of Europe from 400 to 1000.* London: Allen Lane.

Wiemer, H.-U. 2006. "Staatlichkeit und politisches Handeln in der römischen Kaiserzeit - einleitende Bemerkungen." In *Staatlichkeit und politisches Handeln in der römischen Kaiserzeit*, edited by Wiemer, H.-U., 1–40. Berlin: Walter de Gruyter.

Winterling, A. 1999. *Aula Caesaris: Studien zur Institutionalisierung des römischen Kaiserhofes in der Zeit von Augustus bis Commodus (31 v. Chr.–192 n. Chr.).* Munich: Oldenbourg.

———. 2001. "'Staat', 'Gesellschaft' und politische Integration in der römischen Kaiserzeit." *Klio* 83:93–112.

———. 2005. "Dyarchie in der römischen Kaiserzeit: Vorschlag zur Wiederaufnahme der Diskussion." In *Theodor Mommsens langer Schatten: Das römische Staatsrecht als bleibende Herausforderung für die Forschung*, edited by W. Nippel and B. Seidensticker, 177–198. Hildesheim: Olma.

Witschel, C. 2011. "Der Kaiser und die Inschriften." In *Zwischen Strukturgeschichte und Biographie: Probleme und Perspektiven einer neuen Römischen Kaisergeschichte, 31 v. Chr.–192 n. Chr.*, edited by A. Winterling, 45–112. Munich: De Gruyter Oldenbourg.

Woolf, G. 2012. *Rome: An Empire's Story.* Oxford: Oxford University Press.

Yavetz, Z. 1969. *Plebs and Princeps.* Oxford: Clarendon Press.

Zanker, P. 1988. *The Power of Images in the Age of Augustus.* Ann Arbor: University of Michigan Press.

Zuiderhoek, A. 2009. *The Politics of Munificence in the Roman Empire: Citizens, Elites and Benefactors in Asia Minor.* Cambridge: Cambridge University Press.

CHAPTER 6

Territorializing Iran in Late Antiquity: Autocracy, Aristocracy, and the Infrastructure of Empire

RICHARD PAYNE

In late antiquity, the architects of the Iranian Empire superimposed a mythical geography on the Near East that gave way, over the four centuries of its existence, to partially territorialized, infrastructural powers that far surpassed those of their ancient Near Eastern predecessors. More frequently known as the Sasanian Empire after its ruling dynasty, replacing the adjective "Sasanian" with "Iranian" foregrounds the centrality of a mythical conception of time and space to its organization of the empire, and also gives preference to the self-designation of its elites over scholarly convention. The Iranian court and its aristocrats understood themselves as the rulers of Ērānšahr, or "Iran" as a shorthand, a mythical-geographical entity that was the re-instantiation of the cosmically apposite political order that had pertained at the origins of a once-unified world during the era of Zoroaster, the bringer of true religion to humanity. As such, the idea of Iran entailed two distinct illusions of time and space: firstly, that Iranian rulers in the present acted in concert with their mythical predecessors in the past; secondly, that the empire they created corresponded with the mythical territory of Ērānšahr, located at the center of the world and distributing power throughout its confines. In asserting its universal sovereignty, the court of the first Sasanian, Ardashir I, still scarcely in command even of its core cities and regions, made what Seth Richardson calls a presumptive claim, more indicative of imperial ambition and fantasy than an actual achievement.¹ Its illusion of mythical-geographical sovereignty would nevertheless eventually enable the court to establish territorial control, however imperfectly, over islands within the imagined space Ērānšahr designated. The relationship between presumptive claims and infrastructural powers in discontinuous, archipelagic territories is the concern of the present chapter.

The history of the empire can be written as an account of how the illusions of Iran enabled the court to surmount the massive cultural and environmental obstacles to the integration of the Near East from Northeastern Arabia to Bactria, in order to sustain the most enduring and extensive continental political system of the ancient world. Iran, in a word, was a useful lens through which to perceive, to structure, and to unify geographically disparate lands with neither a sea nor an agrarian heartland at its center. In light of the central position of space in Iranian political thought, the relationship between geographies imagined and real accounts for the unique shape of the infrastructural apparatus through which the Iranian court ruled its territories and subordinate populations. The renewal of archaeological research, in particular, allows for the recovery of the dynamic interplay of natural landscapes and geographical conceptions and for the reconstruction of a process of the territorialization of Iranian sovereignty, in a constellation of infrastructures across its 3000 km axis. Viewed from its constituent landscapes, the palpable effects of a mythical geography in the making of the Iranian Empire can be discerned.

A focus on infrastructures places the shifting relations of kings of kings and aristocrats—the central drama of Sasanian history—in a geographical context. The Iranian court has often seemed, to contemporary Roman, medieval Muslim, and modern observers alike, to have embodied despotic power in its archetypal form, with kings of kings exercising command over their subjects without the constraints of laws, organized communities, or rival political authorities, by means of a docile and efficient bureaucratic apparatus. This representation derives ultimately from the rulers themselves, who were portrayed at court and in various media as the sovereigns of the world standing in the place of Ohrmazd, the supreme deity, on earth. And the image of a highly sophisticated Iranian administration, especially influential under the Abbasids, had its foundation in the revamping of the fiscal system in the late Sasanian period.² But Iranian despotism is a chimera. A well-entrenched aristocracy, often tracing its origins to the Parthian period, with autonomous sources of wealth and status constrained the Sasanians continually to renegotiate the terms of their autocracy.³ This was a Janus-faced political system with two distinct, if interdependent, forms of rule, autocratic and aristocratic.[4] The relations of aristocrats and autocrats have been explained episodically and prosopographically, and a more or less reliable narrative of the political history of the various dynasties—that nevertheless leaves a number of questions unanswered—has emerged over the past several decades.[5] What these studies definitively demonstrate is that any power the Sasanians acquired was accumulated by means of, rather than at the expense of, the aristocracy. Some historians have recently taken the ongoing strength of the aristocracy as an indication of the inherent weakness of an Iranian court that depended on the cooperation of noble houses to field its armies and to exploit its resources.[6] Such studies have, however, either downplayed or ignored the large-scale territorial interventions of the court, ranging from the construction of cities in the third century to the large-scale infrastructural projects that transformed the regions of Azerbaijan and Gorgan in the late Sasanian period, ca. 450–636 C.E.[7] The objective of this chapter is to locate the ongoing constitution and reconstitution of Iranian political order in the spaces in which claims to autocratic sovereignty were territorialized—that is, were translated into infrastructures that sustained the rule of the court irrespective of the capacity of individual kings of kings to act despotically. Analyzing the Iranian Empire from the perspective of such processes of territorialization helps to escape the historiographical deadlock that narratives of Iranian weakness have precipitated.

The study of the production of sovereign space moves beyond the vagaries of personal politics to discern how the powers of autocracy could expand within an aristocratic order. To speak of space as "produced" is to evoke a sociological and geographical literature that has taken its inspiration from the work of Henri Lefebvre.[8] The central insight of these scholars is that space is an active agent in historical development, not the canvas on which events occurred. The spaces of empires, cities, and other political formations were artificial and fluid rather than stable, fixed, or pre-given. They had to be created. The creation of a space, in other words, was not necessarily a precondition for a sovereign state, but the very process through which states were constructed and reconstructed.[9] And the processes through which state spaces were produced themselves restructured the relations of their human authors. The term "territory" refers to a particular form of state space, to "a bundle of political technologies" that allowed rulers to demarcate and control terrain.[10] The process of territorialization involves the establishment and maintenance of boundaries, the continuous authority of a sovereign, and the containment and exploitation of its material resources. The making of a territory requires the dismantling of preexisting boundaries, authorities, and claims to resources, and thus the process of territorialization requires a form of deterritorialization. States can therefore be conceived as entities that effectively deterritoralize and reterritorialize in the shifting political and economic circumstances they encounter.[11] These approaches to sovereign space are particularly salient in discussions of ancient empires that aspired to transcend the particularities of place while simultaneously entrenching structures of domination in particular regions. Unlike the post-Westphalian states on whose models ancient historical analyses have often implicitly been based, they aimed not to create territorially continuous sovereign spaces, but rather to disrupt pre-existing spatial orders in favor of a theoretically deterritorialized imperial order that actually operated through an archipelago of territories reorganized in their service.[12] Given the constraints of ancient technologies of communication and transportation, the continuous exercise of authority throughout the extent of the Assyrian, Achaemenian, Roman, or Iranian empires was impossible. Even modern states depend on artificially constructed, "miniaturized" spaces in which the extensive authority of their aspirations can be intensively exercised.[13] What was needed for the functioning of an empire were conceptions of space and structures of territory that allowed them to achieve a balance between extensive and intensive rule through a network of—often discontinuous—territorialized sovereign spaces.

At its inception, Ērānšahr entailed a mythical-geographical conception of rule extending universally throughout the world, from the empire that comprised its center and its source of legitimate political authority into the subordinate states arrayed around Iran, to whose rulers the Iranians were believed to have delegated powers. The "territory (šahr) of the Iranians (ērān)" referred to a mythical kingdom, known in the Avesta as Airyana Vaējah, the homeland of Zoroaster.[14] If modern scholars typically locate the historical origin of Zoroaster in the eastern Iranian world around 1000 B.C.E., for ancient Zoroastrians neither chronological nor geographical precision were of importance for a complex of myths whose usefulness resided precisely in its malleability.[15] The idea of Iran announced on the earliest coins of the kings of kings rendered the members of the ruling Sasanian dynasty the successors of the mythical rulers of the homeland of Zoroaster, by virtue of their reestablishment of the mythical territory of Airyana Vaējah/Ērānšahr.[16] The empire was the central region of the world's seven climes, over which the Iranians exercised their rule indirectly through subordinate kings, such as the Roman emperors who were styled as tributary "Caesars" (*kēsar*).[17] The Iranian rulers described themselves, from the reign of Shapur I, as "the kings of kings of Iran and non-Iran."[18] Iranian sovereignty was constituted through the subjugation of the rulers of non-Iranian territories (*anērān*)—especially the Romans—through martial or diplomatic encounters and, perhaps more importantly, the communication of the successful subordination of outside powers to the kings of kings through the media the court produced. In the rock reliefs of the third century, for example, the kings of kings represented themselves as having subjected the rulers of Rome and India to themselves by force.[19] By the end of the fifth century, the collection of tributary payments from the Romans and the reception of envoys from as far afield as the Northern Wei and Sui dynasties of China came symbolically to underpin the universal sovereignty of the Sasanians more reliably than military victories.[20] Ērānšahr thus implied territorial limits between Iran and non-Iran, the management of which was as important as the establishment of universal authority for the successful exercise of kingship. If the space of Iran was defined with respect to its exterior limits, the role of the court in maintaining the appropriate relationship between Iran and non-Iran offered opportunities for the reorganization of space within its frontiers.

Within this framework of extensive rule, the court created spaces of intensive rule in particular regional landscapes that territorialized its powers. In the following sections, two distinct stages will emerge in the territorializing of Iran. The early Sasanian stage, circa 226–438, punctuated the preexisting landscape of Parthian subkingdoms with cities—often named for their royal founders—as islands of imperial authority, without creating the infrastructural capacities to constrain the aristocracy. The late Sasanian stage, circa 438–636, witnessed the creation of infrastructural complexes of cities, interlocking fortifications, and attendant systems of irrigation in strategic regions—Gorgan (at the southeast corner of the Caspian Sea), Azerbaijan, and perhaps others—that not only maximized the exploitation of resources on behalf of the court, but also effectively caged the aristocracy within walls of their own making. The rescaling of the empire in the fifth century took place in precise political circumstances: the arrival of nomadic imperialists, the Huns, on Iran's northern and northeastern frontiers. After conquering the province of Bactria as well as Sasanian satellites in Kabul and Gandhara, the Huns formed an existential threat to an empire with few geographical boundaries separating its core provinces from the Central Asian steppes. The resulting reorganization of imperial resources resulted in a recalibration of the relations of autocracy and aristocracy that the infrastructural projects of the fifth century embodied and entrenched. The political crisis the Huns provoked ultimately gave way, through the creation of new forms of sovereign space on the part of the court, to an autocracy with significantly expanded powers of coercion. If the greater strength of the late Sasanian court in comparison with its early Sasanian predecessor is a truism in virtually all accounts of the empire's history, a focus on spatial transformations places the conventional explanations of the shift in a longer-term, more gradual infrastructural rescaling. The more efficient fiscal and military administrations of the sixth century were as much the products of this transformation as its causes, and accounts of their establishment in terms of the personal politics of individual rulers, such as a Husraw I that medieval and modern historians alike have idealized, miss the newly established territorial structures that made them possible.

The Two Faces of Iranian Power

The Iranian ideology of empire contained models for the configuration of the political order that preserved aristocratic autonomy within an autocratic structure. The *ēr* of Ērānšahr were not simply the mythical-historical ancestors of the Sasanians, but also their aristocratic associates, the Parthian and other houses that claimed to have descended from the great nobles of Airyana Vaêjah.[21] The universal sovereign was to cooperate with aristocratic allies who were equally indispensable to the cosmic struggle. In practice, this entailed the inclusion of the Parthian aristocracy—such as the great noble houses of Mihrān, Surēn, and Karin—in the Iranian political order with their ancestral territories and authorities intact.[22] The relationship between autocratic and aristocratic forms of rule was therefore a central concern of Iranian political thought, preoccupying the artistic and literary specialists of the court. In the early Sasanian rock reliefs, there were attempts to harmonize the autocratic power of the kings of kings with the aristocratic power of their nobles. On the one hand, the kings of kings were presented as cosmic rulers whom the gods had entrusted to organize human collective action on their behalf.[23] If not gods themselves, they enjoyed intimate access to the divine and served as intermediaries between the supernatural and natural realms.[24] This proximity to the divine distinguished the kings of kings from all other men, whether aristocratic or common, and the Sasanians successfully established a monopoly on *xwarrah*, the manifestation of divine sanction, for the four centuries of their rule.²⁵ On the other hand, the kings of kings were dependent on an aristocracy that could be conceived and represented as a partner in rule. In the reliefs of Ardashir I and Shapur I, aristocratic cavalrymen were portrayed accompanying the kings of kings at their investitures and military victories, most dramatically at Bishapur (relief III), where they appear in serried ranks providing the martial power necessary for Shapur I to establish political order.²⁶ The Sasanians, the court insisted in such reliefs, could not fulfill their cosmological functions without an aristocracy, a variegated coalition of men who placed their own localized forms of rule in the service of an overarching, universalist project. At this early stage, the court of Shapur I portrayed the emerging empire as an amalgam of autocracy and aristocracy.

The historically specific meanings of these two analytical terms require unpacking. The etymologies of autocracy and aristocracy recall the importance of identifying the source of the raw power—*kratos*—that animates a particular political order. Iranian autocracy evolved from ancient Near Eastern traditions of kingship that granted the power to command men and commandeer materiel to a divinely sanctioned ruler, on whom the establishment of peace and prosperity was incumbent. Its sources of power were twofold: the complex of religious institutions that subordinated a population to kings and the material resources—including humans—placed at their disposal within an ideological system that predisposed subjects to obey a single individual granted *kratos*, the "autocrat." As Richardson argues in this volume, the capacity of autocrats to command was remarkably minimal in the absence of territorialized infrastructures and sometimes in inverse proportion to their ideological claims. Distinguishing the Iranian autocracy from its predecessors was not only the Zoroastrian religion, but also its co-constitution with aristocracy. "The rule of the best" describes the exercise of power on the part of a group that defined itself as superior in value—ethically, physically, and/or religiously—to the subjects under its command.²⁷ It is, in essence, a collective autocracy. The sources of its power were identical, even if its scale was usually more localized than the rule of a king. Aristocratic formations seem incompatible with autocracy only superficially, and in fact the relationship between the two forms of rule was normally symbiotic, at least in the imperial polities of the Near East from the Iron Age onward. Autocratic at the supra-regional level, the Achaemenian, Roman, and Iranian empires were aristocratic at local levels. They could be imagined as Chinese boxes, in which nested aristocracies combined to form an autocratic whole. The political order was indeed represented as the layering of aristocrats extending from the ground to the heavens in the relief of Shapur I at Bishapur. Wherever discernible in the sources, the exploitable earth and its laboring population appear uniformly under the authority of aristocrats in the Iranian Empire, ranging from comparatively humble "free man" (*āzād*) who might command little more than a modest domain, a handful of laborers, and a horse, to Parthian great nobles who commanded entire regions and armies composed of such *āzād*. Autocratic at the center, the Iranian Empire was an aristocracy all the way down.

On account of the power of aristocratic dynasties sometimes as rich in land and men as the early Sasanians, recent accounts of the empire regard its structure as inherently frail. The great houses, especially the Parthians, are supposed to have obstructed the attempts of the court to develop organizational capacities that surpassed their own. The recent publication of seals showing that the leading military commanders and religious officials were drawn from the ranks of the great houses and were as proud of their aristocratic lineages as of their imperial offices has reinforced a narrative of the Iranian court as haplessly dependent on refractory aristocrats more interested in their own autonomy than in empire. According to Parvaneh Pourshariati and Zeev Rubin, the Parthians and other aristocrats were relentlessly opposed to the centralization of power. They regularly withdrew their cavalrymen from Iranian military campaigns, rejected the Zoroastrian religion and the imperial ideology, and prevented the officials of the court from levying taxes on their lands.[28] To borrow the phrase of William Novak, the apparent contradictions of autocracy and aristocracy have underpinned a "myth of the weak Iranian state," an account that underestimates the power of the imperial apparatus on the basis of its failure to develop the salient features of an idealized, highly centralized, and bureaucratic state.[29] Critiques of this minimalist account of Iranian power equally endorse the Weberian state as the model against which the strength of an ancient empire should be measured. At the opposite end of the historiographical spectrum, this alternative view contends that the Iranian court effectively centralized power at the expense of the aristocracy in the fifth and sixth centuries, creating a bureaucracy that executed royal dictates, levied taxes, organized and distributed resources, and commanded elites consistently throughout the territories of the empire.[30] The maximalists envision the imperial apparatus as a hegemonic, homogenous, and omnipresent structure.[31] The reforms of Kawad I and Husraw I are supposed to have brought a *Dienstadel* into being, an elite wholly dependent on the court for its status.[32] While the minimalists abandon the terms state and empire in favor of confederacy, the maximalists insist on describing the political system as a state, without qualification. Neither approach fully captures the dynamics at work in Iranian politics.

As Novak has suggested for studies of the American state, recovering the historically particular logic governing the acquisition, distribution, and articulation of power can resolve the apparent contradictions in the structure of a given political system. In the Iranian conception of political order, autocracy and aristocracy were interdependent, and this arrangement allowed the court to penetrate provincial societies and landscapes to an unprecedented degree through the co-optation of localized forms of rule. With underdeveloped technologies of control, discipline, and surveillance, the court depended on local powerbrokers for its organizational capacities. If the Sasanians were successful at centralizing power, they did so paradoxically through a simultaneous decentralization, the widespread authorization of landowning elites to act in the name of the court and to adopt its insignia and language. Rather than despots, the kings of kings were coordinators of aristocrats. The most successful of them consolidated and expanded aristocratic networks, instead of disrupting them. Persuasion, not coercion, was their primary instrument of rule. The collaborative relationship of autocracy and aristocracy was safeguarded through a set of constitutional norms governing the accession, rule, and deposition of kings of kings. The major aristocratic houses participated in the selection of the ruler from among the members of the house of Sasan. The deliberative processes through which they achieved consensus were publicly disclosed at the accession of the king of kings Narseh in 293, in the *Inscription of Paikuli*.[33] Here aristocrats gathered in a "council" (Middle Persian: *hanjaman*) to select the most "righteous" (Parthian: *rʾštstr*) candidate for the throne, the Sasanian best equipped to subject the Romans and secure peace and prosperity for Ērānšahr.[34] The promulgation of the procedures in an inscription at Paikuli, a major crossroads between Mesopotamia, the Iranian plateau, and the Caucasus, was intended to constitute norms that rendered a king of kings legitimate through the collective consent of the aristocracy as a whole, rather than merely the Sasanian dynasty or another subgroup of the imperial elite. A king of kings claiming the throne without broad-based aristocratic support was henceforth self-evidently illegitimate. Implicit in the claim to select their rulers on the basis of their righteousness was the authority to evaluate the ethics of royal action, to ensure the justice of Iranian rule. A frequently exercised right of rebellion thus accompanied the aristocratic appointment of kings of kings.[35] The great majority of Sasanians perished at the hands of rebellious nobles, who with only two short-lived exceptions always placed another member of the house of Sasan on the throne. The collaboration of autocracy and aristocracy was at times highly antagonistic, as the ruling elite competed for powers and privileges in a zero-sum game that often resulted in the executions of autocrats and aristocrats alike. But their commitment to Ērānšahr was stable at a structural level. If individual kings of kings were ephemeral, the adherence of the aristocracy to the ruling house was remarkably consistent across four centuries, making the Sasanians the most successful dynasty in the Near East since the Neo-Assyrians.[36] The co-constitution of autocracy and aristocracy at Paikuli remained in place until the Arab conquests.

The sources of autocratic and aristocratic power nevertheless evolved at different rates, with the court accumulating technologies of communication, economic resources, the rudiments of bureaucracy, and, above all, territorial infrastructures on a scale even the grandest of aristocratic houses could not achieve. There were two institutional roles the aristocracy accorded to the kings of kings that allowed them to transform their autocratic rule into territorialized powers that could be exercised over, rather than merely through, aristocrats: the first is their organization of military campaigns against Iran's neighbors, the subordination of which supported their claims to universal sovereignty and brought an influx of prestige goods and human labor in the form of captives; the second is their augmentation of Iran's material prosperity, through the creation of urban centers that served as sites of production and exchange. Peace and prosperity appear as the signature contributions of kings of kings to Ērānšahr in the *Inscription of Paikuli* and elsewhere. If the source of Iranian military power always remained the aristocracy, the economic resources of the court were autonomous from the beginning. The so-called cities the kings of kings founded throughout the empire were primarily conceived as centers of administration and industrial production, in which deported captives, such as Roman artisans, were settled to produce high-value commodities for markets as well as military supplies.[37] *Bazār* is, after all, a Middle Persian word of Sasanian origin.[38] The human resources expropriated from the Roman world were royal property, and the commodities they produced provided the court with the silver vessels, ceremonial gold, and brocade textiles for the gift economy through which the court consolidated its relations with the aristocracy. More important for economic growth was the construction of irrigation systems at the initiative of the court in Mesopotamia, Khuzestan, and, as will be discussed in greater detail, Azerbaijan and Northeastern Iran. As Robert Adams demonstrated, Sasanian canals increased the arable lands of Mesopotamia and Khuzestan to their greatest extent in antiquity.³⁹ The verdant plains of these regions reinforced the ideological claim of the kings of kings to have been restoring the world, while filling royal coffers with ever-increasing revenues in silver from the land tax. The aristocracy was directly involved in these developments, participating in transregional trade and constructing irrigation systems in their own patrimonies.⁴⁰ But the royal domination of Mesopotamia and Khuzestan, as well as the regions of late Sasanian infrastructural projects, ensured that economic growth gradually strengthened autocracy vis-à-vis aristocracy, in terms of both its economic and ideological resources of power, even as the court continued to depend on aristocratic cavalrymen to conduct its campaigns.

The differential development of aristocratic and autocratic powers manifests itself most clearly in their distinct territorial forms. The basis of the rule of kings of kings and aristocrats alike was the *dastgird*, "what is held under the hand," a patrimonial territory a dynasty administered and exploited directly.⁴¹ To return to Paikuli, the *dastgird* is the source of power under contestation between the two factions of the elite, between the supporters and opponents of Narseh: the usurping party promised to expropriate the *dastgird* of the aristocrats opposing their candidate for the throne, in order to augment their own domains and to secure their authority in the future. The inscription of Shapur I on the Ka'ba of Zoroaster referred to the territories under direct Sasanian control as the "*dastgird* of the king," suggesting these units could be transregional and discontinuous.⁴² In the third-century inscriptions, the empire appears as a network of *dastgird* over which autocrats and aristocrats were functionally autonomous, and the extension of the *dastgird* was the upshot of victory in political struggles such as the contestation of the throne in 294. The scale of the *dastgird* varied enormously from the house of an *āzād* to the Sasanians, but the nature of territorial control was more or less identical. Even at this early stage, however, two spatial entities were invoked to define distinctly royal spheres of authority that encompassed or complemented the *dastgird*: Ērānšahr itself, and the royal cities. The king of kings possessed the "rule of the realm" (*šahr xwadāyīh*) over Ērānšahr, an authority primarily associated with the maintenance of security.⁴³ The court (*dar*) from which this authority was exercised was located in a "city" (*šahrestān*) in central Mesopotamia known as Wahrām-Šāpur, "Victory of Shapur," likely in commemoration of Shapur I's victories over the Romans. Such a geographically extensive authority rooted in a localized center indicates an incipient process of territorialization. But the infrastructural capacities of the court were evidently minimal at the end of the third century. The allies of Narseh established what appear to have been makeshift "border watch-posts" (*pāhrag*) to prevent their enemies from seizing the royal center in Asōrestān, central Mesopotamia, in the absence of preexisting mechanisms of regulating movement within Iran.[44] The journey of Narseh from Armenia to Mesopotamia to take the throne brought him through the domains of "border people and the mountain dwellers" (*marzīg ud kōfyār*), groups evidently beyond the control of the court.[45] In the third century, the court could exercise territorial control only irregularly in lowlands, and the highlands remained beyond its remit. Iranian rule would remain discontinuous, with wide swathes of the Zagros and the Alborz Mountains as well as the deserts of the Iranian plateau often in the hands of poorly known groups—such as the Daylamites, "Kurds," and Alans—that participated only intermittently in empire and occasionally interrupted to plunder its perquisites.[46] In the cultivable lowlands that were the primary concern of agrarian empire, however, the Iranian court sought to exercise greater control through territorial interventions in the form of shrines, cities, and, in the fifth century, regional infrastructural complexes. The cumulative effect of these processes was to transform the idea of Iran into a landscape that simultaneously communicated imperial ideology and controlled the resources of the court.

The Infrastructures of Iran: Shrines and Šahrestān

The shrines and cities the early Sasanians constructed endowed the nascent court with limited, localized infrastructures that distinguished their rule from their Parthian royal predecessors as well as from the aristocracy. Among the first acts the king of kings Ardashir I was believed to have accomplished was the destruction of the temples of the Parthians and the erection of new shrines in their place.[47] Despite substantial overlap in Parthian and Sasanian Zoroastrian religious practice, the court sought to empower a priestly elite drawn from the ranks of its aristocratic associates, which was institutionalized in so-called fire temples that were sites for the performance of the Yasna ritual. The leader of this network of religious specialists in the third century, the *mowbed* Kirdir, boasted of having established fire temples throughout the empire, a claim that, in light of current archaeological research, appears to have been exaggerated.[48] What is clear is that the court constructed at least five regional religious centers that served as sites of royal ritual, pilgrimage, and administration, and that structured the movements of elites through imperial space.

They were administrative centers of particular consequence in regions where the infrastructural footprint of the early Sasanians was either minimal or nonexistent: Azerbaijan, Khurasan, and Sistan.[49] In the early Sasanian period, however, they functioned more to disseminate imperial ideology than to levy taxes on regions in which the aristocracy retain a high degree of autonomy. The shrines commemorated politically potent events from the mythical past in regional landscapes, connecting the Kayanian and Sasanian dynasties in space as well this time. Of the known regional shrines, the two sites of Kayānsīh (Kuh-e Khwaja) in Sistan and Ādur Gušnasp (Takht-e Suleyman) in Azerbaijan have been excavated, revealing vast temple complexes with administrative as well as ritual functions. Kayānsīh was likely constructed in the third century, while Ādur Gušnasp only became a shrine of almost urban proportions in the course of the fifth, with a renovation in the sixth.[50] By the fifth century, Ādur Gušnasp was a destination of royal pilgrimage at the accession of kings of kings and at moments of religious significance such as military victories.[51] Other shrines similarly attracted not merely royal, but also elite pilgrims at regular or irregular intervals, instilling a shared subjective experience of Ērānšahr as a network of shrines at which the mythical time-space of the Iranians was reenacted. Visitors to Ādur Gušnasp, for example, recalled the gods granting universal rulership on Kay Husraw, a Kayanian ancestor of the Sasanians, at the mythical lake Čēčast. The shrines territorialized the myths of Iranian ideology while housing an embryonic imperial apparatus of Zoroastrian priests.

Šahrestān were, in material terms, the most important initial anchors of Ērānšahr. To recall the names of the urban centers the early Sasanian kings of kings established is to list the slogans of imperial ideology. Ardašīr-Xwarrah ("The Supernatural Glory of Ardashir"), Bīšāpur ("The Divine Shapur"), and Ērān-xwarrah-Šāpur ("The Supernatural Glory of Shapur of the Iranians") offer a handful of the dozens of cities founded in the third and fourth centuries that constituted emblems of Ērānšahr.[52] The translation of *šahrestān* as "city," in the most general sense, designates the concentration of populations in fortified centers of political authority. They were, however, hardly cities in the Hellenistic sense. They were typically new foundations built according to plans that themselves reinforced the ideological content of their titles: the concentric plan of Ardašīr-Xwarrah with irrigation channels radiating outward rendered the city a kind of paradise, while large-scale fire temples stood at the centers of Bīšāpur and perhaps other hitherto unexcavated cities.[53] As their names suggest, they were closely linked with royal authority, serving the administrative and economic functions that have already been outlined. Often hewn from pristine landscapes, they were the earliest instances of Sasanian territorialization, the nodal points of heavily irrigated hinterlands on which the kings of kings wielded direct authority, likely forming components of the royal *dastgird*.[54] Laboring captives provided the bulk of the population of early Sasanian *šahrestān*, which were thinly settled within their walls and whose functions were primarily economic. They were concentrated in Mesopotamia, Khuzestan, and Fars, in fertile regions that also supervised movement in and out of the Iranian highlands and plateau, effectively forming a constellation of cities extending from the Roman frontier at Nisibis (itself a Sasanian city from 363) to Dārābgird at the southwestern borderlands of Fars. Trade was, accordingly, nearly as important as agricultural production in augmenting the fisc of the urban Sasanians. Accompanying their *bazār* were mints that issued the silver coinage of consistently high quality that was characteristic of Sasanian rule.[55] As centers of production, market, and minting, cities gave the kings of kings control of the lucrative transregional exchange that linked the often isolated provinces of a continental empire. The cities of the early Sasanians were ideal sites for communicating to aristocrats the benefits of their rule. The court facilitated the growth of arable land through irrigation, population through deportation, and liquid capital through the minting of silver of unprecedented purity. These were interrelated phenomena that benefited not only the court, but also its aristocratic allies, who sold their agrarian commodities and invested in trade in urban markets with a privileged, tax-free status and received salaries and/or gifts in silver.[56] The grandiose ideological claims the names of cities announced were thus not without basis, as they served to crystallize the relations of autocrats and aristocrats around a shared vision of the political order that the wealth of the *šahrestān* underpinned.

The infrastructural capacities of the cities were nevertheless minimal. They could serve to invite aristocrats to participate in their economic structures, but could in no way constrain the actions of elites who could easily circumvent them in their transregional movements. The aristocracy, after all, never exchanged their rural estates for urban residence.[57] This was an infrastructure of persuasion rather than compulsion. Cities were, moreover, notably absent from the great bulk of the landmass that Ērānšahr was supposed to have encompassed. As Pourshariati has recently emphasized, the early Sasanians failed to establish cities in Azerbaijan, Khurasan, Sistan, or the Caspian regions of Tabaristan and Gorgan, forming an arc from the northwestern corner of the empire to its southwestern frontiers.⁵⁸ In the northeastern quadrant of the empire, Merv, Nishapur ("The Good of Shapur"), and—sometimes—Balkh anchored Sasanian power, but there were few infrastructural traces of their rule in the vast intervening territories.⁵⁹ These were precisely the regions known to have been the strongholds of the great aristocratic houses. The major urban center, Rayy (to the south of modern Tehran), retained its Parthian plan and exhibited substantial archaeological continuity from the Parthian through the Sasanian periods.⁶⁰ The Mihranids were centered in the districts of Rayy, the Surenids in Sistan, and the Karinids in Khurasan.⁶¹ The highlands of the Caucasus and Azerbaijan remained in the hands of Armenian and Albanian dynasties of Parthian origin throughout the Sasanian period.⁶² Cities within these regions were known for their fractiousness, as staging grounds for aristocratic rebellion. Husraw II ultimately resorted, at least reportedly, to destroying Rayy, at the geographical heart of the empire, for undermining Sasanian rule.⁶³ Until the fifth century, the kings of kings abstained from even attempting to establish cities in these regions, in a tacit acknowledgment of the limitations of their capacities. The first known city to have been constructed in the name of a king of kings in the northern regions of the empire—Šahrestān-Yazdgird, a foundation of Yazdgird II (438–457), identified with the site of Torpakh-Kala on the Caspian coast, twenty kilometers south of Derbend in modern Dagestan—was a harbinger of the development of new forms of infrastructural power that would fundamentally recalibrate the relations of autocrats and aristocrats.⁶⁴

The Infrastructures of Iran: The Complexes of Gorgan and Azerbaijan

Large-scale infrastructural projects in the fifth century territorialized Iranian power on a significantly grander scale than the *šahrestān* and shrines of the early Sasanians. There are two interconnected regions that recent archaeological research has shown to have been transformed on the part of the court simultaneously, circa 430–480: Gorgan, a strip of arable land at the southeast corner of the Caspian between the Alburz and Kopet Dagh Mountains; and Azerbaijan, known as *ādurbādagān* in Middle Persian, a much larger, more amorphous geographical entity that extended roughly from Lake Urmia to where the Caucasus Mountains meet the Caspian at Derbend.⁶⁵ On both sides of the Caspian, the court combined extensive walls, fortified settlements, and irrigation systems in a package of territorial interventions that inscribed its authority in landscapes in which the autocracy had previously been largely invisible. In Gorgan, a robust, mudbrick wall extended 180 km from the Caspian Sea into the highlands of the Kopet Dagh, with a string of thirty-six fortresses that were continually occupied throughout the fifth and sixth centuries.[66] Behind the wall, as many as sixteen fortified settlements (roughly 45 ha in size; their tent pegs are still visible) housed mobile cavalry units, as well as, in some cases, centers of military and fiscal administration.[67] The construction of irrigation canals augmented the arable land in Gorgan and in neighboring Dehistan, just beyond the wall.[68] In Azerbaijan, a similar assemblage of walls, fortified settlements, and irrigation systems took shape, encompassing a wider swathe of territory from the fertile Mughan Steppe, the modern frontier between Iran and Azerbaijan, to the so-called Caspian Gates at Derbend, roughly 500 km to the north, the only overland point of access available for a cavalry-based army from the steppes of what is now southern Russia to enter Iran and Anatolia.[69] A mudbrick wall 8 m thick was erected between the Caucasus mountains and the sea at Derbend in the middle of the fifth century and rebuilt in stone in the course of the sixth, when the wall was extended, together with upward of a dozen fortresses, 42 km into the highlands.[70] Two other walls extended inland from the Caspian to the highlands, 150 km to the south: Ghilghilchay, a 4 m thick mudbrick wall with upward of 300 towers, and Besh Barmaq, a secondary defensive wall that remains to be surveyed.[71] A series of fortresses and fortified settlements adjoined these walls, and Šahrestān-Yazdgird was located in the plain between Derbend and Ghilghilchay. At the same time, a network of at least nine fortified settlements ranging from 10 to 70 ha in size was constructed in the Mughan Steppe, roughly 300 km to the southwest of Ghilghilchay.[72] The largest of these, the heavily fortified Ultan Qalası, was erected rapidly, according to a preconceived plan, in the middle of the fifth century.[73] Ancillary to these military strongholds, structures of irrigation were established, including canals as long as 150 km.

The package of walls, fortified settlements, and systems of irrigation constituted infrastructural complexes through which the Iranian court intensified its rule—through the simultaneous concentration of military forces and increased exploitation of economic resources—across vast geographical spaces that dwarfed the *šahrestān* of the early Sasanian period. Significantly, these structures were installed in regions that were traditionally associated with the Parthian aristocratic houses, marking the assertion of autocratic power in zones of aristocratic autonomy. At the symbolic level, the erection of walls constituted "theatrical act[s]" that embodied a renegotiation of the limits of autocracy in the northern and northeastern regions of Iran.[74] But the walls bounded regions, much as fortified perimeters bounded *šahrestān*, albeit on a scale of hundreds of kilometers rather than hectares. This rescaling of imperial space was a response to a specific political crisis that enabled the kings of kings to assert their territorial authority more directly in the northern and northeastern regions, with aristocratic assent: the arrival of the Huns. After 350, nomadic imperialists challenged the Iranian claim to universal sovereignty, conquering the regions of Kabul and Bactria and leaving the heart of the empire exposed to the steppe.[75] With the cities of Sogdia, Bactria, and the South Caucasus as their bases, the various Hun dynasties combined the resources of sedentary and nomadic state making, allowing them to maintain armies that reliably humbled their Iranian counterparts throughout the fourth, fifth, and sixth centuries.[76] It was only with the assistance of the Turks that the Iranian court eventually dislodged the Huns from Bactria in 557, and the Turks took the region for themselves only shortly thereafter. The loss of the Iranian East posed an infrastructural as well as an ideological dilemma to the kings of kings. At the same time that territorial losses undermined the spatial illusion of Ērānšahr, the court needed to reorganize its resources to prevent the overrunning of Iran and, where possible, to reconquer formally Iranian cities and regions.

In particular, the court had to continually position and to provision cavalry forces on frontiers whose defensibility the Huns—and later the Turks—regularly tested. This required aristocratic warriors accustomed to fighting only a few months a year to remain stationary in encampments at a great distance from the residences and patrimonies to which they were attached. Apart from the infantrymen and federate forces—often Huns or Turks—that played subsidiary roles in support of the cavalry, the vanguard of the Iranian military consisted of the same aristocratic levees that had waged war against the Romans, who were now constrained to be stationed in the north or northeast, whether in the third century or the sixth.[77] The martial leaders and cavalrymen stationed in the fortified barracks along the walls, or in satellite settlements such as Tureng Tepe or Ultan Qalasi, were drawn from the aristocratic houses of Parthia, Fars, Armenia, and elsewhere, who in turn convened and commanded their middling and lesser noble subordinates. The process of mobilization is discernible in the sixth-century Armenian history of Ełiše, according to whom the king of kings Yazdgird II delivered orders to the leaders of the major aristocratic houses to join their counterparts from other regions of the empire on campaigns against the Huns in the northeast, in Gorgan and Khurasan.[78] The lesser nobles, known in Armenian as *azat*, could form contingents of as many as 2,000 cavalrymen; and the great noble houses of Parthia and Fars would likely have had many more dependent nobles, members of the so-called *dahigān* class who were landowners of noble lineage tied through relations of friendship and fosterage with the greater nobles of their respective regions. Such levies could easily have provided the upward of 30,000 men estimated to have campaigned in Gorgan in the sixth century.[79] In the third- and fourth-century wars against the Romans, the convened aristocrats participated in summertime campaigns in the highly urbanized provinces of the eastern Roman Empire, in battle against Roman field armies who conducted themselves in predictable, even homologous ways.[80] The campaigning armies on both sides expected to return to their bases—and, in the Iranian case, to their homes—before the onset of winter.

Such seasonal campaigning was wholly inadequate to repulse the Huns. According to Ełišē, Yazdgird II began with a campaign two years in length before establishing himself and his cavalrymen semipermanently in Gorgan for seven years, 441/2–448/9.[81] The requirement that nobles remain at the frontiers for multiple years of campaigning in a row came as a shock to the Iranian aristocracy. The households of great noble families were anxious, and even vulnerable, in the absence of a paterfamilias serving as a military commander in the distant north or northeast.[82] The campaigning of kings of kings themselves for years at a time interrupted the rhythms of courtly life in the imperial capital. During the course of these decades of permanent campaign during the middle of the fifth century, the court began to erect self-sustaining structures that supported not only the practice of war, but also the authority of the kings of kings in comparatively remote regions.

The complexes of Gorgan and Azerbaijan provided the infrastructures that transformed the seasonal campaign into a permanently mobilized military. The walls straightforwardly deterred their enemies from entering Iranian territory either from the steppes of Dehistan, to the north of Gorgan, or through the Caspian Gates, compelling them to confront the Iranians directly in Khurasan. To the east of Gorgan, Merv and Nishapur functioned as highly fortified nodal points, in the frontiers of which military confrontations were most likely to occur. Rather than a frontline, the Great Wall of Gorgan demarcated a staging ground, a space in which military forces could be concentrated on a permanent basis without fear of incursion. The geographically more extensive complex of Azerbaijan included two such staging grounds, one located between the walls of Derbend and Ghilghilchay, the other in the network of fortified settlements in the Mughan Steppe. The defenses served to facilitate less the immediate waging of war, and more the creation of multipurpose settlements and intensification of agricultural production, which in turn allowed for the continuous provisioning of armies on permanent campaign within striking distance of the front lines in Khurasan, Bactria, and beyond the Caspian Gates.[83]

The convening of elites from across Iran for multiple seasons marked a profound shift in the position of the aristocracy within the empire. Men of various backgrounds—Zoroastrians and Christians, speakers of Armenian, Aramaic, Middle Persian, and Parthian—combined to form a recognizably imperial elite in the common cause of repulsing the Huns and Turks. It was notably in the context of fifth-century campaigning that the problem of Christian Armenian cultural difference first presented itself at the court.[84] Aristocrats were placed, moreover, under the authority of imperial commanders, *marzbān* and *spāhbed*, as a collective for years at a time, even if regional units remained distinct. The deracination of the aristocrats occupying the complexes of Azerbaijan and Gorgan reinforced already existing tendencies toward increased identification with the court, most apparent in the seals of the sixth century that juxtaposed imperial offices with aristocratic lineages. This phenomenon was, at least in part, an effect of the newfound capacity of the court to coerce its elites.

In addition to their defensive and offensive functions, the infrastructural complexes caged the elites that entered their walls. If the study of the fortifications has concentrated on their role in conflicts with intruders from the steppe, the regulation of movement within the empire was an equally important concern of their architects. The walls accompanying Derbend and Gorgan cut through lands that were always part of Iran: Tammishe separated Gorgan from Tabaristan, while Ghilghilchay and Besh Barmaq divided northeastern Azerbaijan.[85] They served two basic military functions: preventing the raiding of the highlanders of the Alborz, in the case of Tammishe; and providing secondary and tertiary lines of defense if Derbend were to be penetrated, in the cases of Ghilghilchay and Besh Barmaq. They monitored the movement—particularly of nomadic warrior elites—between regions.[86] They may also have served as "prepared arena[s] of combat" in which enemies could be entrapped.[87]

But they equally served to enclose and entrap uncooperative aristocrats. As Owen Lattimore has observed with respect to Inner Asia, walls bound populations within particular spaces as often as they excluded them. On China's northwestern frontiers during the pre-imperial and Han periods, they consolidated control over populations that were oriented more toward the steppe than to central China, while enhancing its defensive and offensive capacities vis-à-vis nomadic powers.[88] Such multifunctionality also pertained in the case of the Iranian walls. The laboring population of Azerbaijan and Gorgan included captives from the Roman Empire and elsewhere whose flight into either the highlands or the steppe the walls foreclosed.[89] More important, however, was the regulation of the movement of aristocrats who had hitherto possessed the liberty of returning from a campaign under circumstances of their own choosing. When they sought to depart for their patrimonies, the Armenian aristocrats stationed at Derbend found themselves in a "secure and inescapable prison."[90] Yazdgird II had ordered the commanders of the fortification to prevent their passage into Albania and Armenia. The control over the movement of the elite that the walls gave the court was particularly consequential in the context of frontier regions known as the empire's most refractory. The highlands of the Caucasus and the Caspian were the leading sites of rebellion in the late Sasanian period, notably in 450 and 482 when the Armenian, Georgian, and Albanian aristocracies contested the extent of imperial authority in the Caucasus.[91] These rebellions specifically targeted Derbend, and its reconstruction in stone was likely as much a response to threats from within Iran as from the steppe.[92] The alliances the aristocrats of the Caucasus formed with the Huns suggests the infrastructural complexes were constructed more to keep the aristocracy at the frontiers within the orbit of the court than to repulse invaders, in accordance with Lattimore's model of the Chinese center preventing its frontier populations "from coalescing into centrifugal bodies."[93] The greatest anxiety at the court in Seleucia-Ctesiphon was the possibility of putatively loyal aristocrats taking advantage of their position at the frontiers to forge personal alliances with the Huns.[94]

Interlocking fortifications, together with the presence of elites of varied backgrounds, caged aristocrats whose cooperativeness was flagging. For every rebellious Armenian aristocrat in the sixth-century accounts, there was another who remained loyal to the Sasanians, as well as nobles from beyond the Caucasus with few ties to the aristocracy of the region. Those who nevertheless withdrew from Sasanian service had to confront and to conquer not only the walls and fortified settlements, but the trans-regional forces that occupied them. The court came to enjoy, for the first time in its history, substantial coercive power over the aristocracy through infrastructural complexes that rendered Iranian sovereignty territorial in a manner that was no less potent for its discontinuities. From Gorgan and Azerbaijan, the court sought to exercise greater authority over the aristocracy of neighboring regions, reconstituting the relationship between the two forms of Iranian rule. Again, the evidence is most revealing for Armenia. There the court replaced the client king with an imperial military commander, a *marzbān*, conducted a cadastral survey to facilitate the exaction of taxes, and—most shockingly to the clerical authors of our sources—installed Zoroastrian fire temples in a predominantly Christian region.[95] It is likely that similar extensions of autocratic authority took place elsewhere, in particular in the Caspian regions between Azerbaijan and Gorgan.[96] From the Caucasus Mountains to the steppes of Khurasan, Iran's richest agricultural lands outside of Mesopotamia and Khuzestan were either within infrastructural cages, or within their reach. Iranian rule, however, did not emanate outward, like an ink stain, from its capital to its frontiers, encompassing the intervening spaces in homogenous structures that operated regularly and predictably in the service of the kings of kings. Heterogeneity characterized the elites and the infrastructures of an imperial apparatus that always granted its aristocratic houses a high degree of autonomy in their own patrimonies and adapted to the limitations of local circumstances, whether geographical, social, or cultural in nature. While retaining its resources and privileges, the aristocracy was now caged through territorialized infrastructures that rendered their cooperation with the court as much the result of compulsion as of the persuasion that characterized the political dynamic of the early Sasanian period.

The Late Sasanian Recalibration of Autocracy and Aristocracy

The kings of kings tested the limits of their coercive power over the aristocracy, sometimes despotically. Yazdgird II forcibly castrated a group of elites in his service, compelled non-Zoroastrian aristocrats to venerate the deities of "the Good Religion," and, most importantly, suppressed the aristocratic privilege of annually presenting petitions to the court in the 450s.[97] Possibly to undermine the patrilineal foundation of aristocratic power, Kawad I imposed the institution of wife sharing on at least some elites, during his first reign 488–496.[98] Throughout the sixth and early seventh centuries, Husraw I, Ohrmazd IV, and Husraw II disciplined the aristocracy through violence to an unprecedented degree, executing scores of nobles on account of their supposed religious deviance, rebelliousness, or, in short, political rivalry.[99] In their visual self-representation, the late Sasanian kings of kings eschewed images of collaboration in favor of reliefs that depicted them as exclusive sovereigns, such as the sculpture of Husraw II at Taq-e Bustan.[100] In the literature of the court, Wahram V (r. 420–438) was arguably the last king of kings to have emphasized the collaborative nature of Sasanian rule on the model of Narseh at Paikuli. It was on account of the despotic undertakings and representations of the late Sasanians that the sixth century has been envisioned as an era of bureaucratic centralization, through which a service aristocracy defanged and disciplined the great noble houses. But, as has been noted, acts of suppression and assertions of autocratic authority took place within the framework of a political order that could not dispense with aristocratic sources of power. Each episode of Sasanian despotism was short-lived. There are no reported forced castrations after Yazdgird II; the communal sharing of women almost immediately resulted in a rebellion that reestablished the patrilineal status quo; and late Sasanians only occasionally used the sword against the aristocratic houses from which they continued to recruit their military commanders, fiscal administrators, and religious officials. What took place in the late Sasanian period, as a consequence of territorialization, was neither the elimination nor the erosion of aristocracy, but rather a recalibration of its authority and sources of power in relation to the court.

A restructuring of military and fiscal administration accompanied the development of the regional complexes alongside the preexisting infrastructures of cities and shrines. By the middle of the sixth century, the court had instantiated a hierarchical organization of offices that permitted a remarkably high degree of oversight, effectively constraining the maneuvering room of aristocratic officials who had previously enjoyed greater autonomy. Seals and bullae document the operation of the more centralized Sasanian administration in the sixth century, even if the origins of the system are impossible to date with exactitude. With respect to the military, a division of authority placed four military commanders, *spāhbed*, each in charge of one of the cardinal directions, four territorial circumscriptions radiating outward from Seleucia-Ctesiphon.[101] This system replaced the office of the *ērān-spāhbed*, which had placed military power under the authority of a single aristocrat. The quadripartition not only facilitated the conduct of war on multiple frontiers simultaneously, but also enabled the court to deploy one *spāhbed* against another in cases of revolt.[102] The revamped military administration was thus an effect as well as an instrument of the coercive power of the court: the office of *spāhbed* was held at the behest of the kings of kings, and aristocratic commanders could be dispatched to regions distant from their patrimonies.¹⁰³ The fiscal reforms similarly placed officials acting on behalf of the court in a supervisory role over provincial aristocrats, who had previously controlled the collection of the land tax, regularly or irregularly, in their territories. Crucially, the recurrence of anonymous cosignatories on the official documents of the leading military and fiscal officials points to the presence of agents of the court supervising their activities.¹⁰⁴ The overlapping fiscal and military administrations were mutually reinforcing: expanding revenues enabled the court to compensate its soldiers, to conduct ever more ambitious campaigns, and to invest further in infrastructural projects, such as the reconstruction of the great shrine of Ādur Gušnāsp, the unfinished transformation of the region around Mount Bisutun along the royal road into a complex of imperial palaces and monuments, and the extension of fortifications in the borderlands.¹⁰⁵

The architects of the enhanced administrative capacities of the court were the very aristocrats they constrained. Known *spāhbed* bore the names of the great house of Mihrān on their seals, alongside their titles as "great noble *spāhbed* of the Iranians" (*wuzurg ērān spāhbed*).¹⁰⁶ Other officials similarly boasted of their noble genealogies in their seals, through the listing of house (Kāren, Warāz), regional origin (*pārsīg* [from Fars], *pahlav* [from Parthia]), status as "great noble" (*wuzurg*), or patronymic.¹⁰⁷ What compelled the aristocracy to participate in the extension of the powers of the court? On the one hand, the package of ideological and material incentives that had co-opted the aristocratic houses in the early Sasanian period remained persuasive. The threat from the steppes had, as we have seen, united aristocrats around the ruling dynasty, and the Sasanian reestablishment of political supremacy in the Near East vis-à-vis Rome in the sixth century only further consolidated the imperial network. Even in rebellion, the leading aristocratic houses of the sixth century perceived their commitment to be to the idea of Iran, if not to the house of Sasan. On the other hand, the infrastructural complexes that endowed the court with the entirely novel capacity to monitor, regulate, and obstruct the movements of men across the strategically crucial axes extending from Seleucia-Ctesiphon to the Caucasus and to Central Asia. If the walls of Gorgan and Azerbaijan caged the aristocrats who found themselves within their confines, on a larger, pan-imperial scale, the combination of cities in Mesopotamia, Khuzestan, and Fars and complexes in the north caged aristocrats in the intervening spaces between the readily defensible islands of imperial authority and the fortified staging grounds of imperial military forces. This spatial, geographical situation of the aristocracy will have had a persuasive power of its own, with or without the court exercising its capacities of coercion. But, as the army always remained under the leadership of aristocrats, the great houses could still potentially restrict the ability of the court to take advantage of its geographical infrastructures. Negotiation rather than coercion therefore continued to characterize the relations of autocrats and aristocrats throughout the late Sasanian period, as they redefined the limits of their respective authorities. Nevertheless, the infrastructural capacities of the imperial apparatus raised the stakes during the rebellions that were a routine feature of Iranian political culture, the traditional means for the aristocracy to renegotiate its interests with the court. Rebellions in the sixth century became contests not simply for shares in the perquisites of empire, but rather for control of the territorialized powers the court had created in the fifth century, and for the return of a territorial autonomy the aristocracy had lost.

The revolts of the late sixth century challenged the ideological and infrastructural foundations of Iranian political order, precisely on account of their territorial ambitions, whereas previous interventions had sought to modify existing institutional arrangements, for example through the replacement of one Sasanian with another member of the dynasty. The rebellion of Wahram Chobin, a *spāhbed* of the north, against Ohrmazd IV and Husraw II 590 was the first of only two attempts to supplant the house of Sasan with another ruling dynasty, in this case the house of Mihrān.[108] It was short-lived in comparison with the rebellion of Wistaxm, a *spāhbed* of the northeast, which took control of Azerbaijan, the Caspian regions, Khurasan, and Rayy for at least five years in the 590s. In the first instance, the infrastructural complexes of the north served to support aristocratic rebellion rather than autocratic powers, indicating their potential for subversion in the hands of military commanders. Already ruling Azerbaijan as *spāhbed* of the north, Wahram Chobin began the rebellion after leading Iranian armies to victory in the northeast against the Turks, that is, while his authority encompassed the infrastructures of Gorgan and Khurasan. In control of these complexes as well as their satellite cities, the noble regarded himself as capable of seizing Seleucia-Ctesiphon and supplanting the Sasanians with his own house of Mihrān. He overestimated, however, the capacities of infrastructures and his own army alone, without the cooperation of the other houses. Husraw II returned to power after only a few months, on the strength of aristocratic loyalties to the ruling house Wahram Chobin was unable to break. Tellingly, a supporter of the anti-Sasanian rebellion had advised the *spāhbed* to consolidate a rival state in the northeastern regions that were as defensible against assaults from within the empire as without.[109] This was the approach of the more successful Wistaxm, whose polity, organized around a capital at Rayy, only succumbed to a campaign that reconquered Gorgan. In designating the general dispatched to quell the rebellion the commander of Gorgan, rather than Khurasan or another neighboring region, Husraw II recognized the centrality of its infrastructure to establishing political control over the entire northeastern corner of the empire. With a loyal commander ensconced in Gorgan by 600 at the latest, the king of kings could confidently initiate the most ambitious of Sasanian campaigns in 603: the conquest of the Eastern Roman Empire. At the head of Iranian forces was a *spāhbed* drawn from the selfsame house of Mihrān that had supported the rebellions of Wahram Chobin and Wistaxm, marking the immediate return of even the most recalcitrant of nobles to the service of the court.

The political conflicts of the late sixth century thus centered on control of the infrastructural complexes. They were extreme instances of aristocratic response to the territorialization of the power of the court. They were exceptional crises in the relationship of aristocracy to autocracy in an era that witnessed ever more concerted cooperation on the part of the great nobles in the extension of imperial structures. The role of territorialized infrastructures in the unfolding of the rebellions nevertheless indicates their importance in the recalibration of powers that brought the more robust administrative apparatus of the sixth century into being. Where the rebellions of the third, fourth, and fifth centuries targeted the cities of Mesopotamia, the late sixth-century revolts effectively instrumentalized the infrastructural complexes of the north to establish alternative Irans in the name of Parthian dynasties. The usurpers overestimated the coercive powers at their disposal in Azerbaijan and Gorgan, as Wahram Chobin fatefully discovered almost as soon as he attempted to incorporate Mesopotamia into his nascent realm. Wistaxm's polity endured somewhat longer, but collapsed in the face of the network of nobles loyal to the Sasanians that successfully took Gorgan. What these struggles for Iranian political order make plain is that the operation of Iranian autocracy always required a network of aristocrats commanding their own sources of power working in concert throughout its domains, as well as infrastructural, territorialized powers of its own. The usurping aristocrats were unable to establish a network of aristocratic allies as extensive as what the Sasanians were consistently able to maintain, even if they appropriated the regional bases of autocratic power. The analytical opposition of autocracy and aristocracy has prevented historians of Iran in late antiquity from appreciating the imbrication of the two forms of rule (and the ongoing redefinition of their spheres of authority) that structured Sasanian politics. Just as a Sasanian could not have ruled without the great nobles, so too was a great noble unable to rule without a Sasanian. The creation of infrastructural complexes never allowed the court to dispense with aristocracy, and the transformation of the imperial apparatus in the late Sasanian period should be seen as recalibrating the balance of power between autocracy and aristocracy in favor of the former, without necessarily diminishing the political authority or economic resources of the great nobles. Indeed, the differential development of powers might have allowed the great nobles to become stronger, in political and economic terms, even as their kings of kings became stronger still.

Conclusion

The third-century mythical-geographical concept of Ērānšahr presumed an empire, "a territory of the Iranians," that only gradually took its characteristic, archipelagic form in the physical landscape of the Near East over the subsequent four centuries. The *šahr* over which the kings of kings claimed to rule, as the representatives of the collective of *ēr*, encompassed myriad territorial forms—ranging from the highland fastnesses of pastoralist warriors to the patrimonies of great noble houses—that would always elude the direct wielding of imperial authority. The translation of the idea of Iran into territorialized infrastructures resided in its envisioning of the collaboration of two forms of rule—the autocracy of the kings of kings and the aristocracy of the nobles—whose authorities and territorial forms could complement, and even reinforce, one another, without suppressing their conflicts of interest. That is, the augmenting of Iranian autocratic power either simultaneously advanced the interests of aristocracy or left its preexisting sources of power intact. The territorialization of Ērānšahr through a network of shrines, cities, and infrastructural complexes proceeded with the consent of an aristocracy that granted the kings of kings the authority to serve as an intermediary with the gods, to bring prosperity, and to secure peace on behalf of the ruling class of "Iranians." Cumulatively, the territorialized infrastructures through which the autocrats fulfilled these roles gave the court powers of coercion as well as persuasion vis-à-vis the aristocracy. The creation of the complexes of Gorgan and Azerbaijan in the fifth century marked an important stage in the rescaling of imperial space, a transition from infrastructures of persuasion to infrastructures of coercion. The bounding of entire regions between walls and fortified settlements enabled the court not merely to exploit the resources of the most fertile lands outside of Mesopotamia and Khuzestan, but also to discipline elites within and between the infrastructural complexes. But if the late Sasanians occasionally exhibited despotic tendencies, these acts were interventions in an ongoing negotiation of the roles of autocrats and aristocrats in an Iran that could dispense with neither. The infrastructural complexes compelled elites to cooperate in an ever more concerted fashion, to create the more efficient and pervasive military and fiscal administration of the sixth century, while granting the aristocracy novel opportunities to expand its powers in official capacities. In consolidating its control over frontier zones that defined Iran in relation to non-Iran, the court territorialized Ērānšahr internally, through a horizontal archipelago of infrastructures.

NOTES

The author would like to thank Cliff Ando, Damián Fernández, Myles Lavan, James Osborne, Seth Richardson, and John Weisweiler for their critical comments on various versions of this chapter.

1. Richardson 2012. The claim to have become the "king of the Iranians" (*šāh ērān*) appears soon after the coronation in the recently conquered Ctesiphon in 226/227: Alram and Gyselen 2003, 24–25.

2. See Rubin 1995, for the reform and its Abbasid accounts.

3. Nikonorov 2005, 146–47; Pourshariati 2008; Wiesehöfer 2010b, 137–39; McDonough 2011, 299–300.

4. This approach to the empire as a hybrid, whose workings are best examined through the interplay of two seemingly contradictory forms of rule, draws on Rana 2010.

5. Pourshariati 2008, 59–160, offers the most comprehensive account, to be read alongside Gyselen 2009. But for the early Sasanians, see Weber and Wiesehöfer 2010 and Mosig-Walburg 2010.

6. Rubin 2000; Pourshariati 2008. The arguments are discussed more fully in the following section.

7. As James Howard-Johnston has consistently demonstrated in Howard-Johnston 1995; Howard-Johnston 2008; Howard-Johnston 2012. Pourshariati 2008, 38–41, acknowledged Sasanian control of cities, without regard for their political potency.

8. Lefebvre 1991; Brenner 1999, 39–45.

9. Scott 1998, 186–189. Adam Smith's influential concept of the "political landscape" makes the production, reproduction, and contestation of space the essence of ancient

politics (2003). For a review of recent archaeological approaches to the politics of space and territory, see VanValkenburgh and Osborne 2013.

10. Elden 2013, 322–23.

11. Brenner 1999, 60–63.

12. Osborne 2013, 787, has emphasized the necessarily discontinuous nature of ancient sovereign spaces: "The phenomenon of patchy . . . political authority, what I have called malleable territoriality, constituted a form of territoriality in which authority was not evenly distributed across the landscape, nor contained within a fixed order."

13. Scott 1998, 257–61.

14. Daryaee 2005.

15. See Gnoli 1980, 23–57, for the various attempts to identify the sites of the Avesta's mythical geography.

16. The mythical-historical Avestan dynasty of the Kayanians did not feature in Iranian ideology before the fifth century; see Shayegan 2011, 14–29.

17. "Inscription of Shapur I on the Ka'ba-ye Zardusht," 25–27.

18. Ibid., 22; Alram, Blet-Lemarquand, and Skjaervø 2007.

19. Grenet 2005; Canepa 2009, 53–78.

20. Ecsedy 1979; Payne 2013.

21. For the mythical-historical significance of *ēr*, see Gnoli 1989, 139. It was only in the courtly historiography of the sixth century that Parthian aristocrats were explicitly given Kayanian genealogies; see Pourshariati 2008, 116–18; Payne 2014: 292–93.

22. "Inscription of Paikuli," 56–58; Lukonin 1969, 39–40; Nikonorov 2005, 146–47; Pourshariati 2008, 37–59.

23. Canepa 2009, 59–62; Overlaet 2013.

24. Panaino 2009.

25. The *xwarrah* became increasingly important in the representation of the kings of kings in the course of Sasanian history; see Shenkar 2013, 430–33.

26. Canepa 2009, 57–58.

27. The cultural superiority of an aristocracy underpinned the economic domination normally emphasized in definitions of this form of rule, such as Kautsky 1982, 24: "An aristocracy . . . is a ruling class in an agrarian economy that does not engage in productive labor but lives wholly or primarily off the labor of peasants."

28. Rubin 1995; Rubin 2000; Pourshariati 2008, 59–160, 321–95.

29. Novak 2008.

30. Howard-Johnston 2008; Wiesehöfer 2010a.

31. Characteristic is the description of "un système administratif des provinces tout à fait cohérent . . . établi sur tout le pays"; Gyselen 1989, 96. Howard-Johnston 2014 speaks of an "effective and efficient governmental system, under the firm control of an imperial center," while McDonough 2011, 299, claims the Sasanians "sought to centralize authority through bureaucratization."

32. Wiesehöfer 2010a, 122–23; Wiesehöfer 2010b, 141; McDonough 2011: 299. Howard-Johnston, on the other hand, recognizes the continuity of the "old aristocratic order" (2008, 128).

33. The accession marked the return of one branch of the house of Sasan to the throne and thus a renegotiation of the ruler relations with the aristocracy; see Weber and Wiesehöfer 2010.

34. "Inscription of Paikuli," 56–58.

35. Rubin 2004.

36. For the "millennium of sovereignty" the Assyrian dynasty achieved, see Radner 2010, 26.

37. Morony 2004.

38. Daryaee 2010.

39. Adams 1981, 200–214. For Khuzestan, see Wenke 1975–1976 and Walstra, Heyvaert, and Verkinderen 2010.

40. For a case study of elite investment and irrigation in Fars, see Hartnell 2014. There is also an example of such an episode in the highlands to the north of Khuzestan in a sixth-century East Syrian hagiographical work: "Martyrdom of the Captives," 323–24.

41. Pigulevskaya 1963, 150–53; Skalmowski 1993; Kennedy 2011, 54–58. When its history as an autonomous kingdom under the Arsacid dynasty was recalled, Armenia itself could be described as a *dastgird*: Ełišē 1957, 72; Ełišē 1982, 123.

42. "Inscription of Shapur I on the Kaʿba-ye Zardusht," 43.

43. "Inscription of Paikuli," 32, 35, 36, 55.

44. Ibid., 31.

45. Ibid., 35.

46. Howard-Johnston 2012, 96; Potts 2014, 120–23. For a hitherto neglected early fifth-century account of highlanders from the Alborz raiding the region of Rayy, see "Martyrdom of Miles," 275. The only attempt to reconstruct the social relations of highland communities in the Iranian world concerns the Alans of the North Caucasus, who appear to have experienced increased social stratification in the hands of "noble military leaders" from the fifth century onward; see Korobov 2003.

47. "Letter of Tansar," 22; Boyce 1968, 47.

48. "Inscriptions of Kirdir," 54 and 66–57. Shapur I also boasted of the shrines he had erected; see "Inscription of Shapur I on the Kaʿba-ye Zardusht," 45–48. Hallier 1972 has identified at least one fire temple—at Nakhlak, 240 km to the northeast of Isfahan—securely dated to the third century. Kleisss 2015, 148–53, provides an overview of known fire temples. For the role of fire temples in structuring the experience of regional landscapes, at least from the fifth century, see Huff 1995. Significantly, as the case study of Huff emphasizes, they were often constructed at the behest of the aristocracy.

49. Zoroastrian religious specialists played a leading role in the imperial administration, in the domains of justice, surveillance, and taxation; see Shaked 1990. Christian religious specialists would similarly be enlisted in the administration from 410 onward; see McDonough 2008.

50. Canepa 2013, 70–76, 80–84.

51. Canepa 2009, 15.

52. Metzler 1977, 219–59; Schwaigert 1989, 280–300.

53. Huff 2008, 45–52; Callieri 2009, 53.

54. Lukonin 1969, 42. Imperial cities were sometimes re-foundations, or located alongside preexisting cities, such as Weh-Ardašīr across from the Parthian capital of Ctesiphon; see Huff 2008, 52. With their heavily irrigated hinterlands, *šahrestān* fit James Osborne's model of the more powerful, more deeply territorialized imperial city, in contrast with city-states (2015).

55. Howard-Johnston 2014.

56. The privilege of undertaking transactions in the *bazār* tax-free with emphasized in the *Kārnāmag ī Ardašīr*, a sixth-century account of the first Sasanian directed at an aristocratic audience; see "Kārnāmag ī Ardašīr," 78–79.

57. Kennedy 2006, 12–14.

58. Pourshariati 2008, 41.

59. Nishapur appears to have been founded at the end of the fourth or early fifth centuries; see Rante and Collinet 2013, 9–10, 53. Simpson 2014 provides an overview of Merv under Sasanian rule. Though the center of the Kushano-Sasanian dynasty in the third and fourth centuries, Balkh entered into the hands of the Huns, only to return to Iranian control for brief periods in the late fifth and late sixth centuries; see Gyselen 2003.

60. Rante 2008.

61. Pourshariati 2008, 64.

62. The Sasanians seem to have brought an Arsacid house to the Albanian royal throne, as subordinate kings, in the early fourth century, and they continued to reign until the end of the fifth; see Gadjiev 2015. But of course even after the end of autonomous Armenian and Albanian kingships, in 428 and circa 510, respectively, aristocratic houses of Parthian lineage occupied the provincial military commanderies, with the exception of a mid-fifth-century interlude to be discussed below; see Garsoïan 2009.

63. Firdawsī 1987–2008, v. 8, 233–39.

64. Gadjiev 2008, 284–85.

65. Similar structures, albeit on a smaller scale, appear to have been erected on the southwestern and southeastern frontiers, but they wait archaeological analyses; see Howard-Johnston 2012, 63–65. For textual references, see Mahamedi 2004.

66. Howard-Johnston 2012, 100–101; Sauer et al. 2013, 156–243.

67. Sauer et al. 2013, 303–81.

68. For the extension of irrigation in Dehistan and the ambiguous nature of political authority in the region, see Lecomte 2007, 305–8.

69. The numerous kurgan burials in northern Dagestan dating from the late fourth through fifth centuries attest to the concentration of nomadic military elites in the districts immediately to the north of Derbend; see Gadjiev and Malashev 2014.

70. Gadjiev 2008, 2012.

71. Aliev et al. 2006.

72. Alizadeh and Ur 2007, 151–54.

73. Alizadeh 2011, 74.

74. Squatriti 2002, 17, with reference to the role of the construction of ditches and dikes in the consolidation of the kingdoms of early medieval Europe.

75. Grenet 2002; Howard-Johnston 2010, 41–51.

76. Payne 2016. On the urban centers of the Huns, see Gadjiev 1995 and Grenet 2010.

77. Nikonorov 2005, 153–56; Howard-Johnston 2012, 113–14. The use of federate forces has been taken to indicate the Sasanian pursuit of extra-aristocratic sources of military power; see McDonough 2011, 300. But they operated alongside the aristocrats, who consistently appear in literary and documentary sources as the leaders of the military and its principal cavalrymen.

78. Ełišē 1957, 9–11; Ełišē 1982, 63–65. The roughly contemporary historian Łazar Paʿrpecʿi described the obligation to fulfill such commands as "service and obedience"; see Paʿrpecʿi 1904, 49; Paʿrpecʿi 1991, 87.

79. Howard-Johnston 2012, 110; Sauer et al. 2013, 230–34.

80. Lee 2013, 719, notes Sasanians avoidance of pitched battles on their Roman campaigns.

81. Ełišē 1957, 12; Ełišē 1982, 66.

82. See Bedjan 1987, 644–49, for the case of a fifth-century Mihranid house.

83. On the activities of the Iranian military in the North Caucasus, beyond Derbend, see the study of a Sasanian fortress and possible Middle Persian inscription along the Kuban River in Gadjiev 2013, 57–63.

84. The Armenian historians emphasized the contradictions between Christian and Zoroastrian practices and beliefs in the context of political cooperation. Yazdgird II, for example, was supposed to have required Christian aristocrats to venerate fire; see Paʿrpecʿi 1904, 49; Paʿrpecʿi 1991, 87. If their accounts of Zoroastrian persecution of Christians were exaggerated, intended to support their own visions of orthodoxy, the court viewed religious difference within the aristocracy as a potential problem. Yazdgird II sought not the conversion of Armenian aristocrats, but rather professions of loyalty to the empire in religious terms some Christian leaders could not accept; see McDonough 2006, 73–74. Such dilemmas were products of the increased inter-aristocratic intimacy of the fifth-century campaigns.

85. Sauer et al. 2013, 252–72. On the late Sasanian administration in Tabaristan, a geographical term from the early Islamic period for a series of provinces, see Gyselen 2012.

86. As Lecomte 2007, 310–11, suggests, "far from blocking the advancing tide of nomads at the northern frontiers of the empire, [the walls] rather played the role of obligatory passage in order to control the progressive infiltration of populations who are beginning to settle over all the territory of Hyrcania." Malashev, Gadzhiev, and Ilyukov 2015, 9–10, 137–158, emphasize a Sasanian interest in co-opting nomadic groups, while documenting their withdrawal from the Caspian rural south of Derbend in the course of the wall's construction.

87. Howard-Johnston 2012, 104.

88. Lattimore 1940, 480–83. For an updated discussion that focuses on the multiple functions of the Chinese walls, see Di Cosmo 2002, 138–58.

89. For deportees in Gorgan, see Fiey 1971, 332.

90. Ełišē 1957, 19; Ełišē 1982, 72. Armenian nobles were similarly trapped within the city gates of Nishapur; see Paʿrpecʿi 1904, 93; Paʿrpecʿi 1991, 140–41.

91. On the rebellions, see Garsoïan 2009.

92. Ełišē 1957, 78; Ełišē 1982, 129–30; Paʿrpecʿi 1904, 66; Paʿrpecʿi 1991, 108.

93. Lattimore 1940, 482. Ełiše 1957, 12, 78; Ełiše 1982, 66, 129–30; Pa'rpec'i 1904, 66; Pa'rpec'i 1991, 108.

94. The mere accusation of such an alliance resulted in the removal of the *marzbān* of Armenia, Vasak, from office: Łazar Parpʻecʻi, *Patmutʻiwn Hayocʻ*, ed. Ter-Mkrtchean, 83, and trans. Thomson, 192.

95. Ełiše 1957, 22; Ełiše 1982, 75. The fire temples installed were probably private shrines within elite residences, like the one established at Dvin in 560, the only archaeologically documented Zoroastrian shrine in Sasanian Armenia; see Kalantarian 1996, 39–40, 69–71.

96. It is notable that the representative of the dynasty in Tabaristan is the voice of aristocratic criticism of the late Sasanian court in a sixth-century debate on the limits of autocratic power; see "Letter of Tansar," 4–5, and Boyce 1968, 29–31.

97. Bedjan 1891, 519; McDonough 2006.

98. Crone 1991.

99. Kolesnikov 1970, 43–48. See the criticism of royal violence in "Letter of Tansar," 16–17;, and Boyce 1968, 41–42.

100. Huff 2008, 39.

101. Gyselen 2002; Howard-Johnston 2012, 115–23.

102. Pourshariati 2008, 94–97.

103. Gyselen 2007, 51–52; Pourshariati 2008: 97.

104. Gyselen 2007, 10–11.

105. Howard-Johnston 2004, 94–96; Canepa 2013, 83–84.

106. Gyselen 2007, 256, 272–74.

107. Ibid., 248, 252–70, 284–86, 298, 304–310.

108. Czeglédy 1958; Pourshariati 2008, 122–30; Payne 2013, 22–30.

109. Pourshariati 2008, 130.

BIBLIOGRAPHY

Primary Sources

Elišē. 1957. *Vasn Vardanantsʻ ew Hayocʻ Paterazmin*. Edited by E. Ter-Minasean. Yerevan: Izdatelstvo Akademii Nauk Armyanskoi SSR.

———. 1982. *History of Vardan and the Armenian War*. Translated by Robert W. Thomson. Cambridge, Mass.: Harvard University Press.

Firdawsī. 1987–2008. *Šāhnāme, v. 1–8*. Edited by Jalal Khaleghi-Motlagh. New York: Bibliotheca Persica.

"History of Karka d-Beit Slok and Its Martyrs." 1891. In *Acta martyrum et sanctorum II*, edited by Paul Bedjan, 507–53. Leipzig: Harrassowitz.

"Inscriptions of Kirdir." 1991. In *Les quatre inscriptions du mage Kirdir: Textes et concordances*, edited and translated by Philippe Gignoux. Paris: Association pour l'Avancement des Études Iraniennes.

"Inscription of Paikuli." 1978–1983. In *The Sasanian Inscription of Paikuli*, edited and translated by H. Humbach and Prods O. Skjaervø. Wiesbaden: Harrassowitz.

"Inscription of Shapur I on the Ka'ba-ye Zardusht." 1999. In *Die dreisprachige Inschrift Šābuhrs I. an der Ka'aba-i Zardušt (ŠKZ)*, edited and translated by Philip Huyse. London: Corpus Inscriptionum Iranicarum.

"Kārnāmag ī Ardašīr." 2003. In *La geste d'Ardashir fils de Pâbag*, edited and translated by Frantz Grenet. Die: Éditions A Die.

"Letter of Tansar." 1932. In *Nāmah-e Tansar bih Jushnasf*, edited by Mojtaba Minovi. Tehran: Matba'ah-e Majlis.

"Martyrdom of the Captives." 1891. In *Acta martyrum et sanctorum II*, edited by Paul Bedjan, 316–24. Leipzig: Harrassowitz.

"Martyrdom of Miles." 1891. In *Acta martyrum et sanctorum II*, edited by Paul Bedjan, 260–75. Leipzig: Harrassowitz.

P'arpec'i, Łazar. 1904. *Patmut'iwn Hayoc'*. Edited by G. Ter-Mkrtchean. Tbilisi: Tparan Ōr.N. Aghaneani.

———. 1991. *The History of Łazar P'arpec'i.* Translated by Robert W. Thompson. Atlanta, Ga.: Scholars Press.

Secondary Works

Adams, Robert McC. 1981. *Heartland of Cities: Surveys of Ancient Settlement and Land Use on the Central Floodplain of the Euphrates Chicago.* Chicago: University Of Chicago Press.

Aliev, Askar A., et al. 2006. "The Ghilghilchay Defensive Long Wall: New Investigations." *Ancient West & East* 5:143–77.

Alizadeh, Karim. 2011. "Ultan Qalasi: A Fortified Site in the Sasanian Borderlands (Mughan Steppe, Iranian Azerbaijan)." *Iran* 49:55–77.

Alizadeh, Karim, and Jason Ur. 2007. "Formation and Destruction of Pastoral Irrigation Landscapes of the Mughan Steppe, North-Western Iran." *Antiquity* 81 (311): 148–60.

Alram, Michael, Maryse Blet-Lemarquand, and Prods Oktor Skjaervø. 2007. "Shapur, King of Kings of Iranians and Non-Iranians." In *Des Indo-Grecs aux Sassanides: Données pour l'histoire et la géographie historique*, edited by Rika Gyselen, 11–40. Bures-sur-Yvette: Groupe pour l'Etude de la Civilizsation du Moyen-Orient.

Alram, Michael, and Rika Gyselen. 2003. *Sylloge Nummorum Sasanidarum, v. I: Ardashir I.—Shapur I.* Vienna: Verlag der österreichischen Akademie der Wissenschaften.

Bedjan, Paul, ed. 1897. *History of Rabban Mar Saba: Acta martyrum et sanctorum II, 635–80.* Leipzig: Otto Harrassowtiz.

Brenner, Neil. 1999. "Beyond State-Centrism? Space, Territoriality, and Geographical Scale in Globalization Studies." *Theory and Society* 28:39–78.

Callieri, Pierrancesco. 2009. "Bishapur: The Palace and the Town." In *Trésors d'Orient: Mélanges offerts à Rika Gyselen*, edited by Philippe Gignoux, Christelle Jullien, and Florence Jullien, 51–65. Paris: Association pour l' Avancement des Etudes Iraniennes.

Canepa, Matthew P. 2009. *The Two Eyes of the Earth: Art and Ritual of Kingship between Rome and Sasanian Iran.* Berkeley: University of California Press.

———. 2013. "Building a New Vision of the Past in the Sasanian Empire: The Sanctuaries of Kayānsīh and Great Fires of Iran." *Journal of Persianate Studies* 6 (1–2): 64–90.

Crone, Patricia. 1991. "Kavad's Heresy and Mazdak's Revolt." *Iran* 29:21–42.

Czeglédy, Karol. 1958. "Bahram Čōbīn and the Persian Apocalyptic Literature." *Acta Orientalia Scientiarum Hungaricae* 8 (1): 32–40.

Daryaee, Touraj. 2005. "Ethnic and Territorial Boundaries in Late Antique and Early Medieval Persia (Third to Tenth Century)." In *Borders, Barriers, and Ethnogenesis, Frontiers in Late Antiquity and Middle Ages,* edited by Florin Curta, 123–37. Turnhout: Brepols.

———. 2010. "Bazaars, Merchants, and Trade in Late Antique Iran." *Comparative Studies in South Asia, Africa, and the Middle East* 30 (3): 401–9.

Ecsedy, I. 1979. "Early Persian Envoys in the Chinese Courts (5th–6th Centuries A.D.)." In *Studies in the Sources on the History of Pre-Islamic Central Asia,* edited by J. Harmatta, 153–62. Budapest: Akadémiai Kiadó.

Elden, Stewart. 2013. *The Birth of Territory.* Chicago: University of Chicago Press.

Fiey, Jean Maurice. 1971. "Les provinces sud-caspiennes des églises syriennes." *Parole de l'Orient* 2:329–43.

Gadjiev, Murtazali. 1995. "O Mestopolozhenii Varachana." *Rossiiskaya Arkheologiya* 2:29–35.

———. 2008. "On the Construction Date of the Derbend Fortification Complex." *Iran and the Caucasus* 12 (1): 1–15.

———. 2012. "O Funktsionirovanii Oboronitelnoi Sistemi Dar-bari v Arabskii Period." *Islamovedenie* 3:93–107.

———. 2013. "Khumara: Nekotorie Stroitelnie Paralleli i Problema Datirovki Ukreplenii." In *Ocherki Srednevekovoi Arkheologii Kavkaza: K 85-Letiyu so Dnya Rozhdeniya V.A. Kuznetsova,* edited by V. I. Kozenkova, 51–65. Moscow: Institut Arkheologii RAN.

———. 2015. "Khronologiya Arshakidov Albanii." In *Albania Caucasica,* edited by Alikber K. Alikberov and Murtazali Gadjiev, 68–75. Moscow: Institut Vostokovedeniya RAN.

Gadjiev, Murtazali, and Vladimir Yu. Malashev. 2014. "'Knyazheskie' i Elitnie Voinskie Pogrebeniya Pozdnesarmatskovo i Gunnskovo Vremeni v Dagestane." *Kratkie Soobshcheniya Instituta Arkheologii* 234:9–24.

Garsoïan, Nina. 2009. "La politique arménienne des Sassanides." In *Trésors d'Orient: Mélanges offerts à Rika Gyselen,* edited by Philippe Gignoux, Christelle Jullien, and Florence Jullien, 67–79. Paris: Association pour l' Avancement des Etudes Iraniennes.

Gnoli, Gherardo. 1980. *Zoroaster's Time and Homeland: A Study on the Origins of Mazdeism and Related Problems.* Naples: Istituto Universitario Orientale.

———. 1989. *The Idea of Iran: An Essay on Its Origin.* Rome: Istituto Italiano per il Medio ed Estremo Oriente.

Grenet, Frantz. 2002. "Regional Interaction in Central Asia and Northwest India in the Kidarite and Hephthalite Periods." In *Indo-Iranian Languages and Peoples,* edited by Nicholas Sims-Williams, 203–24. Oxford: British Academy.

———. 2005. "Découverte d'un relief sassanide dans le nord de l'Afghanistan." *Compte Rendus de l'Académie des Inscriptions et Belle-Lettres* 149 (1): 115–35.

———. 2010. "A View from Samarkand: The Chionite and Kidarite Periods in the Archaeology of Sogdiana." In *Coins, Art and Archaeology II: The First Millennium C.E. in the Indo-Iranian Borderlands*, edited by Michael Alram et al., 267–81. Vienna: Verlag der Österreichischen Akademie der Wissenschaften.

Gyselen, Rika. 1989. *La géographie administrative de l'empire sassanide: Les témoignages sigillographiques.* Paris: Groupe pour l'Étude de la Civilisation du Moyen-Orient.

———. 2002. "Lorsque l'archéologie rencontre la tradition littéraire: les titres militaires des *spāhbed* de l'empire sassanide." *Comptes rendus de l'Académie des Inscriptions et Belle Lettres* 145 (1): 447–58.

———. 2003. "La reconquête de l'est iranien par l'empire sassanide au VIe siècle, d'après les sources 'iraniennes.'" *Arts Asiatiques* 58:162–67.

———. 2007. *Sasanian Seals and Sealings in the A. Saeedi Collection.* Louvain: Peeters.

———. 2009. "Primary Sources and Historiography of the Sasanian Empire." *Studia Iranica* 38 (2):163–90.

———. 2012. "Le Tabaristān: Lieu de mémoire sassanide." In *Objets et documents inscrits en pārsīg*, edited by Rika Gyselen, 109–22. Bures-sur-Yvette: Groupe pour l'Étude de la Civilisation du Moyen-Orient.

Hallier, Ulrich W. 1972. "Fort, Atashgah und Chahar Taq von Nakhlak: Überreste einer sasanidische Bergbausiedlung." *Archäologischer Mitteilungen aus Iran* 5:285–307.

Hartnell, Tobin. 2014. "Agriculture in Sasanian Persis: Ideology and Practice." *Journal of Ancient History* 2 (2): 182–208.

Howard-Johnston, James. 1995. "The Two Great Powers in Late Antiquity: A Comparison." In *The Byzantine and Early Islamic Near East, v. III: States, Resources, and Armies*, edited by Averil Cameron, 157–226. Princeton, N.J.: Darwin Press.

———. 2004. "Pride and Fall: Khusro II and His Regime, 626–628." In *La Persia e Bisanzio*, edited by Antonio Carile et al., 93–113. Rome: Accademia Nazionale dei Lincei.

———. 2008. "State and Society in Late Antique Iran." In *The Sasanian Era: The Idea of Iran Volume III*, edited by Vesta Sarkhosh Curtis and Sarah Stewart, 118–29. London: I.B. Tauris.

———. 2010. "The Sasanians' Strategic Dilemma." In *Commutatio et contentio: Studies in the Late Roman, Sasanian, and Early Islamic Near East*, edited by Henning Börm and Josef Wiesehöfer, 37–70. Düsseldorf: Wellem Verlag.

———. 2012. "The Late Sasanian Army." In *Late Antiquity: Eastern Perspectives*, edited by Teresa Bernheimer and Adam Silverstein, 87–127. Oxford: Gibb Memorial Trust.

———. 2014. "The Sasanian State: The Evidence of Coinage and Military Construction." *Journal of Ancient History* 2 (2): 144–81.

Huff, Dietrich. 1995. "Beobachtungen zum Čahartaq und zur Topographie zum Girre." *Iranica Antiqua* 30:71–92.

———. 2008. "Formation and Ideology of the Sasanian State in the Context of Archaeological Evidence." In *The Sasanian Era: The Idea of Iran Volume III*, edited by Vesta Sarkhosh Curtis and Sarah Stewart, 31–59. London: I.B. Tauris.

Kalantarian, Aram. 1996. *Dvin: Histoire et archéologie de la ville médiévale*. Neuchâtel: Recherches et Publications.

Kautsky, John H. 1982. *The Politics of Aristocratic Empires*. Chapel Hill: University of North Carolina Press.

Kennedy, Hugh. 2011. "Great Estates and Elite Lifestyles in the Fertile Crescent from Byzantium and Sasanian Iran to Islam." In *Court Cultures in the Muslim World: Seventh to Nineteenth Centuries*, edited by Albrecht Fuess and Jan-Peter Hartung, 54–79. London: Routledge.

———. 2006. "From Shahristan to Medina." *Studia Islamica* 102–3: 5–34.

Kleiss, Wolfram. 2015. *Geschichte der Architektur Irans*. Berlin: Dietrich Reimer Verlag.

Kolesnikov, Ali I. 1970. *Iran v Nachale VII Veka*. Moscow: Palestinskii Sbornik.

Korobov, D. S. 2003. *Sotsialnaya Organizatsiya Alan Severnovo Kavkaza IV–IX vv*. St. Petersburg: Aleteiya.

Lattimore, Owen. 1940. *Inner Asian Frontiers of China*. New York: American Geographical Society.

Lecomte, Olivier. 2007. "Gorgân and Dehistan: The North-East Frontier of the Iranian Empire." In *After Alexander: Central Asia before Islam*, edited by Joe Cribb and Georgina Herrmann, 295–312. Oxford: British Academy.

Lee, A. D. 2013. "Roman Warfare with Sasanian Persia." In *The Oxford Handbook of Warfare in the Classical World*, edited by Brian Campbell and Lawrence A. Tritle, 708–25. Oxford: Oxford University Press.

Lefebvre, Henri. 1991. *The Production of Space*. Oxford: Blackwell.

Lukonin, Vladimir. 1969. *Kultura Sasanidskovo Iran v III–V vv.: Ocherki po Istorii Kulturi*. Moscow: Nauka.

Mahamedi, Hamid. 2004. "Walls as a System of Frontier Defense during the Sasanid Period." In *The Spirit of Wisdom: Essays in Memory of Ahmed Tafazzoli*, edited by Touraj Daryaee and Mahmoud Omidsalar, 145–59. Costa Mesa, Calif.: Mazda.

Malashev, V., Murtazali Gadzhiev, and L. Ilyukov. 2015. *Strana Maskutov v Zapadnom Prikaspii i Kurgannie Mogilniki Prikaspiiskovo Dagestana III–V vv. n.e.* Makhachkala: Mavraev.

McDonough, Scott. 2006. "A Question of Faith? Persecution and Political Centralization in the Sasanian Empire of Yazdgard II (438–457 CE)." In *Violence in Late Antiquity: Perceptions and Practices*, edited by Hal A. Drake, 69–81. Aldershot: Ashgate.

———. 2008. "Bishops or Bureaucrats? Christian Clergy and the State in the Middle Sasanian Period." In *Current Research in Sasanian Archaeology, Art and History*, edited by Derek Kennet and Paul Luft, 87–92. Oxford: Archaeopress.

———. 2011. "The Legs of the Throne: Kings, Elites, and Subjects in Sassanian Iran." In *The Roman Empire in Context: Historical and Comparative Perspectives*, edited by Johann P. Arnason and Kurt A. Raaflaub, 290–321. Malden, Mass.: Wiley.

Metzler, David. 1977. *Ziele und Formen königlicher Innenpolitik im vorislamischen Iran*. PhD dissertation, Universität Münster.

Morony, Michael. 2004. "Population Transfers Between Sasanian Iran and the Byzantine Empire." In *La Persia e Bisanzio: Convegno internazionale, Roma 14–18 ottobre 2002*, edited by Antonio Carile et al., 161–79. Rome: Accademia dei Lincei.

Mosig-Walburg, Karin. 2010. "Königtum und Adel in der Regierungs Zeit Ardashirs II., Shapurs III., und Wahrams IV." In *Commutatio et contentio: Studies in the Late Roman, Sasanian, and Early Islamic Near East*, edited by Henning Börm and Josef Wiesehöfer, 133–58. Düsseldorf: Wellem Verlag.

Nikonorov, Valery P. 2005. "K Voprosu o Parfyanskom Nasledii v Sasanidskom Irane: Voennoe Delo." In *Tsentralnaya Aziya ot Akhemenidov do Timuridov: Arkheologiya, Istoriya, Etnologiya, Kultura*, edited by V. Nikonorov, 141–79. St. Petersburg: Institut Istorii Materialnoi Kulturi.

Novak, William J. 2008. "The Myth of the 'Weak' American State." *American Historical Review* 113 (3): 752–72.

Osborne, James F. 2013. "Sovereignty and Territoriality in the City-State: A Case Study from the Amuq Valley, Turkey." *Journal of Anthropological Archaeology* 32 (4): 774–90.

———. 2015. "Ancient Cities and Power: The Archaeology of Urbanism in the Iron Age Capitals of Northern Mesopotamia." *International Journal of Urban Sciences* 19 (1): 7–19.

Overlaet, Bruno. 2013. "And Man Created God? Kings, Priests and Gods on Sasanian Investiture Reliefs." *Iranica Antiqua* 48:313–54.

Panaino, Antonio. 2009. "The King and the Gods in Sasanian Royal Ideology." In *Sources pour l'histoire et la géographie du monde iranien*, edited by Rika Gyselen, 209–56. Bures-sur-Yvette: Groupe pour l'Etude de la Civilizsation du Moyen-Orient.

Payne, Richard. 2013. "Cosmology and the Expansion of the Iranian Empire, 502–628 CE." *Past & Present* 220 (1): 3–33.

———. 2014. "The Reinvention of Iran: The Sasanian Empire and the Huns." In *The Cambridge Companion to the Age of Attila*, Michael Maas, 282–99. Cambridge: Cambridge University Press.

———. 2016. "The Making of Turan: The Fall and Transformation of the Iranian East." *Journal of Late Antiquity* 9 (1): 4–41.

Pigulevskaya, Nina. 1963. *Les villes de l'état iranien aux époques parthe et sassanide: Contribution à l'histoire sociale de la Basse Antiquité*. Paris: Mouton & Co..

Potts, D. T. 2014. *Nomadism in Iran: From Antiquity to the Modern Era*. Oxford: Oxford University Press.

Pourshariati, Parvaneh. 2008. *Decline and Fall of the Sasanian Empire: The Sasanian-Parthian Confederacy and the Arab Conquest of Iran*. London: I. B. Tauris.

Radner, Karen. 2010. "Assyrian and Non-Assyrian Kingship in the First Millennium BC." In *Concepts of Kingship in Antiquity: Proceedings of the European Science Foundation Exploratory Workshop*, edited by Giovanni B. Lanfranchi and Robert Rollinger, 25–34. Padua: S.A.R.G.O.N. Editrice e Libreria.

Rana, Aziz. 2010. *The Two Faces of American Freedom*. Cambridge, Mass.: Harvard University Press.

Rante, Rocco. 2008. "The Iranian City of Rayy: Urban Model and Military Architecture." *Iran* 46:189–211.

Rante, Rocco, and Annabelle Colline. 2013. *Nishapur Revisited: Stratigraphy and Ceramics of the Qohandez*. Oxford: Oxbow Books.

Richardson, Seth. 2012. "Early Mesopotamia: The Presumptive State." *Past & Present* 215 (1): 3–49.

Rubin, Zeev. 1995. "The Reforms of Khusro Anushirvan." In *The Byzantine and Early Islamic Near East, v. III: States, Resources, and Armies*, edited by Averil Cameron, 227–97. Princeton, N.J.: Darwin Press.

———. 2000. "The Sassanid Monarchy." In *Cambridge Ancient History, vol. 14: Late Antiquity: Empire and Successors, A.D. 425–600*, edited by Averil Cameron et al., 638–61. Cambridge: Cambridge University Press.

———. 2004. "Nobility, Monarchy and Legitimation Under the Later Sasanians." In *The Byzantine and Early Islamic Near East, vol. VI: Elites Old and New in the Byzantine and Early Islamic Near East*, edited by John Haldon and Lawrence I. Conrad, 235–73. Princeton, N.J.: Darwin Press.

Sauer, Eberhard, et al. 2013. *Persia's Imperial Power in Late Antiquity: The Great Wall of Gorgān and Frontier Landscapes of Sasanian Iran*. Oxford: Oxbow Books.

Schwaigert, Wolfgang. 1989. *Das Christentum im H̲ūzistān im Rahmen der frühen Kirchengeschichte Persiens bis zur Synode von Seleukeia-Ktesiphon im Jahre 410*. PhD dissertation, Philipps-Universität Marburg.

Scott, James C. 1998. *Seeing like a State: How Certain Schemes to Improve the Human Condition Have Failed*. New Haven, Conn.: Yale University Press.

Shaked, Shaul. 1990. "Administrative Functions of Priests in the Sasanian Period." In *Proceedings of the First European Conference of Iranian Studies: Part I, Old and Middle Iranian Studies*, edited by Gherardo Gnoli and Antonio Panaino, 261–73. Rome: Istituto Italiano per il Medio ed Estremo Oriente.

Shayegan, M. Rahim. 2011. *Arsacids and Sasanians: Political Ideology in Post-Hellenistic and Late Antique Persia*. Cambridge: Cambridge University Press.

Shenkar, Michael. 2013. "Ob Ikonografii Xvarənah i Evo Roli v Ideologii Drevnikh Irantsev." In *Poslednii Entsiklopedist: K Yubeleyu B. A. Litvinskovo*, edited by G. Yu. Kolganova, A. A. Petrova, and S. V. Kullanda, 427–51. Moscow: Institut Vostokovedeniya RAN.

Simpson, St John. 2014. "Merv, An Archaeological Case Study from the Northeastern Frontier of the Sasanian Empire." *Journal of Ancient History* 2 (2): 116–43.

Skalmowski, Wojciech. 1993. "On Middle Iranian *dstkrt(y)*." In *Medioiranica: Proceedings of the International Colloquium*, edited by Wojciech Skalmowski and Alois Van Tongerloo, 157–62. Leuven: Peeters.

Smith, Adam T. 2003. *The Political Landscape: Constellations of Authority in Early Complex Polities*. Berkeley: University of California Press.

Squatriti, Paolo. 2002. "Digging Ditches in Early Medieval Europe." *Past & Present* 176 (1): 11–65.

VanValkenburgh, Parker, and James F. Osborne. 2013. "Home Turf: Archaeology, Territoriality, and Politics." In *Territoriality in Archaeology*, edited by Parker VanValkenburgh and James F. Osborne, 1–27. Hoboken, N.J.: American Anthropological Association.

Walstra, Jan Vanessa, Mary An Heyvaert, and Peter Verkinderen. 2010. "Assessing Human Impact on Alluvial Fan Development: A Case Study from Lower Khuzestan (SW Iran)." *Geodinamica Acta* 23 (5–6): 267–85.

Weber, Ursula, and Josef Wiesehöfer. 2010. "König Narsehs Herrschaftsverständnis." In *Commutatio et contentio: Studies in the Late Roman, Sasanian, and Early Islamic Near East*, edited by Henning Börm and Josef Wiesehöfer, 89–132. Düsseldorf: Wellem Verlag.

Wenke, R. J. 1975–1976. "Imperial Investments and Agricultural Developments in Parthian and Sasanian Khuzestan, 150 BC to AD 640." *Mesopotamia* 10–11:31–221.

Wiesehöfer, Josef. 2010a. "The Late Sasanian Near East." In *The New Cambridge History of Islam, v. I: The Formation of the Islamic World, Sixth to Eleventh Centuries*, edited by Chase Robinson, 98–152. Cambridge: Cambridge University Press.

———. 2010b. "King and Kingship in the Sasanian Empire." In *Concepts of Kingship in Antiquity: Proceedings of the European Science Foundation Exploratory Workshop*, edited by Giovanni B. Lanfranchi and Robert Rollinger, 135–52. Padua: S.A.R.G.O.N. Editrice e Libreria.

CHAPTER 7

Kinship and the Performance of Inca Despotic and Infrastructural Power

R. ALAN COVEY

> I admit the Inca as an exception, where logistically reinforced militarism played a greater role in the origins of civilization than elsewhere, and where civilization (viewed through the eyes of the other civilizations) seems uneven in its achievements.
>
> —Mann (1986, 123)

Within his broader IEMP typology of social power in states, Mann (1986, 27) finds it useful in discussing the "actual power of state elites" to distinguish between "the range of actions that the ruler and his staff are empowered to attempt to implement without routine, institutionalized negotiation with civil society groups" (*despotic* power) and "the capacity to actually penetrate society and to implement logistically political decisions" (169–70).[1] The schematic representation of how these qualities manifest in different state types (for example, Mann 1984, 2008) suggests that they reflect geographical and historical differences in state power. Despotic power is a measure of heterogeneity across state territory—the power of the center to coordinate different aspects of daily and political life using ideological power sources. By contrast, infrastructural power reflects the capacity of states, particularly modern ones, to supersede the logistical boundaries inherent to governing distant and diverse areas and to coordinate local life on the basis of other sources of social power.² Mann considers infrastructural power to be "real" political power, and he suggests a trajectory for its emergence, articulation, and proliferation.³

Mann's general model for the emergence of infrastructural power struggles to account for the Inca empire of Andean South America, which flourished c. 1400–1535. This is partly because the rulers of the Inca dynasty conquered and ruled across a territory unlike any other early empire—a world of considerable local environmental and cultural variation whose main axis ran north-south along the Andes Mountains, from the equatorial tropics of southern Colombia to temperate latitudes in central Chile some 4,000 km away. Unlike the cereal cultivators who built the early Old World empires, the Inca empire did not depend primarily on irrigation agriculture, and local fishing, farming, and herding strategies offered variable opportunities for aspiring elites to circumscribe and dominate subject populations. These were especially limited in the highlands, where the Incas exercised their most intensive administrative practices—intensive maize agriculture could only be developed in certain valley-bottom areas, and upland horticultural and herding economies could easily evade state capture (cf. Scott 2009). Inca highland statecraft was not an obvious continuity of a deep Andean tradition; rather, it arose from the long-cold ashes of the Wari and Tiwanaku states, in a world of climatic uncertainty and widespread conflict among decentralized kin-based societies (see, for example, Covey 2008). The Inca state emerged where other states had failed, and its imperial strategies flourished precisely where local societies had rejected urban life, economic specialization, and social hierarchies for centuries.

The Incas also challenge Mann's general model because their infrastructural power did not come from the kinds of sources that enabled Old World states to appropriate distributive power, generate collective power, and coordinate civil society (Mann 1984). Although the Incas were great road builders (Hyslop 1984), they lacked wheeled vehicles and animals that could bear human riders—they were a pedestrian empire in a world where most waterways imposed obstacles rather than offering low-cost transport options. They also did not use coins or other currency for economic exchanges or taxation, or written language for storing a broad range of social information.⁴

These apparent constraints to civilization building beg the question: was the Inca achievement all it appears to be? Mann (1986, 123) gives a brief consideration to the apparent ease of the Spanish conquest before concluding that Inca highways, storage facilities, and way stations communicate an infrastructural power unlike that of less-advanced societies, such as Neolithic monument builders. This conclusion raises a second question that Mann does not confront in his magnum opus—*how* did the Incas establish such a considerable degree of infrastructural power without relying on the means commonly propelling Old World state-building? This chapter addresses these two fundamental questions using a more intensive reading of the ethnohistoric and archaeological corpus, concluding (1) that the trajectory of Inca infrastructural power lasted longer, but had a much more modest impact than many historians have thought; and (2) that Inca infrastructural power was strongest in the central highlands because it presumed to work within an established idiom of kinship, cyclical labor, and reciprocity. The Inca reliance on kinship to establish and deploy infrastructural power encourages a reconsideration of definitions of the state that rely on social stratification as a prerequisite. The degree of infrastructural power established by the Incas in just a century of state expansion and consolidation suggests that literacy and currency-based economics were not the only option for early state building.

The Despotic Vision of the Inca Nobility

The Incas called their empire "Tawantinsuyu," which in Quechua literally means "the Unity of the Four Regions." Scholars recognize the quadripartite structure of Inca provincial space as grounded in Andean principles of duality and the pairing of upper (*hanan*) and lower (*hurin*) parts.[5] The names of the principal provincial regions (*suyu*) also correspond to groups living in the main ecological zones of the Andes (Julien 2002). The great northern provincial region of Chinchaysuyu bore the name of the Chincha kingdom of the coastal desert, where urban populations of specialized fishers, farmers, and merchants served a powerful and wealthy lord. Condesuyu was a small region of intermontane valleys, a land of small-scale farmers. The high-plateau camelid herders of the Qolla group gave their name to Collasuyu, a province that stretched southward to central Chile and northwest Argentina. Finally, the tribes of the humid Amazonian slope, known collectively as Antis, occupied Andesuyu, the region of cloud forest and jungles found along the eastern escarpment of the Andes Mountains.[6]

In many ways, *tawantinsuyu* was more an aspirational element in Inca elite ideology, rather than a description of a functioning administrative apparatus (cf. Richardson 2012). Inca rule utterly transformed some areas, but in others the traces of state influence are ephemeral at best. Although the Incas sought to encompass the cultural and environmental diversity of their principal *suyu* regions, the archaeological evidence attests to the variable intensity of Inca rule across the broader region (see Covey 2006b). Coastal kingdoms offer very limited evidence of Inca rule, and many local rulers appear to have remained in power as Inca clients. Frontier regions have the remains of Inca garrisons and colonies, but they lack strong material evidence for the institutions that would facilitate state administration.[7] Inca dominance is most clearly articulated along a highland road network linking Quito, Cuzco, and La Paz, but even in the central highlands canonical expressions of Inca material culture (for example, architecture or pottery) are rare and frequently ambiguous at a distance from the royal highway (*qhapaqñan*) and its associated messenger posts, way stations, and administrative centers.

Imperial messages resonated not only in specific places, but only at designated times—outside of periodic festivals and royal visits, many Inca administrative centers were only partially occupied (for example, Morris, Covey, and Stein 2011). Pronouncements of Inca dominance may have been deafening in the moment of imperial encounters, but they decayed or became garbled at a distance of space and time. Inca provincial congregations achieved a strategic state of legibility (*sensu* Scott 1998), but they left space for participants in imperial encounters to read flows of power and expressions of sovereignty in multiple ways. The empire proclaimed unmatched power along its network, but it appears to have made only limited inroads in local contexts—both in the domains of existing state societies, as well as in upland areas less amenable to state exploitation.[8]

Tawantinsuyu was a presumptive universal socioecological claim of the Inca ruler, but it was simultaneously a dynamic noble domain fundamental to the negotiation and implementation of despotic and infrastructural power in the Inca state. The region surrounding Cuzco, the imperial capital, united the peripheral regions and stood apart from them as the center of a cosmological quincunx (see, for example, Pease 1986; cf. Julien 2002). Ritual actions delimited the Cuzco region as an Inca heartland, and in the early sixteenth century its inhabitants included Inca nobles, people of honorary Inca status, and an array of retainers, craft specialists, and labor colonists of provincial origin. The Cuzco region was itself *tawantinsuyu*, and the Inca sovereign represented himself as the personification of Cuzco, especially during ceremonies held in Cuzco's central Awkaypata plaza.⁹

Sources for Reconstructing Inca Governance

In some ways, the distance that separates Cuzco from the Inca provinces derives from the Spanish sources used to reconstruct the Inca past. The Incas had no written record before the European invasion, relying instead on the *khipu* (a knotted cord device) for administrative record keeping.¹⁰ Noble memory specialists maintained special *khipu* for recounting life histories of key dynastic figures, which were performed regularly in dances and praise songs. The "official" Inca history was a dynamic assemblage of lineage narratives that materialized periodically in public ceremonies where the descendants of deceased rulers brought the mummified remains of their forebears (or their lithic personifications) to the central plaza in Cuzco to be placed in order under the gaze of the current ruler.¹¹

The physical structure of the *khipu* offers some perspectives on Inca spatial conceptualizations and programs to make political and ideological power more legible. A *khipu* consists of a central cord from which emanate subsidiary cords of different fibers and colors that represented specific categories of information (see Urton 2003). Value-laden knots (representing numbers) interrupt the line of the subsidiary cord at intervals that are consistent in some registers but idiosyncratic in others. The *khipu* can be an account in both the numerical and narrative senses of the word, and it can be arranged physically to represent networks and mnemonics that constitute political and sacred landscapes.¹² A *khipu* could be unfurled to serve as a map of local shrine systems, such as the *ceque* system of Cuzco.¹³ Cords and knots could also help to reproduce the geography of mythical journeys, or to link bureaucratic records with units of labor tribute and state facilities for the production and storage of goods.¹⁴

Despite recent advances in the study of the *khipu*, we still cannot decode these devices entirely, so contemporary scholars turn to early Colonial documents and archaeology to flesh out narratives of Inca power and how it mapped onto local landscapes. The Inca canon is historiographically complex, and its variegated narratives expose the prevailing concerns of Europeans and Andeans as the ascendant Spanish empire positioned itself to administer the remains of the Inca realm. Inca nobles participated in the production of histories of the Cuzco region as a means of safeguarding special privileges under Spanish rule, and their accounts offer a potent concoction of narrative detail and elite/state-oriented bias that could be appropriated for the purposes of both champions and critics of Inca order.

Andeanists have long recognized the dangers of extrapolating conditions in Inca Cuzco onto the broader Andean region (for example, Rowe 1946, 183), but many researchers today continue to view the elite landscapes of the imperial heartland as the canonical template for the empire. Archaeologists face a similar challenge in interpreting material evidence for Inca state power and influence. As Inca artistic traditions have become better understood, many researchers continue to treat the imperial architectural remains and material culture of the Cuzco region as the *Bauplan* for provincial rule. Rather than seeing the capital region as a unique expression of Inca aesthetics and ideology, they interpret the imperial heartland as an imperial microcosm, which can lead to problematic interpretations of Inca power and influence in the periphery. An emphasis on the distribution of state canons can elide the multitude of in-between places where such material traces are not in evidence—just as imperial myths focus on significant places more than the spaces lying between them. Returning to the *khipu* at a metaphorical level, it is just as important to understand the qualities of the cord as it is to be able to decipher the message of the knots.

Although Spanish officials granted a measure of legitimacy to Inca *khipu* records, most of what we know about Inca society before the European invasion comes from the testimonies of men who belonged to (and in many cases, claimed to represent) one of the royal Inca lineages (*panaqa*). According to Inca succession practices, a royal brother-sister pair from the ruling family founded a new *panaqa* each generation, pooling their labor tribute to construct palaces and estates that remained in the hands of all of their descendants, except for the pair who would rule in the following generation.[15] In assembling dynastic king lists, Spanish writers failed to appreciate the temporal dimensions of the Inca system of split inheritance—the descendants of the most recent ruling pairs referred to each other by specific kin terms and owed service to the current rulers, whereas the descendants of the earliest rulers were potentially much more numerous and related only through the fiction of shared descent from the founding ancestors.

Inca Imperial Networks and the Power to Summon

The Inca sovereign claimed to be a peerless king (*sapa qhapaq*) whose ritual and political power completely dominated imperial territories, and whose military might continued to push frontiers outward against uncivilized peoples.[16] Although the power of the Inca was unmatched, it was not unlimited, and the imperial reality was one of periodic and strategic displays of hard power designed to limit governing costs and to promote the spread of Inca soft power.[17] The construction of state infrastructure amplified Inca state's capacity to build social power and distribute it flexibly and quickly, and, like Mann, archaeologists have long recognized the significance of an extensive network of roads, messenger posts (*chaskiwasi*), way stations (*tampu*), and administrative centers. It is important to note, as Hyslop (1984) does in his authoritative review of the Inca road system, that not all Inca roads were imperial constructions, and only certain parts of the network bore the full armature used for direct rule. For example, even though an Inca route passed along the Pacific coast, the state societies of the region—which had more ancient traditions of statecraft, more developed arrangements of economic specialization and exchange, and distinct religious ideologies—remained only indirectly governed by Cuzco (see, for example, Hayashida 2003; Morris and Santillana 2007).[18]

Even in the central highland provinces, archaeologists often struggle to find evidence of state dominance when they look at local communities and regional settlement patterns. Regional survey projects identify Inca-era sites based on the presence of imperial polychromes or local styles known to date to the period of Inca occupation, and in some survey regions—especially those near Inca administrative sites, ritual locations, and roads—there is evidence for population increases under imperial rule.[19] As Table 7.1 shows, there are also numerous regions located at a distance from Inca infrastructure where the paucity of Inca-style material culture creates the impression of significant population declines.[20] The decline in Inca site counts might represent site abandonment in some cases, but in many parts of the highlands it probably reflects the lack of local penetration of Inca state canons—that is, the continued use of vernacular ceramics creates the impression of a strictly pre-Inca occupation.[21]

The paucity of Inca ceramics in local contexts suggests limits to the power of the Inca state, and the architectural evidence reinforces the impression that state officials and institutions were not present in the everyday life of most highland communities. Except for a few examples of hybrid constructions, Inca rectangular forms and masonry styles are completely absent from settlements not lying on an Inca road or at a shrine location.[22] The near-universal absence of state administrative and religious architecture suggests that Inca officials were only occasionally present in local communities, which suggests

Table 7.1. Late Intermediate Period (LIP) and Inca Site Counts for Selected Highland Surveys

Region	Nearest Significant Inca Site	LIP Sites	Inca Sites	References
Tarama-Chinchaycocha (~1300 km^2)	Pumpú (20+km) Hatun Xauxa (20+km)	77	19	Parsons et al. 2000, 120
Wanka (435 km^2)	Hatun Xauxa (0+km)	77	82	Parsons et al. 2013, 100-101
Andahuaylas (~300 km^2)	Vilcashuamán (30+km), Curamba (10+km)	202	76	Bauer et al. 2010
Upper Vilcanota (~300 km^2)	Cacha (0+km)	84	18	Dean 2005
Huancané-Putina (~1000 km^2)	Paucarcolla (50+km)	433	319	Stanish and de la Vega 2004
Chucuito-Cutimbo (200 km^2)	Chucuito (0 km+)	52	110	Frye 2005
Juli-Pomata (360 km^2)	Copacabana (25+km)	140	242	Stanish et al. 1997
Taraco Peninsula (85 km^2)	Tiwanaku (10+km)	83	125	Bandy 2001
Island of the Sun (21 km^2)	Island was an Inca pilgrimage destination	22	78	Stanish and Bauer 2004
Tiwanaku Valley (400 km^2)	Tiwanaku was a sacred site with small Inca occupation	964	492	Albarracin-Jordan and Mathews 1990
Katari Valley (102 km^2)	Tiwanaku (10+km)	145	79	Janusek and Kolata 2003; Bandy and Janusek 2005

a much lower level of infrastructural power than many scholars have assumed. This archaeological reading of the material remains of Inca canons is consistent with early Colonial narratives in which an Inca official called a *tukuyrikhuq* ("the one who sees all") conducted periodic inspections across provincial regions. Ordinarily, everyday administration involved local officials who participated actively in kin-based subsistence activities.

Although the Inca ruler used his proxies to extend his all-seeing gaze to the local level on occasion, his actual administrative power relied more on an ability to summon his subjects to state labor projects, and for encounters at sites on the imperial network. The Incas established about ten new provincial capitals in the central highlands, to which tens of thousands of people traveled at times ordained by the state ritual calendar.[23] In assembling his vassals, the Inca ruler performed a political act that echoed the supernatural work of the creator at the dawn of time, as well as the social labor of parents to rally their kin and allies to attend a child's first haircutting ritual. By drawing tributaries to imperial spaces at a time of his choosing, the Inca claimed a power to govern that was linked to the concept of creation.[24] As provincial people left the familiar places of their own landscapes for the state road system, they witnessed the material signs of Inca generative power—carved rock outcrops, cut-stone structures, terraced hill slopes, stone-lined canals—encouraging them to see themselves as participants in a political assemblage that congregated the diverse peoples whom the Creator had dispersed at a time far beyond memory. This gathering-in not only closed a cycle of creation, but it also evoked the affective pull that well-connected people could use to create, reinforce, and extend their social networks.[25] The summoning Inca simultaneously played the role of creator and distant relative while staging an encounter in which his representatives would transform those assembled into subjects.

The Theater of Inca State Congregations

Annual festive encounters at Inca provincial centers constituted a social flowing-together (*tinkuy*) that was understood as a political form of antagonistic complementarity. Colonial sources use the verb *tinkuy* to describe a paired relationship in which both partners are completed (for example, black/white or woman/man), as well as the unpredictable event in which those partners confront one another (see, for example, Covey 2002; Morris, Covey, and Stein 2011). Several scholars have described inter-community *tinku* events in the Colonial period and ethnographic present that take the form of ritual battles and dance competitions that reinforce social identities and fulfill ritual functions in potentially unpredictable ways.[26] Inca administrators at highland centers sought an orderly display of provincial subjectivity, which required the transformation of preexisting local identities and relationships under the state gaze. As discussed above, dislocation from local landscapes and travel on the Inca network would remove people from their lived places, but it is clear that participants in state encounters still arrived as non-Inca peoples.[27] The Incas designed the layout of their highland centers to channel subjects into a state-supervised confluence, so that processions into Inca plazas recapitulated imperial conquest histories and reinforced provincial boundaries and administrative units.

For example, Cristóbal de Molina (2011 [1575], 48) describes the arrival of provincials to the central plaza in Cuzco for the imperial Situa ceremony: "The next day in the morning, all the nations that the Inca had subjected would enter [the plaza]. They came with their *huacas* [sacred objects] and dressed in the clothing of their lands, the finest that they could have . . . Reaching the plaza, they entered according to their areas from the four *suyos* [regions] and offered reverence to the Creator, Sun, Thunder [and] Huanacauri, [which was the] *huaca* of the Incas, and then to the Inca, who by that time was already in the plaza. In this way, they would go arrange themselves in their previously assigned positions." Several important points can be made from this short account. Local people probably did not journey from their homes in their best clothes, but they came to imperial encounters as individuals dressed in their finest and representing a multiplicity of non-Inca identities. The streets that brought people into the plaza grouped them into Inca regional units, and ordered them according to state purposes. Finally, all participants knew where to go in the Inca plaza, which served as a living map of the empire with the ruler and most powerful sacred objects established on a platform (*usnu*) in the center. The event was scripted in advance so that people arrived at their prescribed place in their proper order at a time ordained by the Inca ruler.

The procession into an Inca center replicated an ideal imperial history and geography, establishing a subject population that could be viewed, rewarded, punished, and redefined by the Inca ruler or his representatives. The actual work of government followed this performance, much of it focused on reviewing tribute assignments, assessing changes in the subject population, and celebrating state-sponsored festivities. Inca governors used annual festivals as an occasion to select preadolescent girls to be cloistered in the *aqllawasi* until they were ready for marriage, and to take young women out of that cloister to pair them with single men in mass marriage ceremonies that created new tributary households (Morris, Covey, Santillana n.d.). These governors also inspected older men and women to see if they were too old to travel for state labor service (*puriy ruku*). As they moved households into and out of service, Inca officials also met with local officials (*kurakas*) to review the labor assignments of their units and to punish serious crimes and failure to fulfill tributary work.[28] The creation of decimal administrative units appropriated the ceremonial and strategic power of kin groups to celebrate individual passage through gendered lives, and it undermined the relevance and efficacy of the kin-based reciprocal labor systems that maintained local agropastoral economies.[29]

The imperial encounter at an Inca center not only transformed kin groups into tributary units, but it also used tropes of kinship to reinforce unequal relationships between individual and ruler. The ruler was *qhapaq*—rich, powerful, and possessing strong kin connections—and he and his wife claimed to be generous patrons of people who were *waqcha*, or poor and without kin or rights to land and reciprocal labor.[30] The imperial gathering was an occasion to overwhelm the poor relations of the ruling couple, but it was also an event in which state biopower was on display.[31] By intervening in marriage and reproduction, the Inca arrogated the power to assemble individual social networks, making individuals kin-poor and then strategically bestowing or withholding the full status of a married adult.

The Inca highland center at Huánuco Pampa illustrates some of the spatial aspects of the preceding, highlighting the temporary nature of Inca administrative performances and the potential for multiple interpretations of such events.[32] The Incas laid out Huánuco Pampa to be a space for state encounters with tens of thousands of locals who lived in the surrounding valleys. The site lies on the highland road from Cuzco to Quito, which cuts across a huge central plaza (550 x 350 m) with a large masonry *usnu* platform at its center. Long structures delimit the plaza, and a few restricted gateways offer access to state complexes that include an administrative palace, a cloister, and probably a sun temple. From the *usnu*, Huánuco Pampa looks like an Inca city, albeit one that was only partially occupied for most of the year. Behind the facade of great halls and ornamental masonry, however, there is much less evidence of state dominance to be found in terms of urban planning or the distribution of Inca canons (Morris, Covey, and Stein 2011, 30–31).[33]

Highland centers like Huánuco Pampa represent the epitome of Inca infrastructural power, but outside of festive occasions they appear to have functioned more or less as way stations on the highways connecting Cuzco to the imperial frontiers. From this perspective, the everyday function of such sites falls in the domain of military power, with brief political performances that were couched in ideological terms that resonated with local highland worldviews in both an ultimate (creation) and everyday (kinship) sense.

The Transformation of Inca Subjects at Cuzco

The same principles that undergirded provincial performances were on display in Cuzco, which acted as a higher-order destination for assembling people and things from the provinces to transform them, imbue them with Inca power, and send them to an appropriate destination. Inca officials serving as the stand-ins (*rantiq*) for the Inca ruler and his wife selected exotic raw materials, sacred objects, sacrificial victims, and people with the potential to serve in a variety of capacities, sending them to the capital.[34] Cuzco functioned as an imperial capital through regular festive performances joining Incas and provincial populations, but the city was also the center of the Inca people (Bauer 2004). The public events held there reflect a second kind of power claimed by Inca royals, as well as a distinct kin-based configuration of power.

Whereas military campaigns and provincial tribute levies relied on the decimal authority of the *kuraka*—an appointed lord over vassals—the maintenance of the social and moral well-being of the Inca community of Cuzco depended on the power of the Inca and his wife as *yaya* and *mama*, or lord and lady of servants.[35] This was a much more ancient form of power, one that had been developing for several centuries in the Cuzco region (see, for example, Covey 2006b). The early chroniclers suggest that the ruling pair treated the city of Cuzco as its domain but emphasized the self-sufficiency of the noble and commoner households residing there (see, for example, Betanzos 1999 [1550s]). The royal household was established physically through the construction of a new urban palace, and it grew over time through polygynous marriage alliances and by the addition of retainers (*yanakuna*), craft producers (*kamayuqkuna*) and *mamakuna*. During a lengthy reign, a royal household would become increasingly capable of appointing its own members to oversee military and administrative leadership in provincial contexts, but it continued to function as an intermediary with Inca supernatural patrons, and to perform acts of respect and generosity for the mummies of earlier rulers.[36]

A complete review of the kinship basis of Inca power in Cuzco lies beyond the scope of this chapter (see Covey 2015b), but it is useful to note that the relationships among the noble Inca *panaqas* were distinct from the *ayllu*-oriented kin values on display in provincial encounters. The empire assembled its highland subjects in the role of a distant but well-connected relative, performing regular tributary reviews as if marking individual social movement through the different stages of the life cycle. In Cuzco, kinship was more concrete and oriented around the performance of ancestry, especially through the relationships between the different founding couples of the noble households. Inca kinship engendered dynastic history.

The Civilization of Sovereign Landscapes in the Imperial Heartland

As discussed above, the Inca network inscribed state mnemonics onto an emerging imperial landscape, sending regular visual cues that travelers were moving across Inca space and time. In the region surrounding Cuzco, Inca canons are much more prevalent (although not ubiquitous), and they appear to be part of a broader noble project to "civilize" the hinterland of the Inca capital and extend the domain of royal *panaqas*. Whereas the ruler and his wife treated the city of Cuzco as their household, they engaged in projects in rural Cuzco to promote themselves as founding ancestors whose civilizing acts created the resources necessary to support a new royal house (Covey 2011).

The royal civilization trope diverged from the cyclical themes that were central to highland representations of agropastoral patterns and human life—building a noble house meant permanently transforming land, water, and people into new forms. According to Spanish chroniclers, at least six generations of royal pairs engaged in estate building in the countryside surrounding Cuzco. These projects involved first identifying lands as "wild" (*purum*) and thus open for civilizing acts. Before Inca transformation, lands were said to have been unpopulated, unproductive, or the domain of faithless or rebellious people. Labor by people related to or subject to the Inca ruling pair transformed barren lands into terraces and diverted water from streams into irrigation canals. Significantly, estate lands tended to be worked not by tributary labor, but by *yanakuna*, who were often rebellious provincial subjects who had been transformed into perpetual servants of the noble house.

At the time of the European invasion, royal estate projects had altered large areas of valley-bottom farmland, and the resources and rural palaces associated with many of these projects were integrated into the performance of noble leisure and political factionalism in the capital. A major part of the aesthetic program on display at sites such as Pisac or Machu Picchu reflects noble statements about the power of *panaqas*—a distinct form of messaging from the deployment of imperial canons along the road network. Growing beyond a focus on maize lands and pasture for camelids, royal estates extended into the humid coca lands lying to the north of Cuzco, producing large amounts of the ritual crop. Although it is important to recognize the self-interest in noble Inca narratives in the early Colonial period, it is difficult to identify "the state" in the distribution of people and resources in the Inca imperial heartland. Beyond the resources of the state religion, the way stations on the royal roads to the provinces, and the installations of tributary laborers engaged in new construction projects, virtually all the resources that would ordinarily be classified as constituting the political economy lay in the domain of noble estates.

Kinship and the Dynamics of Inca Despotic and Infrastructural Power

The linguistic and ethnohistoric evidence suggests that two distinct kinds of kinship figured prominently in the central organizing principles of the Inca state. The creation of new households occurred at the royal, ethnic, and political level, and even though the empire devised a new kin conceptualization for provincial decimal administration—the *apu/mama* interplay at highland centers took the place of the *yaya/mama* performances on display in Cuzco—it emphasized kin relations and the fulfillment of reciprocity.[37] The strongest manifestations of Inca infrastructural power seem to have worked because Inca officials treated statecraft as an extension of kinship rather than an institutional interruption of it. Kin ties extended the despotic power of the Inca ruler, and as his representatives journeyed from the center to the periphery, they reconstituted the presumptive state as a presumptive family.

Having noted the continuing prominence of Inca kinship in imperial statecraft, we return to the exceptional nature of the Inca in Mann's general model. To a certain extent, the Inca exception can be explained by a new generation of research that shows Inca power to be more ancient within the Cuzco region and less continuous and intense in many peripheral contexts. The heterogeneity of Inca imperial strategies and diverse local manifestations of imperial social power expose flaws in the Weberian definition of the state as possessing monopolies over some kinds of power within a bounded territory. The continuing role of kinship for organizing the Inca elite and for aiding the administrative structuring of provincial populations challenges theoretical expectations of stratification as a prerequisite for state formation. In the Inca case, infrastructural power claimed to represent the family values of highland communities, and the top officials in emerging institutions were relatives of the ruling couple. Kin-based rule could be placed within Mann's category of despotic power, although it represents ideological power of a different sort than is expected in a focus on the universal pronouncements of the Inca ruler.[38] Instead, the Inca case encourages treating kinship as an enduring form of social power that is not necessarily displaced by political institutions as states develop infrastructural power.

NOTES

1. Mann 1984 defines the state from a Weberian perspective, as a territorially bounded society with centralized and specialized institutions, including a monopoly over law and violence. Because he defines "state elite" as "those who control the state" (1986, 27), Mann ultimately addresses the nature of statecraft in the despotic/infrastructural formulation. The Weberian presumption of a monopoly of violence ties military power to the political domain, but the process by which societies move from an absence of coercive power to a monopolistic state control over violence requires explanation and articulation with the despotic/infrastructural distinction (1986, 10–11, 46–49). This is particularly relevant for the Inca case, given that coerced labor—considered by Mann to be militaristic—was the currency of the Inca political economy.

2. Mann chooses early states for his "low-infrastructure" examples, with feudal Europe as the "low despotic power" example and imperial China as the "high despotic power" case. His "high-infrastructure" examples are the United States (democracy) and the Soviet Union (single-party) as low and high dimensions of despotic power, respectively. Assuming that early states had limited infrastructural power, the feudal/despotic distinction resembles the scalar binary that some archaeologists make, for example Trigger's (2003) city-state/territorial state distinction.

3. Mann (1986) describes a general evolution of modest social inequality (ranking), from which states originated, as leaders in areas of circumscribed irrigation agriculture appropriated disproportionate shares of distributive power and coerced subordinate social groups to increase collective power. As elites extended their power beyond "caged" areas, they relied on military and economic power, as well as on the despotic ideological power discussed above. The infrastructural power of state elites grew over the very long term, as institutions became more specialized and better coordinated, aided by the enhancement of the capacity to store and transport information and economic value more easily (Mann 1984). For a historical review of Western theories of state formation, see Lull and Micó 2011. Flannery and Marcus (2012) offer a more robust treatment of social evolution from the perspective of processual archaeology.

4. A caveat should accompany this statement. Spondylus bead bands (*chaquira*) and metal "money axes" served as currency in parts of the Inca periphery, and early colonial accounts of coastal kingdoms identify specialized maritime merchants that moved exotic goods along the coast (e.g., Hosler, Lechtman, and Holm 1990; Salomon 1987). Although the Inca *khipu* cannot be considered "writing," it fulfilled record-keeping functions and aided in the performance of royal histories and cyclical rituals (see below).

5. Structuralist theory undergirds contemporary conceptualizations of Inca social organization (e.g., Wachtel 1966; Zuidema 1964), even though most researchers acknowledge that these divisions were imagined and historically contingent.

6. In addition to these great regions, the Inca recognized smaller *suyu* divisions, including (1) Colesuyu, an area of dispersed coastal fishers in southern Peru and northern Chile (Rostworowski 1986); (2) Urqusuyu, a region of Aymara-speaking "hill people" in the Titicaca Basin; and (3) Umasuyu, a complementary Aymara-speaking region of lakeside or valley people (Bouysse-Cassagne 1978).

7. Inca imperial military power is said to have begun as a generational display to uphold the paramount status of the Inca sovereign (e.g., Betanzos 1999[1550s]), but over time it shifted conceptually to the reconquest of rebellious groups, and then to the establishment of a militarized frontier and a demilitarized interior, linked by the imperial road network.

8. Scott's 1998 and 2009 books explore the interplay between state "modernization" projects and the ways that "upland" peoples have flourished in areas resistant to such schemes. To view the Inca case through this lens, an ideology of universal sovereignty might be used in place of the concept of "high modernism," but the ecological arrangement of archipelagoes of intensive agriculture surrounded by hard-to-govern uplands is apt for the Andes. It should be noted that the most circumscribed agricultural landscapes were in the coastal valleys of northern Peru, where the Incas achieved indirect control over existing state governments.

9. Ramírez 2005 discusses the identification of the Inca paramount as "the Cuzco," but rulers regularly vested close relatives with their military power, or as regents when they were absent from Cuzco. Morris and Covey 2003 describe the Inca use of central plaza spaces for the spatial resolution of municipal and administrative relationships. Recent scholarship emphasizes that the center of the Inca could be replicated. Another person or object could act as the stand-in (*rantiq*) for the Inca (Covey 2006a), and the center itself was architecturally reproduced at some provincial sites said to have been "other Cuzcos" (Coben 2006).

10. For example, see chapters in Quilter and Urton 2002. Model-building and counting devices also aided in this work, and there are descriptions of a painted record of the Inca dynasty, although few Colonial witnesses claim to have seen this latter register (see Covey 2006a).

11. Chroniclers such as Pedro de Cieza de León (1985 [c. 1550, chapter 12]) and Juan de Betanzos (1999 [1550s, part I, chapter 31]) describe praise songs and commemorative dances. Cristóbal de Molina 2011 [1575] and Pedro Pizarro 1978 [1571] are among the authors who mention the spatial ordering of the mummies in the Inca dynasty.

12. Astuhuamán 2011 draws the parallel between the *khipu* and an archipelagic model of the Inca administrative network. Such a vision of strategic statecraft can draw interpretive value from Tuan's (1977) distinction between place and space, and we should remain mindful that state projects of place-making have temporal dimensions and occur across existing landscapes of space/place.

13. Zuidema's (1964) classic presentation of the 328 shrines in Cuzco's municipal sacred landscape focuses on a schematic spatial vision that could be easily reproduced using a *khipu*, whereas Bauer's (1998) toponym survey of the shrines shows the more complicated sacred geography on the ground.

14. For example, Betanzos (1999 [1550s, part 1, chapter 2]) provides an account of universal creation by the deity Viracocha (see Pease 1986). After creating the first men and women at the ancient site of Tiwanaku, Viracocha travels the Inca road to Cuzco, stopping at different places along the way. This myth is essentially a recounting of the shrines to Viracocha lying along the Inca road from Cuzco to Tiwanaku, which could easily be encoded on a *khipu* cord.

15. See Covey 2006b and 2011 for a discussion of *panaqas* and estate building in the Cuzco region.

16. Transcribing accounts of his Inca affines, Betanzos (1999 [1550s]) offers an early treatment of Inca sovereignty, as well as the circumstances under which noble factions worked to facilitate or challenge it. Inca society united to face threats to the peerless status of the Inca ruler (e.g., part 1, chapter 20), but in times of peace the "lords of Cuzco" claimed a power that could supersede the will of the monarch (e.g., part 1, chapter 17).

17. Nye's (2011, 20–21) distinction between hard (military and economic) and soft power is useful, as it recognizes a spectrum of state strategies that lie between the extremes of coercion and persuasion. Soft power constitutes the attractive power of the state society, which may grow state political power without the need to cage and coerce peripheral populations.

18. Hyslop (1984, 37–59) concludes that many sections of the coastal road were pre-Inca constructions, and the Incas reused the road and many sites along it. Where they built new sites, the Incas used local construction techniques, and Hyslop argues that there is no written or archaeological evidence of the construction of administrative sites like those found on the main Inca road in the neighboring highlands. The Incas ruled most of the coastal region using despotic forms of power, although in some instances they restructured the political and economic power of coastal rulers by resettling ruling elites and appropriating craft specialists who produced high status elite goods.

19. For a comparison of highland regions, see Covey 2012 and Covey 2015a.

20. Similar results have been observed in smaller surveys, including Asto (Lavallée 1973), Pampas-Qaracha (Valdez and Vivanco 1994), and Sondondo (Schreiber 1993).

21. Some Inca sites have been effaced by Colonial and contemporary settlement, which accentuates some of the appearance of site-count drops. In some regions, the LIP site count is probably artificially inflated by the rough chronology of the period (ca. 1000–1400 C.E.).

22. Hyslop (1990, 244–69) discusses hybrid forms in a section on "local-Inca" settlements. A few examples of hybrid architecture include the modification of Inca canons in the house of a high-ranking local administrator at the site of Ichu in the Huánuco region (Morris and Thompson 1985, 138–43), as well as the local appropriation of Inca-style masonry in the construction of local funerary towers at Sillustani in the Qolla region (Julien 1983, 254–55).

23. As noted above, such sites are not present on the coast or Amazonian slope, nor are they found in the southern part of the empire. This discussion is based on the archaeology and the kinship systems of the central highlands, and does not apply to other parts of the Inca empire.

24. *Kamay*, "to create," becomes "to govern" with the addition of the causative "-chi" (Cusihuamán 2001, 199–200). Literally, *kamachiy* means "to make someone else create." For the administrative reconfiguration of wild/civilized, see Morris and Covey 2003.

25. In the ethnographic literature of the central highlands, Isbell (1977) describes how on festive occasions local officeholders (*varayuqkuna*) use a network of people whom they call *khuyaq* (the one who loves me) to provide resources for them. A local official described this network as members of one's *ayllu*, one's distant kin (*karu ayllu*), and social allies (*compadres*). These are the same people that Colonial authors describe assembling at key moments in the individual life cycle (first haircutting, onset of menses, first house construction for newly married couples) (see Covey 2013).

26. Morris and Covey (2003) note that intramural encounters taking place within social spaces often have a more scripted result, whereas those involving different communities in "wild" spaces can lead to mayhem and death. The positive interpretation of bloodshed in these latter events—as necessary to nourish the earth for the coming tuber cultivation season—exposes a sacrificial function that should be contrasted with the carnivalesque subversion of order at state-sponsored festivals (e.g., Bakhtin 1984 [1965]).

27. Early chroniclers such as Cieza de León (1985 [c. 1550]) emphasize the Inca attempt to maintain clear local identity markers in contradistinction to those of Inca people. The invention of an imperial alterity made it easier to see who was in charge—the conquering Spaniards called Inca nobles *orejones* ("big-ears") for their privilege of wearing large earspools, and when meeting a person with enlarged earlobes, they understood that they were dealing with a person of political authority. This divide between Inca and *suyuruna* (tributary) also reflects the ambivalence of imperial enculturation practices (*sensu* Bhabha 1984)—the need for a colonizing power to promote its cultural practices while at the same time maintaining distance from its subjects.

28. Inca decimal administration created standard units from 10 to 10,000 households, administered by a hierarchy of officials called *kuraka*, a kin term used to refer to older sons, and which references the power of a lord over vassals. Given the idiom of kinship at play in provincial encounters, it is worth noting that the Inca ruler delegated power to these "older sons," whereas he sent his actual kin, often brothers, to serve as governing lords (*apu*) bearing his orders for them and the power to enforce them (Covey 2006a).

29. After these imperial gatherings, many households went to the site of their rotational labor service assignments. For example, Chupaychu households from the Huánuco region went to Cuzco, Quito, and the Chachapoyas province, as well as to areas on the Amazonian slope (Julien 1988). Rather than in the presence of Inca officials or institutions in local communities, Inca state power was more apparent in the *absence* of families from local networks of kin-based labor.

30. The seventeenth-century Huarochirí manuscript (Salomon and Urioste 1991, 57–59) describes a legend about a poor man named Huatya Curi who is summoned to a competition with his rich brother-in-law, who wishes to shame him. The event consists of drumming and dancing, drinking, display of costumes, and house building. With supernatural aid, Huatya Curi plays a drum that causes an earthquake, serves a potent maize beer that robs his opponents of their senses, dazzles the assembled people with a snow garment, and builds a house with the help of wild animals rather than kin and allies. This myth articulates the kind of divide that Inca nobles would seek to accentuate in state festivals—elaborate performances of music and dance in which royal histories were performed, the service of massive quantities of maize beer, and the display and distribution of fine craft goods. All of this was choreographed in a context of monumental state construction.

31. I use "biopower" in the sense of Foucault (2007 [1978], 1), noting the strategic Inca state intervention in the life cycle of some subjects (Morris, Covey, and Santillana, forthcoming). This includes cloistering girls until marriage age, conducting mass marriages, prohibiting some men from marrying or remarrying, and castrating some men to use them as eunuch guards of the *aqllawasi* cloister. An Inca governor was known as wife giver (*warmikuq*) for his power to generate new households during provincial assemblies.

32. See Morris and Thompson 1985 for an overview of the site and the broader region. Morris, Covey, and Stein (2011) offer a more detailed presentation of the central plaza and administrative palace at the site.

33. Local incised pottery constituted 31 percent (167/555) of the decorated feature sherds from excavations outside of the Inca palace and cloister, whereas researchers identified imperial polychrome designs on 38 percent (209/555) of decorated feature sherds from these areas. Although there are clear Inca-style structures and complexes located off the central plaza, unplanned vernacular constructions are common in many parts of the site. The ambiguity of state power across Huánuco Pampa should give scholars pause, given that Inca centers of this scale are rare in the Andes. Rather than representing a "typical" case of Inca provincial rule, the site is a maximal portrait of state power in one of the most directly governed regions in the central highlands.

34. As discussed already, Inca governors possessed some power to select and set apart (*aqllay*) people, animals, and raw materials. The female ritual specialists (*mamakuna*) in the cloister and Sun temple carried out transformative acts of different kinds, including changing girls to women in the *aqllawasi* cloister and rendering harvested corn into maize beer and different sacred foods that were essential for state festivals and religious rituals.

35. Note that the latter are Quechua kin terms for father and mother, respectively, which Santo Tomás (1995 [1560], 142) says are used by distant kin for elders. There is an incongruous gender structure for kin-based sovereignty terms—*mama* applies to members of the class of female ritual specialists in institutional and provincial contexts, whereas the corresponding male term (*kuraka*) relates to a son, rather than a father. Domingo de Santo Tomás distinguishes between lordship over vassals (*vasallos*) and servants (*siervos*) in his 1560 Quechua dictionary. These Castilian terms conform to the Latin *servus* (Nebrija 1979 [1492]) and Medieval Latin (*vasallus*), the latter overlapping with *cliens* and *subditus* (Real Academia Española 1739). Essentially, they distinguish between power over a slave versus a subject. Betanzos (1999 [1550s]) describes Inca law as the creation of the Inca ruler who rebuilt Cuzco as an imperial capital, and judgment as consisting of annual public reviews of the city's population. MacCormack (1997) has discussed the historiography of Inca law as presented by Betanzos and later chroniclers.

36. To return to the power of kinship—Inca marriage practices imposed a multi-generation incest taboo with a concomitant set of kin terms and obligations that differed for the mother's and father's families (see Covey 2006b). The ruling *panaqa* interacted closely with the houses of the preceding two or three generations on the basis of concrete kin relations, but with other *panaqas* on the basis of fictive kinship (i.e., shared descent from the founding ancestors). For the houses of early rulers, marrying women from their line into the ruling *panaqa* could reinvigorate (and complicate) the long-term kin relationship.

37. Sahlins's (1972, 193–96) description of the relationship between reciprocity and closeness of a kin relationship is useful for the Inca case. The Incas practiced *generalized reciprocity* in their noble houses, whereas cycles of labor service and state feasts emphasized the *balanced reciprocity* found in different formulations of the concept of *ayni*. The Incas claimed only to practice *negative reciprocity* against rebels and those who transgressed against the Inca, as well as "savage" lowland peoples lying beyond the frontier. These were people who lacked a kin relation to the Inca, unless they were brought to Cuzco as *yanakuna* assigned to a royal house.

38. In his category of ideological power, Mann (1986) distinguishes between meanings, norms, and aesthetic/ritual practices, which could be contrasted with Bourdieu's (1980) description of kinship as an element of *habitus*.

BIBLIOGRAPHY

Albarracin-Jordan, J., and J. E. Mathews. 1990. *Asentamientos prehispánicos del valle de Tiwanaku*, vol. 1. La Paz: Producciones CIMA.

Astuhuamán González, C. W. 2011. "The Concept of Inca Province at Tawantinsuyu." *Indiana* 28:79–107.

Bakhtin, M. 1984 [1965]. *Rabelais and His World*. Translated by Hélène Iswolsky. Bloomington: University of Indiana Press.

Bandy, M. S. 2001. *Population and History in the Ancient Titicaca Basin*. PhD dissertation, Department of Anthropology, University of California, Berkeley.

Bauer, B. S. 1998. *The Sacred Landscape of the Inca: The Cuzco Ceque System*. Austin: University of Texas Press.

———. 2004. *Ancient Cuzco: Heartland of the Inca*. Austin: University of Texas Press.

Bauer, B. S., L. C. Kellett, and M. Aráoz Silva. 2010. *The Chanka: Archaeological Research in Andahuaylas (Apurimac), Peru*. Cotsen Institute of Archaeology, Monograph 68. Los Angeles: Cotsen Institute of Archaeology Press.

Bauer, B. S. 2004. *Ancient Cuzco: Heartland of the Inca*. Austin: University of Texas Press.

Bakhtin, M. 1984[1965]. *Rabelais and His World*. Translated by Hélène Iswolsky. Bloomington: Indiana University Press.

Betanzos, J. de. 1999 [1550s]. *Suma y naración de los incas*. Cusco: Universidad Nacional de San Antonio Abad del Cusco.

Bhabha, H. 1984. "Of Mimicry and Man: The Ambivalence of Colonial Discourse." *October* 28:125–33.

Bourdieu, P. 1980. *The Logic of Practice*. Translated by R. Nice. Palo Alto, Calif.: Stanford University Press.

Bouysse-Cassasgne, T. 1978. "L'espace aymara: urco et uma." *Annales, histoire, sciences sociales* 33 (5–6): 1057–80.

Cieza de León, P. de. 1985 [c. 1550]. *Crónica del Perú, segunda parte*. Lima: Pontificia Universidad Católica del Perú.

Coben, L. S. 2006. "Other Cuzcos: Replicated Theaters of Inka Power." In *Archaeology of Performance: Theaters of Power, Community, and Politics*, edited by T. Inomata and L. S. Coben, 223–70. Lanham, Md.: AltaMira Press.

Covey, R. A. 2002. Mediation, Resistance, and Identity in Colonial Cuzco: A Review Essay. *Comparative Studies in Society and History* 44 (2): 395–401.

———. 2006a. "Chronology, Succession, and Sovereignty: The Politics of Inka Historiography and Its Modern Interpretation." *Comparative Studies in Society and History* 48 (1): 166–99.

———. *How the Incas Built Their Heartland: State Formation and the Innovation of Imperial Strategies in the Sacred Valley, Peru*. Ann Arbor: University of Michigan Press.

———. 2008. ""Multiregional Perspectives on the Archaeology of the Andes during the Late Intermediate Period (c. AD 1000–1400)." *Journal of Archaeological Research* 16 (3): 287–338.

———. 2011. "Landscapes and Languages of Power in the Inca Imperial Heartland (Cuzco, Peru)." *SAA Archaeological Record* 11 (4): 29–32, 47.

———. 2012. "The Development of Society and Status in the Late Prehispanic Titicaca Basin (Circa AD 1000–1535)." In *Advances in Titicaca Basin Archaeology III*, edited by A. Vranich, E. A. Klarich, and C. Stanish, 291–302. Ann Arbor: University of Michigan Museum of Anthropology.

———. 2013. "Inca Gender Relations from Household to Empire." In *Gender in Cross-Cultural Perspective*, 6th edition, edited by C. Brettell and C. Sargent, 70–76. New York: Pearson.

———. 2015a. "Inka Imperial Intentions and Archaeological Realities in the Peruvian Highlands." In *Diversity and Unity in the Inka Empire: A Multidisciplinary Vision*, edited by I. Shimada, 83–95. Austin: University of Texas Press.

———. 2015b. "Kinship and the Inca Imperial Core: Multiscalar Archaeological Patterns in the Sacred Valley (Cuzco, Peru)." *Journal of Anthropological Archaeology* 40:183–95.

Cusihuamán, A. 2001. *Gramática quechua: Cuzco Collao*. Cusco: Centro de Estudios Rurales "Bartolomé de las Casas."

Dean, E. M. 2005. *Ancestors, Mountain shrines, and Settlements: Late Intermediate Period Landscapes of the Southern Vilcanota River Valley, Peru*. PhD dissertation, Department of Anthropology, University of California, Berkeley.

Flannery, K., and J. Marcus. 2012. *The Creation of Inequality: How Our Prehistoric Ancestors Set the Stage for Monarchy, Slavery, and Empire*. Cambridge, Mass.: Harvard University Press.

Foucault, M. 2007 [1978]. *Security, Territory, Population: Lectures at the Collège de France, 1977–1978*. Edited by M. Senellart. Translated by G. Burchell. New York: Picador.

Frye, K. L. 2005. "The Inca Occupation of the Lake Titicaca Region." In *Advances in Titicaca Basin Archaeology I*, edited by C. Stanish, A. B. Cohen, and M. S. Aldenderfer, 197–208. Los Angeles: Cotsen Institute of Archaeology Press.

Hayashida, F. M. 2003. "Leyendo el registro arqueológico del dominio inka: reflexiones desde la costa norte del Perú." *Boletín de arqueología PUCP* 7:305–19.

Hosler, D., H. Lechtman, and O. Holm. 1990. *Axe-Monies and Their Relatives*. Studies in Pre-Columbian Art and Archaeology, 30. Washington, D.C.: Dumbarton Oaks Research Library and Collection.

Hyslop, J. 1984. *The Inka road System*. New York: Academic Press.

———. 1990. *Inka Settlement Planning*. Austin: University of Texas Press.

Isbell, B. J. 1977. "'Those Who Love Me': An Analysis of Andean Kinship and Reciprocity Within a Ritual Context." In *Andean Kinship and Marriage*, edited by R. Bolton and E. Mayer, 81–105. Washington, D.C.: American Anthropological Association.

Janusek, J. W., and A. L. Kolata. 2003. "Prehispanic Rural History in the Río Katari Valley." In *Tiwanaku and Its Hinterland: Archaeological and Paleoecological Investigations of an Andean Civilization*, vol. 2, edited by A. L. Kolata, 129–71. Washington, D.C.: Smithsonian Institution Press.

Julien, C. J. 1983. *Hatunqolla: A View of Inca Rule from the Lake Titicaca Region*. University of California Publications, Anthropology vol. 15. Berkeley: University of California Press.

———. 1988. "How Inca Decimal Administration Worked." *Ethnohistory* 35 (3): 257–79.

———. 2002. "Identidad y filiación por *suyu* en el imperio incaico." *Boletín de arqueología PUCP* 6:11–22.

Lavallée, D. 1973. "Historia de los Asto." In *Asto: curacazgo prehispánico de los Andes centrales*, edited by D. Lavallée and M. Julien, 25–47. Lima: Instituto de Estudios Peruanos.

Lull, V., and R. Micó. 2011. *Archaeology of the Origin of the State: The Theories*. Translated by P. Smith. Oxford: Oxford University Press.

MacCormack, S. G. 1997. "History and Law in Sixteenth Century Peru: The Impact of European Scholarly Traditions." In *Cultures of Scholarship*, edited by S. C. Humphreys, 277–310. Ann Arbor: University of Michigan Press.

Mann, M. 1984. "The Autonomous Power of the State." *Archives européennes de sociologie* 25:185–213.

———. 1986. *The Sources of Social Power. Volume I: A History of Power from the Beginning to A.D. 1760*. New York: Cambridge University Press.

———. 2008. "Infrastructural Power Revisited." *Studies in Comparative International Development* 43, (3–4): 355–65.

Molina, C. de. 2011 [1575]. *Account of the Fables and Rites of the Incas*. Translated by B. S. Bauer, V. Smith-Oka, and G. E. Cantarutti. Austin: University of Texas Press.

Morris, C., and R. A. Covey. 2003. "La plaza central de Huánuco Pampa: espacio y transformación." *Boletín de arqueología PUCP* 7:133–49.

Morris, C., R. A. Covey, and P. Stein. 2011. *The Huánuco Pampa Archaeological Project, Volume I: The Plaza and Palace Complex*. American Museum of Natural History Anthropological Papers, 96. New York: AMNH.

Morris, C., R. A. Covey, and J. I. Santillana. Forthcoming. *The Huánuco Pampa Archaeological Project, Volume II: The Aqllawasi Complex*.

Morris, C., and J. I. Santillana. 2007. "The Transformation of the Chincha Capital." In *Variations in the Expression of Inka Power*, edited by R. L. Burger, C. Morris, and R. Matos Mendieta, 135–63. Washington, D.C.: Dumbarton Oaks Research Library and Collection.

Morris, C., and D. E. Thompson. 1985. *Huánuco Pampa: An Inca City and Its Hinterland*. New York: Thames and Hudson.

Nebrija, E. A. de. 1979 [1492]. *Diccionario Latino-Español (Salamanca 1492)*. Barcelona: Puvill-Editor.

Nye, Jr., J. S. 2011. *The Future of Power*. New York: Public Affairs.

Parsons, J. R., C. M. Hastings, and R. Matos M. 2000. *Prehispanic Settlement Patterns in the Upper Mantaro and Tarma Drainages, Junín, Peru. Volume I: The Tarama-Chinchaycocha Region, Part 1*. Memoirs of the Museum of Anthropology, University of Michigan, 34. Ann Arbor, Mich.: UMMA.

———, eds. 2013. *Prehispanic Settlement Patterns in the Upper Mantaro, Junín, Peru. Volume 2: The Wanka Region*. Memoirs of the Museum of Anthropology, University of Michigan, 53. Ann Arbor, Mich.: UMMA.

Pease G. Y., F. 1986. "Notas sobre Wiraqocha y sus itinerarios." *Histórica* 10 (2): 227–35.

Pizarro, P. 1978 [1571]. *Relación del descubrimiento y conquista de los reinos del Perú*. Lima: Pontificia Universidad Católica del Perú.

Quilter, J., and G. Urton, eds. 2002. *Narrative Threads: Accounting and Recounting in Andean khipu.* Austin: University of Texas Press.

Ramírez, S. E. 2005. *To Feed and Be Fed: The Cosmological Bases of Authority and Identity in the Andes.* Palo Alto, Calif.: Stanford University Press.

Real Academia Española. 1739. *Diccionario de la lengua castellana en que se explica el verdadero sentido de las voces, su naturaleza y calidad, con las phrases o modos de hablar, los proverbios o rephranes, y otras cosas convenientes al uso de la lengua.* Madrid: Real Academia Española.

Richardson, S. 2012. "Early Mesopotamia: The Presumptive State." *Past and Present* 215 (1): 3–49.

Rostworowski, M. 1986. "La región de Colesuyu." *Revista Chungará* 16–17:127–35.

Rowe, J. H. 1946. "Inca Culture at the Time of the Spanish Conquest." In *Handbook of South American Indians, 2: The Andean Civilizations,* edited by J. Steward, 183–220. Washington, D.C.: Bureau of American Ethnology.

Sahlins, M. 1972. *Stone Age Economics.* New York: Aldine de Gruyter.

Salomon, F. 1987. "A North Andean Status Trader Complex Under Inka Rule." *Ethnohistory* 34 (1): 63–77.

Salomon, F., and G. L. Urioste, tr. 1991. *The Huarochirí Manuscript: A Testament of Ancient and Colonial Andean Religion.* Austin: University of Texas Press.

Santo Tomás, D. de. 1951 [1560]. *Lexicon o vocabulario de la lengua general del Perú.* Lima: Institito de Historia.

———. 1995 [1560]. *Grammatica, o arte de la lengua general de los indios de los reynos del Perú.* Cuzco: Centro Bartolomé de Las Casas.

Schreiber, K. J. 1993. "The Inca Occupation of the Province of Andamarca Lucanas, Peru." In *Provincial Inca: Archaeological and Ethnohistorical Assessment of the Impact of the Inca State,* edited by M. Malpass, 77–116. Iowa City: University of Iowa Press.

Scott, J. C. 1998. *Seeing like a State: How Certain Schemes to Improve the Human Condition Have Failed.* New Haven, Conn.: Yale University Press.

———. 2009. *The Art of Not Being Governed: An Anarchist History of Upland Southeast Asia.* New Haven, Conn.: Yale University Press.

Stanish, C., and B. S. Bauer. 2004. "The Settlement History of the Island of the Sun." In *Archaeological Research on the Islands of the Sun and Moon, Lake Titicaca, Bolivia: Final Results from the Proyecto Tiksi Kjarka,* edited by C. Stanish and B. S. Bauer, 23–42. Monograph 52. Los Angeles: Cotsen Institute of Archaeology Press.

Stanish, C., and E. de la Vega. 2004. *Informe final: prospección arqueológica del sector bajo de la Cuenca del Ramis (Ríos Azángaro y Ramis), Puno.* Report submitted to the National Technical Commission of Archaeology, National Institute of Culture, Peru.

Stanish, C., E. de la Vega, L. Steadman, C. Cháves Justo, K. L. Frye, L. Onofre Mamani, M. T. Seddon, and P. Calisaya Chuquimia. 1997. *Archaeological Survey in the Juli-Desaguadero Region of Lake Titicaca Basin, Southern Peru.* Fieldiana anthropology 29.

Trigger, B, G. 2003. *Understanding Early Civilizations: A Comparative Study.* Cambridge University Press, Cambridge.

Tuan, Y. 1977. *Place and Space: The Perspective of Experience.* Minneapolis: University of Minnesota Press.

Urton, G. 2003. *The Social Life of Numbers: A Quechua Ontology of Numbers and Philosophy of Arithmetic.* Austin: University of Texas Press.

Valdez, L. M., and C. Vivanco. 1994. "Arqueología de la cuenca de Qaracha, Ayacucho, Peru." *Latin American Antiquity* 5:144–57.

Wachtel, N. 1966. "Structuralisme et histoire: A propos de l'organisation sociale de Cuzco." *Annales. Histoire, sciences sociales* 21 (1): 71–94.

Zuidema, R. T. 1964. *The Ceque System of Cuzco: The Social Organization of the Capital of the Inca.* Translated by Eva M. Hooykaas. Leiden: Brill.

CHAPTER 8

Statehood, Taxation, and State Infrastructural Power in Visigothic Iberia

DAMIÁN FERNÁNDEZ

At the end of the seventh century, an anonymous writer produced a hagiographical text on the life of Fructuosus (d. 665), a monk-bishop from Braga in Portugal. The saint preached an ascetic Christianity that found support in many aristocratic and sub-aristocratic groups, although other elite members of the Visigothic kingdom (including some of his own relatives) rejected him with equal force. According to his *Life*, the impulse toward asceticism arose in the young Fructuosus while he was visiting the mountains of El Bierzo (León, Spain) with his father, a commander of the royal army. It occurred to Fructuosus that the solitude and wilderness of these mountains formed the perfect environment for a monastic foundation. The reason why his father was visiting El Bierzo is succinctly explained in the *Life of Fructuosus* as follows: he was there to "ask [shepherds] for an account of their flocks."[1] Was he collecting revenue to support the army from lands he had received in exchange for service to the king?[2] Or was he in the countryside of El Bierzo as a landowner who collected rents from his tenant shepherds?[3] Perhaps neither, as the story may have been created to convey the image of a wild and remote region only suitable for pastoral life, in order to give credibility to the hagiographical narrative.

The anecdote was meant to communicate clear meaning to its contemporary audience, many of whom may have repeatedly experienced tax or rent collection from one side (or both sides) of the relationship. Whether

Fructuosus's father was a state official or a private landowner, his dealings with local shepherds are at the core of scholarly reconstructions of statehood in Visigothic Iberia—traditionally understood as a "weak state." The weakness of the Visigothic kingdom of Toledo, which spanned the mid-sixth to the early eighth centuries, is to have resulted from the power held by individuals such as Fructuosus's father: landed military aristocrats, powerful landowners, or both. Throughout this chapter, I will challenge the idea of the supposed weakness of the Visigothic state and suggest that we must consider the role played by supposedly non-state actors in the construction of the state's infrastructural power. Specifically, I will look at the role of taxation in spreading state power into the social fabric of Visigothic Iberia. Landowners like Fructuosus's father and bishops like Fructuosus himself introduced state power in the various regions of Visigothic Iberia in ways that defy modern conceptions of statehood, although they were not less effective in implementing state imperatives. By recognizing its own infrastructural limits, the Visigothic monarchy encouraged the participation of non-state-appointed officials in the administration of the tax system. These social actors, in turn, incorporated the language and the practice of taxation as part of their own social and political persona. The authority of the Gothic monarchy was thus able to reach every corner of the kingdom, while non-administrative agents asserted their own social prominence at the local level.

Visigothic State and Taxation: Between Weakness and Strength

The historiography of the state during the Visigothic kingdom of Toledo has traditionally fallen under the shadow of debates on "feudalization." This debate tackles the question of whether, and to what extent, certain proprietary, legal, and administrative practices associated with the high medieval (and predominantly post-Carolingian) kingdoms were already present in the polities that immediately followed the collapse of the Roman administration in the Peninsula. Thus scholarly examinations of the nature of the Visigothic state have paid particular attention to issues such as "private" armies, the proprietary status of land given to the Church or high officials, and fidelity oaths. As a result of these stimulating debates, we have inherited a well-established scholarly tradition according to which statehood in the post-Roman world is measured against the real or presumed impact of the privatization of public power and the patrimonialization of political authority.[4]

A more recent trend approaches the dynamics of statehood in the Peninsula in terms of central and local powers. This approach offers the possibility, at least on the surface, of bracketing the question of feudalism and feudalization, which ultimately seems tainted with teleology. While the late Roman Empire would have maintained the central-local balance in favor of a "central power" (the late Roman state), the post-Roman world began to alter this picture. After the fifth century, local men of authority (bishops included) appropriated, to various degrees, the spheres of influence once reserved to the more commanding Roman state—including military, tributary, and political attributes. Collaboration between central and local powers existed, but they remained two distinct sets of actors.[5] These local powers constituted the substratum of authority even during the late Roman period, but fully emerged once the imperial administration vanished in the fifth century.[6]

The idea of a separation between central and local powers presents a certain attractiveness. For one thing, it offers a powerful causality for the "failure" of the Visigothic state in the early eighth century. According to this interpretation, socially dominant figures with little political or symbolic attachment to the monarchy decided to negotiate with the Arab and Berber newcomers, who offered advantageous conditions to those willing to accommodate a new central government. This conglomerate of landed potentates deprived Toledo's monarchy of the economic and military resources to face the invasion of Arab and Berber troops after 711.[7] Moreover, the distinction between local and central powers accommodates a neo-Weberian reading according to which distinct forms of domination, patrimonial and bureaucratic, struggled to prevail over each other. The administrative machinery of the late Roman state, with its intrusive tax system, provincial administration, and military structure, represented a stronger and more unassailable form of statehood than the supposedly weak Visigothic kingdom. The Gothic monarchy relied on revenues from royal lands rather than taxes and on private armies of dependents and slaves rather than a standing salaried army, although rulers made presumptuous claims to administer as effectively as the late Roman state.

However, it is not an easy task to reconcile the supposed intrinsic weakness of the Visigothic state with its noteworthy longevity, relative military success, and its ideological assertions of rulership. The monarchy of Toledo "survived" over a century and a half and in fact almost three centuries if we start counting from the first permanent settlement of the Visigoths in 418 near Toulouse. Of all the "first-generation" (fifth-century) post-Roman kingdoms, (the Visigothic, Vandal, Ostrogothic, Suevic, and Burgundian kingdoms), the Visigoths were the only group still ruling when the second wave of kingdoms (Franks, Lombards, Anglo-Saxons, etc.) redrew the map of Western Europe. The Visigothic kingdom successfully faced a crushing military defeat against the Franks in 507 (admittedly with an important territorial loss in Gaul to the Frankish kingdom) and resisted the Byzantine armies more effectively than its Vandal and Ostrogothic neighbors. Furthermore, King Leovigild (r. 568–586) swallowed the Suevic state in northwestern Iberia in a single military campaign in 583.[8] To be sure, royal succession was not smooth—in fact there were few cases of peaceful accessions to the throne. But the Visigoths could at least boast that their kingdom remained unified in the long run contrary to the constant partition of their Frankish peers. The sophisticated ceremonial developed in the sixth and seventh centuries made their authoritative claims of central power a match for the ideological assertions of the contemporary Byzantine court.[9] As Chris Wickham has noted, contrary to the other post-Roman kingdoms, the Visigothic state seems to have grown stronger rather than weaker over time.[10] The history of the Visigothic kingdom, then, hardly fits any historiographical reputation as the sick man of early medieval Europe, waiting for the Arab and Berber armies to give it the final blow.

What needs to be assessed is to what extent this state succeeded in transmitting practices of political domination to social actors traditionally perceived as non-statal agents. There are good reasons to believe that the Visigothic state was more than an empty shell of centrally appointed office-holders ruling over a rebellious civil society of landowners. Even the conceptual separation between state apparatus and local powers must be questioned. In a previous work, I argued that the Visigothic state as an ideological enterprise from the 470s onwards granted the state a form of strength apparently denied by the monarchy's under-bureaucratization.[11] From very early on in the history of the Visigothic kingdom, so-called local powers may have found a language of interaction with the central monarchy, beginning a path-dependent cycle of mutual legitimacy. The language and practices of social and political legitimacy changed throughout the kingdom's history, but the ideal of a Visigothic king ruling over Iberia and its local elites was firmly established within a generation after imperial legitimacy faded from the Peninsula in the second half of the fifth century. We should ask ourselves what was the impact of the Visigothic state project on shaping the language and practice of agents who did not, strictly speaking, belong to the despotic state apparatus as defined by the monarchy itself.

The ultimate reach of state bureaucratic power can be approached from a different angle than the clash of compartmentalized central and local powers. To borrow Michael Mann's terminology, the despotic nature of the Toledo monarchy collided with (some) interests of men and women of local ascendancy, but the state's infrastructural power could work through them to meet the interests of state reproduction.[12] In more concrete terms, the sphere of action of royally appointed officials (the "despotic branch" of the Visigothic kingdom) only reveals part of the state's operation and reach. It is only when we consider how non-bureaucratic agents operated, in this case, "local powers," that the reach of the Visigothic state acquires a new dimension, permeating thickly into the fabric of Iberian society. The use of non-state agents with state purposes was the result of a tacit acknowledgement of the limits that the Visigothic state faced in building stable domination mechanisms. Through the use of despotic power proclaimed, for instance, in royal legislation, the monarchy of Toledo gave various agents the opportunity to build infrastructural power—sometimes not necessarily along the lines expected by the original legislator.

The ability to mobilize material resources (mainly manpower and tributes in kind and coin) is at the core of the "despotic" apparatus of every ancient state. In the absence of modern bureaucracies, "infrastructural" power becomes crucial to obtain such resources. Indeed, tax collection in the Visigothic kingdom is an area in which bureaucratic and non-bureaucratic agents intervened at various moments. Not surprisingly, the role of taxes within the post-Roman kingdoms has been at the center of debates over state strength. Chris Wickham is justly credited with the establishment of the current orthodoxy on state and taxation in the post-Roman West.[13] While the late Roman empire was a tax-raising state, the post-Roman kingdoms increasingly relied on landed elites to raise armies and maintain their bureaucratic apparatus. The consequence was a drop in the proportion of revenue flowing from taxes, and a reduction in the elaborate bureaucratic structure that had supported state revenue collection during the late Roman empire. If we limit our understanding of state strength to bureaucratic numbers, the post-Roman kingdoms would have thus been "weaker" states that the late Roman empire, as they relied less on a centralized administration and more on the collaboration of landed potentates. The western states lacked the "strength" of the contemporary tax raising of the Byzantine Empire and of the later Islamic caliphates.[14] This model (presented here as an oversimplified description of a much more nuanced explanation) works satisfactorily in the case of the

Iberian Peninsula. The importance of taxes to state income was very likely more reduced than during the empire, as armies were raised by different mechanisms. Likewise, the tax-collecting bureaucracy was simplified compared to the elaborate late Roman system, although some of its basic elements were present in the Visigothic kingdom.

What deserves more attention, however, is linking the "weakness" or "strength" of a state to the permanence or transience of certain bureaucratic features. In this chapter, I will advance two interrelated arguments vis-à-vis state strength/weakness. I will first argue that the Visigothic monarchy utilized a language of authority that emphasized the state's despotic power in the process of tax collection, in line with the presumptive bureaucratic nature of state power. The power of the state is often presented in these documents as an order-seeking force, which expects to successfully face the intervention of certain wicked subjects who disrupt the king's government. The historiographical model of collision between central and local powers largely derives from the language of these sources.

However, and this will be my second argument, the kingdom of Toledo relied (and perhaps successfully so) on the collaboration of other agents—predominantly bishops, landowners, and estate managers, that is, "local powers." Although these actors were never presented as tax collecting agents, they nevertheless performed crucial actions without which the monarchy and its officials would have not been able to raise economic resources, as proclaimed in the despotic language of the laws. Statehood existed beyond the self-proclaimed boundaries of state administration and incorporated several actors whose presence was crucial to the operation of tax collection. The supportive role of these actors was far from detrimental to their social pursuits. Yet while they potentially could and effectively did use the power granted by the state to advance their own interests, at the same time they built in state infrastructural practices throughout Visigothic society. Before focusing on the various actors involved in tax collection, let us take a quick glimpse at the taxation system of Toledo and its possible development throughout the sixth, seventh, and early eight centuries.

Taxation in the Visigothic Kingdom of Toledo

Several tributary practices of the kingdom of Toledo mirrored Roman antecedents and contemporary Byzantine examples. The most fundamental similarity was the crucial role of land tax (assessed in kind but commutable to coin). However, taxation in post-Roman Iberia seems to have had less uniformity and impact than the late Roman and Byzantine systems. For one thing, it is very likely that tax collection varied considerably according to regional and, more importantly, micro-regional lines. To borrow a concept developed by Shane Bjornlie in the case of Ostrogothic Italy, the sixth- and seventh-century Iberian Peninsula may have been dotted by "oases of taxes" rather than a uniform, all-encompassing tax system.[15]

While the Iberian evidence is less copious than the Ostrogothic documentation, there are some indications of a less than uniform tax scheme. To take one of the best-documented examples, centrally organized fiscal institutions such as mints show an uneven distribution throughout the kingdom. Northwestern Iberia, the former Suevic kingdom, had a disproportionate number of mints until the mid-seventh century in relation to the number of important cities and the size of its territory.[16] Several of these mints were in small towns that could not even boast an episcopal see of their own. The most satisfactory explanation of this uneven distribution remains, in my opinion, Pablo Díaz's argument that these mints represent an institutional inheritance from the Suevic kingdom after its conquest by Leovigild.[17] Coinage was intimately related to tributary cycles, which hints at the presence of a denser network of tax collection in this region than in other parts of the Peninsula. This does not mean they paid *more* taxes overall, but rather that state agents operated at a more local level than in other regions.

Grand state proclamations about taxation were also confronted with highly varying micro-realities. There were probably disparities regarding what type of land was subject to tax. Although much has been written about the Visigoths being exempt of taxes after their settlement within the empire, the current *communis opinio* asserts that Goths and Romans, however we want to define these groups, were subject to similar state demands (or lack thereof) by the late sixth century. Tax exemptions were thus granted on an individual basis rather than on collective ("ethnic") principles.[18] Moreover, some land was probably not subject to tax. A law from the reign of Chindaswinth (r. 642–653) aimed at securing a steady flow of taxes by preventing the sale of land subject to tribute. In the event that such a transaction took place, however, the *LV* V.4.19 mandated that the purchaser or beneficiary of lands subject to tribute pay the taxes associated with that particular land—even if, presumably, the purchaser had no obligation to pay taxes on any other lands he owned.[19] Nothing in the law indicates the ethnic "affiliation" of either side of the transaction, but rather examines their tax status. One side was responsible for the supply of horses and the payment of taxes, while the other, apparently, did not have the same liability and wanted to extend that privilege to newly acquired property. The Visigothic monarchy was forced to seek the cooperation of local notables to secure the documentation required by a centralized tax system. This law also enforced the notarial culture of non-state agents. As will presently be discussed, royal legislation ordered that land transfers, and likely tax assessments, be maintained by the municipal institutions that were predominantly controlled by local landowners.

The historical contingencies of the Visigothic kingdom also forced the central administration to engage different non-state agents over time. Leovigild's reign represents the first moment of political unity in the Peninsula since the withdrawal of the Roman administration. With the exception of a coastal strip under Byzantine control and, perhaps, the highlands in the Basque country, Leovigild could claim to rule over the whole of Iberia and Septimania after a series of military campaigns that occupied most of his reign. It is improbable that this conquest imposed a tax system *ex novo*; rather, it is likely that state authorities became more intrusive in a process that had remained until then largely under the control of local hands.[20] Evidence indicates that the reign of Leovigild's son and successor, Reccared (r. 586–601), had to deal with the friction that this intrusiveness created. The complaints of taxpayers were addressed in royal legislation: "A count, his deputy, or a royal estate overseer shall not dare to oppress the people with taxes, tributes, labor or, compulsory requisitions for their own benefit; nor shall they receive their allotted payment from a city or its territory; for . . . when we appoint officials, we also provide them with an income from our munificence. By the same command, we order the governor of the province, the count of the royal patrimony, and the administrators of our properties that they have no power over free people and they shall not harass them."[21]

The Visigothic state vigorously pursued the safeguarding of the state's despotic dimensions in the area of taxation. Regardless of the actual impact of tributes on state income, these stipulations reveal a tax system at work. Reccared did not decree that taxes should not be collected; rather, he wanted to prevent royal officials and estate managers from collecting taxes *for their own benefit*. Royal officials were manipulating the tax system to demand payments for what they could claim to be their services as administrators. These officials were not only local representatives of the king, as counts were in the cities. The group also included administrators of royal properties, which hints at the potential association between estate management and tax collection (a question to which I will return presently). As a mechanism to prevent abuses, local communities were to elect two officials—a *defensor* and a *numerarius* (with judicial and financial authority respectively).[22] The appointment of these local officials was left to the bishops and the people of each city, and may have remained the focus of political life into the seventh century in various regions of the Peninsula.[23] In addition, the law ordered bishops to oversee royal officials and denounce abuses or "they shall be liable to the sentence imposed by the council and shall be compelled to make reparation from their own property for such losses as the poor may have suffered through their silence."[24]

This is not the only document from Reccared's reign appointing bishops as overseers of royal agents. In 589, the III Council of Toledo (the same council in which Reccared publicly professed his Nicene Christianity) ordered that provincial synods should meet once every year. Royal officials as well as the administrators of the royal estates were to be present "so that they come to know how carefully and rightfully they must conduct themselves with the people and they neither burden free people nor oppress public slaves with superfluous tasks or requisitions."[25] Together with the *LV* XII.1.2, this canon of III Toledo sheds light on taxpayers' complaints about the role of state-appointed officials in the tax collection process. The monarchy intervened in what appears to be the demands of the taxpaying base on a specific issue (the role of the state officials) rather than proposing a radically new taxation structure. These clues help us piece together a situation in which a more intrusive state apparatus began to alter previous tributary practices, making it difficult for the population to separate this intrusion from Leovigild's military conquests. Reccared's administration offered potential solution to this dissatisfaction, by defining the limits of the spheres of action of various administrative agents. At the same time, as we shall soon see, this intrusion relied on the mobilization of the episcopate as a nonofficial actor in the process of tax collection.

A partial reorganization of the tax system took place during the reign of Chindaswinth and his son and successor Recceswinth (r. 653–672). Chindaswinth's consecration resulted from a conspiracy of Gothic nobles to overthrow the previous king, which led to a series of land expropriations and political assassinations. Chindaswinth attempted to reinforce central authority within the kingdom by issuing legislation.[26] His centralizing tendencies also manifested themselves in an endeavor to reorganize the tax system. The number of mints sharply declined, from fifty-four during Sisebut's reign (r. 612–621) to eleven during Recceswinth's reign, which suggests an attempt to centralize the coinage issued in provincial capitals and a few other cities.[27] Chindaswinth's reign also witnessed an attempt to stabilize and even increase the gold content of the *tremis*—the fraction of the Roman golden *solidus* that was minted in post-Roman Iberia.[28] Finally, one of the few laws that tackled question of taxation in the Visigothic kingdom dates from Chindaswinth's reign—the above-mentioned *LV* V.4.19 on transfers of subject-to-tax land. The king's concern was not, as was the case for Reccared's legislation, with abuses by royal officials. Rather, it aimed at preventing abuses by taxpayers, particularly tax evasion after the transfer of lands by sale or donation. Overall, the central years of the seventh century witnessed an effort to affirm the state's authority in tributary assessment and collection.

A third moment of change in tax practices took place in the last decades of the Visigothic kingdom, especially in the last two decades of the seventh century. The evidence suggests a real break in the impact of taxation on state finances and this was reflected in the reorganization of the military that seems to have taken place after the reign of Erwig (r. 680–687). King Erwig issued a law requiring that all free men respond to the call to arms, and imposing an obligation on landowners to bring a tenth of their slaves to fight with them.[29] Whereas previous readings of this law insisted that it merely represented continuity with previous practices, Amancio Isla has recently suggested that, in fact, we might be in the presence of a significant reorganization of the army—and, therefore, of its material (that is, tributary) support.[30] Although the Visigothic monarchy probably levied both paid and landed armies throughout the history of the kingdom, the latter became more important than the former by the late seventh century.[31] Given this preference, Erwig's decree of 683 condoning tax arrears (but only until 680) may be regarded as an indication of the declining importance of taxes in the maintenance of the army, since the monarchy no longer needed that income to pay for a standing army.[32] Also, the mention of a likely new royal official, the Count of the Treasury (*comes thesaurorum*) in 683 may reflect a reorganization of state finances.[33] However, as "late" as 693, a royal decree by Egica (r. 687–702) tried to secure tax payments from lands under direct episcopal jurisdiction and prevented bishops from requesting that rural churches pay for the taxes owed by the lands of their own sees.[34] In any event, Erwig's military law seems to have altered the proportion of tax and land in the army's resources—and, hence, their relative impact on the maintenance of the largest state expense in premodern states. The reigns of Reccared, Chindaswinth/Recceswinth, and Erwig/Egica suggest an active state policy vis-à-vis taxation that involved readjustments between fiscal bureaucracy and local notables. In any case, the despotic claims of the Visigothic state were confronted with the limits posed by unavoidable collaboration with non-statal agents.

This overview indicates that the Visigothic court was concerned with taxation and aimed at regulating various aspects of this process, including the composition of the taxpaying base and the modalities of tax collection. Uniformity may not have prevailed, but this does not reveal any less interest by Visigothic kings in implementing state power to define the operation and boundaries of the tax system. The Visigothic monarchy, acting as a "despotic agent," claimed its right to establish, maintain, and modify taxpaying practices. It may have done so in grandiloquent language contrasting with the dwindling impact of taxes within the state income structure.[35] That language was inherited from the despotic phrasing of late Roman law and, perhaps, contemporary Byzantine legislation since the ceremonial life of the kingdom appropriated Constantinopolitan patterns.[36] Ultimately, the central administration of the kingdom never ceased to see taxation as a prerogative of the king and his appointed officials. The grandiose language of the laws left several aspects of tax collection deliberately undetermined—especially how taxes were to be collected and how tax assessment was to be controlled. This should not surprise us, since the post-Roman kingdoms were much less bureaucratized states than their late Roman predecessor. The Visigothic monarchy, I would like to suggest, showed considerable awareness of the challenges that this situation presented to its presumptive claims of tax collection. The smooth cycle of tax assessment, collection, and transportation depended on the active involvement of a larger group of actors, whose intervention we can only reconstruct through discrete references in the extant fragmentary evidence.

Taxation and Its Various Agents

Tax collection under the Visigothic kingdom mobilized various agents, as it had during the late Roman Empire. Nevertheless state bureaucracy in this area was certainly less complex than it had been in the fourth and early fifth centuries, although it did not abandon all of its hierarchies and practices.[37] Royal fiscal officials are attested to in several sixth- and seventh-century documents. The structure of the tax-collecting bureaucracy may have changed over time, but it seems that there was a centrally appointed court official who oversaw the tributary cycle. In some documents, this official appears as "count of the royal patrimony" (*comes patrimonii*). His functions are never clearly described, but it is assumed that they included the management of revenues from both land tax and royal properties. Other officials, known as *numerarii*, were in charge of tax collection at a more local level—perhaps with jurisdiction over a city or a group of cities.[38] *Numerarii* probably had aides who helped them in their task, although we cannot tell whether they were professional staff or personal (private) assistants.[39] *Numerarii* also appear in the Reccared's law, mentioned earlier, which mandates that they be appointed by the bishop and the people.[40] The evidence suggests that the urban leadership jealously protected appointments to this fiscal position. During the reign of Wamba, Theudemund, a commander of the king's personal guard (*spatarius*), was appointed *numerarius* over Merida. His appointment was "against his lineage and social status" as well as "against the norms." Nevertheless, King Egica asked the bishops gathered at XVI Toledo protect Theudemund and his descendants from any judicial claim because his appointment had been decided by the bishop Faustus and taxpayers.[41]

Less clear is the role played by military and administrative officials (dukes and counts) in the process.[42] Taken together, the legislation discussed above shows efforts throughout the history of the kingdom of Toledo to keep military officials away from tributary administration. But the same laws warn against the abuses perpetrated by these officials on taxpayers, making plain that "para-legal" tributary demands existed and created tensions with local communities. These demands could have been tied to royal officials' obligations to support the army and solve legal disputes, which presumably included tax disputes.[43] Thus, based on the dukes' and counts' military, administrative, and judicial roles, it is not difficult to imagine how their functions may have widened to encompass at least some aspects of the tributary cycle, such as resolving tributary disputes or organizing the army supply.

This situation may have led to abuses and, occasionally, political threats. The central government had limited resources to check royally appointed officials, and in this area relied on the collaboration of non-bureaucratic agents. The episcopate had a particularly relevant role, as it provided a body of influential men of local esteem in every corner of the kingdom. As we saw above, bishops oversaw some aspects of tax collection, especially after the conversion of Reccared to Nicene Christianity.[44] They were not in charge of collecting taxes but, rather, of preventing royal officials from committing abuses. A document from 592, also dating from Reccared's reign, offers insight into this particular role. Four bishops of northeastern Iberia addressed the *numerarii* appointed by the *comes patrimonii* to collect taxes in the region in a letter known as *De fisco Barcinonensi*. The letter aimed at establishing limits to the amount of coin (assessed in *siliquae*) the tax collectors could demand from those who wanted to commute their taxes in dry measures of grain (in barley *modii*).

> We decide . . . that you shall demand eight *siliquae* . . . for one legal *modius* [of barley], and one *siliqua* [each?] for your work, and four *siliquae* for inevitable losses or the exchange rate between kind and coin, which makes a total of fourteen *siliquae* with respect to the barley. . . . However, if somebody refused to obey according to our agreement or managed to pay you in kind less than what is due to you, he shall be compelled to pay his fiscal dues. And if your representatives obtained anything beyond what our agreement gives account of, you will order it corrected and restored to those from whom it was unlawfully taken.[45]

This text fits very well within the spirit of abovementioned Canon 18 from III Toledo, according to which bishops are supposed to meet with royal officials and give them an admonition on good government. Moreover, Reccared's law on bishops denouncing abuses can also provide context for this letter (if the law was actually issued before 592). The role that both royal and conciliar legislation assigned to the episcopate—preventing abuses—led bishops to control the exchange rate between kind and coin, to address what had been a source of arbitrariness during the late empire.[46] In other words, the expression of moral expectations of good government adopted the form of tributary norms, enforcing customary exchange rates of taxes in kind. Bishops did not become state agents in the "despotic" sense, however. They never determined taxes and they did not collect taxes. Perhaps they did not even determine the *adaeratio* rate, and instead merely sanctioned the agreement previously negotiated between the *numerarii* and local taxpayers. And yet at a time of recently imposed and more intrusive state presence, their intervention must have been fundamental to secure the flow of tributes to the crown. The intervention of bishops, therefore, may not have been a sign of state "weakness." Rather, the letter shows that the central monarchy effectively transmitted the norms of state (tax) administration. The bishops shaped their role as overseers of good government by regulating the practice of *adaeratio* and tacitly collaborating in the smooth process of tax collection. The letter itself, therefore, shows the success, rather than the weakness, of the despotic ambitions of the state while, at the same time, indicating its infrastructural limits and reliance on noncentrally appointed groups.

The combination of state reach without extensive infrastructural means can also be observed in the taxpaying base, a usually neglected group in the analysis of the Visigothic kingdom's tributary history. To be sure, little evidence survives in terms of who paid taxes in the Visigothic kingdom. As I mentioned before, traditional scholarship focused on those who were presumably exempt—the "Goths" and the Church. This interpretation ascribes later, medieval concerns to the Visigothic state. This is not to say that tax exemptions did not exist. The model of "islands of taxations" admits the possibility (and, very likely, the reality) of areas or groups whose tributary relationship with the state was not structured around tax payments. What cannot be demonstrated is the collective nature of such groups, such as a hypothetical Gothic nobility as an exempt group based on descent.

The taxpaying base, as in most premodern states, consisted of landowners, from small peasants to great landowners. Other taxes are attested to (especially customs taxes), but the bulk of tax revenue came from the land.[47] The late Roman category of the taxpaying farmer (*colonus*) vanished from the Visigothic legal codes after the fifth century, although it survived in a few legal formulaic texts.[48] Instead, the law of Chindaswinth mentions urban leaders (*curiales*) and free landowners in general (*privati*) as the taxpaying base obligated to pay taxes to the royal fisc. The law made it clear that the assessment was based on land itself. It ordered that following any transfer of land through purchase, donation, or other means, the new owners had to register their names in public documents. As Paul King once suggested, these registers were probably the same documents that recorded the names of former slaves of Jewish owners to ensure that the newly freed would become subject to taxation, according to a law enacted by Sisebut.[49]

The law of Chindaswinth suggests the very likely existence in seventh-century Iberia of a type of civic government common in the post-fifth century Roman Empire and some successor kingdoms—government by notables.[50] The Visigothic monarchy did not collude with this group but did rely on it to support state infrastructural power. The existence of urban tax registries was, among other things, an acknowledgement of the governmental role played by these notables. Moreover, it is not difficult to imagine that great landowners were responsible for local tax collection, gathering taxes from tenants and small peasants. This practice was not unheard of in late antiquity: landowners acting as tax collectors vis-à-vis their tenants and small peasants were a recurrent feature of the late Roman countryside.[51] As Cam Grey recently argued, landowners who collected taxes were the concrete expression of state interaction for most peasants in the fourth and fifth centuries throughout the Mediterranean.[52] In the next section, I would like to suggest that tax collection by landowners also existed in the Visigothic kingdom of Toledo. Without necessarily arguing that there was a straight continuity between the two states, one can contend that the central administration of Toledo recognized the limits of its despotic power as much as its late Roman predecessor. Tax collection was a highly localized affair, one that would have involved a bureaucratic apparatus even in the context of a limited number of "islands of taxation."

Landowning and Tax Collection

In order to address this question, I propose to look at a series of documents, a unique set of texts known as *pizarras visigodas* (Visigothic slates). In recent years, the potential to study these documents has expanded thanks to the lexical analysis provided by Isabel Velázquez in her carefully edited collection of slates.[53] The texts written on the slates offer a window into the rural life of central Iberia from whence most of them come. They reveal a functional Latin used for daily record keeping. Some of them may have been used as permanent records (such as slates recording contracts of sale).[54] Their individual archaeological contexts are difficult to reconstruct, although the areas in which they have been found present a particular settlement pattern: few and small cities, fortified hilltop sites, and a rural landscape that combined dispersed settlements with a few peasant villages—villages that increased in number throughout the seventh century.[55] These slates deal with various topics, from religious prayers and copies of psalms to alphabets that have been interpreted as school exercises; from an oath in a judicial case about swine to a letter concerning the harvest of olives on an unknown property. One subgroup of slates only registers a series of numbers and are very likely related to some type of accounting.[56] Overall, some 160 textual slates offer a glimpse into a buoyant rural world engaged in diverse economic activities, legal disputes, and a practical Christianity.[57]

One group of no more than twenty textual slates has been the subject of controversy—a controversy that pertains to the impact of taxation on seventh-century Iberia. These slates consist of lists of (presumed) payments in kind.[58] For instance, seventh-century Visigothic slate no. 45, from Diego Alvaro in the province of Ávila, lists a series of otherwise unknown characters paying dry measures (*sextaria*, sg. *sextarium*) of grain, as is mentioned in the first few lines from one side of the slate:[59]

> [—] one (?) sextarium.
> The son of Elianus, one (?) sextarium
> Erugio, one sextarium
> Murilda, one sextarium
> Domnus the elder, one sextarium   5
> Domnela, by command of her master [—]
> W[—]la, one sextarium [—]
> Half, Valeria, one sextarium
> Serena, by command of her (?) master [—]
> one sextarium [—]   10
> by command, Teodadus [—]
> one sextarium Aiutor
> Feruodus, in another tenancy/property (?) [—]

We are able to trace other types of payments in these type of slates, like cash or animals. A good example is the fragmentary Visigothic slate no. 76, from the same area and period:[60]

> [—] and
> [—] received one *solidus* [—]
> [—] one sheep (for?) Letorius [—]
> [—] one sheep for Valerius
> One sheep for the plowed fields, Pa[—]   5
> [—]eriuo, five *modii* for [. . .]

Finally, another subgroup lists names and amounts, such as slate no. 1:[61]

> Vicentius, two
> Bonifatius, two
> Bitorius, one
> Profidentius, one
> Ferbodus, one   5
> Perias [—]

Scholarly interpretations of these texts are split into two camps. In the first interpretation, the Visigothic slates recording payments are accounts from rural estates. They reveal a manorial administration interested in keeping records of rents paid by tenants (free or unfree) working on large properties.[62] In the second interpretation, these same slates are records of tax payments in kind (or occasionally in coin) collected at the local level by state agents. These "state agents" could have been royal officials or, as Iñaki Martín Viso has suggested, clerics and landowners, who thus asserted social, semi-autonomous power in the countryside.[63]

I would like to suggest that there might be no contradiction between these interpretations. Indeed, these slates might indicate that tax collection was, at its foundation, tied to the property structures of large landownership. In other words, great landowners may have been in charge of collecting taxes at the local level before these taxes reached the royal administration, as the "tributary" interpretation of the slates argues, and they would have used the slates both for internal record keeping and tax collection purposes. It is less clear that this practice developed from an interest in manipulating socioeconomic relationships. The interest in record keeping more likely resulted from state requirements to control the process of tax collection at the local level and the interest of landowners in documenting this process in the face of potential state demands. Peasant exploitation existed and taxes could occasionally be unlawfully appropriated. But laws on taxation were more than just an ideological construct to affirm state power. Or, perhaps, ideological constructs were powerful enough to translate into concrete requirements. On the other hand, these state requirements offered the possibility of maintaining (and perhaps developing) managerial practices to assist estate administration, which would partially concur with the "manorial" interpretation of the slates. Therefore some of these varied and fragmentary accounting slates could be tax registers, others manorial records, and yet others could be both. In all cases, however, they reveal a tributary world intimately related to large properties.

Let me illustrate this suggestion with one example. Visigothic slate no. 5 dates from the late sixth or seventh century—that is, it could date from anytime during the kingdom of Toledo. It was found near Paralejos de Solís, in the province of Salamanca, although the exact place of origin and its archaeological context is unknown. Both sides of the slate are inscribed. On one side, we find a series of numbers. On the other side, the text presents a series of payments in kind (both in *modii* and *sextaria*) together with names. Although part of the document is missing, the remaining portions can be reconstructed as follows:⁶⁴

[—] six s(extaria)
[—] and Simplicius, one modius
[—] Masetus, six sextaria
[—] gave ropes for one modius
[—] and Sigerius and Iustina, one modius   5
[—] Precurasor, three modii
[—] (. . .)deo, eight modii
[—] John [—(took?)] sixty modii for the services
[—]ota twelve (modii?)
[—]   10
[—] adds for Sigerius to the modii from Lebaia
sixteen modii of sowing seeds, [—] modii of wheat
To Flascinus, two modii; to Flaina, six sextaria with [—]
her co-freedwomen. Flaina, one sextarium, Maxima, four sextaria
Manno, one modius, Procula, three sextaria, Bonus and
  Flamnus   15
and Nonnus the elder and Patricius, one modius
John took/paid (*exprendit*) for the horses
thirty-three modii. Masetius two modii
In (?) Bodenecas, three modii

This slate presents some intriguing features. For instance, we find certain people who are presumably making payments, while others, Flascinus and Flaina, are receiving grain.⁶⁵ Moreover, different types of payments are recorded. One payment is made in ropes, but assessed in grain. In one instance, there is an explicit reference to the type of grain being paid (wheat), which may indicate that the other payments of grain were made in barley, or even cash but assessed in grain. Also, a certain Sigerius pays in sowing seed, maybe as a repayment of a seed loan. None of these hypotheses are, of course, easy to corroborate based solely on the information provided by the slate itself. However, it is very likely that this variety of payments to and from different people reveals the work of an estate manager who keeps track of payments, loans, and expenses at the center of a large property.

The lines in which "John" is mentioned pose an interesting challenge. Although they could refer to two different Johns, I believe the Johns of lines 8 and 17 are the same person. Not only is he mentioned together with the largest grain quantities (sixty and thirty-three *modii*), but his actions are also the only ones for which we have a specific description in this document. The verb is missing in line 8 (only the last letters survive and indicate a verb in the past tense), while it did survive in line 17. In line 8, he is dealing with *angariae*, which I translated ambiguously on purpose as "services." In certain high medieval texts, *angariae* refers to labor rents or corvées.[66] So if we follow the manorial interpretation of the slate, John would be paying rent *and* buying or renting horses from the estate owner.

However, in this context I believe *angaria* takes the more classical meaning of "compulsory services," usually performed at the request of the state.[67] Indeed, the law of Reccared against the abuses of royal officials prohibited officials from requesting taxes, tributes, and *angariae* for their own benefit. Likewise, the canon of the Third Council of Toledo mentions *angariae* as a source of abuses by royal officials and administrators of royal properties.[68] I believe we must read the *angariae* of Visigothic slate no. 5 as a tributary demand commuted to grain—or as a synonym of tax altogether.

Moreover, lines 17-18, which indicate that John took or paid grain for horses, may also specify a tributary practice. Chindaswith's law on land sales, which might be contemporary to the slate, may help us reconstruct an alternative meaning for these "horses." As I mentioned before, the Visigothic monarchy wanted to secure the collection of taxes over certain types of land in case they were sold or transferred. "Urban leaders and free people, who customarily supply horses and pay taxes in the public treasury, shall never sell, donate, or transfer their property through any type of exchange. However, if it happens that they convey all their property, out of either desire or need, by sale, donation, or transfer, he who receives it shall pay the assessed tax of the person from whom he received (that property)."[69] Zeumer, the editor of the Visigothic laws, believed that "horses" refers to the *cursus publicus*, the state-organized transportation system of the late Roman empire.[70] We do not have other specific evidence of this system working in the Visigothic period, so the law may also be referring to a specific tax with an unknown purpose. If it refers to the *cursus publicus*, it is also possible that not all taxpayers provided horses, but some among them may have supplied fodder or coin in exchange for payment. In any event, when we read Visigothic slate no. 5 against the background of this law, the actions of John can be framed within the context of the tributary system of Toledo.

Since the verb in line 8 is missing, and the verb in line 17 could be interpreted as either "took" (presumably from the estate granary) or "paid" (again, presumably into the estate granary), we can consider two possible scenarios. In the first case, an estate manager is recording rent and/or tax payments *from* tenants, payments or loans *to* other peasants, and tax payments made by a local, perhaps small, free landowner named John. In the second scenario, the estate manager keeps records of rents and/or tax payments from smaller peasants, loans, and disbursements of the estate's assigned taxes through an estate employee/manager/slave named John. In both cases, however, the document highlights the crucial role of large landownership in the process of tax collection.

If my interpretation is correct, we need to read the Visigothic slates within the context of estate management *and* state tributary demands. The despotic ambitions of the Visigothic state relied on manorial practices of record keeping. Record keeping in the rural areas of central Iberia (and the Peninsula as a whole) had the double purpose of administering property and keeping track of tax payments. This double goal may explain why these slates, especially those listing payments, are strictly contemporary to the Visigothic kingdom of Toledo. Indeed, they started being produced in the late sixth century, when, as I have argued before, tributary practices were reorganized under Leovigild and Reccared, and they had ceased to be written by the turn of the eighth century, either as a result of the impact of Erwig's military law or—perhaps as a consequence of the Visigothic kingdoms' defeat by Islamic armies—new tributary practices. Be that as it may, state requirements during the sixth and most of the seventh century led to the development of managerial practices of record keeping that could be used for a different purpose, namely estate management. In other words, as in the case of episcopal intervention in the tax collection process, the adoption of state practices in the post-Roman countryside built in "infrastructural habits," which would, in turn, benefit the state.[71]

The association between large property structures, managerial techniques, and tax collection may explain why abuses in the tributary system were not only associated with royal officials but also royal estate administrators (*vilici* and *actores*) in Visigothic legislation.[72] Four decades ago, Luis García Moreno had already called attention to the potential fiscal role that royal estate administrators may have had in taxation, although he correctly believed these *vilici* were not royal functionaries in charge of tax collection.[73] Royal legislation includes them as potential appropriators of undue taxes as late as 683, when king Erwig names them together with other officials in his decree on tax arrears.[74] This decree seems to reveal that royal estate administrators did not only collect rents from servile-status peasants working the lands of the crown.

They were also probably involved in the collection of taxes from nearby alodial land in the remote corners of the Iberian countryside.

The Visigothic slates should therefore be seen both as documents registering tax payments and as estate accounts. Individual slates may refer to one of each category or, as in the case of PV 5, both. For the purposes of this chapter, it is important to stress that both types of activity were part of a common managerial world of large properties in the northern plateau. They indicate that the Visigothic monarchy could rely on preexisting social structures to spread state power through society, operating on the tacit recognition that it lacked de facto despotic power to do so. Rent and tax collection could operate on the same proprietary principles and, as John Haldon has argued, they could become indistinguishable from the point of view of class relations.[75] The abuses by royal estate managers mentioned in Visigothic legislation lend support to the possibility that tax collection could be used by landowners as another mechanism of economic exploitation.

State reliance on great landowners for tax collection—or, better yet, on property structures—can then be approached with a different model than the opposition between state "weakness" and "strength." Moreover, landowners incorporated notarial practices of tax collection into the administration of their estates. Like the bishops in *De fisco Barcinonensi*, landowners were also able to employ tax language to assert non-state modes of domination. Their role in the maintenance of urban tax and property registers as well as their practices as infrastructural state agents in the countryside could eventually become mechanisms to assert their claims to legitimate ascendancy over their own communities—a legitimacy that could not be solely based on economic grounds.

Conclusion: Was the Visigothic State a "Weak State"?

In the preceding pages, I have argued that the Visigothic kings of Toledo claimed a monopoly on the process of tax collection and direct control over the centralized agents in charge of tax collection (*comes patrimonii, numerarii*, etc.), regardless of the actual impact that taxes may have had on state finances. The laws of the period present the tributary cycle as a highly harmonious process only interrupted by the wicked forces of cheating taxpayers and abusive officials. The monarchy offered remedies for both of these evils, specifically by applying the king's justice through its local branches (judges and counts) or by direct intervention of the monarch.

The solution to these problems, however, required more than just judicial intervention. After all, legal remedies depended on the ability to access the king's justice, which was mediated by the same actors that the language of the law assumed could interfere against the fisc: taxpayers (especially great landowners), judges (counts and other administrative officeholders), military commanders, and notables in general. Furthermore, family, friendship, and patronage relationships tied together some members of all these groups in social networks, which may have undermined any attempt to create autonomous state power. Facing these limitations, kings encouraged the intervention of non-bureaucratic agents, especially bishops but also other local notables (such as the *defensores* of individual cities). Moreover, the state demanded that taxpaying entities adopt record-keeping practices, some of them public (such as city polyptychs) and, as I have argued, others more private in character (such as records of private tax collection). The state's "despotism" brought potentially undermining agents into performing power practices associated with state authority. Whether consciously or not, these individuals brought the state, as it were, at least in its tax-extracting capacity, to numerous corners of the Visigothic kingdom. The question is how this was possible.

As the central/local powers model posits, the interests of royal officials and local landowners could, and occasionally did, collide. Nevertheless, state despotic power opened up possibilities of power practices that could be used for the advantage of those actors involved at the local level. Landowners were able to follow managerial strategies that asserted both their economic ascendancy in the countryside and their social and political leadership over their communities. Likewise, bishops could use their supervisory powers to affirm their leadership in relation to other competitors (royal officials, local notables, and clergy) by expanding their public interventions to issues affecting a large number of people under their pastoral care. However, the development of what appeared to be autonomous practices by local elites ultimately reinforced the infrastructural dimensions of state power. By accepting the role that legal norms gave them (tacitly or explicitly), various social actors built up state power in the crucial area of tax collection.

If this interpretation is correct, the history of taxation during the Visigothic kingdom of Toledo shows a successful attempt by the monarchy to build state power throughout its territory. Paraphrasing Seth Richardson's conception of early Mesopotamian states, while at the beginning of the period the Gothic monarchy may not have completely held sovereignty in the field of taxation, it chased after this sovereignty for most of its history, and, I am inclined to believe, successfully so.[76] The importance of tax revenue to state finances probably declined throughout the sixth century. Yet we do not necessarily need to see this decline as a failure of the state to tax subjects. Instead, it may have been the consequence of a reform in military organization, or a combination of multiple factors. Thus, for the purposes of this chapter, it does not matter how much land was taxed but rather to what extent the state could incorporate important social actors into the acceptance of the principle that the despotic rulings of the king were to be accepted as normative practice.

The Visigothic kingdom, like most premodern states, could not compete with modern nation states in terms of developed bureaucratic power. Post-Roman kingdoms in particular witnessed a downsizing of centralized bureaucratic institutions compared to the despotic late Roman empire. But what needs to be questioned is to what extent the dwindling of the central state apparatus represented a weakening of statehood. As I argued in this chapter, state power was consolidated by the intervention of non-bureaucratic agents through the embedding of despotic decisions into practices of specific social actors. In the case of taxation, the monarchy relied on the existing habitus of bishops, city-based notables, and landowners to achieve its goals. Consciously or not, and regardless of the fact that they could also use the powers attributed by the state's strategy for their own social and economic advantage, these groups built an infrastructural statehood at the local level on an everyday basis. In this sense, the actions of Fructuosus's father in the remote areas of El Bierzo could very well have been perceived as a form of state interaction at the local level, whether he was collecting taxes or rents from his domains. Looking at these capillary networks of invisible state power, the "weakness of the Visigothic monarchy" begins to fall as an appropriate hermeneutical model.

NOTES

1. Gregum suorum requireret rationes (*Vita Fructuosi*, II).
2. Vigil and Barbero 1970.
3. Martin 2003, 178–79.
4. Sánchez-Albornoz 1971, 255–375; Barbero and Vigil 1978. More recently, Wickham 2005, 98–99.
5. For a structurally conflictual relationship between state and aristocracies, see Díaz and Valverde Castro 2000. An interpretation emphasizing "conflict-cum-dialogue" (though limited to northwestern Iberia) can be found in Castellanos and Martín Viso 2005. Cf. Díaz and Menéndez Bueyes 2005, who argue that in certain areas, such as the

Cantabrian basin, these local powers consisted mostly of indigenous communal structures without much of an aristocratic element. I myself followed this line of interpretation in previous work (Fernández 2006, 222–24). See Arce 2011, on the power of bishops over the monarchy.

6. This is a model put forward in Van Dam 1985, 48–53.

7. Manzano Moreno 2006, 29–34. Cf. Arce 2011, 299.

8. Iohan. Bicl., *Chron.*, 66.

9. Ripoll 2000, 390–91; Arce 2011, 59–72.

10. Wickham 2005, 93.

11. Fernández, forthcoming.

12. Mann 1984.

13. Wickham 1984 and a more recent and expanded elaboration in Wickham 2005, 56–150.

14. Wickham 2005, 56.

15. Bjornlie 2014.

16. Pliego Vázquez 2009, 128–44.

17. Díaz 2011, 191–206.

18. García Moreno 1971, 236–40. King 1972, 65–67. Gothic "immunity": Sánchez-Albornoz 1971, 134–40. Hendy 1988, 51. Cf. Thompson 1969, 133–34.

19. See infra, n. 68.

20. Martín Viso 2013, 73–75. A pessimistic assessment of the survival of the Roman tax system in the late fifth century can be found in Jiménez Garnica 2011.

21. Ut nullis indictionibus, exactionibus, operibus vel angariis comes, vicarius vel vilicus pro suis utilitatibus populos adgravare presumant nec de civitate vel territorio annonam accipiant; quia . . . quod, dum iudices ordinamus, nostra largitate eis compendia ministramus. Simili auctoritate iubemus rectorem provincie sive comitem patrimonii aut actores fisci nostri, ut nullam in privatis hominibus habeant potestatem nullaque eos molestia inquietent (*LV* XII.1.2).

22. For *numerarii* in the late Roman empire, see Jones 1964, 450. For the *defensor* in Visigothic legislation, see King 1972, 79–84. For the role of the *defensor* in the post-Roman world, see Schmidt-Hofner 2014.

23. Kulikowski 2004, 307–8.

24. Sacerdotes vero, quos divina obtestatione conmonemus, si excessus iudicum aut actorum scierint et ad nostram non retulerint agnitionem, noverint se concilii iudicio esse plectendos, et detrimenta, que pauperes eorum silentio pertulerint ex eorum rebus illis restituenda.

25. Ut discant quam pie et iuste cum populis agere debeant, ne in angariis aut in operationibus superfluis sive privatum onerent sive fiscalem gravent (III Toledo, 18).

26. For the administrative reforms of the mid-seventh century, see Martin 2003, 175–91.

27. The most current study on Visigothic coinage can be found in Pliego Vázquez 2009. However, as the author herself has pointed out, the large number of mints during

the period of Sisebut could also be the result of the larger number of surviving pieces from that period.

28. Ibid., 199.
29. *LV* IX.2.9.
30. Isla 2010, 54–68.
31. García Moreno 1974, 65–66. Isla 2010, 9–22
32. XIII Toledo, *Lex edita*.
33. XIII Toledo, *De uiris illustribus officii palatini*. However, this court official may have existed in earlier times, although there is no definite evidence (Valverde Castro 2007, 247–49). Cf. Arce 2011, 83–94.
34. XVI Toledo, *Tomus*. Cf. XVI Toledo 5. Isla 2010, 95.
35. Valverde Castro 2000, 238-241.
36. McCormick 1986, 297–327. Valverde Castro 2000, 181–95. But see Collins 1995, 126–27, on some noticeable differences between Visigothic and Byzantine legislation.
37. Jones 1964, 411–62. Tax assessment and collection: Grey 2011, 189–97.
38. García Moreno 1974, 35–54. King 1972, 53–53.
39. *De fisco Barcinonensi* (ut tam vos quam agentes, sive adiutores vestri).
40. City *numerarii* and *comites patrimonii* are attested as late as 693, in the case of Mérida (XVI Toledo, *Lex edita in conformatione concilii* and *Suscriptiones*).
41. XVI Toledo, *Lex edita in conformatione concilii*. For the role of *spatarii* in the Visigothic court, see Isla 2002, 833–36.
42. Counts: Martin 2003, 161–65. Dukes: Isla 2002, 836–43.
43. Martin 2003, 151–59.
44. Fernández 2006. For a somewhat different interpretation of the document, see Martín Viso 2013, 76–77.
45. Decrevimus, ut tam vos quam agentes, sive adiutores vestri pro uno modio canonico ad populum exigere debeatis, hoc est siliquas octo, et pro laboribus vestris siliquam unam, et pro inevitabilibus damnis vel inter pretia specierum siliquas quatuor quae faciunt in uno siliquas quatuordecim inibi hordeo. . . . Si quis sane secundum consensum nostrum acquiescere noluerit vel tibi inferre minime procuraverit in specie, quod tibi convenerit, fiscum suum inferre procuret. Quod si ab agentibus vestris aliqua superexacta fuerint, quam huius consensi nostri tenor demonstrat, vos emendare et restituere cui male ablata sunt ordinetis.
46. Mazzarino 2002, 143.
47. For other taxes, see García Moreno 1974, 54–65. Cf. *PV* 2 and 97.
48. Castellanos 1998. *FV* 36.
49. *LV* XII.2.13. King 1972, 64–65.
50. Laniado 2002, 131–223; Liebeschuetz 2001, 124–36; Schmidt-Hofner 2014.
51. Mirković 1996. *CTh*, XI.22.4. Tax collecting was considered a compulsory service (*munus*) in laws from 365 and 386 (*CTh*, XII.6.6 and XII.6.20). Another law from 364 (*CTh*, XII.6.7) established that these *susceptores* could not be members of the curial order, but

must possess the appropriate "reputation and property" (*moribus quam facultatibus*) to perform this task.

52. Grey 2011, 185–86.

53. Velázquez 2000, 2004. The examples in this chapter are taken from the latter edition.

54. For instance, *PV* 8, from Galinduste, Salamanca, records the sale of an unknown good for three *solidi* or *PV* 40 (I), in which a certain Gregory sells a plot of land to his nephew, Desiderius, for an unknown number of *solidi*.

55. Martín Viso 2006, 276–83. For village archaeology in Spain, see Vigil-Escalera Guirado 2007.

56. Díaz and Martín Viso 2011.

57. Velázquez 2004, 84–113.

58. For a description of these slates, see Martín Viso 2006, 266–70.

59. II. [—]uuomi s(e)s(tarium) [I?] | filius Eliani s(e)s(statium) [I?] | Erugio s(e)s(tarium) I | Murildi s(e)s(tarium) I | Domnus magior s(e)s(tarium) I | Domnella p(er) mandato sui d[om]ni [—] | uu[—]la [—]s sesta[rium unum?—] | semis Valeria sestarium u[num—] | Serena p(er) ma[n]dato domn[I sui?—] | sestarium unu[m—] | mandato Teodatus [—] | unum Aiutor | Feruodus in alio cus[so—].

60. [—] et p+u[—] | [s]uscepto solido uno [—] | [—]+ius uerbice uno Letori[o?—] | [—uer]bice uno Valerio uerbi | ce uno pro arata Pa[—] | [—]eriuo modius V pro[—].

61. Vincentius II | Bonifatius II | Bitorius I | Profidentius I | Ferbodus I | Perias [—].

62. Velázquez 2004, 85–101. Wickham 2005, 223–26.

63. The standard "taxation interpretation" is in Martín Viso 2006, 283–90.

64. I.——| [—] s(estaria VI | [—]s et Simplicius mod(ium) I | [—]+sus Maseti s(e)s(taria) VI | [—]+s dedi licias mod(ium) I | [—]s et Sigerius et Iustina mod(ium) I | [—] Precurasor mod(ios) III | [—]deo mod(ios) VIII | [—]uit Ioannis in angarias mod(ios) LX | [—]ota XII |——| [—] [[om ad oc]] | [—]n+etum adicie p(er) Sigerius ad mod(ios?) a Lebaia | semertura mod(ios) XVI, tritico mod(io)s [—] | Flascino mod(ios) II, Flaine s(estaria) VI cum a[—?] | suas conlibertas Flaina s(estarium) I, Maxima s(estaria) IIII | Manno mod(ium) I, Procula s(estaria) III, Bonus et Flamnus | et Nonnus maior et Patricius mod(ium) I | exprendit Ioannis ad kaballos mod(ios) | XXXIII, Masetius mod(ios) II | ad Bodenecas mod(ios) III.

65. Isabel Velázquez does not rule out the possibility that the dative is a mistaken nominative, and that therefore, Flascinus and Flaina are also making payments (Velázquez 2004, 138–39).

66. Wickham 2005, 293–99.

67. For *angariae* as compulsory transportation services in the Roman Empire, see Mitchell 1976. For a similar meaning in the Carolingian context, see Goffart 1982, 7.

68. See supra, n. 25.

69. Curiales igitur vel privati, qui caballos ponere vel in arca publica functionem exolvere consueti sunt, numquam quidem facultatem suam vendere vel donare vel commutatione aliqua debent alienare. Tamen si contigerit, aut voluntate aut necessitate, eos

alicui, sive vinditione aut donatione seu commutatione, omnem suam facultatem dare, ille, qui acceperit, censum illius, a quo accepit, exolvere procurabit (*LV* 5.4.19).

70. Also, King 1972, 64–65.
71. I owe the suggestion of this concept to Seth Richardson.
72. *LV* VIII.1.9, IX.1.8, X.1.16, and XII.1.2.
73. García Moreno 1974, 28–35. See also Martin 2003, 159–61.
74. Si quisquis ille dux, comes, tiufadus, numerarius, vilicus aut quicumque curam publicam agens tributa exacto sbe comisso annis singulis pleanrio numero non exegerit aut exacta apud se retinuerit (XIII Toledo, *Lex edita*).
75. Haldon 1993, 75–87.
76. Richardson 2012, 14.

BIBLIOGRAPHY

Arce, J. 2011. *Esperando a los árabes. Los visigodos en Hispania (507–711)*. Madrid: Marcial Pons.

Barbero, A., and M. Vigil. 1978. *La formación del feudalismo en la Península Ibérica*. Barcelona: Crítica.

Bjornlie, S. 2014. "Law, Ethnicity and Taxes in Ostrogothic Italy: A Case for Continuity, Adaptation and Departure." *Early Medieval Europe* 22 (2): 138–70.

Castellanos, S. 1998. "Terminología textual y relaciones de dependencia en la sociedad hispanovisigoda. En torno a la ausencia de coloni en las Leges Visigothorum." *Gerión* 16:451–60.

Castellanos, S., and I. Martín Viso. 2005. "The Local Articulation of Central Power in the North of the Iberian Peninsula (500–1000)." *Early Medieval Europe* 13:1–42.

Collins, R. 1995. *Early Medieval Spain: Unity in Diversity, 400–1000*. Basingstoke: MacMillan.

Díaz, P. 2011. *El reino suevo, 411–585*. Madrid: AKAL.

Díaz, P., and Menéndez Bueyes, L. 2005. "The Cantabrian Basin in the Fourth and Fifth Centuries: From Imperial Province to Periphery." In *Hispania in Late Antiquity: Current Perspectives*, edited by K. Bowes and M. Kulikowski, 265–97. Leiden: Brill.

Díaz, P., and Martín Viso, I. 2011. "Una contabilidad esquiva: Las pizarras numerales visigodas y el caso de El Cortinal de San Juan (Salvatierra de Tormes, España)." In *Between Tax and Rent. Fiscal Problems from Late Antiquity to Early Middle Ages*, edited by P. Díaz and I. Martín Viso, 221–50. Bari: Edipuglia.

Díaz, P., and M. Valverde Castro. 2000. "The Theoretical Strength and the Practical Weakness of the Visigothic Monarchy of Toledo." In *Rituals of Power: From Late Antiquity to the Early Middle Ages*, edited by F. Theuws and J. Nelson, 59–93. Leiden: Brill.

Fernández, D. 2006. "What Is the De Fisco Barcinonensi About?" *Antiquité Tardive* 14:217–24.

———. 2016. "Persuading the Powerful in Post-Roman Iberia: King Euric, Local Powers, and the Formation of a State Paradigm." In *Motions of Late Antiquity. Essays on Religion, Politics, and Society in Honor of Peter Brown*, edited by H. Remitz and J. Kreiner, 107–128. Turnhout: Brepols.

García Moreno, L. 1971. "Algunos aspectos fiscales de la Península Ibérica durante el siglo VI." *Hispania Antigua* 1:233–56.

———. 1974. "Estudios sobre la organización administrativa del reino visigodo de Toledo." *Anuario de Historia del Derecho Español* 44:5–155.

Goffart, W. 1982. "Old and New in Merovingian Taxation." *Past and Present* 96:3–21.

Grey, C. 2011. *Constructing Communities in the Late Roman Countryside*. Cambridge: Cambridge University Press.

Haldon, J. 1993. *The State and the Tributary Mode of Production*. London: Verso.

Hendy, M. 1988. "From Public to Private: The Western Barbarian Coinages as a Mirror of the Disintegration of Late Roman State Structures." *Viator* 19:29–78.

Isla, A. 2002. "El officium palatinum visigodo. Entorno regio y poder aristocrático." *Hispania* 62:827–47.

———. 2010. *Ejército, sociedad y política en la Península Ibérica entre los siglos VII y XI*. Madrid: CSIC.

Jiménez Garnica, A. 2011. "Aproximación a la situación tributaria durante el reinado autónomo de Eurico (475–484)." In *Between Taxation and Rent. Fiscal Problems from Late Antiquity to Early Middle Ages*, edited by P. Díaz and I. Martín Viso, 39–50. Bari: Edipuglia.

Jones, A. H. M. 1964. *The Later Roman Empire, 284–602. A Social, Economic, and Administrative Survey*. Norman: University of Oklahoma Press.

King, P. 1972. *Law and Society in the Visigothic Kingdom*. Cambridge: Cambridge University Press.

Kulikowski, M. 2004. *Late Roman Spain and Its Cities*. Baltimore: Johns Hopkins University Press.

Laniado, A. 2002. *Recherches sur les notables municipaux dans l'Empire protobyzantin*. Paris: Association des amis du Centre d'histoire et civilisation de Byzance.

Liebeschuetz, J. H. W. G. 2001. *Decline and Fall of the Roman City*. Oxford: Oxford University Press.

Mann, M. 1984. "The Autonomous Power of the State: Its Origins, Mechanisms and Results." *European Journal of Sociology* 25 (2): 185–213.

Manzano Moreno, E. 2006. *Conquistadores, emires y califas. Los Omeyas y la formación de al-Andalus*. Barcelona: Crítica.

Martín, C. 2003. *La géographie du pouvoir dans l'Espagne visigothique*. Villeneuve d'Ascq: Presses Universitaires du Septentrion.

Martín Viso, I. 2006. "Tributación y escenarios locales en el centro de la península ibérica: algunas hipótesis a partir del análisis de las pizarras 'visigodas.'" *Antiquité Tardive* 14:263–90.

———. 2013. "Prácticas locales de la fiscalidad en el reino visigodo de Toledo." In *Lo que vino de Oriente. Horizontes, praxis y dimensión material de los sistemas de dominación*

fiscal en Al-Andalus (ss. VII–IX), edited by X. Ballestín and E. Pastor, 72–85. Oxford: Archaeopress.
Mazzarino, S. 2002. *Aspetti sociali del quarto secolo: richerche di storia tardo-romana.* Milan: Biblioteca Universale Rizzoli.
McCormick, M. 1986. *Eternal Victory: Triumphal Rulership in Late Antiquity, Byzantium, and the Early Medieval West.* Cambridge: Cambridge University Press.
Mirković, M. 1996. "Autopragia and the Village of Aphrodito." *Zeitschrift der Savigny-Stiftung für Rechtsgeschichte. Romanistische Abteilung* 113:346–57.
Mitchell, S. 1976. "Requisitioned Transport in the Roman Empire: A New Inscription from Pisidia." *Journal of Roman Studies* 66:106–31.
Pliego Vázquez, R. 2009. *La Moneda Visigoda.* Seville: Universidad de Sevilla.
Richardson, S. 2012. "Early Mesopotamia: The Presumptive State." *Past and Present* 215 (1): 3–49.
Ripoll, G. 2000. "Sedes regiae en la Hispania de la Antigüedad tardía." In *Sedes regiae (ann. 400–800)*, edited by G. Ripoll and J. Gurt, 371–401. Barcelona: Reial Acadèmia de Bones Lletres.
Sánchez-Albornoz, C. 1971. *Estudios visigodos.* Rome: Instituto storico italiano per il Medio Evo.
Schmidt-Hofner, S. 2014. "Der defensor civitatis un die Entstehung des Notabelnregiments in den spätrömischen Städten." In *Chlodwigs Welt. Organisation von Herrschaft um 500*, edited by M. Meier and S. Patzold, 487–522. Stuttgart: Franz Steiner.
Thompson. E. A. 1969. *The Goths in Spain.* Oxford: Oxford University Press.
Valverde Castro, M. 2000. *Ideología, simbolismo y ejercicio del poder real en la monarquía visigoda: Un proceso de cambio.* Salamanca: Universidad de Salamanca.
———. 2007. "Monarquía y tributación en la 'Hispania' visigoda: el marco teórico." *Hispania Antigua* 31:235–52.
Van Dam, R. 1985. *Leadership and Community in Late Antique Gaul.* Berkeley: University of California Press.
Velázquez, I. 2000. *Documentos de época visigoda escritos en pizarra, siglos VI–VIII.* Turnhout: Brepols.
———. 2004. *Las pizarras visigodas: entre el latín y su disgregación: la lengua hablada en Hispania, siglos VI–VIII.* Burgos: Fundación Instituto Castellano Leonés de la Lengua.
Vigil, M., and A. Barbero. 1970. "Algunos aspectos de la feudalización del reino visigodo en relación a su organización financiera y military." *Moneda y Crédito* 112:71–91.
Vigil-Escalera Guirado, A. 2007. "Granjas y aldeas tardoantiguas y altomedievales de la Meseta. Configuración espacial, socioeconómica y política de un territorio rural al norte de Toledo (ss. V–X d.C.)." *Archivo Español de Arqueología* 80:239–84.
Wickham, C. 1984. "The Other Transition: From the Ancient World to Feudalism." *Past and Present* 103:3–36.
———. 2005. *Framing the Early Middle Ages. Europe and the Mediterranean, 400–800.* Oxford: Oxford University Press.

CHAPTER 9

Did the Byzantine Empire Have "Ecumenical" or "Universal" Aspirations?

ANTHONY KALDELLIS

The infrastructural capabilities of the Byzantine state have not yet become the subject of sustained and explicit debate. Instead, one encounters divergent views in different studies, but these have not yet been rubbed together. Thus, one study of provincial authority finds only a distant state, or court, interested primarily in tax collection and leaving almost no other footprint locally;[1] others see the empire as little more than a set of personal relations centered on the emperor;[2] and others still find, correctly in my view, that

> the government and court, in spite of often dramatic transfers of political power from ruler to ruler and their supporting factions and vested interests, remained stable and continued to function. . . . A standing army was maintained through an administrative apparatus whose resources were independent of the imperial household. . . . Even in the worst of crises [when an emperor was killed in battle] the state was hardly shaken. . . . The state's fiscal and administrative machinery was kept running with barely a murmur of unease. . . . Institutional stability of this sort was deeply rooted, and the state and its apparatus were embedded in the social-political order.[3]

It has also been said that "the authority of the Byzantine state and its internal articulation were second to none for most of the middle ages."[4]

I intend separately, in a book-length study, to uphold the maximalist view and document how it played out on the ground. In the terms employed in this volume, what we call Byzantium—the eastern Roman empire, or *Romanía* as it was called by its inhabitants—was not a weak state. Not only was it capable, within the limits of a premodern economy, of impressive feats of infrastructural competence on a fairly regular basis, its structures of administration permeated provincial society to the exclusion of alternatives, as did the mentalities that those structures required and inculcated. The main vector and matrix of this infrastructural penetration was the Byzantines' Roman identity, which was defined, in addition to cultural criteria, by an acceptance of the normative political order of New Rome. The operations of despotic power in Byzantium rested on that infrastructural bedrock but were checked, sometimes violently, when they attempted to subvert that normative order.[5]

The Problem of Ecumenism Between Weak and Strong Conceptions of the State

The present chapter is not going to enter this debate directly, as that would require more documentation than can be provided here. It will examine instead an alleged peculiarity of Byzantine ideology which has sometimes led historians to think of Byzantium as something other than an infrastructural state: I refer to its claim to "ecumenicity" or "universality," terms that have become mandatory in modern expositions of Byzantine political ideology. They are never defined precisely, but leave the vague impression that the Byzantine empire had claims or aspirations to rule or somehow preside over the entire world, or at least over a larger portion of it than was at any time directly governed by its state apparatus. The terms thereby introduce a conceptual and even ontological gap between Byzantium's historical and infrastructural reality on the one hand and its ideology or ideal existence on the other. On a strong—but ultimately ahistorical—reading, this claim undermines the idea that it was a state at all: it becomes something more like a theological abstraction that emanated from Constantinople. But, more commonly, "universal" has become a catchword for referring to the empires of late antiquity, even though precise definitions are lacking here too. Having a big "imperial" state in partnership with a religion approvingly labeled "universal" seems to suffice. In some models the Sasanian Persian empire, with its state-endorsed Zoroastrian religion, and the Muslim caliphate also qualify as "universal empires," making late antiquity an age of universalism in both the religious and imperial spheres.[6]

The current celebration of late antique ecumenism ameliorates previous models that emphasized cultural decline and imperial failure in the later Roman period. But it comes at considerable cost to its heir, Byzantium. A common view is that Byzantium retained the ecumenical ideology of its predecessor but was so reduced a state, after losses in the west and east, that the gap between ideology and reality drove the culture insane. Scholars depict Byzantium as trapped in a "myth" of ecumenicity, a "monstrous fable," "ostrich-like attitude," "beliefs that contradicted reality,"[7] "egocentric fantasies,"[8] "ideological 'schizophrenia,'"[9] "the myth and outdated nostalgic history,"[10] the "illusion of a dominant position in the world,"[11] and so on. In 1961, one scholar had to remind his readers that "on occasion educated Byzantines kept their heads up and their eyes open," that they were not only "so many ostriches hiding their heads in the sands of past imperial glories" or "inhabiting an antiquarian fool's paradise." According to this model, the Byzantines' sanity can be redeemed, if only partially, by showing that some of them knew "that the Roman empire did not encompass the whole *oecumene*, not even at the peak of its might."[12] But the idea remains entrenched that Byzantine ideology "was no longer even plausible as an account of reality," though it was "celebrated by art and ceremonial."[13] These discussions postulate a different ontological gap at the heart of imperial ecumenism, one between late Roman "universalism" and the diminished Byzantine present that fostered only nostalgic illusions, which may also correlate to the gap between ideal and real.

This gap corresponds to two different views of the empire today. On the one hand, it is widely believed that the Byzantines viewed the existence and historical role of their state in theological and even apocalyptic terms. An article that is frequently cited in support of this thesis even asserts that they were *mentally incapable* of thinking about it in secular or worldly terms, in terms of state infrastructure.[14] On the other hand, it is known that Byzantium, one of the longest-lived states in history, survived a difficult millennium by implementing effective institutions of governance, administration, taxation, diplomacy, and war, and flexibly adjusting to circumstances. Whatever they may have affirmed in their theology of empire, its rulers were pragmatic, even cynical in dealing with subjects and neighbors. They kept normal diplomatic relations with the latter, making treaties that specified borders, transit points, and trade policies in detail. To forge alliances, Byzantine officials participated in heathen rituals, putting pragmatism over religious purity. As a historical entity, then, Byzantium was not "in denial." To the contrary, it has proven difficult to find policies, entailing the mobilization of human and material resources, that aimed to realize any *universal* aspirations. The gap between these two views of Byzantium—ideological and universal vs. pragmatic and infrastructural—corresponds to different modes of scholarly analysis that are rarely aligned.

Some historians have tried to bridge the gap between the two. The editor of a recent volume that seems overall to question whether it is helpful to view Byzantium as a state aspiring to "universality" writes that "the retention of a rhetorical, artistic, and symbolic performance of 'ecumenicity' across the spectrum does not mean that the Byzantines did not understand the limits of their empire or of their political capabilities. Of course they knew them, and they survived precisely because they took care to accommodate themselves to new geopolitical facts."[15] A contributor to that volume affirms that there was a disconnect between Truth (the emperor as Master of the World) and Reality (a limited state that had to protect its borders): ecumenicity operated on a different level than the practical business of the state. It was "less of a logical construction than an accumulation of words, of representations, and of histories or of legends . . . disparate elements, belonging to different registers."[16] This sounds impressive, but it resolves the problem only through a verbal trick.

A way forward is provided by Seth Richardson's Babylon, a city-state that claimed lordship over more territory than it effectively controlled.[17] For this model to work in the Byzantine case, we need to distinguish between territories under direct administration and putative aspirational claims beyond them: within the former analytical framework, we are dealing with a relatively strong state, whereas in the latter with a relatively weak one. I define as internal all territory visited by imperial surveyors and tax collectors, where imperial laws were promulgated and expected to be enforced. This was also roughly the same as the territory delimited by the outermost provinces to which governors were sent by the court and guarded by the imperial armies. Beyond this territory, these overlapping layers of infrastructural penetration largely disappeared, probably abruptly. But some imperial institutions reached marginally past the frontiers, exerting "soft power," such as the distribution of court titles to foreign client-rulers, the never-ending stream of embassies, and the system of bishoprics under the patriarch of Constantinople.[18]

This chapter has two goals. First, it will attempt to provide some clarity regarding the scope and nature of Byzantine ecumenism. A society whose view of itself does not match reality is not surprising (the opposite would be quite a find). What is frustrating in our case is how little we understand the *contents* of Byzantine ecumenicity. What beliefs exactly did they hold that were so at odds with reality? What we will find is that the Byzantines' ecumenical claims pose no threat to the specific ethno-political integrity of Romanía as a state circumscribed by bounded institutions and infrastructures—whether that state be seen as weak or strong. Second, it will partially redeem the pragmatic and historical function of these universal claims by arguing that they did promote state projects beyond the border. Byzantium, like Richardson's Babylon, earned long-term dividends from its allegedly "delusional" ecumenical claims. The analysis will thereby bring a different perspective to the exploration in this volume of the gap between the authority claimed by states and what they could actually control in fact. The focus here is not on how that gap manifested itself in the empire's *internal* governance, the strength and penetration of which, as stated, remains an open question. Instead, it examines a set of rhetorical or ideological gestures that supposedly inflected the empire's relations with the outside world.

Christian and Roman Ecumenicities

Historians generally do not specify whether Byzantine universal claims stemmed from the aspirations of the state (*imperium sine fine*), the Church ("make disciples of all nations"),[19] or some combination of the two. Schematically, I will divide the analysis between concepts of *Christian* and *Roman* universalism, though some permutations combined the two. I will divide each category between *internal* and *external*, that is, whether the operational sphere of each universalist ideology was within or outside the territory of direct infrastructural control. As my primary interest is in external versions of universalist ideology, I begin with the others.[20]

Modern rhetoric about late antique universalism stems largely from Christian views of Christianity. Its apologists saw and still see Christianity as a religion that aims to spread one faith to all people and thus create "unity." An empire that accepts Christianity can, then, be called a Universal Empire, in the sense that it universally accepts Christianity. And the later Roman emperors did not only accept Christianity, they sought to persuade or compel their subjects to accept it, too, in order to create a unified Christian society under their rule. We need not review this process, except to make two observations. First, the spread of Christianity in late Roman society entailed a greater use of state institutions than religious scholars are often willing to grant; they view the process primarily as a chapter in spiritual rather than state-infrastructural history. Second, it is not clear that Christianity introduced anything new here, or that it was in the lead rather than in the wake of key developments. Cliff Ando has exposed the prior Roman (pagan) moves that made it possible.[21] Specifically, the Roman landscape of empire postulated a distinctive form of worship for each political community: each city had its gods. With the universal extension of Roman citizenship in 212, the empire became a vast Roman community under the obligation to practice Roman religion. When the emperor Decius required all *Romans* to pray for him and the empire, he was addressing a universal audience of all his subjects. The one-people one-religion mentality was loosened briefly after the recognition by Galerius and then Constantine of Christianity as an alternative option available to Roman citizens, but slammed shut again when Christianity was prescribed as the only permissible religion. Thus, Christian universalism was but a variation on a prior Roman universalism that had not been merely latent. Christian-imperial intolerance was rooted in pagan thinking.[22]

But Christian proselytism was not limited to Roman subjects of the emperors. The Byzantines, as Christians, implicitly had ecumenical religious commitments, namely, to convert even barbarians to the Orthodox faith and way of life. It used to be thought that they were *actively* committed to this goal (for example, "the Christian Roman emperor had the divine task of spreading Orthodoxy on a world-wide scale").[23] But this notion has recently been downsized. Church writers hoped for barbarian conversions, but the Byzantines generally, and the court in particular, showed little interest in the project, which was associated with the office of the emperor rarely and only for specific rhetorical effect.[24] When it came to actual missions, the emperors were largely passive. If they received a request from a foreign people, they would send missionaries to help them convert. But the Roman state never developed an infrastructure for such activity, nor expressed an interest in having one. "There was no corps of experienced missionaries at the disposal of the government . . . there is minimal evidence of an urge to go out and save souls on the part of the culturo-religious elite of the metropolis."[25] "The initiative for the conversions of barbarian peoples in the ninth and tenth centuries seems to have come mainly from their leaders."[26] And even after a people had converted, the Byzantines generally still did not regard them as civilized. They were not motivated by an ideology of Christian brotherhood, and the emperors did not make the protection of Orthodox minorities abroad a major part of their image. A few made gestures in that direction, but no more.[27] The emperor was the *basileus* of the Romans, not of the Christians. There was no gap between ideal and reality here, only an absence of Christian universalism in practice.

A looser form of Christian ecumenism might be the perception by the Byzantines of their spiritual affinity with other Orthodox peoples and states, especially those who had received their religion from Constantinople. Dimitri Obolensky branded this cultural-religious continuum as "the Byzantine Commonwealth," basically a Slavic-Orthodox version of "Christendom."[28] The thesis has recently been challenged on many fronts for sins of both omission and commission. Here I draw attention to a specific problem that relates to Byzantine mentalities. Obolensky could find no evidence that the Byzantines themselves or anyone else at the time believed that they lived in such a Commonwealth, nor that the Byzantines held a higher view of Christian barbarians than of heathens or Muslims, or that they tended naturally to form alliances or other state projects with Orthodox peoples. Although many Byzantine authors generally declared that Christians should stick together and avoid bloodshed, or that Christians are superior to pagans, when it came to any particular foreign Christians Byzantine writers and the court regarded them as little more than unredeemed barbarians barely fit to receive Scripture. They had nothing to say about the missions that had converted them (most surprisingly, virtually nothing about Cyril and Methodios), and the Byzantine state did not develop any policies or infrastructure to promote such ecumenical visions. Obolensky could not deny these facts, so he put them down to "Greek" chauvinism (in reality, Roman). At any rate, chauvinism is not "schizophrenia," and so here we lack *both* an ideology and a reality, given that the Commonwealth, if presented as a medieval mentality, is largely a modern fiction.[29]

Turning to Roman imperial versions of universalism, I begin with its internal forms, though they are not what scholars mean by Byzantine ecumenism. After 212, the law of all the subjects of the empire was Roman law, their previous laws becoming only local customs.[30] This contributed decisively to the increasing sociocultural uniformity of the empire, and eventually to the relatively homogeneous society of Byzantium. Early Byzantine writers expressed an awareness that there was one universal system of law in force throughout the empire, though not outside of it, where barbarian anarchy or tyranny prevailed.[31] It was Rome's own legal institutions that created "universal empire" in late antiquity.[32] Whereas modern notions of ecumenism like to transcend state boundaries, this version tended to strengthen them by diluting internal differences and thereby highlighting the contrast between Romans and barbarians. The emergence of this unified Roman world was seen as form of ecumenism, for it fused previously separate subject groups into one: what was previously a multiethnic empire now increasingly became Romanía, the land of the Romans, an *oikoumene* in its own right. The rise of this Roman-imperial universalism, then, paralleled that of Christian universalism, which emerged at the same time, and their valence was largely "domestic." When modern scholars use the term ecumenical, they are gesturing toward ideals that transcend state boundaries, but when the Byzantines used the term *oikoumene*, they tended to mean Romanía. Consider the emperor Justinian's claim regarding the scope of his law's authority in *Novel* 7 (epilogue): "over the entire earth (ἐπὶ πάσης τῆς γῆς), where Roman law holds sway as well as the rule of the Catholic Church."[33] This conception of "the entire earth" was defined by the jurisdiction of Roman institutions of governance.

A State-Delimited Oikoumene

When Byzantines referred to the emperor as ruling the entire world, which world did they mean?

Oikoumene is an ambiguous term. It means "the entire inhabited world." The ancient geographer Strabo defined it as "the part of the world that we live in,"[34] but who are we? If "we" are all human beings, this may refer to the entire world, but in political texts "we" are usually a more limited community, the part of the world that matters, the properly settled or civilized part as opposed to what lies beyond. Thus, in Byzantine political texts *oikoumene* refers most commonly to Romanía, that is, the part of the world that was controlled by the imperial government. A slightly more expansive sense included various client states along the periphery, encompassing areas where the emperor might expect his orders to have some pull with local rulers (though he could not give them orders as he did to his own functionaries). Or *oikoumene* might refer to the entire world, over which the emperor was understood to preside in some way that has not yet been specified. Let us take these senses in turn, starting with the first, which was by far the most common Byzantine understanding of *oikoumene* even though it gives no comfort to modern visions of ecumenism.

The modern argument about Byzantine "delusion" and "schizophrenia" rests on the premise that the Byzantines believed that their emperor did, would, or should rule the entire world. But if *oikoumene* for them meant the portion of the world that he did rule, the "limited" Romanía of which he was the emperor, the problem disappears. And it does seem that "it had come to mean the empire itself, not, as it literally meant, the whole inhabited world."[35] The Byzantines had ways of signaling this "limited" conception of the *oikoumene*, and they had key precedents for it in canonical texts.

The Gospel of Luke famously states that just before Jesus was born, Caesar Augustus sent a decree that a census was to be taken of "the entire *oikoumene*."[36] A fiction, of course, but every Byzantine who heard the story would conclude that *oikoumene* was the part of the world that was governed by the agents of the imperial state, where the census and land surveys were conducted. This was an *oikoumene* defined by imperial infrastructure. Geographical definitions could have the same effect. In the 1060s, Psellos praised the emperor Doukas for standing in the middle of the *oikoumene* and patrolling its outer circuit, which he specifies as the Danube and Euphrates frontiers, where the barbarians are. "The barbarian fears you upon the edges, while we take heart seeing you at the center."[37] Here too the *oikoumene* is the empire. It is effectively the same division that Psellos makes elsewhere when he divides the world into τὸ Ῥωμαϊκὸν and τὸ βάρβαρον, wishing that they were not so confused as they were becoming in those days of barbarian invasions.[38] The Danube was generally perceived as the northern edge of the *oikoumene*.[39] In another oration Psellos says that the city of Trebizond is the first to greet the sun in the morning.[40] Here geography is determined by state boundaries: he means the first city in *our* world.

The equation of the Roman empire with "the world" was made already in the early centuries: a state that stretched from Britain to Arabia was big enough to count as a world in itself. In his edict of universal citizenship (212 C.E.), the emperor Caracalla said that he was giving Roman citizenship to all *xenoi* (non-Romans) in the *oikoumene* (that is, the empire).[41] The third-century historian Cassius Dio distinguished between the city of Rome and its *oikoumene*.[42] The fifth-century ecclesiastical historian Sozomenos highlighted the spread of Christianity "throughout the entire *oikoumene* of the Romans."[43] The emperor Constantine likewise subjected the entire *oikoumene*, "from end to end," to his power, then divided his imperial authority among his sons in geographical terms: west, middle, and east.[44] The *oikoumene* is here the territory that was subject to the βασιλείας ἀρχή (in the words of Eusebios), which could be divided in dynastic succession. In later texts, Constantine's defeat of his Roman rivals was presented as "bringing peace to the *oikoumene*."[45] In all these texts, the *oikoumene* can logically be understood only as the part of the world under imperial control.

In the twelfth century, the historian Zonaras, writing about the events of 350 C.E., said that the empire was too big for one man to rule seeing as it reached "almost (σχεδὸν) from one end of the earth to the other."[46] (Make note of that "almost": we will return to it below.) In another of his *Novels*, Justinian claimed that the Romans, by their arms and laws, had "acquired the entire *oikoumene*, so to speak"—another interesting qualifier. That *oikoumene* was for him nothing other than the Roman *res publica* (that is, Romanía).[47] Let us give some later Byzantine parallels. According to a tenth-century historian, the civil war in the 820s between Michael II and Thomas the Slav filled the entire *oikoumene* with evil.[48] The fourteenth-century treatise on the antiquities of Constantinople (*Patria*) by pseudo-Kodinos recounts how the subjects of Leon I (457–474), "whether Constantinopolitans or provincials from the entire *oikoumene*," posted grievances on a column, which would then be delivered to him.[49] A saint's life from the tenth century equates, in the course of a few words, the *oikoumene* with "the land of the Romans" and, finally, with "us."[50]

This persistent equation of *oikoumene* and Romanía removes any gap between ideal and reality. The Byzantines were not "deluded" about what their emperor actually ruled. Indeed, most of the time they may not have thought that the rest of the world mattered, a view with ancient Roman precedent.[51] This should influence how we interpret attestations of the term that are not specifically limited. An inscription on Samos honors the emperor Theophilos (829–841) as the "*autokrator* [emperor] of the entire *oikoumene*" in one line and as "ruler of the Romans" in the next.[52] These two functions are probably equivalent rather than distinct, though we will consider the possibility below that the former encoded added prestige. Before we turn to those more "ecumenical" meanings (in the modern sense), let us consider some verbal mechanisms by which they could be contained, to keep the *oikoumene* limited to Romanía.

The first we have already encountered: the qualifier "almost," matching Justinian's "so to speak." From the middle period we have the patriarch Photios (ninth century) praising Constantinople as ruling "almost, by just little, over the entire *oikoumene*," and the emperor Konstantinos VII Porphyrogennetos claiming that ancient Roman armies conquered "almost the entire *oikoumene*, falling short by just a little."[53] There was "just a bit" out there that was not in

Romanía. An equivalent technique was to say ἡ καθ' ἡμᾶς οἰκουμένη: "our own *oikoumene*," "the *oikoumene* according to us," the version "limited to us." This had appeared already in late antiquity and became common in the Byzantine period.[54] It could be used to designate even more limited locales. In the eleventh century, the bishop of Ohrid, Theophylaktos, a Roman, referred to the "barbarous καθ' ἡμᾶς οἰκουμένη" to which he had been posted, that is, Bulgaria.[55]

Thus, when emperors are called "lords of the sea and earth and of every human nation and race," or "rulers of the entire *oikoumene*," we have warrant to take this in a "narrow" Roman sense, rather than a modern, truly "ecumenical" one.[56] In some cases the crucial qualification lies just around the textual corner. Celebrating the reconquest of Crete from the Arabs in 961, Theodosios the Deacon first says that Romanos II will now rule over "the entire earth," but later this is replaced by the realistic claim that territory has been restored that had once belonged to the Romans.[57] Psellos forecasts in a speech for Konstantinos IX Monomachos that "the circle of your authority may become equal to the entire *oikoumene*, and the Roman empire may then extend over the entire earth."[58] In two later orations to the same emperor he tones it down: "you have moved the καθ' ἡμᾶς οἰκουμένη to the north" and "expanded our frontiers."[59]

The Oikoumene Beyond Romanía

Still, this "limited" Roman *oikoumene* does not fully domesticate the latent universal aspirations of imperial rhetoric. For starters, there is tension between the evident desire in the texts to refer to "the whole earth" without qualification and their mechanisms for then "containing" that implication. This ambiguity in the meaning of *oikoumene* was obvious, yet many persisted in using it in place of Romanía or the "*arche* of the Romans." They *wanted* to imply that more was at stake, even if they were never deluded about the actual extent of imperial power. "There seems to be, at some level, a false consciousness in this, as if one is speciously passed off as the other."[60] *Imperium sine fine* hovered over the articulation of Roman power. Second, there are texts and images in which the scope of imperial authority does extend transliminally. In many cases these referred to the reconquest of recently lost territory, where modest reacquisitions were amplified by court rhetoric. A striking image of such expansion was based on Psalm 80(79).8–11. The nation of Israel is there compared to a vine brought from Egypt that replaces the gentiles (τὰ ἔθνη), fills up the new land from the mountain to the sea, but is now being fed on by wild beasts. Court orators lifted this imagery, comparing the emperor to a vine that will grow, defeat the nations (ἔθνη), and expand the power of Rome. Prodromos predicted to Ioannes II (1118–1143) that "all the lands and cities of the nations will be subjected to you . . . you will increase the vine of New Rome as far as the sea."[61]

Sometimes the imagery or language of world dominion is explicit. We have, for example, images of the emperor holding the globe (with or without a cross). According to Prokopios, this signified that "the entire earth and sea had been subjected to him by the Creator."[62] Court acclamations praised emperors as a vine from which the entire *globe* drew delight (but this might refer only to Roman society).[63] Referring to the nations that attacked the empire during the reign of her father Alexios I Komnenos (1081–1118), including the Normans, Pechenegs, Turks, and Venetians, Anna notes that they all had their sights trained on "the monarchy of the Romans because it is by nature the *despotis* [mistress or queen] of all other nations, and so they, who are its slaves, are hostile to it."[64] Georgios Akropolites, in the thirteenth century, deployed a traditional motif of panegyric when he compared the emperor to the sun, adding that he illuminated "*not only* the land of the Romans *but also* the farthest points of the *oikoumene*."[65] Here the latter is clearly not limited to the Roman state. As late as 1393, when the empire was limited to Constantinople, the patriarch could claim that the emperor was preeminent over other Christian rulers.[66]

These images suggest that the Romans believed that they occupied a preeminent position among the rulers and nations of the world. Modern historians tend to treat them as relics inherited from earlier Roman tradition, or fossils embedded within their discourse. Ancient Romans also claimed that the emperor did (or should) rule or preside over the entire *oikoumene* (in whatever fashion).[67] Certainly, imperial titles are conservative (the crown of England claimed France until 1800). But rather than treat these claims, like everything classical passing through Byzantium, as an antiquarian fossil that could not interface with the Byzantines' lived reality or have real meaning for them,[68] we must interpret them within their living context as semantically meaningful and politically useful to those who employed them. The Byzantines chose what to keep from the past because it was useful to them.[69] It should not need to be stated, but in this case it must, that they were purposive agents in the construction of their matrices of meaning.

The second part of this chapter will examine how projections of universal preeminence facilitated state projects beyond the borders of Romanía. But a final word must be added to this more conceptual section. Byzantine ecumenism had an apocalyptic dimension, though it occupied a more limited ideological space than modern studies imply (some make it coextentional with imperial ideology as a whole).[70] Briefly, in some discursive contexts the Byzantines presented their polity as the culmination of epochal and teleological processes that took place within a divine dispensation of ancient history. This need arose in the (circumscribed) context of explaining how Roman imperial and Christian millenarian ideologies could coexist. According to the scheme that Christian theorists invented to solve this problem, the absolute or universal legitimacy of Romanía had been established by the coincidence of the birth of Christ and the reign of Augustus, the subsequent conversion of the empire, and the foundation of New Rome by Constantine, the first Christian emperor, in the east. These conjunctions linked a series of narratives that were (inevitably) cast in the form of national and political histories (of Jews, Greeks, Romans, and Christians). Their result, the Christian Roman empire, would last until the End Times, when Christ would (perhaps) reassert the empire's supreme standing in the world.[71] No development subsequent to the foundation of Constantinople had abrogated any of the elements of this picture, not Islam and not the Roman pretensions of the upstart Frankish world. That is because the teleological narrative was transposed to a higher conceptual level, as "the first step in the transformation of earthly imperial order into the universal kingdom of God . . . a new ontological paradigm . . . an entirely new religio-political category."[72]

A number of apocalyptic texts grant the empire a prominent role in such scenarios of the End Times. These texts were rarely associated with or generated by the court, so it is unfortunate that scholars have used them to reinforce the image of delusional Byzantines who held to "a vision of an ecumenical empire which, with divine assistance, was destined to expand to the ends of the earth so that all people could embrace the One True Faith," an outlook that is then immediately found to conflict with "reality."[73] This is an excessive reaction. Imperial apocalypticism was merely a rhetorical form of Byzantine exceptionalism (like that of modern empires which, after ruling some part of the world, subsequently believe that the foundations of their own culture furnish a universal standard by which all may be measured). What interests us here is the fact that no projects involving the use of state infrastructure can be associated with these fantastic scenarios and metaphysical views of history, and their invention and promulgation owed more to "freelance" religious writers than to the court. In the following section we turn to state projects in the area of foreign policy, and ask how they were facilitated in pragmatic ways by concepts of imperial ecumenism.

The Dividends of Ecumenical Rhetoric

Can we redeem Byzantine universalism in terms of state projects correlating to tangible infrastructural mechanisms and outcomes? The remainder of this chapter will explore ways in which ecumenical ideologies promoted imperial projects. First, they enabled the Byzantines to represent and legitimate the reconquest of limited territories within the former Roman *oikoumene*; second, they created client states (which may or may not have been subsequently annexed); and, third, they projected the preeminent authority of the emperor internationally for diplomatic advantage.

First, *irredentism*. The productive contrast was not between fantasy and reality, but between past and present versions of the Roman *oikoumene*. Romanía experienced two phases of sudden contraction: the loss of the west in the fifth century, and the loss of the east and much of the Balkans in the seventh. These events destabilized the Roman definition of *oikoumene*: did it refer to the current boundaries of the state or to those before the loss? Historical texts and institutional memory kept past "glories" alive in Byzantine ideology. Even the more narrow understanding of the emperor as lord of the (Roman) *oikoumene* gestured potentially toward lost territories. As it happens, before 1100 the Byzantine empire also experienced two phases of imperial expansion: the reconquest of parts of the west by Justinian in the mid-sixth century, and the slower but better managed conquest of the Balkans (including Bulgaria), Crete, Cyprus, eastern Anatolia, most of Armenia and Georgia, Cilicia, northern Syria-Mesopotamia, and southern Italy between 700 and 1050. Historians are so used to viewing Byzantium through the rubric of the long decline and fall that they often fail to realize that it was an expansionist state. We need not discuss the motives and circumstances of these acquisitions. The key point is that in each instance they targeted former territories of the Roman *oikoumene* in a previous incarnation. Thus conquest could be seen as *re*conquest: described as an ecumenical ambition, it nodded to the restoration of the previous boundaries of the Roman *oikoumene*. We saw above how Theodosios the Deacon, Psellos, and Prodromos celebrated recent acquisitions in the tenth–twelfth centuries in such "ecumenical" terms. Likewise, after the success of his first land grab (North Africa), Justinian also reached for a rhetoric of restoration to justify what he had done and was about to do to Italy: he was liberating lost Roman provinces that had fallen under the illegitimate rule of barbarian usurpers. His success gave him "hope that God would grant him dominion also over the other lands that the ancient Romans had ruled between the limits of the two oceans but that were subsequently lost through [the] indolence [of previous emperors]."[74] This might gesture toward Spain and Gaul but not Germany or Persia.

But pragmatism always prevailed. It is not the case, as is sometimes asserted, mostly on the basis of that same handful of apocalyptic texts, that the Byzantines had a master plan or even a grand vision for the reconquest of the Roman world and, indeed, the entire world.[75] Byzantine military strategy was, as is more commonly and correctly described, defensive, and its attitude toward war was reluctant.[76] Yet when the opportunity presented itself, say, a vacuum of power in a neighboring region (Greece in the eighth century, southern Italy in the ninth) or the collapse of a rival's stability (the caliphate in the tenth century, Bulgaria in the eleventh), territory could be annexed. It is likely that Justinian too lacked an advance plan for the conquest of the west; the opportunity presented itself a year before the first expedition in 533.[77] Moreover, military emperors did not bite off more than they could chew: those who could have conquered more territory prudently did not, for example Ioannes Tzimiskes (969–976) and Basileios II (976–1025).[78] When it came to conquest, therefore, Byzantines were not carried away by apocalyptic fantasies. Psellos says that the emperor Isaakios I Komnenos (1057–1059) turned down offers by local foreign lords who wanted to surrender their lands to him, "not because he begrudged the Roman empire the expansion of its borders, but because he knew that such additions require lots of money, formidable garrisons, and preparation in advance, and that in the absence of these things addition is actually loss."[79] Most Byzantine planners shared this outlook: infrastructural viability trumped ideological fulfillment. Ecumenicity was never at the helm; it never interfaced with the gears of administration and control.

Within that context, however, the restoration of Roman "ecumenicity" was a useful rhetorical trope for normalizing the acquisition of new territories and putting them on a path of full absorption into Romanía (with greater success in Greece, say, than in Bulgaria). These tropes were supported by auxiliary mechanisms, such as calling the conquered (or notionally subordinated) peoples occupying former Roman lands by the classical ethnonyms of nations who had been conquered by the ancient Romans, thus reinscribing contemporary relations in the irredentist terms of classical Roman dominion.[80] Another was labeling the former rulers of conquered peoples as "tyrants," that is, illegitimate claimants.[81] "Tyranny" created a notional political void to be filled by the emperor as the ruler of the (old Roman) *oikoumene*, which could theoretically extend as far as the Danube, Euphrates, or Naples. A third trope that could be activated as necessary against barbarian interlopers was the quasi-legal argument of prior ownership: that's our land you're on.[82] These tropes satisfied "the ineluctable necessities of conquest and government," namely "to understand (or to believe that one understands) the physical space that one occupies or hopes to dominate."[83]

We must resist the temptation of crystalizing these rhetorical tropes into a doctrine that we must then treat as an essential component of Byzantine thinking or a fixed motivation for their actions. These rhetorical tropes were but options within a spectrum of views relating to Roman power that the court could activate when they were useful. The Byzantines controlled the deployment of those options; they were not trapped by them into nostalgic delusions.

Second, *the creation of client rulers along the periphery*. Many of the peoples who settled within former Roman territory or along the periphery of Byzantine control had either been previous Roman clients, or their settlement had been accompanied by real, fictive, or retroactive grants of imperial permission. These warbands or proto-states were typically tribal confederacies with little by way of state infrastructure to start with, and their subsequent development relied heavily on the adaptation of Roman modes of governance. In the fifth-sixth centuries, this enabled the emperors at Constantinople to pose as the nominal overlords of the kings of the Goths in Italy and even of the Franks, who were ruling over sub- or post-Roman polities. Theoderic the Goth was presented as a delegate of the emperor Zenon (474–491),[84] and Clovis was sent Roman titles and insignia of office by Anastasios (491–518).[85] It should be noted that one of these two realms was liquidated in a spectacular fashion by its ostensible Roman overlords, who claimed that they were taking back what had always been theirs. This was the context, and the consequences, of early Byzantine "imperial ecumenism."[86]

Byzantine emperors made similar claims in the middle period too. In his military manual, Leon VI (886–912) regarded the Bulgarians as somehow subjects of the empire—at a time when their king Symeon was on hostile terms and winning the war. Leon also thought that the Hungarians were on the verge of submitting to his authority and that even the Franks were loyal allies and basically subjects of the crown.[87] His son Konstantinos VII (944–959) expressed similar views in his writings about the Dalmatian cities and the Georgian and Armenian principalities.[88] Konstantinos wanted his son to be attended by the foreign nations and adored by all people who inhabit the earth.[89] Emperors of this period, most aggressively Nikephoros II Phokas (963–969), likewise asserted that the Lombard dukes of Salerno and Capua-Benevento were imperial subjects or "slaves."[90]

When these claims were made, the territories or states in question were *not* under Byzantine control, something that modern scholars insist on and cite as proof of the "fantastic" and "ideological" view of the world that the emperors cultivated, a result of their ecumenical delusions. In reality, all the emperors did was grant court titles to local rulers and their top men, which the latter accepted readily because Byzantine titles came with impressive cash salaries that could not be generated through the primitive fiscal mechanisms that those local lords commanded. Thus—the standard view goes—the court gave titles and pretended that this subordinated titulars to the authority of the emperor; for their part, local lords accepted these titles but otherwise operated independently, sometimes even against the empire.

But the joke may not have been on the empire. In time, the Dalmatian cities, Bulgaria, and most of Georgia and Armenia, places where the emperors had distributed titles and cash, *did* come under direct imperial control, a process that was more or less complete by the mid-eleventh century. In some cases, for example, Basileios II's annexation of Bulgaria, Tao, and Vaspurakan, we know that the ground had been prepared ahead of annexation through the creation of a cadre of local officials invested with Byzantine ranks and titles.[91] Again, this was not a master plan. The emperors routinely gave out titles to local lords in many realms and then pretended that this gave them nominal suzerainty over them, across the Roman border. Those realms were not slated for conquest. But when the ground had been sufficiently prepared *and* the opportunity arose, they could be annexed, depending on pragmatic decisions. Previously rhetorical claims thereby became reality. Crucially, the mechanisms of foreign annexation were, in this case, drawn from the domestic infrastructure of the empire itself: its ability to generate cash more effectively than its neighbors, and the hierarchy of its court titles, which created a presumptive Romanocentric framework for anyone taking that cash. And these policies paid dividends even before annexation: pro-Roman factions could split foreign elites and prevent concerted action against the empire;

talent, leadership, and manpower could be drained away into Roman territories and institutions, especially the army, where they would eventually become assimilated to Roman norms; and Orthodox (that is, Chalcedonian) communities could be defended, subsidized, and expanded so as to promote imperial interests within client states. In the relationship between the empire and its peripheral states, these exchanges typically happened in only one direction, underscoring the regional seniority of the Roman emperor.

There is no reason to scoff at the idea that the Lombard duchies and even Venice itself might have also come under direct imperial control. For all that these states are regarded today as belonging to the "west," the dukes' allegiance oscillated during the tenth century between the western and the eastern emperors, and were at times visited by Byzantine armies. Constantinople even managed to impose its own popes on Rome in the later tenth century,[92] though they are of course regarded as anti-popes in the western tradition. The Venetian doges also accepted court titles. In the twelfth century, at a time when they were well past the point of tutelage and had begun to attack the empire as an independent power, Manuel I Komnenos (1143–1180) correctly claimed in a letter that the Venetians "used to be vagabonds and poor before they poured into the polity of the Romans, toward whom they now behave arrogantly.... That nation did not merit a name of its own name in the past and has only recently become known, solely on account of the Romans."[93] These newcomers were not only interlopers on Roman territory, they had matured under Byzantine tutelage and previously accepted court hierarchies. This made them nominal subjects, if not of the emperor's direct political control, at least of his moral authority. We saw above how Manuel's aunt, Anna, believed that the empire was the true *despotis* of all these peoples, including the Venetians. The present analysis has tried to explain how this made good Byzantine sense, without imputing fantastic notions to the imperial leadership. To this degree, at least, the Byzantine state resembled the Babylonian one discussed by Richardson in that it brought capacities into being by first claiming them.

Third, *enhancing imperial prestige*. Though scholars of Byzantine political ideology have generally been skeptical of its ecumenical pretensions, those who study the impact of Byzantine culture, art, and even political symbolism on the regimes of medieval Europe have come to strikingly more positive results. Many areas of western art are seen as influenced by Byzantine forms and precedents; more importantly, regimes attempted to imitate the manners of the court in order to access a living version of the Roman imperial tradition that they were all eager to emulate.⁹⁴ These studies vindicate the claim of Akropolites (see above) that the emperor was like the sun who illuminated "not only the land of the Romans but also the farthest points of the *oikoumene*." What future research needs to restore is a sense of the Byzantines' own agency in this process, their deliberate cultivation of an image of cultural diffusion as solar emanation. Surely the emperors knew what they could accomplish through the strategic deployment of soft power, including diplomatic gifts and the reception of foreign travelers. Imperial ecumenism included a component of cultural and diplomatic politics which presented the emperor as "surpassing all rulers on the earth"—to use the words of a twelfth-century poem welcoming a western bride to the court.⁹⁵

The emperors sought to reinforce this image of transliminal importance in their correspondence with other rulers by referring to them as their "sons." This practice has unfortunately been turned by scholars into a theory or a doctrine of international relations, the so-called Family of Kings. There was no theory or doctrine. There was only a rhetorical-cum-ceremonial practice from which we have constructed the fiction of a theory.⁹⁶ But this practice—again, a set of rhetorical options—also transcended the limits of Romanía by elevating the emperor above his peers, at least when he could get away with it. In moments of weakness, he had to upgrade some of his "sons" to "brothers." But there was a period during which the Byzantine emperor was the "father" of a more expansive *oikoumene*. Projections of such symbolic centrality were central to Clifford Geertz's study of the kings of Bali. "If the reach of their government was limited, their fame would travel wider to make them an axis mundi or 'center of centers'—the hub from which the spokes in the wheel of the world would protrude."⁹⁷ This was accomplished through precisely the types of displays, claims, rhetoric, and protocol employed by the Byzantine emperors within their *oikoumene*.

Conclusion

Studies of Byzantium as a historical society have been enervated by its alleged ecumenical ideology. Compared to its cosmic claims, its state infrastructure is bound to appear laughably weak, and comparison to ancient Rome only makes things worse. Moreover, by defining its imperial culture in "ecumenical" terms, we lose sight of the distinction between the sphere of strong control exerted domestically by its institutions of governance on the one hand and the zones of diminishing influence beyond that, which could only be influenced indirectly, unless armies were physically deployed. This chapter has argued, by contrast, that Byzantine "ecumenism" is not the key to the empire's political self-awareness and historical ontology. It points to no gap between reality and ideal and cannot turn the Byzantine state into a theological abstraction. Exactly the opposite: in most instances, the Byzantines saw their "world" in terms defined by state institutions. Its horizons were those of Romanía. This by itself, and before any infrastructural analysis, underscores the extent to which the Roman order shaped mentalities. Beyond those horizons, by contrast, lay a world that could usually be tamed only in rhetorical ways. The Byzantines were acutely aware of the limits of their sway, yet when it came to the outside world too ecumenical rhetoric was not purely nostalgic: it created notional cradles for the furtherance of imperial projects and prestige. It was a successful investment of soft power in areas where the state was weak.

NOTES

I thank Cliff Ando, Ilias Anagnostakis, and Charis Messis for valuable suggestions and corrections.

1. Neville 2004.
2. Haldon and Brubaker 2011, 724; Cheynet 2002.
3. Haldon and Brubaker 2011, 796.
4. Wickham 2013.
5. Kaldellis 2015.
6. Rather than cite copious bibliography, I refer to a recent textbook: Cline and Graham 2011, chapter 13: "Universal Empires and Their Peripheries in Late Antiquity." It is not clear what they mean by the term, esp. at 294–97, 320–21. "Empire" has also not been well defined when used for these states.
7. Nicol 1967.
8. Obolensky 1971, 354.
9. Koder 2005, 38.
10. Ahrweiler 2005, 18–19; the shift from reality (later Rome) to myth (Byzantium) shapes her book, *L'idéologie politique de l'Empire byzantin* (1975); see also Ducellier 1976. The same in Patoura-Spanou 2008, 22. The dichotomy theory-reality is applied to the western medieval empire by Folz 1969, xi, 122.
11. Angelov 2007, 84.

12. Ševčenko 1961, 170, 183.

13. Louth 2007, 209.

14. Alexander 1962; cf. Mango 1965. Response: Kaldellis 2015, 185–98.

15. Chrysos 2005, 78. Read closely, Chrysos seems to reject the view that Byzantium had ideological delusions. Cf. Fowden 1993, 12–14: "Clearly 'the whole world' was a relative concept. . . . The Romans knew full well that there was no such thing as *imperium sine fine*. . . . When it came to the question of what was strategically indispensable to the existence of empire, the Romans and all the other successful imperial nations of antiquity were complete realists." Also Cameron 2006, 37: "The tension between show and reality is a familiar one in all periods, and the Byzantines were nothing if not pragmatic."

16. Dagron 2005.

17. Richardson 2012.

18. My study in preparation will push back against the current fashion for regarding Byzantine borders as fluid and permeable to the point of nonexistence.

19. Matthew 28:19.

20. To save space, I will not discuss two relevant ecclesiastical titles: Ecumenical Patriarch (i.e., of Constantinople) and Ecumenical Council, which do not undermine the analysis given below (their function was to differentiate one patriarch from his peers and those Councils from their rivals).

21. Ando 2012, 123–24; see also Scheid 2013.

22. Athanassiadi 2010, also with reference to 212 and Decius.

23. Simeonova 2000, 230.

24. Ivanov 2002; Kaldellis 2013, 119–25.

25. Shepard 1998, 179.

26. Shepard 2007, xxxiv–xxxv.

27. Constantine in Sozomenos, *Ecclesiastical History* 2.15.5; and Justinian in *Novel* 78.4.1; Prokopios, *Wars* 3.10.18; and on behalf of Catholics in the Gothic kingdom of Italy.

28. Obolensky 1971.

29. Kaldellis 2013, 39–43, 126–39, citing previous studies.

30. See the papers by T. Honoré and P. Garnsey in Swain and Edwards 2004; and Ando 2012, ch. 4.

31. Kaldellis 2007, 48–49, 102; for views of barbarian societies, see idem 2013.

32. Capogrossi Colognesi 2014, xxiii, 271.

33. Chrysos 2005, 64–65, cites Ammianus Marcellinus, *Res Gestae* 18.4.5, on the *termini iurisdictionis Romanae*. Cf. Justinian, *Novel* 109: the patriarchs of the entire *oikoumene* are those of Rome, Constantinople, Alexandria, Antioch, and Jerusalem.

34. Strabo, *Geography* 1.4.6; at 2.5.13 he refers to a possible "other *oikoumene*" beyond our knowledge on another part of the globe; see Romm 1992, 37.

35. Runciman 1977, 52.

36. Luke 2.1: ἐξῆλθεν δόγμα παρὰ Καίσαρος Αὐγούστου ἀπογράφεσθαι πᾶσαν τὴν οἰκουμένην.

37. Psellos, *ep. KD* 29.

38. Psellos, *ep. KD* 207, 239.
39. Stephenson 2000, 255; Kazhdan and Constable 1982, 38–39.
40. Psellos, *Oration for Xiphilinos* 3.
41. Buraselis 1989; Sherwin-White 1973, 283, 286–87.
42. Cassius Dio, *Roman History* 78(79).26.1.
43. Sozomenos, *Ecclesiastical History* 2.6.1.
44. Eusebios, *Life of Constantine* 4.51.
45. Texts cited by Koder 2005, 34.
46. Zonaras, *Chronicle* 13.10 (v. 3, 49). A similar expression in Metochites, *Essay* 93 (p. 593).
47. Justinian, *Novel* 24, preface. In Prokopios' *Secret History* 25.15, "the entire earth" is the empire governed by Justinian.
48. Theophanes Continuatus 2.9 (p. 49).
49. Pseudo-Kodinos, *Patria* 2.31.
50. *Life of Nikolaos the Younger* 3.
51. Ando 2000, 320–35. The Roman claims to world rule did not entail "belief" in such a thing; see Nicolet 1991, esp. ch. 2.
52. Schneider 1929, 139.
53. Photios, *Homily* 3.3 (*On the Rus' Attack*); and Konstantinos VII, *On the Themes* pr. 8–14 (p. 59); see also *Souda* s.v. Παράστημα ψυχῆς. For similar qualifiers in the early period, see Nicolet 1991, 34–35.
54. E.g., Psellos cited by Koder 2005, 39; Pachymeres in Angelov, 2007, 83 n. 28.
55. Theophylaktos, *ep.* 13.
56. These are, respectively, from the Councils of Chalcedon (451) and Constantinople II (553): *Acta Conciliorum Oecumenicorum*, v. 1.2.3, p. 45(404) and v. 3, p. 30. See also Agapetos, *Hortatory Chapters* 2 (the emperor's παγκόσμιος πολιτεία); and Skylitzes, *Synopsis*, p. 123 (κύριον πάσης τῆς γῆς, a prophesy about the rise to power of Basileios I). For a sampling of more expressions, albeit with no analysis, see Radošević 1993.
57. Theodosios the Deacon, *On the Capture of Crete* 467 and 995 (pp. 19 and 38).
58. Psellos, *Panegyrical Oration* 4.125–27 (p. 60).
59. Psellos, *Panegyrical Orations* 6.242–43 and 7.125-130; 97 and 104.
60. Parker 2008, 218; at 243 called "a sleight of hand."
61. Prodromos, *Imperial Poems* 4.76–79; 16.169–82; on whom see Magdalino 1993, 421–22 (for "amplification"); cf. Konstantinos VII, *Book of Ceremonies* 1.2 (v. 1, p. 40). I owe these references to Ilias Anagnostakis.
62. Prokopios, *Buildings* 1.2.1–12.
63. Konstantinos VII, *Book of Ceremonies* 1.78 (v. 1, p. 375).
64. Anna Komnene, *Alexiad* 14.7.2 (φύσει γὰρ οὖσα δεσπότις τῶν ἄλλων ἐθνῶν ἡ βασιλεία Ῥωμαίων ἐχθρωδῶς διακείμενον ἔχει τὸ δοῦλον).
65. Akropolites, *Funeral Oration for Ioannes III Doukas Batatzes* 21 (v. 2, p. 29, emphasis added).
66. Patriarch Antonios IV, *Letter to the Grand Prince of Moscow*. By that point the idea was being explicitly criticized; see Ševčenko 1961, 183.

67. Mastino 1986; Whittaker 1994, 14–26; Koder 2005, 27–28; Parker 2008, 204–27, 240–50.

68. Statues: Spivey 1996, 11: "essentially meaningless." Classical philosophy: Gutas 2012, 250: "without life and soul." Roman political rituals: Kaegi 2003, 83: "an antiquarian and vestigial sense."

69. Kaldellis 2012.

70. Sivertsev 2011, within its remit, is an excellent study.

71. Konstantinos VII, *On the Image of Edessa* 4.

72. Sivertsev 2011, 10–11, 15, 34–35, 40.

73. Caseau 2006, 313. The basic study is Podskalsky 1972; see also Mango 1965. A survey of these texts is in Alexander 1985. P. Magdalino has made them central to Byzantine mentality, e.g., Magdalino 2003.

74. Justinian, *Novel* 30.11; for Roman restoration, see Agathias, *Histories* pref. 24, 30, and 4.15.3, 5.14.1. For Justinian's propaganda of liberation, see Pazdernik 2000.

75. Ahrweiler 1975, 46: world rule expressed the "deepest convictions" of the "average Byzantine." Haldon 1999, 35, acknowledges that this theory rests on the apocalyptic texts. The desire for world conquest is an *accusation* in Prokopios, *Wars* 2.2.6 (a speaker). I recognize but bypass T. Lounghis's view (in many publications, e.g., Lounghis 1993) that the high command was divided between proponents of limitless and limited universal reconquest. I am still not sure what the thesis rests on.

76. Haldon 1999, 13–33, 43–44, 45–47; Treadgold 2006.

77. Haldon 1999, 35; Heather 2013, 137–43.

78. Kaldellis 2017.

79. Psellos, *Chronographia* 7.50.

80. Stephenson 2000, 253–56.

81. E.g., Totila in Justinian's pragmatic sanction on Italy (Appendix 7 of the *Novels*, 799–802). For similar claims, see Cheynet 1990, 178.

82. Verosta 1964 [1966], 564; Chrysos 1987; Laiou 2002, 1126.

83. Nicolet 1991, 2.

84. For the debate over his status, see Arnold 2014; Swain 2014, ch. 4.

85. Gregory of Tours, *History of the Franks* 2.38; see Mathisen 2012.

86. Chrysos 1978; Harris 2003.

87. Leon VI, *Taktika* 18.44, 18.76, 18.79 (the Slavs too).

88. Konstantinos VII, *De administrando imperio*, esp. 27–36, 43–46. For Georgia, see Martin-Hisard 2000; for Armenia, Greenwood 2010.

89. Konstantinos VII, *De administrando imperio*, pref. 38–39.

90. Liudprand, *Embassy to Constantinople* 15, 18, 27, 36. The situation was complex: Loud 2000; Mayr-Harting 2001.

91. Kaldellis 2017. For the foreign-policy use of titles, see Neville 2004, 28–30.

92. Vlysidou 2005.

93. Kinnamos, *History* 6.10.

94. For various aspects, see Ciggaar 1996; Raffensperger 2011, ch. 1; and Hilsdale, 2014.

95. Hilsdale 2005, 467.
96. See now Moysidou 1995; Chrysos 2005, 74–77.
97. Bang 2012, 65.

BIBLIOGRAPHY

Primary Sources

I have not included here full references to cited texts that can conveniently be found in the Loeb Classical Library or *Sources chrétiennes* series.

Acta Conciliorum Oecumenicorum, ed. E. Schwartz. Berlin: De Gruyter, 1914 ff.
Agapetos, *Hortatory Chapters*, ed. R. Riedinger, *Agapetos Diakonos: Der Fürstenspiegel für Kaiser Iustinianos*. Athens: Etaireia filon tou laou, 1995.
Agathias, *Histories*, ed. R. Keydell, *Agathiae Myrinaei Historiarum Libri Quinque*. Berlin: De Gruyter, 1967.
Akropolites, Georgios, *Funeral Oration for Ioannes III Doukas Batatzes* 21, ed. A. Heisenberg, rev. P. Wirth, *Georgii Acropolitae opera*, v. 2. Stuttgart: Teubner, 1978.
Antonios IV, Patriarch, *Letter to the Grand Prince of Moscow*, ed. F. Miklosich and J. Müller, *Acta et diplomata graeca medii aevi sacra et profana*, v. 2, 188–92. Vienna: C. Gerold, 1862.
Justinian, *Novels*, ed. R. Schoell and G. Kroll, *Corpus Iuris Civilis*, v. 3: *Novellae*. Berlin: Weidmann, 1899.
Kinnamos, Ioannes, *History*, ed. J-P. Migne, *Patrologia Graeca* v. 133.
Komnene, Anna, *Alexiad*, eds. D. R. Reinsch and A. Kambylis, *Annae Comnenae Alexias*. Berlin: De Gruyter, 2001.
Konstantinos VII Porphyrogennetos, *Book of Ceremonies*, ed. and tr. A. Moffatt and M. Tall, *Constantine Porphyrogennetos: The Book of Ceremonies*. Canberra: Australian Assocation for Byzantine Studies, 2012.
———, *De administrando imperio*, ed. and tr. G. Moravcsik and R. J. H. Jenkins, *Constantine Porphyrogenitus: De administrando imperio*. Washington, D.C.: Dumbarton Oaks, 1967.
———, *On the Image of Edessa*, ed. E. von Dobschütz, *Christusbilder: Untersuchungen zur christlichen Legende*, 39**–85**. Leipzig: J. C. Hinrichs, 1899.
———, *On the Themes*, ed. A Pertusi, *Costantino Porfirogenito de Thematibus*. Vatican City: Biblioteca apostolica vaticana, 1952.
Leon VI, *Taktika*, ed. G. T. Dennis, *The Taktika of Leo VI*. Washington, D.C.: Dumbarton Oaks, 2010.
Life of Nikolaos the Younger, ed. D. Sophianos, Ἅγιος Νικόλαος ὁ ἐν Βουναίνῃ. Athens: Ethnikon kai Kapodistriakon Panepistēmion Athēnōn, Philosophikē Scholē, 1972.
Metochites, Theodoros, *Essays*, ed. M. C. G. Müller and M. T. Kiessling, *Theodori Metochitae Miscellanea philosophica et historica*. Leipzig: F. C. G. Vogelli, 1821.

Photios, *Homilies*, ed. B. Laourdas, *[Φωτίου λόγοι]*=Ἑλληνικά: Παράρτημα 12 (1966): Thessalonike.

Prodromos, Theodoros, *Imperial Poems*, ed. W. Hörandner, *Theodoros Prodromos: Historische Gedichte*. Vienna: Austrian Academy of Sciences, 1974.

Psellos, Michael, *Chronographia*, ed. S. Impellizeri, tr. S. Ronchey, *Michele Psello: Imperatori di Bisanzio (Cronografia)*, 2 vols. Milan: L. Valla, 1984.

———, *ep. KD*, ed. E. Kurtz and F. Drexl, *Michaelis Pselli scripta minora*, v. 2. Milan: Vita e pensiero, 1941.

———, *Oration for Xiphilinos*, ed. I. Polemis, *Michael Psellus: Orationes Funebres*, vol. 1. Berlin: Teubner, 2014.

———, *Panegyrical Orations*, ed. G. T. Dennis, *Michaelis Pselli orationes panegyricae*. Leipzig: Teubner 1994.

Pseudo-Kodinos, *Patria*, ed. T. Preger, *Scriptores originum Constantinopolitanarum*, v. 2, 135–289. Leipzig: Teubner, 1907.

Skylitzes, Ioannes, *Synopsis of Histories*, ed. J. Thurn, *Ioannis Scylitzae Synopsis Historiarum*. Berlin: De Gruyter, 1973.

Theodosios the Deacon, *On the Capture of Crete*, ed. H. Criscuolo, *Theodosii diaconi De Creta Capta*. Leipzig: Teubner, 1979.

Theophanes Continuatus, ed. I. Bekker. Bonn: E. Weber, 1838.

Theophylaktos of Ohrid, *ep.*, ed. P. Gautier, *Theophylacte d'Achrida*, v. 2: *Lettres*. Thessalonike: Association de recherches byzantines, 1986.

Zonaras, Ioannes, *Chronicle*, ed. M. Pinder and T. Büttner-Wobst, *Ioannis Zonarae Epitomae historiarum*, 3 vols. Berlin: E. Weber, 1841–1897.

Modern Scholarship

Ahrweiler, H. 1975. *L'idéologie politique de l'Empire byzantin*. Paris: Presses universitaires de France.

———. 2005. "Παγκοσμιότητα του Βυζαντίου: Από τα έργα στα λόγια." In *Το Βυζάντιο ως Οικουμένη*, edited by E. Chrysos, 13–23. Athens: National Hellenic Research Foundation.

Alexander, P. 1962. "The Strength of Empire and Capital as Seen Through Byzantine Eyes." *Speculum* 37 (3): 339–57.

———. 1985. *The Byzantine Apocalyptic Tradition*. Berkeley: University of California Press.

Ando, C. 2000. *Imperial Ideology and Provincial Loyalty in the Roman Empire*. Berkeley: University of California Press.

———. 2012. *Imperial Rome, AD 193 to 284: The Critical Century*. Edinburgh: Edinburgh University Press.

Angelov, A. 2007. *Imperial Ideology and Political Thought in Byzantium, 1204–1330*. Cambridge: Cambridge University Press.

Arnold, J. 2014. *Theoderic and the Roman Imperial Restoration*. Cambridge: Cambridge University Press.
Athanassiadi, P. 2010. *Vers la pensée unique: La montée de l'intolérance dans l'Antiquité tardive*. Paris: Les Belles Lettres.
Bang, P. F. 2012. "Between Aśoka and Antiochos: An Essay in World History on Universal Kingship and Cosmopolitan Culture in the Hellenistic Ecumene." In *Universal Empire: A Comparative Approach to Imperial Culture and Representation in Eurasian History*, edited by P. F. Bang and D. Kołodziejczyk, 60–75. Cambridge: Cambridge University Press.
Buraselis, K. 1989. *ΘΕΙΑ ΔΩΡΕΑ: Μελέτες πάνω στὴν πολιτικὴ τῆς δυναστείας τῶν Σεβήρων καὶ τὴν Constitutio Antoniniana*. Athens: Academy of Athens.
Cameron, A. 2006. *The Byzantines*. Malden, Mass.: Wiley-Blackwell.
Capogrossi Colognesi, L. 2014. *Law and Power in the Making of the Roman Commonwealth*. Translated by L. Kopp. Cambridge: Cambridge University Press.
Caseau, B. 2006. "La vie religieuse." In *Le monde byzantin*, v. 2: *L'empire byzantin (641–1204)*, edited by J.-C. Cheynet, 313–21, 325–33. Paris: Presses universitaires de France.
Cheynet, J.-C. 1990. *Pouvoir et contestations à Byzance (963–1210)*. Paris: Publications de la Sorbonne.
———. 2002. "Les limites du pouvoir à Byzance: une forme de tolérance?" In *Ανοχή και καταστολή στους μέσους χρόνους: Μνήμη Λένου Μαυρομάτη*, edited by A. Nikolaou, 15–28. Athens: National Hellenic Research Foundation.
Chrysos, E. K. 1978. "The Title ΒΑΣΙΛΕΥΣ in Early Byzantine International Relations." *Dumbarton Oaks Papers* 32:31–75.
———. 1987. "Die Nordgrenze des byzantinischen Reiches im 6. bis 8. Jahrhundert." In *Die Völker Südosteuropas im 6. bis 8. Jahrhundert*, edited by B. Hänsel, 27–40. Berlin: Südosteuropa-Ges. u.a.
———. 2005. "Το Βυζάντιο και η διεθνής κοινωνία του Μεσαίωνα." In *Το Βυζάντιο ως Οικουμένη*, edited by Chrysos, E. K., 59–78. Athens: National Hellenic Research Foundation.
Ciggaar, K. N. 1996. *Western Travellers to Constantinople: The West and Byzantium, 962–1204*. Leiden: Brill.
Cline, E. H., and M. W. Graham. 2011. *Ancient Empires from Mesopotamia to the Rise of Islam*. Cambridge: Cambridge University Press.
Dagron, G. 2005. "L'oecuménitcité politique: droit sur l'escape, droit sur le temps." In *Το Βυζάντιο ως Οικουμένη*, edited by E. Chrysos, 47–57. Athens: National Hellenic Research Foundation.
Ducellier, A. 1976. *Le drame de Byzance: idéal et échec d'une société chrétienne*. Paris: Hachette.
Folz, R. 1969. *The Concept of Empire in Western Europe from the Fifth to the Fourteenth Century*. Translated by S. A. Oglivie. New York: Edward Arnold.
Fowden, G. 1993. *Empire to Commonwealth: Consequences of Monotheism in Late Antiquity*. Princeton, N.J.: Princeton University Press.

Greenwood, T. 2010. "Patterns of Contact and Communication: Constantinople and Armenia, 860–976." In *Armenian Constantinople*, edited by R. G. Hovannisian and S. Payaslian, 73–99. Costa Mesa, Calif.: Mazda.

Gutas, D. 2012. "Arabic into Byzantine Greek: Introducing a Survey of the Translations." In *Knotenpunkt Byzanz: Wissenformen und kulturelle Wechselbeziehungen*, edited by A. Speer and D. Wirmer, 246–64. Berlin: De Gruyter.

Haldon, J. 1999. *Warfare, State and Society in the Byzantine World, 565–1204*. London: University College London Press.

Haldon, J., and L. Brubaker. 2011. *Byzantium in the Iconoclast Era, c. 680–850: A History*. Cambridge: Cambridge University Press.

Harris, A. 2003. *Byzantium, Britain and the West: The Archaeology of Cultural Identity, AD 400–650*. Stroud: Tempus.

Heather, P. 2013. *The Restoration of Rome: Barbarian Popes and Imperial Pretenders*. Oxford: Oxford University Press.

Hilsdale, C. 2005. "Constructing a Byzantine 'Augusta': A Greek Book for a French Bride." *Art Bulletin* 87 (3): 458–83.

———. 2014. *Byzantine Art and Diplomacy in an Age of Decline*. Cambridge: Cambridge University Press.

Ivanov, S. A. 2002. "Casting Pearls Before Circe's Swine: The Byzantine View of Mission." *Travaux et mémoires* 14 (1): 295–301.

Kaegi, W. 2003. *Heraclius: Emperor of Byzantium*. Cambridge: Cambridge University Press.

Kaldellis, A. 2007. *Hellenism in Byzantium. The Transformation of Greek Identity and the Reception of the Classical Tradition*. Cambridge: Cambridge University Press.

———. 2012. "The Byzantine Role in the Making of the Corpus of Classical Greek Historiography: A Preliminary Investigation." *Journal of Hellenic Studies* 132:71–85.

———. 2013. *Ethnography After Antiquity: Foreign Lands and People in Byzantine Literature*. Philadelphia: University of Pennsylvania Press.

———. 2015. *The Byzantine Republic: People and Power in New Rome*. Cambridge, Mass.: Harvard University Press.

———. 2017. *Streams of Gold, Rivers of Blood: The Rise and Fall of Byzantium, 955 AD. to the First Crusade*. Oxford and New York: Oxford University Press.

Kazhdan, A., and G. Constable. 1982. *People and Power in Byzantium: An Introduction to Modern Byzantine Studies*. Washington, D.C.: Dumbarton Oaks.

Koder, J. 2005. "Η γεωγραφική διάσταση της βυζαντινής Οικουμένης." In *Το Βυζάντιο ως Οικουμένη*, edited by E. Chrysos, ed., 25–45. Athens: National Hellenic Research Foundation.

Laiou, A. E. 2002. "Economic Thought and Ideology." In *The Economic History of Byzantium from the Seventh Through the Fifteenth Century*, vol. 3, edited by A. E. Laiou, 1123–44. Washington, D.C.: Dumbarton Oaks Research Library and Collection.

Loud, G. A. 2000. "Southern Italy in the Tenth Century." In *The New Cambridge Medieval History*, vol. 3, edited by T. Reuter, 624–45. Cambridge: Cambridge University Press.

Lounghis, T. 1993. *Η ιδεολογία της βυζαντινής ιστοριογραφίας*. Athens: Herodotos Press.

Louth, A. 2007. *Greek East and Latin West: The Church AD 681–1071*. Crestwood, N.Y.: St. Vladimir's Seminary Press.

Magdalino, P. 1993. *The Empire of Manuel I Komnenos, 1143–1180*. Cambridge: Cambridge University Press.

———. 2003. "The Year 1000 in Byzantium." In *Byzantium in the Year 1000*, edited by P. Magdalino, 233–70. Leiden: Brill.

Mango, C. 1965. "Byzantinism and Romantic Hellenism." *Journal of the Warburg and Courtauld Institutes* 28:29–43.

Martin-Hisard, B. 2000. "Constantinople et les archontes du monde caucasien dans le Livre des Cérémonies, II, 48." *Travaux et mémoires* 13:359–530.

Mastino, A. 1986. "Orbis, kosmos, oikumene: Aspetti spaziali dell'idea di impero universale da Augusto a Teodosio." In *Popoli e spazio romano tra diritto e profezia*, 63–162. Naples: Edizioni scientifiche italiane.

Mathisen, R. 2012. "Clovis, Anastasius, and Political Status in 508 C.E.: The Frankish Aftermath of the Battle of Vouillé." In *The Battle of Vouillé, 507 C.E.: Where France Began*, edited by R. Mathisen and D. Shanzer, 79–110. Berlin: De Guyter.

Mayr-Harting, H. 2001. "Liudprand of Cremona's Account of His Legation to Constantinople (968) and Ottonian Imperial Strategy." *English Historical Review* 116 (467): 539–56.

Moysidou, J. 1995. *Το Βυζάντιο και οι βόρειοι γείτονές του τον 10ο αιώνα*. Athens: Basilopoulos.

Neville, L. 2004. *Authority in Byzantine Provincial Society, 950–1100*. Cambridge: Cambridge University Press.

Nicol, D. 1967. "The Byzantine View of Western Europe." *Greek, Roman, and Byzantine Studies* 8:315–39.

Nicolet, C. 1991. *Space, Geography, and Politics in the Early Roman Empire*. Translated by H. Leclerc. Ann Arbor: University of Michigan Press.

Obolensky, D. 1971. *The Byzantine Commonwealth: Eastern Europe, 500–1453*. London: Widenfield & Nicholson.

Parker, G. 2008. *The Making of Roman India*. Cambridge: Cambridge University Press.

Patoura-Spanou, S. 2008. *Χριστιανισμός και παγκοσμιότητα στο πρώιμο Βυζάντιο*. Athens: National Hellenic Research Foundation.

Pazdernik, C. F. 2000. "Procopius and Thucydides on the Labors of War: Belisarius and Brasidas in the Field." *Transactions of the American Philological Association* 130:149–87.

Podskalsky, G. 1972. *Byzantinische Reichseschatologie*. Munich: W. Fink.

Radošević, N. 1993. "L'Oecuménè byzantine dans les discours imperiaux du XIe et XIIe siècle." *Byzantinoslavica* 54:156–61.

Raffensperger, C. 2011. *Reimagining Europe: Kievan Rus' in the Medieval World*. Cambridge, Mass.: Harvard University Press.

Richardson, S. 2012. "Early Mesopotamia: The Presumptive State," *Past and Present* 215 (1): 3–49.

Romm, J. 1992. *The Edges of the Earth in Ancient Thought*. Princeton, N.J.: Princeton University Press.

Runciman, S. 1977. *The Byzantine Theocracy.* Cambridge: Cambridge University Press.
Scheid, J. 2013. *Les Dieux, l'État et l'individu: Réflexions sur la religion civique à Rome.* Paris: Seuil.
Schneider, A. M. 1929. "Samos in frühchristlicher und byzantinischer Zeit." *Mitteilungen des deutschen Archäologischen Instituts, Athenische Abteilung* 54:96–141.
Ševčenko, I. 1961. "The Decline of Byzantium Seen Through the Eyes of Its Intellectuals." *Dumbarton Oaks Papers* 15:167–86.
Shepard, J. 1998. "Byzantine Relations with the Outside World in the Ninth Century: An Introduction." In *Byzantium in the Ninth Century: Dead or Alive?*, edited by L. Brubaker, 167–80. Aldershot: Ashgate.
———, ed. 2007. *The Expansion of Orthodox Europe: Byzantium, the Balkans and Russia.* Aldershot: Ashgate.
Sherwin-White, A. N. 1973. *The Roman Citizenship.* 2nd ed. Oxford.: Oxford University Press.
Simeonova, L. 2000. "Foreigners in Tenth-Century Byzantium: A Contribution to the History of Cultural Encounter." In *Strangers to Themselves: The Byzantine Outsider*, edited by D. C. Smythe, 229–44. Aldershot: Ashgate.
Sivertsev, A. M. 2011. *Judaism and Imperial Ideology in Late Antiquity.* Cambridge: Cambridge University Press.
Spivey, N. 1996. *Understanding Greek Sculpture: Ancient Meanings, Modern Readings.* London: Thames and Hudson.
Stephenson, P. 2000. "Byzantine Conceptions of Otherness After the Annexation of Bulgaria (1018)." In *Strangers to Themselves: The Byzantine Outsider*, edited by D. Smythe, 245–57. Aldershot: Ashgate.
Swain, B. 2014. *Empire of Hope and Tragedy: Jordanes and the Invention of Roman-Gothic History.* PhD dissertation, Ohio State University.
Swain, S., and M. Edwards, eds. 2004. *Approaching Late Antiquity: The Transformation from Early to Late Empire.* Oxford: Oxford University Press.
Treadgold, W. 2006. "Byzantium, the Reluctant Warrior." In *Noble Ideals and Bloody Realities: Warfare in the Middle Ages*, edited by N. Christie and M. Yazigi, 209–33. Leiden: Brill.
Verosta, S. 1964 [1966]. "International Law in Europe and Western Asia Between 100 and 650 AD." *Académie de droit international: Recueil des cours* 3:491–617.
Vlysidou, B. 2005. "Η πολιτική του Βασιλείου Λακαπηνού έναντι της Δύσης." *Symmeikta* 17:111–30.
Whittaker, C. R. 1994. *Frontiers of the Roman Empire: A Social and Economic Study.* Baltimore, Md.: Johns Hopkins University Press.
Wickham, C. 2013. "Response." In *Authority in Byzantium*, edited by P. Armstrong, 110. Farnham: Ashgate.

CONTRIBUTORS

Clifford Ando is David B. and Clara E. Stern Professor and Professor of Classics, History, and Law and in the College at the University of Chicago. He is also a Research Fellow in the Department of Biblical and Ancient Studies at the University of South Africa.

R. Alan Covey is Associate Professor of Anthropology at the University of Texas at Austin as well as a faculty associate in the Teresa Lozano Long Institute of Latin American Studies. He is a Research Associate in the Division of Anthropology at the American Museum of Natural History.

Damián Fernández is Assistant Professor in the Department of History at Northern Illinois University.

Anthony Kaldellis is Professor of Classics at The Ohio State University.

Emily Mackil is Associate Professor of History at the University of California, Berkeley.

Richard Payne is Neubauer Family Assistant Professor in the Department of Near Eastern Languages and Civilizations and the Oriental Institute at the University of Chicago.

Seth Richardson is Editor of the *Journal of Near Eastern Studies* in the Oriental Institute at the University of Chicago.

Wang Haicheng is Mary and Cheney Cowles Endowed Associate Professor of Chinese Art and Archaeology at the University of Washington, Seattle.

John Weisweiler is Assistant Professor in the History of the Late Antique Mediterranean at the University of Maryland, College Park.

INDEX OF SUBJECTS

Abbasids, 180
Ādur Gušnap (Takht-e Suleyman), 191, 201
Airyana Vaējah, 182, 184
Akkad, 22, 47n29
ambiguation, strategic, 18, 40–41, 67–68
Ammianus Marcellinus, 149, 160
Anderson, Benedict, 91, 116, 144
Ando, Clifford, 44, 166, 277
Anna Komnene, 283, 289
Apollo Pythion, Temple of, 70, 72
archaeology, of power, 9–10, 64–65, 70, 180, 190–91, 193–94, 221, 223, 225
Ardashir I, 179, 185, 190
Aristotle, 65, 78
Armenia, 195, 198–99, 285, 288
Aššur (city), 22, 23
Aššur (deity), 96
Assyria, 25, 92, 96, 98, 100, 104, 188
Augustus, Roman emperor, 129, 280
Azerbaijan, 181, 183, 191–94, 196–99, 203

Babylon (city), 25
Bactria, 183, 195, 197
Besh Barmaq, 194, 197
bureaucracy, 142, 163–67, 186, 188, 247–48, 253–54, 265. *See also* rationality, bureaucratic

Caspian Gates, 194, 196
Caucusus, 193, 195
census, 100, 108, 140–42, 280
ceremonial, 149, 151, 226–29, 236n30
Cheng, King, 94, 99
Chindaswinth (law of), 249, 251–52, 256, 261
Christians, Christianity, 122, 197, 251, 254, 276–78, 284
citizenship. *See* membership

civil society, 19, 20, 44, 165. *See also* elites, cooptation of; non-state actors, instrumentalization of
claims to power, by state, 17, 24, 42, 145n13. *See also* presumptive state
Claudius, Roman emperor, 125, 127, 139
client kingdoms, 93, 96–98, 100, 199, 221, 275, 279, 287–89
Codex Gregorianus, 163, 171n69
Codex Hermogenianus, 163, 171n70
Codex Theodosianus, 164, 171n73
Cohen, Morris, 72, 75
colonies, 10, 76–77, 99–101, 127–29, 188, 191–92
communication, 6, 117–18
comparison, practice of, 2, 92
Constantine, 157, 164, 277, 280–81
Constantinople, 273, 275, 281, 283
corvée labor, 10, 134–39, 194–96, 225–26, 228
countryside. *See* hinterlands
Cuzco, 221–23, 228–31

debt, 69, 78
De fisco Barcinonensi 255, 263
despotic power, 17, 18, 64, 117, 119, 143–44, 150, 160, 185, 198–99, 218, 234n18, 247, 253, 273
Ding (Yi duke), 99, 105–6
Diocletian, 149, 157, 161–63
distance of state authority, 39–41, 149

elites, cooptation of, 2, 9, 23, 91, 106–108, 118, 119–20, 144, 153–55, 157–58, 162, 180–81, 184, 195–96, 200–201, 225, 231–32, 246, 258–62, 264
empire, theories of, 3, 4, 6, 116–17, 160–61, 182
Ērānšahr, 182, 204
evidentiary regimes, 121

Fars, 192, 196–96
feudalism, 111n63, 238n2, 244
fiscality. *See* taxation
formularies, 5
Franks, 246, 287
Fructosus, 243–44, 265

Gaul, 127–32, 157, 286
Ghilghilchay, 194, 197
Gorgan, 181, 183, 192–94, 196–99, 203
Gortyn, 69–70, 72–76, 79
Goths, 249, 256, 287
governmentality, 7, 9, 41, 100, 118, 141–42, 196. *See also* subjectivity
Great Code of Gortyn, 70, 74, 77

Hammurabi, 22, 23, 31, 34, 40
hinterlands, 4, 12n8, 81n10, 91, 104–8, 115, 119–20, 120–29, 133, 145n6, 156, 162–63, 166, 192, 208n54, 230–31, 233n8
Huns, 183–84, 195–98
Husraw I, 184, 186, 199
Husraw II, 193, 199–200, 202–3

ideal-typical analysis, 1
ideological power, 37, 68, 144, 218, 259
ideology, 18–19, 39–40, 104, 138, 152–60, 179–80, 273, 274
infrastructural power, 9, 17–21, 23, 30, 28–29, 75, 78–79, 117, 142–44, 150–52, 180–81, 183, 218–19, 247, 272–73, 280, 285, 288
institutionalization, 19

Justinian, 279, 281, 285–86

Kant, Immanuel, 66, 79
Khurasan, 191, 193, 196, 197
Khuzestan, 188–89, 192
kinship, 181, 184, 195–96, 201, 220, 227–30, 231–32, 237n35

Larsa, 22, 24, 27, 35
law, 1, 28–43, 66–68, 71, 76, 125, 163–64, 278–79
law, as form of power, 67
law-applying institutions, 1, 35, 38, 77–78, 124
law-making institutions, 1, 34
Laws of Hammurabi (LH), 22, 28–43

legibility, of objects of governance, 27
Leovigild, 246, 249–51, 262

Mann, Michael, 2, 9, 18, 63–64, 65–66, 67–68, 70–71, 79–80, 91–92, 108, 116–19, 144, 151–52, 218–19, 231–32, 247
maps, 129–35
Marduk (deity), 20, 24, 43
membership, 25–28, 72, 75, 125–29, 139, 155–56, 160–61, 277, 278
Mesopotamia, Ch. 1, passim; also 188–89, 192, 203
Mihranids, 184, 193, 202
military power, 23–24, 104, 193–99, 228
monumentalization, 9–10, 65–66

Narseh, 189, 200
non-state actors, instrumentalization of, 118, 246–47, 250, 254–56, 263–64
Novak, William, 2, 9, 72, 118, 165, 186–87

Ostrogoths, 246, 249

Parthians, 180, 186, 190, 194–96
patrimonialism, 189, 244, 245
patronage, of local elites. *See* elites, cooptation of
penetration, of territory by state, 1, 5, 115, 164–67, 221, 224, 249, 255–56, 263. *See also* territoriality
pluralism, within imperial states, 35–36, 41, 160, 180, 224, 235n27, 277–78
polis, 3–4, 9–10, 63–65
politicization, 6, 68, 72, 75, 78, 79, 181–82
Postgate, Nicholas, 91–92, 98, 100, 104
presumptive state, 8, 18, 30, 36, 43–44, 91, 119, 179–80, 221, 248, 275, 289
privileges, granted by imperial state, 26
property, 64, 66, 69, 72–73, 77–80, 189, 249–50, 256, 263
Psellos, 280, 282, 285, 286
Pythion laws, 70, 72–73

Quito, 221, 228

rationality, bureaucratic, 8, 19, 40 107–8, 138, 166–67
Reccared (law of), 250–55, 261
resistance, 2, 187–88, 202–3, 233n7

Richardson, Seth, 2, 7, 8–9, 67, 91, 98, 104, 119, 144, 161, 167, 179–80, 185, 264, 275
roads, 10, 120, 129–40, 219, 224
Roman Empire, 183, 196, 245, 247–48
rural population. *See* hinterlands

Sasan, house of, 157, 187–88, 273–74
Scott, James C., 2, 91, 104, 116, 144
Shapur I, 157, 183, 185–86, 189
sovereignty, 4, 7, 10, 20, 22–23, 27–28, 40, 43–44, 115, 179–83, 221, 223–24, 234n16, 237n35, 263–65
state, in theory, 3–5, 17–20, 66, 100, 115–20, 143–44, 151–52, 181–82, 186, 218–20, 231–32, 232n1, 233n8, 243–48
subjectivity, 7, 17, 19, 28, 44, 52n115, 116, 118, 142, 166, 226

taxation, 20, 25, 43, 78–79, 92, 96, 119, 161–63, 180, 186, 200–201, 227–28, 243, 248–63
temporality, 118, 134, 145n3, 179
territoriality, 1, 21–28, 64, 71, 75–76, 79, 91–92, 98, 180, 181–82, 188, 200–201, 204–5, 274, 275, 280
tribute, 96–98. *See also* taxation

Vespasian, 127, 153–54, 158
villages, 4, 22, 99, 100, 105–8, 115, 120–22, 137–39, 156, 163, 257
violence, monopoly on, 1, 6, 20, 36, 39, 63, 64, 104, 232n1

weakness, of state, 2, 5, 19, 39, 41, 43–45, 63, 186–87, 192, 244, 247–48, 255, 273
Weber, Max, 8, 11n1, 31, 63, 91–92, 144, 186, 232n1, 245
Wen, King, 93–94, 97
Wickham, Chris, 246–47
women, as legal actors, 73, 74, 105–6, 163–64
Woolf, Greg, 129–32, 157
writing and literacy, 66–68, 70–71, 79–80, 219, 220, 233n4
Wu, King, 94, 97, 99

Yazdgird II, 193, 195, 196, 198–200
Yi (people), 97, 99, 102
Yin Eight Armies, 102, 104

Zeng (state), 101–2, 104
Zhou (city; also Cheng Zhou), 92, 94–95, 105
Zoroastrianism, 182, 185–86, 197, 199, 207, 209–10, 274

INDEX OF CITATIONS OF THE LAWS OF HAMMURABI, BY PARAGRAPH

LH ¶ 001, 55n156, 56n163
LH ¶ 002, 50n82, 55n156
LH ¶ 003, 55n156
LH ¶ 004, 55n156
LH ¶ 005, 54nn146–147
LH ¶ 006, 54n141, 55n156
LH ¶ 007, 55n156
LH ¶ 008, 54n141, 55n156
LH ¶ 009, 54n145–146, 55n156
LH ¶ 010, 55nn150, 156
LH ¶ 011, 55nn150, 156
LH ¶ 012, 55n153
LH ¶ 013, 54n146, 55nn150, 156
LH ¶ 015, 31, 54n141, 55n156
LH ¶ 016, 32, 51n94, 54n141, 55n156
LH ¶ 017, 55n153
LH ¶ 018, 54n138, 55n154
LH ¶ 019, 32, 51n94, 55n156
LH ¶ 021, 32, 55n156
LH ¶ 022, 55n156
LH ¶ 023, 49n63, 54nn145, 147
LH ¶ 024, 54n147
LH ¶ 025, 55n156
LH ¶ 026, 32, 54n141, 55n156
LH ¶ 027, 32, 54n141, 55n154
LH ¶ 028, 32, 54n141, 55n156
LH ¶ 029, 32, 55n153
LH ¶ 030, 32, 55n153
LH ¶ 031, 32, 55n153
LH ¶ 032, 31, 32, 54n140, 55n153
LH ¶ 033, 32, 54n141, 55n156
LH ¶ 034, 32, 55n156
LH ¶ 035, 32, 55n153
LH ¶ 036, 32, 38, 55n157
LH ¶ 037, 32, 55n153
LH ¶ 038, 32, 55n153
LH ¶ 039, 32, 55n153
LH ¶ 040, 32, 55n153

LH ¶ 041, 55n153
LH ¶ 042, 55n153, 55n154
LH ¶ 043, 55n153
LH ¶ 044, 55n153
LH ¶ 045, 55n157
LH ¶ 046, 55n153
LH ¶ 047, 55nn150, 153
LH ¶ 048, 55nn150, 157
LH ¶ 049, 55n153
LH ¶ 050, 55n153
LH ¶ 051, 53n124, 54n139, 55n153
LH ¶ 052, 55n153
LH ¶ 053, 55n153
LH ¶ 054, 54n147, 55n154
LH ¶ 055, 55n153
LH ¶ 056, 55n153
LH ¶ 057, 55n153
LH ¶ 058, 55n153
LH ¶ 059, 55n153
LH ¶ 060, 55n153
LH ¶ 061, 55n154
LH ¶ 062, 55n153
LH ¶ 063, 55n153
LH ¶ 064, 55n153
LH ¶ 065, 55n153
LH ¶ 100, 54n145, 55n154
LH ¶ 101, 55n153
LH ¶ 102, 55n153
LH ¶ 103, 54n145, 55n156
LH ¶ 104, 55nn150, 153
LH ¶ 105, 55nn150, 153
LH ¶ 106, 54n145, 55nn150, 153
LH ¶ 107, 54n145, 55n153
LH ¶ 108, 53n128, 55n154
LH ¶ 109, 54n138, 55n156
LH ¶ 110, 55n154
LH ¶ 111, 55n153
LH ¶ 112, 55n153

LH ¶ 113, 55n154
LH ¶ 114, 53n132, 54n148, 55n153
LH ¶ 115, 32, 53n132, 54n148, 55n157
LH ¶ 116, 32, 53n132, 54n147, 55n153
LH ¶ 117, 50n82, 55n153
LH ¶ 118, 55n153
LH ¶ 119, 55n153
LH ¶ 120, 54n145, 55n153
LH ¶ 121, 55n153
LH ¶ 122, 50n82, 55n153
LH ¶ 123, 50n82, 55nn150, 157
LH ¶ 124, 55n153, 55n154
LH ¶ 125, 55n153
LH ¶ 126, 54nn145, 147, 55n153
LH ¶ 127, 54n146, 55nn151, 153, 154
LH ¶ 128, 55n157
LH ¶ 129, 54n137, 55n154
LH ¶ 130, 55n154
LH ¶ 131, 54n145, 55n153
LH ¶ 132, 55n156
LH ¶ 133a, 55n157
LH ¶ 133b, 55n154
LH ¶ 134, 55n157
LH ¶ 135, 55n153
LH ¶ 136, 55n157
LH ¶ 137, 55n154
LH ¶ 138, 50n79, 55n153
LH ¶ 139, 55n153
LH ¶ 140, 55n153
LH ¶ 141, 50n79, 55nn153, 154
LH ¶ 142, 50n79, 54n147, 55nn153, 154
LH ¶ 143, 50n79, 54n147
LH ¶ 144, 55n154
LH ¶ 145, 55n153
LH ¶ 146, 55n153
LH ¶ 147, 55n153
LH ¶ 148, 55n153
LH ¶ 149, 50n79, 55n153
LH ¶ 150, 55nn150, 153
LH ¶ 151, 55nn150, 157
LH ¶ 152, 55n154
LH ¶ 153, 55nn151, 154
LH ¶ 154, 55n154
LH ¶ 155, 55nn151, 154
LH ¶ 156, 55n153
LH ¶ 157, 55nn151, 154
LH ¶ 158, 55n156
LH ¶ 159, 55n153
LH ¶ 160, 55n153
LH ¶ 161, 55n153
LH ¶ 162, 50n79, 55n157

LH ¶ 163, 50n79, 54n142, 55n157
LH ¶ 164, 55n153
LH ¶ 165, 54n148, 55nn150, 153
LH ¶ 166, 54n148
LH ¶ 167, 54n148
LH ¶ 168, 54n146, 55n157
LH ¶ 169, 54n146, 55n154
LH ¶ 170, 55n153
LH ¶ 171, 55nn150, 153
LH ¶ 172, 54nn146, 148
LH ¶ 173, 54n148
LH ¶ 174, 54n148
LH ¶ 175, 55n157
LH ¶ 176a–b, 55n154
LH ¶ 177, 54n146
LH ¶ 178, 54n148, 55nn150, 153
LH ¶ 179, 55n153
LH ¶ 180, 55n153
LH ¶ 181, 55n153
LH ¶ 182, 55nn150, 153
LH ¶ 183, 55n157
LH ¶ 184, 54n148
LH ¶ 185, 55n157
LH ¶ 186, 55n153
LH ¶ 187, 55n157
LH ¶ 188, 55n157
LH ¶ 189, 55n153
LH ¶ 190, 55n153
LH ¶ 191, 55n153
LH ¶ 192, 55nn151, 154
LH ¶ 193, 55nn151, 154
LH ¶ 194, 55nn151, 154
LH ¶ 195, 55nn151, 154
LH ¶ 196, 55nn151, 154
LH ¶ 197, 55nn151, 154
LH ¶ 198, 55n153
LH ¶ 199, 55n153
LH ¶ 200, 55nn151, 154
LH ¶ 201, 55n153
LH ¶ 202, 54n147, 55n156+B192
LH ¶ 203, 55n153
LH ¶ 204, 55n153
LH ¶ 205, 55nn151, 154
LH ¶ 206, 55n153
LH ¶ 207, 55n153
LH ¶ 208, 55n153
LH ¶ 209, 55n153
LH ¶ 210, 55nn151, 154
LH ¶ 211, 55n153
LH ¶ 212, 55n153
LH ¶ 213, 55n153

LH ¶ 214, 55n153
LH ¶ 215, 55n153
LH ¶ 216, 55n153
LH ¶ 217, 55n153
LH ¶ 218, 55nn151, 154
LH ¶ 219, 55n153
LH ¶ 220, 55n153
LH ¶ 221, 55n153
LH ¶ 222, 55n153
LH ¶ 223, 55n153
LH ¶ 224, 55n153
LH ¶ 225, 55n153
LH ¶ 226, 55nn151, 154
LH ¶ 227, 55nn151, 154
LH ¶ 228, 55n153
LH ¶ 229, 55nn151, 155, 156
LH ¶ 230, 55nn151, 154
LH ¶ 231, 55n153
LH ¶ 232, 55n153
LH ¶ 233, 55n153
LH ¶ 234, 55n153
LH ¶ 235, 55n153
LH ¶ 236, 50n80, 55n153
LH ¶ 237, 50n80, 55n153
LH ¶ 238, 55n153
LH ¶ 239, 53n127, 55n153
LH ¶ 240, 54n145, 55n153
LH ¶ 241, 55n153
LH ¶ 242, 55n153
LH ¶ 243, 55n153
LH ¶ 244, 55n157
LH ¶ 245, 50n84, 55n153
LH ¶ 246, 55n153
LH ¶ 247, 55n153
LH ¶ 248, 55n153
LH ¶ 249, 50n84, 54n145, 55n157
LH ¶ 250, 55n157
LH ¶ 251, 55n153
LH ¶ 252, 55n153
LH ¶ 253, 50n82, 55nn151, 154
LH ¶ 254, 50n82, 55n153
LH ¶ 255, 50n82, 55n153
LH ¶ 256, 50n82, 55nn151, 154
LH ¶ 257, 53n127, 55n153
LH ¶ 258, 53n127, 55n153
LH ¶ 259, 55n153
LH ¶ 260, 55n153
LH ¶ 261, 53n127, 55n153
LH ¶ 263, 55n153
LH ¶ 264, 55nn150, 153
LH ¶ 265, 55n153
LH ¶ 266, 54n145, 55n157
LH ¶ 267, 55n153
LH ¶ 268, 55n153
LH ¶ 269, 55n153
LH ¶ 270, 55n153
LH ¶ 271, 55n153
LH ¶ 272, 55n153
LH ¶ 273, 50n81, 53n127, 55n153
LH ¶ 274, 50n81, 53n127, 55n153
LH ¶ 275, 55n153
LH ¶ 276, 55n153
LH ¶ 277, 55n153
LH ¶ 278, 55n153
LH ¶ 279, 55n153
LH ¶ 280, 52n111, 55n153
LH ¶ 281, 52n111, 54n145, 55n153
LH ¶ 282, 55nn151, 153, 56n163
LH ¶ Epilogue, 54n144
LH ¶ gap a, 50n83, 51n93, 55n150, 55n153
LH ¶ gap bb, 55n156
LH ¶ gap c, 55n153
LH ¶ gap cc, 54n145, 55n154
LH ¶ gap e, 55n153
LH ¶ gap g, 55n153
LH ¶ gap h, 55n153
LH ¶ gap l, 55n153
LH ¶ gap m, 55n154
LH ¶ gap n, 55n156
LH ¶ gap r, 55n153
LH ¶ gap s, 55n154
LH ¶ gap t, 53n126, 55n156
LH ¶ gap u, 53n126, 54n139, 55n156
LH ¶ gap v, 55nn150, 156
LH ¶ gap w, 55n153
LH ¶ gap x, 53n128, 55n153
LH ¶ gap y, 55n153
LH ¶ gap z, 55n150, 55n153
LH ¶ gaps l–¶ 107, 51n93
LH ¶ gaps t–cc, 50n83
LH Prologue, 22–23, 40, 47nn27–28, 56n164